Between the Middle East and the Americas

Between the Middle East and the Americas

The Cultural Politics of Diaspora

Edited by
Evelyn Alsultany *and* Ella Shohat

The University of Michigan Press
Ann Arbor

Copyright © by the University of Michigan 2013
All rights reserved

This book may not be reproduced, in whole or in part, including illustrations, in any form (beyond that copying permitted by Sections 107 and 108 of the U.S. Copyright Law and except by reviewers for the public press), without written permission from the publisher.

Published in the United States of America by
The University of Michigan Press
Manufactured in the United States of America
♾ Printed on acid-free paper

2016 2015 2014 2013   4 3 2 1

A CIP catalog record for this book is available from the British Library.

Library of Congress Cataloging-in-Publication Data

Between the Middle East and the Americas : the cultural politics of diaspora / edited by Evelyn Alsultany and Ella Shohat.
    p.   cm.
   Includes index.
   ISBN 978-0-472-09944-3 (cloth : alk. paper)—ISBN 978-0-472-06944-6 (pbk. : alk. paper)—ISBN 978-0-472-02877-1 (e-book)
   1. Arabs—Ethnic identity.   2. Arabs—Social conditions.   3. Arab Americans—Ethnic identity.   4. Arab Americans—Social conditions. 5. Arabs—Western countries—Ethnic identity.   6. Arabs—Western countries—Social conditions.   7. Middle East—Relations—United States. 8. United States—Relations—Middle East.   9. Middle East—Relations—Western countries.   10. Western countries—Relations—Middle East. I. Alsultany, Evelyn.   II. Shohat, Ella, 1959–

DS36.95.B47   2012
305.892'707—dc23   2012033640

In memory of Edward W. Said

Contents

Acknowledgments   ix

INTRODUCTION

1. The Cultural Politics of "the Middle East" in the Americas: An Introduction   3
   Ella Shohat and Evelyn Alsultany

2. The Sephardi-Moorish Atlantic: Between Orientalism and Occidentalism   42
   Ella Shohat

NATION, CULTURE, AND REPRESENTATION

3. Mahjar Legacies: A Reinterpretation   65
   Jacob Berman

4. *Turcos* in the Mix: Corrupting Arabs in Brazil's Racial Democracy   80
   John Tofik Karam

5. From "*Baisanos*" to Billionaires: Locating Arabs in Mexico   96
   Theresa Alfaro-Velcamp

6. Ali Bla Bla's Double-Edged Sword: Argentine President Carlos Menem and the Negotiation of Identity   108
   Christina Civantos

7. They Hate Our Freedom, But We Love Their Belly Dance: The Spectacle of the Shimmy in Contemporary U.S. Culture   130
   Amira Jarmakani

8. From Arab Terrorists to Patriotic Arab Americans: Representational Strategies in Post-9/11 TV Dramas   153
   Evelyn Alsultany

9. When Pakistanis Became Middle Eastern: Visualizing
   Racial Targets in the Global War on Terror   176
   Junaid Rana

   DIASPORA, TRANSNATION, AND TRANSLATION

10. "A Strip, A Land, A Blaze": Arab American Hip-Hop
    and Transnational Politics   195
    Sunaina Maira

11. Muslim Digital Diasporas and the Gay Pornographic
    Cyber Imaginary   214
    Karim Tartoussieh

12. Drawing the Line: A Rhetorical Analysis of the Mohammed
    Cartoons Controversy as It Unfolded in Denmark and the
    United States   231
    Helle Rytkønen

13. *Turcophobia* or *Turcophilia:* Politics of Representing Arabs
    in Latin America   252
    Heba El Attar

14. User-Friendly Islams: Translating Rumi in France and the
    United States   264
    Ziad Elmarsafy

15. "Axising" Iran: The Politics of Domestication and
    Cultural Translation   282
    R. Shareah Taleghani

16. "The Uneven Bridge of Translation": Turkey in between
    East and West   299
    Shouleh Vatanabadi

    Contributors   319

    Index   323

Acknowledgments

Between the Middle East and the Americas: The Cultural Politics of Diaspora is a collaborative project that was probably in the making long before we actually began conceptualizing it in 2003. Growing up in the wake of our families' displacement from Iraq, and having lived in multiple geographies as part of complex familial mixing, we see this project as an attempt to connect what otherwise would be perceived as disparate and disjointed worlds. We have attempted to gather under one "roof" essays on seemingly unrelated cultural geographies that correspond to the various diasporic worlds we have been familiar with, or aware of, but which have hardly travelled together in scholarly publications. Middle Eastern diaspora in the United States is often compared to Europe, while the linked analogies to the rest of the Americas are overlooked. The Arab/Latino interface examined in this book was inspired by similar convergences in our own lives. Our respective familial itineraries, along with Iraq and the United States, in the case of Evelyn Alsultany, have included Cuba and Colombia, while in Ella Shohat's case have included Israel/Palestine and Brazil. It was therefore only a matter of time before we sought to translate our personal trajectories to a book that proposes to view the Americas as a continuum, in terms of both Middle Eastern diasporas and cross-border cultural flows. Finally, the penchant to regard the presence of Arabs, Muslims, or Middle Easterners in the West as a menacing infiltration, on the one hand, or as exotic unattainable people, on the other, was also at the heart of our desire to highlight a long historical cultural syncretism between East and West as well as between North and South. We hope that the volume will contribute to reshaping the discursive premises about the world/s we inhabit.

This journey, however, would not have been possible without the enthusiastic participation and groundbreaking work of the authors who have enriched the itineraries of scholarly inquiry while also making the volume's proposed conceptual framework a textual reality. Taken together, the essays, we believe, offer a multiperspectival understanding of the interconnected cultural geographies. We are immensely grateful to the contributors for their excellent work and remarkable patience throughout this long and winding road. We would also like to acknowledge the superb work of those with whom we were in dialogue concerning the project along the way: Hishaam Aidi, Seyed Alavi, Shiva Balaghi, Doris Bittar, Chaza Charafeddine, Nouri Gana, Deborah Justice, Alex Lubin, Dina Ramadan, and Steven Salaita. We thank our editor at the University of Michigan Press, LeAnn Fields, for her belief in this project from the outset. Despite some raised eyebrows about the relevance of Latin America to the discussion, and despite some doubts about the coherency of such proposed analytical framework, LeAnn supported the scope of the volume throughout the process. At University of Michigan Press, we also thank Marcia LaBrenz, Alexa Ducsay, and the anonymous readers. Over this long period, the project has also benefited from the diligent work of a number of research assistants: Emma Alpert, Camila Bechelany, Benjamin Minh Ha, Leili Kashani, Jennifer Kelly, Diala Khalife, Andrew McBride, Sandra Ruiz, Adam Pascarella, Monika Raj, Michael Sackllah, Mejdulene Shomali, Karim Tartoussieh, Lani Teves, and Eliot Truesdell. We are immensely grateful for their indispensable help.

We are fortunate to be surrounded by supportive friends and colleagues who generously helped the project in various ways. We are deeply grateful to Minoo Moallem for her invaluable comments concerning the volume as well as to Mireille Abelin, Mona El-Ghobashy, and Christine Burmeister-Guivernau for their feedback and support. We would also like to acknowledge the dialogues which we have had over the years with: Rabab Abdulhadi, Thomas Abowd, Deborah Al-Najjar, Anan Ameri, Paul Amar, Sinan Antoon, Kathryn Babayan, Elif Bali, Magdalena Barrera, Moustafa Baymoumi, Yael Ben-Zvi, Michael Bobbitt, Isaura Botelho, Lori Brooks, Dorothy Duff-Brown, Emily Brown, Carlos Augusto Calil, Amy Carroll, Christianne Cejas, Erskine Childers, Luiz Antonio Coelho, Vivia Costalas, Ebony Coletu, Deirdre de la Cruz, Philip Deloria, Nacisse Demeksa, Greg Dowd, Leonor Garcia, Lourdes Garcia, José Gatti, Reem Gibriel, Indepal Grewal, Catherine Groves, Esther Hamburger, Suheir Hammad, Sandra Hanna, Salah Hassan, Rima Hassouneh, Mervat Hatem, Anya Hurwitz, Shaista Husain, Shazia Iftkhar, Amira Jarmakani, Caren Kaplan, John Tofik Karam, Connie Katon, Osman Khan, Lawrence LaFountain-Stokes, Kate Lyra, Sunaina Maira, Ivone Margulies, Randy Martin, Florencia Masri, Joseph Massad, Khaled Mattawa, Anthony Mora, Nadine Naber, Maria del Mar Logrono-Narbona, Marisol Negrón, Sana Odeh, Dahlia Petrus, Douglas

Pineda, Lavinia Pinto, Paulo Pinto, Marcelle Pithon, Richard Porton, Vanessa Primiani, Rachel Afi Quinn, Yvette Raby, Junaid Rana, Yeidy Rivero, Gilda Rodriguez, Lauren Rosenthal, Rasha Salti, Jack G. Shaheen, Shahid Siddiqui, Brad Verebay, João Luiz Vieira, Shouleh Vatanabadi, Penny Von Eschen, and Ismail Xavier. Our warm appreciation and gratitude goes to our families for their vital love: Kamal, Maggie, and Fabian Alsultany; Fatima Chavez, Raul Chavez, Steven Cuevas, Maria Jimenez, Martha Jaramillo; the Ofosu-Benefo family; Rachel and Rahamin Saban; Aziza, Sasson and Jacob Shohat; Juan, Doris, Becky, and Gilberto Stam, and especially Robert Stam whose dialogical generosity enriched the book and Benefo Ofosu-Benefo for his unwavering support. We regret that this project came into completion after the passing of Kamal Alsultany, an Iraqi in the diaspora whose life reflected the cultural geographies charted in this volume, but which also embraced the cross-border affinities aspired by this book.

Between the Middle East and the Americas comes in the wake of years of conference organizing, curating, lecturing, and teaching on these issues—in the case of Shohat for over the past three decades, and in the case of Alsultany over the last decade. The book has been shaped by organizing panels at such associations as the American Studies Association, Middle East Studies Association, and Modern Language Association; curating in such spaces as the Arab American National Museum, Brooklyn Museum, and New Museum of Contemporary Art; and teaching undergraduate courses and graduate seminars; for Evelyn Alsultany at Stanford University and University of Michigan (both Ann Arbor and Dearborn campuses); and for Ella Shohat at the City University of New York, Cornell University, New York University, University of California at Los Angeles, and University of São Paolo, Brazil. For Alsultany such courses have included: "Arab American Studies: Race, Gender, and Representation," "Introduction to Arab American Studies," "Representing the Middle East in Hollywood Cinema," "Perspectives on 9/11," and "The Middle East in American Studies." For Shohat they have included: "Performing Postcolonial Memory," "Imaging Palestine and Israel: Issues in the Politics of Representation," "The Media of Displacement," "'Covering the World:' Visual Culture and the Imperial Imaginary," "Representing the Middle East," "Performing the Orient," "Transnational/Multicultural Feminism," "Diasporic Bodies in Multicultural America," "Belly Dancing and the Politics of Sexuality," "Questions of Displacement: Gender, Diaspora, and Exile," "(Post)Colonial Discourse and the Cinema," "Gender and the Discourses of Discovery," "Gender and the Popular Culture of Empire," "Orientalism and the Cinema: Issues in Ethnic/Racial Representation," and "Jew/ Arab: Issues in Representation."

Teaching these courses has been a vital part of shaping this project and has made this journey meaningful. Finally, we would like to express our gratitude to the artist Pouran Jinchi for generously agreeing to let us use "Untitled 13" from her Entropy series (2010) for the cover of *Between the Middle East and the Americas.*

Evelyn Alsultany
ANN ARBOR

Ella Shohat
NEW YORK

Introduction

ONE

The Cultural Politics of "the Middle East" in the Americas
An Introduction

Ella Shohat and Evelyn Alsultany

The Middle East in the Americas

Shuttling between Rio de Janeiro and Fez, the hit Brazilian soap opera or telenovela *O Clone* tells the tale of the forbidden yet enduring love between a Catholic Brazilian man and a Muslim Moroccan woman. To an audience increasingly curious about Islam and the Middle East, the series, which had its début shortly after 9/11 (on October 1), portrayed two worlds, both bursting with sensuality but also tormented by social and religious restrictions. In contrast to U.S. media representations, it was not a case of fearmongering about "Islamic terrorism" but rather of an Orientalist exoticism rooted in a tropical imaginary long marked by a fascination with a distant Moorish/Iberian past.[1] The telenovela's imagery of harems, veils, nargilas, and belly dancing ignited a Dança do Ventre craze and generated classes in belly dance across Brazil. A CD based on the original soundtrack of *O Clone*'s Arabic music contributed to an already growing music/dance fusion genre, the BellySamba, which gained visibility thanks to the new climate generated by *O Clone*.[2] The ornamented dress of the protagonist, Jade Rachid, was reportedly the most popular costume in the 2002 Rio carnival.[3] It was displayed within the same spirit of carnivalesque hilarity that animated the performance of "Bin Laden's harem," which included sambistas rhythmically lifting their burqas to reveal skimpy Brazilian tangas underneath.[4] Drawing on international news headlines, the performance turned what was usually seen as threatening into a flirtatious scene of ludic corporeality.

O Clone's popularity was not limited to Brazil. The telenovela was dubbed from Portuguese into Spanish in 2002, and broadcast on the U.S. television network, Telemundo, to one of the largest audiences in the history of the Spanish language American channel.[5] Due to popular demand it was rebroadcast in 2004. In addition to its broadcast in Spanish for Latin American countries such as Peru, Argentina, and Venezuela, *O Clone / El Clon* was also dubbed into multiple languages and aired in more than ninety countries, including Turkey, Israel, Russia, Portugal, and Kyrgyzstan.[6] In 2010, Telemundo and TV Globo, the Brazilian network that created the original telenovela, coproduced a completely fresh Spanish-speaking version—*El Clon*—with a new cast. The telenovela's original base-country was now relocated from Brazil to North America. The Latin/Arab or Catholic/Muslim cultural clash of the original novella gave way, in a new transoceanic passage, to the cultural contrasts between the United States and Morocco, and a narrative shuttle between Miami and Fez.

We begin our introduction to *Between the Middle East and the Americas: The Cultural Politics of Diaspora* with *O Clone* as a way of hinting at the multiple geographic and transnational foci of the volume. What representations and discourses about Arabs/Muslims, and about Brazilians/Latinos, were produced by *O Clone / El Clon* in the diverse contexts in which it was translated, circulated, and broadcast? To what extent were these discourses shaped by the discrepant contexts of reception? Within the U.S. Latino submarket, Arabs/Muslims were largely portrayed, just a switch of the channel away, as terrorists. What is most striking in the varying representations of Arabs/Muslims in *O Clone / El Clon* are the distinct yet overlapping significations of Arabness and Muslimness in North vis-à-vis South America. Indeed, the Arabs/Muslims in *O Clone / El Clon* are nowhere marked as potential terrorists. At the same time, they are portrayed within an Orientalist imagery that mirrors familiar European and North American fantasies.

While the figure of the Arab/Muslim in the United States is vital to this volume, the project is deeply concerned with the interconnectedness of regions usually seen as separated.[7] Our multilateral approach focuses, in other words, on the links not only between the Middle East and the United States but also between the Middle East and the Americas as a whole. Within this transnational perspective the volume examines cultural production and dissemination as part of complex cross-border flows where "the-Middle-East-in-the-U.S." constitutes one terminal within a diasporic pan-American network.[8] Generally, the interrelated issues of Arab, Muslim, and Middle Eastern diasporas in North America are discussed in relation only to Western Europe. Indeed, the earlier colonization of the Middle East / North Africa by Western Europe, in conjunction with the later imperialist interventions associated with the United States, form the taken-for-granted backdrop for the anticolonialist critique of "the West," or "the First World," or "the Global North." The partly overlapping discourses of Eurocentrism and Orientalism, meanwhile, make it necessary to stress the representational links between Europe and the United States. In this sense, the United States inherits significant traits of the Old World empires like France and Britain, making all these nation-states the "obvious" object of comparative postcolonial studies as well as of transnational analysis. Despite the specificities of each zone, North America and Western Europe form part of historically related hegemonic formations, which is why Eurocentrism and Orientalism are relevant to both.

The Middle-East-in-Europe, indeed, is often assumed to form the taken-for-granted comparative framework for discussing the Middle-East-in-the-U.S. The postcolonial Arab/Muslim diasporas in Western Europe—North African Muslims in France, Turkish/Kurdish Muslims in Germany, Indian/Pakistani/Bangladeshi/Kashmiri Muslims in Great Britain—have gained visibility over the past three decades, long before the Arab/Muslim gained prominence in U.S. political and media discourses. In Europe, public controversies around such issues as "the veil," "clitoridectomy," circumcision, mosque construction, and the rebellions of the French banlieues have become code words for the "clash of cultures" and "the problem" of immigration and integration. While the multicultural debates in the United States traditionally centered on the relations between empowered whites and the red (Native American), black (African American), and Latino "minorities," the debates in Europe have focused more on religion than on race. For the U.S. Right, the lack of integration of the Muslim/Arab minorities in European countries such as Britain, France, Germany, Holland, Switzerland, Belgium, Sweden, and Spain has been seen as figuring or foreshadowing similar problems for the United States and Canada. Some of the essays here discuss European nation-states, such as France or Denmark, both as comparative points and as terminals in the transnational flow of debates to further illuminate the cultural politics of the Middle East in "the West." The European fear of an Islamic takeover of Europe lurks in the background of the debates in the United States. In this sense, while South Asia might appear to be outside the scope of a volume dealing with Middle Eastern / North African diasporas, the current cultural politics make it necessary to address the ways in which Islamic Asia (Pakistan, Bangladesh, Kashmir, Indonesia, etc.) and the Middle East become conflated. Indeed some of the essays here reflect precisely on present-day constructions of the geography of Islam.

The interface between diasporic communities and the hegemonic society, however, is distinct in each site in the Americas. In the United States, strong expressions of hostility to Muslim/Arabs, for example hate crimes and symbolic acts of violence such as threats to burn the Quran, are relatively recent phenomena, largely a result of tensions around the Middle East and the Israeli/Palestinian conflict, exacerbated, of course, by 9/11, the War on Terror, electoral politics, and the need for a scapegoat in a time of economic crisis. Although the United States, unlike Europe, did not define itself against Arab/Islam (from the Crusades to direct colonialist interventions), what one might call the (shared) colonialist and Orientalist intertext is always already available to be tapped into in moments of crisis.[9] It is fascinating, in this sense, that at the beginning of the Iraq War the Pentagon screened *The Battle of Algiers,* a classic denunciation of French colonialism in North Africa, in order to see what could be gleaned about dealing with a guerrilla insurrection like the one U.S. forces were facing in Iraq. Despite the proclaimed Francophobia of Donald Rumsfeld, Richard Perl, and others, and despite the pretense of not bringing imperialism but only democracy to Iraq, when it comes to imperial wars the assumption is that "we Americans" are "naturally" with the French colonialists. When the Pentagon screens *The Battle of Algiers* it clearly empathizes with the colonialist French paratrooper Mathieu and not with the revolutionary Algerian Ali-la-Pointe. Here we detect a tacit admission, if only by analogy, that despite administration disavowals ("we are not an imperial power!"), the Iraq War was not totally disconnected from French colonial misadventures fifty years earlier in Algeria.

Some of the current fanners of the flames of Islamophobia directly invoke the case of Muslims in Europe as a motive not only for hostility but also even for hate crimes and symbolic acts of violence, such as commemorating the ninth anniversary of 9/11 through holding "Burn a Koran Day."[10] In this version of patriotism, a white Christian "we" strives to forestall a Muslim takeover of America like the one that has already transpired in Europe. For the NeoCons and anti-multiculturalists, the 2004 murder of the Dutch author and filmmaker Theo van Gogh by a Dutch-Moroccan Muslim, Mohammed Bouyeri, and the angry Muslim protests against the Danish newspaper publication of cartoons depicting the Prophet Muhammad as a terrorist, served as a perfect indication of what's wrong with liberal America and with multiculturalism. In this narrative, the open-minded Dutch welcomed Arab-Muslims who then ransacked Holland's liberal polity. Holland, like France and other liberal Western welfare states, has come to constitute the negative paradigm of what "we must prevent in the US." Indeed, the Somali-born Dutch writer and politician Ayaan Hirsi Ali, who worked with Theo van Gogh on the controversial film *Submission* that criticized the treatment of women in Islam, ended up finding refuge in the corridors of NeoCon think tanks in the United States. A fellow at the American Enterprise Institute, Hirsi Ali has come to occupy the role of the insider who speaks knowingly about the true essence of Islam, in the same way that other Muslim women writers, such as Azar Nafisi, the author of the memoir *Reading Lolita in Tehran*, have become favored witnesses to the dangers of Islamicism. Symbolic battles, furthermore, are fought over the history of Muslim-Christian relations. In the political battle over the Islamic Center near Ground Zero, the moderate Sufis behind the project chose the name "Cordoba" to evoke the multiculturalism avant-la-lettre of the Iberian convivencia of Al Andalus. The opponents of the Center, meanwhile, saw it as a sign of Muslim conquest, part of a tradition of establishing mosques to commemorate victories over Christians.

At the same time, for Arab/Muslim American antiracist activists, the European case has also become an object lesson, but in a different sense. While drawing on the long tradition of civil rights–resistant models, Muslim/Arab American mobilization against discrimination—whether against racial profiling and detentions, or against offensive representations of Islam and Arabs—has been performed in solidarity with its counterparts in Europe. Conversely, Muslims/Arabs in Europe have been inspired by the civil rights struggle in the United States. In France, the attractive "pull" of the postwar French prosperity of "les trentes glorieuses," combined with the "push" of postindependence travails in North Africa itself, led to a situation where hundreds of thousands of Algerians, Moroccans, and Tunisians in France came to form the country's "visible minorities." For a period in the 1970s and early 1980s, members of these minorities—and especially the second-generation children of the largely North African migrant workers displaced to the colonial metropole in the 1950s and 1960s—rose up in protest movements against racism and in favor of minority and immigrant rights. The high point was the 1983 "March for Equality against Racism," dubbed by the media "Marche des Beurs" (the verlan word then used for the children of immigrants, from the Maghreb for "Arabe"), modeled on the demonstration, two decades earlier, led by Martin Luther King, Jr. in Washington, DC.

Between the Middle East and the Americas in a sense goes against the grain of much of the writing about Middle Easterners outside of the Middle East. The tendency to compare Arabs/Muslims in the United States and Canada in relation only to Europe has often disconnected these diasporic communities from the rest of the Americas. The political Right tends to bring up such links only in the context of the terrorist threat. The vigilante patrols on the Mexican border have thrown a harsh spotlight on the brown bodies not only of Mexicans, Guatemalans, and Salvadorans but also on potential Middle Easterners "infiltrating our country." The Right (for example, Lou Dobbs) has tried to link defense of the United States from threats on its southern border to dangers emanating from the Middle East. Post-9/11 anxieties about Middle East–based terrorism have come to be superimposed on the xenophobic fears of the Latino "invasion." The right-wing media has even tried to fuse the two fears by warning of "terrorist anchor babies" planted in the United States just after birth, to gain citizenship, who will supposedly later bloom into full-blown terrorists. For the superpatriotic defenders of the border, the wall between Mexico and the United States offers a fortification not only against the Latin South but also against the Arab/Muslim East. And despite some Middle Eastern terrorist scares coming from the Canadian border, it is only the Mexican border that triggers anti-immigrant hysteria. The traditional arrogance toward Latin America as a U.S. "backyard" and the scorn for Mexican-American "greasers" overlaps with both 9/11 and the War on Terror as an overarching rhetorical framework.

While we take for granted the discursive commonalities in the construction of the Arab/Muslim figure in Europe and the United States, we also want to highlight the Americas as a multiracial and multifaith transnational continuum. And while some of the essays in this volume examine the cross-border cultural production between the United States and the Middle East in relation to Europe (e.g., France and Denmark), other essays examine cross-border productions across the Americas. Apart from their common colonial-settler formation, all the nation-states of the Americas share parallel waves of immigration from the Middle East / North Africa dating at least as far back as the late nineteenth and early twentieth centuries, and in many cases much earlier. The dislocations to the Americas from what were the Ottoman Empire or French- and British-dominated North Africa and the Middle East form part of the same historical process. In Latin America, the immigrants were referred to as *Turcos*—a name that indicated their origins in provinces under the Ottoman Empire, although many of them were not culturally or ethnically Turks but largely Armenians, Arab Christians, and Arab Jews from the region of Syria/Lebanon/Palestine. Arriving on the shores of the United States, similarly, the immigrants were called *Turks;* their kilims are now displayed in Ellis Island's Immigration Museum. And at the turn of the century and until the mid-1940s, New York's "Little Syria" referred to Washington Street's vibrant Arab community, just south of what later became the site of the World Trade Center.[11]

The purpose of this volume is to provide a lens not merely onto the parallel and separate immigrations to the Americas but also onto their interconnectedness, demonstrating the linked analogies between the Americas as a whole.[12] Thus the essays address the cultural history of Arab presence in relation to contemporary cultural practices not only in the United States but also in Brazil, Argentina, Chile, Colombia, and Mexico, covering such themes as the dilemmas of diasporic Arab/Muslim identity vis-à-vis hegemonic national discourses; the negotiations of gender and sexuality in novels and memoirs, especially those written by Middle Eastern women, in the face of recurrent tropes of despotism and patriarchal oppression; and the representation of the War on Terror in TV dramas as a contradictory site of Muslim diasporic invisibility and hypervisibility.[13] The essays collectively address a range of issues of resistant diasporic practices within the highly charged politics of representation and cultural translation.

The very notion of "between the Middle East and the Americas" points to the similarly ambivalent place occupied by "the Turk" or "the Arab" within nation-states whose primary menacing "other" had not been historically "the Jew" or "the Muslim," as in Europe, but rather the indigenous people and/or African Americans. Thus despite the right-wing equation of the Arab/Islamic Middle East with terror, our project attempts to offer a more relational perspective on cultural representations and practices throughout the Americas.[14] Just as the history of immigration to the Americas, in sum, requires regarding Arab/Muslim displacements in a way that transcends nation-state spaces, so too the globalized nature of contemporary political discourse and media representation calls for a cross-border transnational analysis. The case of *O Clone*, in this sense, points to the importance of transnationalizing the discussion about Arab/Muslim diaspora, by correlating East/West and North/South geographical imaginaries.

The Paradoxes of the Culture of Displacement

This volume appears in a context where "the Middle East" has become visible not simply "over there" but also "right here." The paranoid demagoguery of the War on Terror, and the anti-Muslim hysteria of the Tea Party activists, has culminated in the current wave of Islamophobia and the unsavory polemics about what is prejudicially called the "Ground Zero Mosque." The increased presence of Middle Eastern peoples in the Americas in the context of the War on Terror has turned Middle Easterners into villains in a kind of horror movie, in ways that have impacted popular opinion. According to a 2005 Gallup Poll of American Households, when asked what they most admire about Muslim societies, the most frequent response was "nothing."[15] According to a 2006 USA Today/Gallup poll, 44 percent of Americans find Muslims "too extreme" in their religious beliefs. Nearly one-quarter of Americans, 22 percent, say they would not want a Muslim as a neighbor. Less than half believe U.S. Muslims are loyal to the United States.[16]

Middle Eastern and Muslim American communities have faced heightened surveillance, deportation, and detention. There has been a significant increase in hate crimes against Arabs, Muslims, Middle Easterners, and Sikhs immediately after 9/11.[17] While the number of hate crimes decreased as 9/11 became a more distant memory, they are still higher than they were pre–9/11. In addition to an increase in hate crimes, Middle Eastern and Muslim Americans have faced a slew of post-9/11 government initiatives including detention of Arab and Muslim immigrant men, the PATRIOT Act, the "voluntary" interview program, special registration, and the targeting of Muslim charitable giving.[18] In the wake of the erosion of civil rights, these communities have come to distrust the U.S. government, experiencing a kind of post–9/11 trauma that has triggered return emigration from the United States.[19]

Written against the backdrop of such tragedies, this volume also strikes a more celebratory note by highlighting the cultural production of the Arab / Muslim / Middle Eastern diasporas. Middle Eastern peoples and cultures have also become a vibrant presence in the United States, and indeed throughout the Americas. Our text highlights the ambivalent and contradictory position of the Middle East in the Americas. It explores a paradoxical situation in which "the Middle East" is at the very kernel of the current state of national anxiety in North America, yet where at the same time "the East" has become increasingly interwoven into the American cultural fabric. Not always obvious or explicit, this interweaving becomes discernable through a historicized study of the politics of culture. The situation, then, is one of disorienting simultaneity, mingling the "worst of times" and the "best of times." This volume in this sense hopes to shed light on the paradoxical nature of a situation where the shameless demagoguery of the Christian Right exists in tandem with the increased visibility of Arab / Muslim / Middle Eastern peoples and cultures in the United States.

This new visibility is multidimensional, reflected in a certain mainstreaming of Middle Eastern culture and of the Arab/Muslim diasporic presence. Post-9/11 Arab / Muslim / Middle Eastern cultural production has drawn media attention and crowds of diverse backgrounds. Screenings of Middle Eastern films dedicated to the region and its diasporas, for example, have grown in popularity, including in the film festivals of Tribeca and Lincoln Center in New York, San Francisco, D.C., and Montréal. The Miss USA pageant, meanwhile, selected a Muslim Arab American, Rima Fakih, as the 2010 winner for the first time in history. On the most mundane level, Middle Eastern cuisine—falafel, hummus, shawarma, couscous—is by now a staple food sold in supermarkets and consumed by Americans of diverse origins. American cities are dotted with halal meat shops, and even halal hotdog carts selling shish kebab and kefta. Home supplies—hand-woven Turkish kilims, Persian handmade silk rugs, Moroccan leather henna-painted lampshades, mother-of-pearl Syrian furniture, and handcrafted colorful ceramic dishes from all across the Middle East / North Africa—are widely sold as house décor or home accessories. Fashion has also incorporated "oriental chic," with elite department stores like Neiman Marcus displaying a Stella McCartney design of "Wrapped Silk Harem Pants," while popular clothing stores, such as H&M, sell the more affordable version of "harem pants," which made a comeback after the Orientalist fantasy projected in *Sex and the City 2* (2010).

The increasingly vibrant presence of the Middle East / North Africa in the United States, then, neighbors with the stubborn persistence of an Orientalist imaginary. In the United States, the Middle East has inspired popular theme-park attractions, drawing on century-old traditions of fairs and expositions. One of Orlando's theme parks features The Holy Land Experience, offering visitors a biblical landscape and reenacted scenes, as well as the pleasure of participating in longstanding American Holy Land mania that dates back to the nineteenth century and included not only actual travel to the Orient but also pilgrimages to theme parks, such as Palestine Park, at Chautauqua, New York. But whether in actual or simulacrum voyages, travelers viewed the biblical land through an Orientalist vision, one that tended to elide the indigenous perspective in favor of biblical romanticism, present even in the work of a satirist such as Mark Twain, or a black traveler such as David Dorr.[20] At Epcot Center, visitors can participate in a different version of Orientalism, in Arab exotica; they can go to the Morocco Pavilion, dine at Restaurant Marrakesh, watch a belly dancing show, shop for rugs and fezzes, and meet Aladdin and Princess Jasmine. At the Aladdin Hotel in Las Vegas (1966–2003, now Planet Hollywood) guests were offered an Arabian Nights experience that included the "Baghdad Theater," "Sinbad's Lounge," and the "Desert Passage" mall. At the same time, trendy Middle Eastern–style cafés have mushroomed in many cities, offering their customers the pleasures of nargila smoking, belly dancing, and Arabic music, while Rai and Arabic pop provide the sound track for chic boutiques. The fluid boundaries between the Orientalist imaginary and Arab popular culture are in this sense especially complex, when Arabian/oriental dreams, in a case of commercially motivated "self-orientalizing,"[21] are marketed and promoted by Middle Easterners themselves. In fact it has been common for Middle Eastern café, club, or restaurant owners to cash in on the desire to enjoy a fantasy night in Arabian dreamland.

Arab / Middle Eastern culture has also gained media visibility in Latin America. Clarin.com, a popular Argentine online newspaper, reports an Arab cultural boom in Argentina since the late 1990s. This cultural boom was reportedly inspired by a combination of Shakira's "fusión árabe-rock latino"—particularly her song "Ojos Asi" and the accompanying belly dance of the hit song "Habibi" by the Egyptian singer Amr Diab—and of the popularity of the telenovela *O Clone / El Clon*.[22] A YouTube video, "Havana Habibi," for example, documents Cuba's first Arabic dance troupe, Groupo Aisha Al-Hanan, consisting of eight women who have embraced belly dancing as an important form of self-expression and empowerment—a discourse reminiscent of North American and Western European belly dancing scenes.[23] And as in the United States and Canada, the engagement with "the Middle East" has been an ambivalent site that cannot be reduced to exoticist appropriation; it simultaneously displays a desire to study what is usually viewed as an unattainable culture by, for example, enrolling in Arabic language classes and organizing academic conferences on topics ranging from Arabic calligraphy to Arab immigration to Latin America.[24]

While the diasporization of populations and the transnational flows of culture have in one sense whetted an already existent appetite for Orientalist voyeurism, in another sense they have shaped new culturally collaborative modes that at times simultaneously incorporate, appropriate, subvert, and reinvent Middle Eastern / North African cultural practices. These tensions and paradoxes trigger questions about the very definition of appropriation and/or artistic dialogue. Music videos, for example, have been incorporating belly dancing, a traditional popular art form in the Middle East / North Africa, but also a fixating trope dating back to the nineteenth-century voyages to the Orient. The music video for U2's "Mysterious Ways" (1992), filmed on location in Morocco, for example, features a belly dancer whose movements enact the words of the refrain: "she moves in mysterious ways." Shakira, the Lebanese-Colombian "cross-over" pop sensation, who already in 1999 opened and closed her South and North America concert "Tour Anfibio" with Arabic music and belly dancing, collaborated with Beyoncé on the music video "Beautiful Liar" (2007). Both dressed in tight black leather, the pair belly dance in a kind of mirror image, to the mixed sounds of pop and Arabized rhythms.

In his song "Big Pimpin'" (2000), rapper Jay-Z sampled the rhythmic music of a leading contemporary Egyptian musician, Hossam Ramzy, specifically "Khusara Khusara" (1997), itself a version of the Egyptian musical star Abdel Halim Hafez's original version in 1957. Such experiments have not gone completely uncontested, however. Rapper Lil Kim, for example, provoked controversy in December 2002 when she appeared on the cover of Russell Simmons's hip-hop fashion/music magazine, *One World,* wearing a bikini while covering her head with a burka. Similarly, Carlos Mencia on "The Mind of Mencia" produced a parodic music video, "The Rich Sheik," in which he tells famous rappers that they are broke compared to him—he has so much money that he paid Bush to attack Iraq and snaps his fingers for his "hos" to get on their backs.

The encounter of multiple diasporas whether within actual geographical or digital spaces, meanwhile, has come to form part of an ingenious artistic dialogue generating new diasporic and transnational cultural work. On the international scene, we find hybrid music featuring multilingual lyrics, mixing multiple musical genres, rhythms, and systems (for example, half- and quartertones). What was marketed in the 1980s as "ethnic music" morphed in the 1990s into "world music." Concerts have featured crossover musicians and singers such as Ilham Al-Madfai (Iraqi-British-Jordanian), Enrico Macias (Algerian-French), Ziad Al Rahbani (Lebanese), Hamza El Din (Nubian-Egyptian-American), Ofra Haza (Yemeni-Israeli), Hassan Hakmoun (Gnawa-Moroccan-American), Cheb Khaled (Algerian-French), Natacha Atlas (Moroccan-Egyptian-Palestinian-British-Belgian), and Alabina (Moroccan-Egyptian-Israeli-Spanish).[25] Conversely, Arabic music, ever since the 1930s and 1940s, has increasingly manifested the impact of Western musical tradition by incorporating such instruments as the piano and the trumpet, founding large orchestras, and stressing halftones. Within the transnational dialogue taking place within Arabic music, the absorption of such genres as tango, jazz, rumba, and bossa nova parallels incorporation of the Arab rhythms into popular musical hybrids throughout the Americas.

Postcolonial dislocations and transnational cultural flows have generated further collaborative artistic dialogues that go beyond the mere question of influence. As cultural practices move between geographies, we must address their complex itineraries. Cuban musician Omar Sosa, for example, created a musical polyphony of genres where Moroccan rhythms dialogue with salsa, samba, jazz, pop, rock, and bolero, winning a Grammy for his album *Sentir* (2003). Sting, meanwhile, collaborated with Algerian-French Rai musician Cheb Mami on the music video "Desert Rose" (1999), sung both in Arabic and English. The Lebanese singer Hanine Abu Chakra collaborated with the Cuban group Son Cubano, singing in Arabic and Spanish. Fusing Arabic and Latin music in a 2002 CD entitled *Arabo Cuban,* Hanine y Son Cubano blended famous Arab songs by Mohammed Abdel Wahab and Farid Al Atrash with Cuban music.[26] Hanine y Son Cubano rearranged the original tango compositions sung by Asmahan, a star of Egyptian musical cinema of the 1930s and 1940s, which were now transformed and recombined with the rhythms of salsa. Some Arabic music critics felt that Hanine's Arab-Cuban blend hurt the purity of Arabic music,[27] ironically ignoring the very fact of an earlier history of Latin/Arab dialogue. This volume is ultimately interested in this question of what constitutes cultural dialogue, hybridity, and syncretism, not merely in the context of uneven East/West or North/South power over representation but also within what could be seen as South-on-South cultural flows.

The poetics of diaspora finds expression in diverse artistic genres. Such work has revealed the indissoluble links between "here" and "there," between the Middle East and the Americas. The poetry of Suheir Hammad, for example, forms part of a burgeoning "spoken word" movement among young people of color and progressive white youth in the New York area. The multiracial coalition of poets generally combines percussive verbal style, performance smarts, and socially conscious lyrics. A Palestinian American who grew up in Brooklyn within a multicultural environment of Blacks, Latinos, and East Europeans, Hammad wrote/performed in the context of the spoken word group Def Poetry Jam, which brought its poetry to Broadway between 2002 and 2007, and was broadcast on HBO. In a poem entitled "first writing since," Hammad gives eloquent expression to the conflicting feelings of a Palestinian American New Yorker after the 9/11 attacks. She speaks of her initial fears that the pilot might be Arab or Muslim, in short someone who resembles her brothers:

> First, please god, let it be a mistake, the pilot's heart failed, the plane's engine died.
> Then please god, let it be a nightmare, wake me now,
> Please god, after the second plane, please don't let it be anyone
> Who looks like my brothers.

The poem scores the ignorance of those Americans who fear generic "orientals," who "do not know the difference / Between Indians, Afghans, Syrians, Muslims, Sikhs, Hindus."

At the same time, Hammad is irritated by the e-mails from leftists and Arab nationalists who say, "Let's not forget US transgressions." She feels resentful about such comments, since "I live here, these are my friends and fam, and it could have been me in those buildings, and we're not bad people, do not support America's bullying. . . . can I just have half a second to feel bad?" She also resents the Arab-haters who ask if she knew the highjackers; or those who say "they had it coming" but assume that "they" did not include the Arabs or Muslims or Mexicans who died in the World Trade Center. Denouncing the media double standard where terror always wears a brown Arab face, she asks: "When we talk about holy books and hooded men and death, why do we never mention the KKK?" And, then, in a sudden turn of association, Hammad makes what might seem to some a surprising claim: "If there are any people on earth who understand how New York is feeling right now, they are in the west bank and the Gaza strip." At the same time, Hammad dissociates herself completely from Bin Laden, whose "vision of the world does not include me or those I love." The poem "first writing since" gives an incandescent sense of what it is to live in the (multi) nation in the age of globalized error and globalized terror, of overlapping and conflicted loyalties to family and community, on the one hand, and to nation-states on the other.[28]

Satire has been another generic vehicle to shed light on the experiences of post-9/11 Arab and Middle Eastern Americans.[29] *The Axis of Evil Comedy Tour*, broadcast on Comedy Central in 2007, was the first comedy show featuring all Middle Eastern American comedians. Dean Obeidallah begins his act by thanking the audience for attending the show, including "the Iranians-slash-Persians, Arabs, white people, FBI, ATF, Homeland Security . . . Homeland Security?" He then provides insight for his audience into the experience of being Arab American after 9/11: "Do you know what it's like being of Arab heritage with a Muslim last name living in America the last few years? I could use a hug." Along with transforming fear and trauma into a source of humor, Dean Obeidallah makes fun of the stubborn stereotyping in the news media. There are two kinds of news stories in which Arabs appear, according to Dean Obeidallah: "There's the bad story where we're described as militant, gunmen, and terrorists and then the occasional positive one where we're described as alleged militant, gunmen, and terrorists." Standup comedian Maz Jobrani also expresses frustration at the representations of Middle Easterners, stating "The U.S. media always shows the crazy dude burning the American flag going: 'Death to America!' Always that guy." Maz Jobrani wishes the media would:

> Show us doing something good, like you know like baking a cookie or something, right? Cause I've been to Iran. We have cookies. Just once I want CNN to be like, "Now we are going to Mohammed in Iran." They go to some guy who's like, "Hello, I am Mohammad and I am just baking a cookie. I swear to God. No bombs, no flags, nothing. Back to you, Bob." That would be the whole news piece. They're never going to do that. Even if they ever did that, they would follow it up with another news piece: "This just in: A cookie bomb just exploded."

Pointing to the fraught and uneven representational terrain in the United States, Jobrani challenges his audience to imagine media reports depicting ordinary Arab and Muslim characters doing nothing more remarkable than baking cookies. Yet, the absence of stories on quotidian spaces reveals a failure of the imagination, since even a potentially imagined quotidian is always-already embedded in Islamophobia.

While cultural and social activism in the American diaspora has a long history, this activism, as some of the essays in the volume demonstrate, is no longer marginal and limited to community centers, or to a few vanguard cultural spaces, as was the case in the decades prior to 9/11.[30] Since then, cultures of resistance have found a location in the United States and Canada not only through political advocacy but also through artistic work. Art centers and media outlets have not simply exhibited cultural production "from" the Middle East but also amplified diasporic voices throughout the Americas, as evident in the opening of the Arab American National Museum in Dearborn, Michigan, in 2005.[31] Film festivals dedicated to Arab and Middle Eastern cinemas, such as the Arab Film Festivals in San Francisco and Minneapolis, have also paid attention to diasporic cinema.[32] Diverse forums for Middle Eastern American filmmakers, writers, performers, and visual artists have multiplied. Books, exhibitions, performances, and film festivals have been featured in the mainstream media in ways hardly imaginable prior to 9/11. In the realm of visual art, museums such as the Guggenheim, the Museum of Contemporary Art, and the Museum of Modern Art, in New York, as well as art galleries such as the National Gallery of Canada, have dedicated exhibitions specifically to the work of Middle Eastern or Middle Eastern diasporic artists, such as Sherene Neshat, Mona Hatoum, Jamelie Hassan, and Emily Jacir.[33] The renaissance of cultural production by this generation of Arab / Middle Eastern Americans, in sum, is visible in diverse realms, where cultural activism ranges from writing novels, plays, or poetry, through making films, media, and online creativity, to scholarly texts. Filmmakers such as Annemarie Jacir, Rola Nashef, Jackie Salloum, Jayce Salloum, and Elia Suleiman; writers such as Alia Malek and Gregory Orfalea; artists such as Doris Bittar and Happy Hyder; playwrights such as Leila Buck, Heather Raffo, and Betty Shamieh; creative writers such as Rabih Alameddine, Laila Halaby, and Randa Jarrar; and poets such as Hayan Charara, Nathalie Handal, Naomi Shihab Nye, and Khaled Mattawa have transformed the field of what constitutes Arab American art and writing.

The emergence of diasporic cultural centers and institutions must be viewed alongside the energized activism of dozens of civil rights and community centers, and the religious organizations that have emerged, such as the American-Arab Anti-Discrimination Committee (ADC), the Council on American-Islamic Relations (CAIR), and Arab Women's Solidarity Association (AWSA).[34] This volume is also produced in the context of another changed institutional landscape—that of the emerging overlapping academic fields of Arab American studies, U.S. Ethnic studies, postcolonial/transnational studies, and transnational Middle Eastern studies. Scholarly publications, academic panels, theme conferences, and exhibits on Arab American experiences and Islam are proliferating around the country. Along with the contributors to this volume, academics such as Rabab Abdulhadi,

Nabeel Abraham, Hishaam Aidi, Amal Amireh, Barbara Aswad, Anny Bakalian, Moustafa Bayoumi, Mehdi Bozorgmehr, Louise Cainkar, Carol Fadda-Conrey, Brian Edwards, Nada Elia, Sarah Gualtieri, Yvonne Haddad, Elaine Hagopian, Salah Hassan, Rosina Hassoun, Mervat Hatem, Sally Howell, Lutfi Hussein, Amaney Jamal, Suad Joseph, Mohja Kahf, Pauline Kaldas, Alex Lubin, Lisa Suhair Majaj, Melani McAlister, Minoo Moallem, Nadine Naber, Hamid Naficy, Sherene Razack, Edward Said, Steven Salaita, Therese Saliba, May Seikaly, Jack Shaheen, Evelyn Shakir, Andrew Shryock, Michael Suleiman, and others have published and created academic spaces from within multiple disciplines including sociology, anthropology, history, political science, and literary and media studies.[35] Such spaces have not merely reflected the cultural and intellectual production of diasporic communities but have also played an important role in the shaping of resistant diasporic identities and identifications. Fostering a certain fluidity between identities "back" home and "elsewhere," such resistant identities must be viewed as deeply linked and mutually constitutive. The negative images in the public sphere have generated new Arab, Muslim, and Middle Eastern American subcultures and critical voices. They do not necessarily argue for a positive image of Arabs/Islam but often deconstruct Orientalist stereotypes, while also generating cultural spaces that articulate the specificities of Arab / Muslim / Middle Eastern diasporic identity. This volume, in this sense, points to the complex negotiation between colonized self-rejection, on the one hand, and empowered self-representation, on the other.

Cross-Border Convergences

Although the formation of U.S. area studies and ethnic studies was premised on specific regional and racial/ethnic categorizations, our volume blurs neat boundaries and categories. Within the realm of mainstream popular culture, for example, Latino-Arab culture draws on very diverse cultural sources, which necessitates the focus on syncretisms that tend to be ignored or marginalized within current ethnic studies and area studies models. Arab-Latino/a figures in popular culture include Lebanese-Colombian singer Shakira; Syrian-Jewish-Brazilian-Canadian-American singer/choreographer Paula Abdul; Lebanese-Mexican actress/director Salma Hayek; and Mexican-Lebanese performance artist and singer Astrid Hadad. In Latin America, the presence of Arab-descended cultural and political figures has often been acknowledged, however ambivalently. In the political realm a number of Latin American leaders are of Arab descent, such as Abdalah Bucaram, president of Ecuador from 1996 to 1997 and Jamil Mahuad, the president of Ecuador from 1998 to

2000. In Colombia, it is not unusual for twenty to thirty members of Parliament and the senate to be of Arab descent.[36] The corruption of some of these powerful figures has contributed to a negative image of "the Arab-Muslim" in general. Carlos Menem, president of Argentina from 1989 to 1999, who is of Muslim-Syrian descent but who converted to Catholicism, offered land valued at $10 million in Buenos Aires during his presidency to build the King Fahd Islamic Center, the largest mosque in Latin America, funded by Saudi Arabia. Some Argentines saw the mosque as reflective of Menem's pro-Muslim bias, pointing out that Saudi Arabia does not allow non-Muslims to build places of worship in Saudi Arabia, and that the bombers of the Israeli Embassy in 1992 and the Argentine-Israelite Mutual Association (Asociación Mutual Israelita Argentina) in 1994 in Buenos Aires were not brought to justice.[37] Such media debates tend to mirror similar North American debates over the equation of all Muslims with terrorism.

In Latin America, multiple organizations and websites have been devoted to Islam, for example, La Organización Islámica Para América Latina and Islam Hoy.[38] News reports indicate that some Cubans are converting to Islam and that Muslim religious events in Havana have been sponsored by Iranian diplomats.[39] The United States has also witnessed increased Latino-Muslim convergences. According to the Latino American Dawah Organization (LADO) website, there are approximately 25,000 to 75,000 Latino Muslims in the United States. The mission of LADO, a nonprofit organization founded in 1997, is to promote Islam among Latinos and provide support for Latino Muslims, while HispanicMuslims.com seeks to educate the public on Latino Muslims.[40] Many newspaper articles have noted the increase in Latino converts to Islam and have published the conversion stories of Latino Muslims.[41] The American-Muslim magazine *Horizons* dedicated a special issue to Latino Muslims in July–August 2002. Recent documentary films, such as *New Muslim Cool* (2009, directed by Jennifer Maytorena Taylor) and *A Son's Sacrifice* (2006, directed by Yoni Brook), focus on the experiences of Latino Muslims. These films highlight the doubly marginalized identity generated by the rhetoric of the War on Terror, which, in the wake of the Jose Padilla episode, made Latino Muslims especially more vulnerable, the objects of racial and religious animosity.

This volume is published at a moment when the Arab and Muslim population is increasing throughout the Americas. Arabs in Venezuela, Argentina, Brazil, and many other countries are largely of Christian-Lebanese descent, although some are of Jewish and Muslim backgrounds.[42] While statistics indicate that 8.5 percent of the population in Argentina is Arab, only approximately 1.5–2.1 percent are Muslim. Roughly a quarter of a million Colombians are of Arab descent, the majority of whom live in Barranquilla and Cartagena, and about 400,000 Arabs live in Venezuela.[43] Approximately 1 percent of the Mexican population is of Arab descent, and an estimated 0.28 percent are Muslim.[44] In Brazil there are approximately nine million people (5 percent of the population) of Middle Eastern descent, and 1.5 million of them are Muslim.[45] Many Arab-Brazilians have attained high status as finance ministers (Ibrahim Abi-Ackel), novelists (Milton Hatoum, Raduan Nassar), filmmakers (Karim Ainouz), theater directors (Antônio Abujamra), and media producers (Ali Kamel). It is often said in Brazil that there are more Lebanese there than in Lebanon, and although most Arab-Brazilians are Christian, there are also fifty-five mosques and Muslim religious centers throughout the country.[46] There are small but growing Muslim populations in Guatemala, Honduras, Belize, Bolivia, Costa Rica, Colombia, Chile, Panama, Nicaragua, Peru, Venezuela, and the Dominican Republic. In the United States, meanwhile, there are approximately three million Arab Americans and seven million Muslims.[47] In Canada, approximately 350,000 people (1.2 percent of the population) are of Arab origin, and 579,640 are Muslim.[48]

In addition to an overlap due to an increase in Arab-Latino convergences through demographics (Latino-Muslims), the mass media (*O Clone / El Clon*), and pop stars (Shakira), the Americas are historically connected particularly since the first wave of Arab immigration from the Ottoman Empire to both North and South America occurred simultaneously in the late nineteenth and early twentieth centuries. Emigrating largely from the region of Greater Syria to cities such as São Paulo, Brazil; Caracas, Venezuela; Veracruz, Mexico; New York City; and Detroit, these early immigrants were predominantly pack peddlers and later small business owners. In the cultural realm, these early diasporic Arabs developed a literary movement, known throughout the Americas as "Mahjar Literature" (or Literature of Immigration). Writers such Gibran Khalil Gibran (U.S.), Ameen Rihani (U.S.), Fauzi al-Maluf (Brazil), Ilias Farhat (Brazil), and Na'um Labaki (Argentina) established newspapers and literary magazines, such as *al-Istiklal* and *al-Jaroda al-Suriyya al-Lubnaniyya / El Diario Sirio-Libanes* in Argentina, *al-Fayha* in Brazil, and *al-Huda* in the United States. In the 1920s and 1930s, they also formed literary societies, such as Al Rabita al-Qalamiyya in the United States, Al-'Usba al-Andalusiyya in Brazil, and al-Rabita al-Adabiyya in Argentina.[49]

What has become of the cultural and racial formation of Arabs in South America compared to North America? While Arabs and Muslims in the United States usually confront the stereotype of the terrorist, Arabs and Muslims in Latin America, due to a different context, confront a different stereotype: that of the corrupt merchant who profits at the expense of "real" Mexicans, or Argentines. Arabs in the United States are excluded from normative notions of national identity based on discourses of either whiteness or Islamophobia, but also by some versions of multiculturalism that have no room for experiences outside of the established ethnic/racial categories of oppression. In the case of Arabs in Latin America, meanwhile, exclusion from the national imaginary operates in relation to discourses of mixed national identity. In the case of Mexico, for example, the figure of the Arab must be seen in conjunction with mestizo identity, in relation to the hegemonic trope of "la raza cósmica."

This volume thus highlights the production, consumption, and circulation of discourses about "the Middle East" in the Americas as a continuum, even while acknowledging the importance of the specificities of national formations. The "Middle East" in the Americas enters a transcultural "contact zone"[50] where cultures meet, clash, and grapple within conditions of inequality. A contradictory site, "the Middle East" is produced and performed against the backdrop of colonial and imperial history as well as of contemporary corporate transnationalism. While some of the essays discuss the ways in which hegemonic discourses position the Arab as an exploitable Other or make Arab culture consumable for a Western audience by diluting, exoticizing, or commodifying it, other essays deal with efforts to imagine more complex understandings of self-representation in diverse cultural practices, e.g., literature, visual culture, cinema, digital spaces, performance, and music. This project explores the de/construction of the idea of "the Middle East," through different cultural sites whether in the national geographies of the United States, Brazil, Mexico, Argentina, Denmark, and France or within transnational digital spaces. Taken together, the essays point to an assemblage of meanings that shift depending on the historical moment and geographic/cultural context. They point to a contradictory field of meaning—where Muslims can be figured as terrorists in the U.S. hegemonic discourse, or as corrupt businessmen in Latin America, yet where such hegemonic discourses can also be defied, as seen in diverse artistic expressions and cultural projects. Even when located in a specific national geography, the volume as a whole suggests that these cultural practices must be understood within a transnational perspective, as exemplified by Arab American hip-hop artists, such as the Narcicyst (Yassin Alsalman), Omar Offendum (Omar Chakaki), and Excentrik (Tarik Kazaleh).

Despite the inaccuracy and even Orientalist history of the term "the Middle East," we use it for a number of reasons, and in multiple ways. In the broadest sense, the term evokes the variegated identities, including Amazigh/Berbers, Arab-Christians, Arab-Jews, Armenians, Assyrians, Chaldeans, Copts, Druze, Kurds, Iranians, Nubians, Turks, which do not easily fall under the "Arab-Muslim" rubric. In this sense, the volume assumes the complexity of Middle Eastern diasporic formations within and in relation to diverse spaces—at their point of departure and at their point of arrival, as well as in their continuous multiple cross-border movements. Although we considered the term "West Asia," we also felt that because it was not the operative term in the academic and public discourse, it therefore would fail to capture the volume's critical engagement with Orientalist representations, especially when one of the purposes of this volume was to highlight what the region signified in popular culture. We echo this common usage of the term, however inaccurate, to include North Africa as well, since within the public sphere "the Middle East" does tend to "cover" the region of North Africa, including in academic organizations, for example, The Middle East Studies Association. Our use of the quotes surrounding the term "the Middle East," in this sense, alludes to **the idea** of the Middle East as signifying a broad geographical spectrum, while acknowledging that it is a problematic rubric. We also surround the term "the Middle East" with apologetic quotation marks to point to its colonial and Eurocentric genealogy. The term reifies the position of Europe as the arbiter of spatial evaluation dividing up "the East" into "Near," "Middle," and "Far."[51]

Between the Middle East and the Americas strives to expand the ways geographies of culture are conceived, imagined, and analyzed. It highlights the way cultural production, consumption, and reception are intimately intertwined, with blurry boundaries made ever more entangled within multiple itineraries. This interdisciplinary project begins from the premise that representation itself is a site of contestation, with profound historical and theoretical implications for area studies, ethnic studies, and American studies. The volume as a whole aims to further illuminate the complex relationship between American studies, ethnic studies, and area studies as it impacts the analysis of the Middle East in the United States and the Americas. In sum, it aims to disentangle conventional geographies of meaning, moving beyond the binarist notion of "here" and "there," in an effort to transcend a ghettoized mapping of the diverse regions of the world by highlighting an inter–area studies perspective.[52]

Both U.S. ethnic studies and area studies, central loci for the production of knowledge on marginalized ethnicities and geographies, have largely ignored Middle Eastern Americans. Ethnic studies, for example, has generally assumed a limited and fixed conceptualization of American race/ethnicity, although this conceptualization has been challenged recently.[53] Ethnic studies, like the census, has defined itself primarily through four ethnic categories: African American studies, Asian American studies, Native American studies, and Chicano/Latino studies. Over the past decade, these hyphenated identities have begun to claim a certain space in American studies, entering the debate on race and ethnicity in the United States. Since 9/11, however, American studies and U.S. ethnic studies have begun to pay attention to the Middle Eastern diaspora, with a growing number of courses on campuses, panels at conferences, and growing scholarship on Arab Americans. The contributors to this volume add to this body of work by examining particular sites in which various discourses of "the Middle East" are produced and performed in the Americas.

The Persistent Struggle over Representation

In addition to bringing these geographies together and challenging area studies and ethnic studies models, we also seek to incorporate postcolonial cultural studies methods into Arab American studies and Middle Eastern studies. Within Arab American studies, while ample work develops historical, sociological, and anthropological approaches, few works take cultural studies approaches or cover both North and South America.[54] And while cultural studies approaches have been incorporated into American studies and Latin American studies, such approaches have been, for the most part, absent in Middle Eastern studies. At the center of our inquiry is the question of how cultural texts generate discourses about "the Middle East," how these discourses circulate and are consumed, and how they change over time and across space. It is not merely who speaks for the Middle Eastern diaspora but also within which conceptual paradigms it is represented. The problem of representation and discourse analysis, as articulated in this volume, is central to the study of cultural politics.

The case of *O Clone / El Clon* could also serve as a metonymy and metaphor for the ongoing battle over the veracity and authenticity of the representation of Arab/Muslim culture, that is, the persistent debate over "the real." Heated website discussions, for example, on Telemundo forum topics, cover a vast array of themes in and around *O Clone*'s portrayal of polygamy, the veil, the Muslim pillars of faith, women's role in Muslim society, and so forth. The question of veracity and accuracy was also on the minds of the Brazilian team that created *O Clone*. The telenovela's writer Gloria Perez and director Jayme Monjardim indicated that although they did not alter the script after 9/11, the event did generate a newfound sense of responsibility to "differentiate Islam from terrorism," especially since "Brazilians are much less exposed to Muslims in their daily lives than Americans or Europeans."[55] On the other hand, they are also less exposed to the War on Terror rhetoric typical of U.S. politicians. In preparation for the script, Perez reportedly immersed herself in research, visiting the Middle East / North Africa to study Muslim rituals of marriage and birth, for example, while Muslim clerics conducted workshops attended by the director and the cast prior to the filming.[56]

Despite the producers' efforts to accurately represent Islam and Arab culture, the reception of the telenovela underlines the politically charged nature of such representational practices. The telenovela elicited a heated international debate on websites, with conflicting responses, deriving, we would suggest, from the tensions and contradictions within the narrative itself, which simultaneously exploits Orientalist topoi while also celebrating Arab culture. Living between Brazil and Morocco, the protagonist Jade is painfully torn between pursuing her desire to be with the Brazilian Lucas and performing her duty to accept an arranged marriage with a Muslim man. Lucas, meanwhile, has to reconcile his passion for Jade, and his desire to play music, as well as the imperative of working for the family business and marrying within the Brazilian elite. Both Jade and Lucas tragically spend most of their lives married to people with whom they are not in love, fulfilling familial or cultural obligations while denying their own desire and longing.

While in *O Clone* Brazilian culture signifies relative freedom, the narrative also suggests that Lucas's life is not completely free. Very much like Jade, Lucas too has to cope with familial and social expectations, in particular the class expectations of a well-to-do son of the Brazilian elite. Although a man enjoying Brazilian-style freedom, Lucas's life eerily mirrors that of Jade. Jade, meanwhile, is the only woman in her family circle who faces cultural and religious conflict; the other women, such as her cousin, shaped by their religious and cultural assumptions, opt willingly for arranged marriages. Unlike Jade, they are not portrayed as oppressed. Jade marries Said, the man her family picks for her, a kind man who falls deeply in love with her, and who is heartbroken at having to try, day after day, to win the heart of a woman in love with someone else. In this sense the narrative complicates binarist representations of both Moroccan and Brazilian cultures. Although *O Clone* is replete with examples of stereotyping and essentializing Muslim-Arab culture, it also incorporates narrative moments and actions that challenge such stereotypes through more rounded and complex portrayals.

Although in one sense both protagonists lead a life of self-denial to satisfy familial and cultural expectations, in another sense the Muslim woman's conflictual existence, given her stringent religious duties, is more profoundly dramatic and devastating. This glaring difference has to do with *O Clone*'s narrative contextualization of the protagonists' ambient cultures. *O Clone* relies on a binary opposition between Moroccan and Brazilian cultures, with Brazil standing in for Western freedom. The telenovela frequently juxtaposes scenes of Muslim women wrapped head to toe in hijab with Brazilian women flaunting tangas on the beach. Arab/Muslim culture is depicted as patriarchal, restrictive, and obsessed with rules, in contrast to Brazilian culture, portrayed as flexible, open, and gender-equal. In *O Clone* all Muslim-Arab women must cover themselves while Brazilian women enjoy wearing sexy clothes; Muslim women are prohibited from dating, while Brazilian women date freely and even have relationships outside of marriage; Brazilians go to discos and dance in the streets, while Arab women belly dance (with great frequency) in the privacy of their homes.

If in *O Clone* the world of Arab/Islam is associated with the struggle with "maktub" (literally, that which is written, or destiny, and the title of the theme song composed by Marcus Viana), the world of Brazil is associated with fighting and even triumphing over fate. The clone of the title refers to the cloning of Lucas's twin brother who was killed in an airplane accident. Through the act of cloning, the Brazilian scientist brings Lucas's lost brother back into the world. Cloning here signifies the ability to create, to generate, and be God-like in breathing new life into the old flesh. In the encounter between "maktub," on the one hand, and science, on the other, Brazil signifies science-friendly modernity—a refusal to simply accept that which is determined or predetermined. The notion of a scripturally foreordained fate, within the Orientalist imaginary, operates in tandem with other topoi and tropes, such as Oriental despotism (which assumes a passive mass subjected to the despot) and the pop psychology of Oriental fatalism, all alongside the formulaic binarism of an active, agential, modern West and a passive, traditional East.

In sum, despite *O Clone*'s attempt to offer a positive portrayal of Arabs and Islam, its narrative nonetheless reproduces a number of paradigmatic Orientalist tropes and binarist oppositions. The telenovela mixes customs and traditions from diverse regions and communities, subjecting the varied regions of the Middle East / North Africa to a "topographical reductionism"[57] that elides the significant differentiations within Arab/Islam's multiple geographies. While the telenovela's theme did feed into a growing Latin American curiosity about Islam, it also provoked discontent about its penchant for a presumably ethnographic representation of polygamy, harems, and veils. One of the telenovela's critics, Morocco's ambassador to Brazil, Abdelmalek Cherkaoui Ghazouani, was especially alarmed by *O Clone*'s image of Morocco. Posting critical comments on his embassy's website bulletin board,[58] he debunked four myths: that polygamy is standard and widely practiced; that women do not study or work outside of the home; that women are subordinate to men; and that belly dancing is how men and women communicate. He clarified that the Moroccan state prohibits polygamy; that women are not confined to the home; and that belly dancing is not the national dance but popular in tourist locations.[59]

The issue of accuracy and distortion is a complex one and can be seen on a number of levels. On the one hand, a fair and adequate representation is vitally necessary within a public and media sphere proliferating in negative images. On the other hand, the discussion must go beyond veristic accuracy and positive images, which revolve around questions of character, to engage issues of voice, discourse, and ideology.[60] For example, often the idea of the "real Arab" is articulated within a set of assumptions and axioms about modernity: "the real" Arab is "the modern" Arab. Such criticisms convey an investment in the metanarrative of modernity, where the Arab nation-state is viewed as a vehicle for emancipation and progress. This volume acknowledges the importance of accuracy but it also points to the complex issues involved in the demand for authentic representation. In terms of sheer factuality, *O Clone* does indeed fail to indicate a basic fact, in this case the Moroccan state prohibition of polygamy. It is also factually problematic to portray all Arab-Muslims as practicing polygamy. In doing so, such narratives elide a potentially more complex conflict having to do with tensions between certain traditions and state prohibitions of those very same traditions. At the same time, such narratives tend to portray Arab/Muslim society as inherently patriarchal, presumably in contrast with nonpatriarchal non-Arab societies. But such a formulation elides the issue of patriarchy in Western societies. While Arab/Islamic culture is presented as a space of polygamy, the more subtle "harem structures"[61] of the differently structured patriarchal societies of the West (for example, the conventional triad of husband, wife, and lover) remain unthematized.

The following questions are thus central to this volume: How are the discourses and ideologies about and from the Middle East imagined and enacted through cultural practices such as literary translation and hip-hop, now also unfolding in digital spaces? What are the social and historical conditions of possibility that produce the simultaneous commodification, demonization, and appreciation of Middle Eastern culture in the Americas? How do meanings about Arab and Muslim identities shift in function of geographical context and historical moment? Within a postcolonial cultural studies approach the volume focuses on significations produced by texts and the ways in which these significations participate in a larger contested field of the politics of representation. Rather than merely studying the object of culture, cultural studies has advanced a poststructuralist methodology of reading hegemonic and resistant practices. Overlapping with the volume's cultural studies concern is also a postcolonial studies perspective that addresses the question of "cultural politics" or "the politics of culture." In this sense the volume engages the ways in which identities become sites of contestation, politicization, and struggle over national narratives, and in the context of transnational cultural flows.

Diaspora and the Politics of Culture

The essays focus largely on contemporary cultural sites, situating them historically within the twentieth-century context of multiple dislocations. The volume is divided into two parts. The first section, "Nation, Culture, and Representation," is composed of essays examining the cultural politics of "the Middle East" in the Americas through narratives of "the Nation." These contributions focus on how representations of the Middle East and its diasporas shape conceptions of nation, nationalism, and national identity. The second section, "Diaspora, Transnation, and Translation," highlights the transnational dimension of these issues by analyzing the ways that representations of the Middle East and its diasporas circulate and translate across national borders. As the purpose of this book is to move beyond nationalist toward transnational analytical perspectives, even essays focused on the Middle Eastern diaspora within a single national zone also deconstruct the hegemonic nationalist narrative by foregrounding the complex diasporic negotiations entailed by multiple belongings.

As a preamble to both sections of the collection, Ella Shohat's essay "The Sephardi-Moorish Atlantic: Between Orientalism and Occidentalism" explores the impact and implications of Edward Said's *Orientalism*. Asking when Orientalism begins, Shohat resituates Said's post-Enlightenment framework, suggesting the Reconquista of Iberia and the Conquista of the Americas—the "two 1492s"—as an alternative starting point. Orientalism, she argues, was constituted in the Americas long before it was applied to the colonized French and British Middle East/North Africa, as part of an historically triangulated relationality between the geographies of Islam, Europe, and the Americas. Pre-existing Iberian phobic discourses about Jews and Muslims—what we would now call an Orientalist ideology—traveled to the Americas, "orientalizing" the indigenous peoples. The reading of Luso-Tropical texts (such as Gilberto Freyre's), meanwhile, reveals that the Sephardi/Moor has co-existed with the opposite anxiety about the "Oriental" element in Iberian blood/culture, resulting in an Occidentalization/de-Orientalization project of cleansing of the Sephardi/Moorish traces from the veins of Latin America. While some Latin American scholars have productively extended Said's critique of post-Enlightenment Orientalism to the representation of Latin America, they have at the same time elided the centrality of the proto-Orientalism of the Reconquista and the ways in which the Conquista itself was already profoundly imbricated in anti-Semitism and anti-Islamism. Occidentalism—in Mignolo's sense—and Orientalism—in Said's sense—are interdependent, and can be seen as branches of Eurocentrism as they are intimately connected and mutually constitutive within the same historical moment. In doing so, Shohat also calls for a capacious and diasporic reconceptualization of area studies (including Middle East studies and Latin American studies) and ethnic studies (including Arab American Studies). Besides being a foundational text for postcolonial studies, *Orientalism,* Shohat argues, is also an Arab American studies text that must be understood within the American historical context in which it was written, against the backdrop of the transformed academic landscape impacted by ethnic studies, women's studies, and Third World studies challenges to Eurocentric protocols. Shohat investigates the contemporary implications of Said's final "Orientalism Now" chapter, noting that the current trend of transnational flows and the diasporization of Middle Eastern peoples call into question reified notions of regional boundaries. Rather than see "the Middle East" as a fixed sign with demarcated boundaries between East and West, Shohat argues that the scope of Middle Eastern studies and Arab American studies has to be mapped transnationally, subjected to a diasporic cross-border critique as a method of reading. What could be called a "diasporic turn" would help us conceptualize all regions in a more flexible and non-finalized manner, wherein each geography constitutes not a point of origin or final destination, but a terminal in a transnational network.

The following essay in the first section, "Nation, Culture, and Representation," is Jacob Berman's "Mahjar Legacies: A Reinterpretation." Berman examines how the writers—members of the first or early generation of Arab immigrants, from 1880 to 1924—conceptualized Arab and Arab American identity. Focusing on mahjar writers Ameen Rihani and Khalil Gibran, Berman asks about the causes for the absence of Arab particularity in such work. Is this absence the legacy of Orientalist representation or early Arab American self-representation? Berman frames the discussion around tensions between the discourse of ethnic particularity and national discourse of assimilation. He discusses the trope of "the Arab street vendor" as one of the only visible representations of Arabs circulating during the period of mahjar writing. Representative of broader U.S. immigration fantasies, the image of the Arab vendor represented both cultural difference and the necessity of eradicating difference through cultural assimilation. Berman examines how Rihani's and Gibran's writings are both complicit in assimilationist U.S. discourses and simultaneously emphasize their difference, thus allowing them to culturally assimilate into whiteness while retaining a modicum of Arab identity. Berman argues that Rihani's and Gibran's approaches to identity can be seen as acts of figurative self-representation, of a constant process of becoming that resists closure and thus anticipates the work of contemporary Arab American writers.

John Tofik Karam's essay, "*Turcos* in the Mix: Corrupting Arabs in Brazil's Racial Democracy," examines the complexities of Arab inclusion in Brazil's self-conception as a "racial democracy," read through the media coverage of the São Paulo city government corruption scandals in 1999 and 2000. In these scandals, corruption was signified as Arab while other groups implicated in corruption were depicted as innocent victims, illuminating deep-seated prejudices about Arabs as fundamentally dishonest and outside the pale of national belonging. Karam examines how elite Arab Brazilians have sought to integrate themselves into the Brazilian national imaginary by narrating themselves as part of Brazil's racial mixture. One such example is the Lebanese Independence Day celebration, an event that Karam reads as exhibiting the Lebanese Brazilian elite's investment in Arab assimilation into the "Brazilian race." The national narrative of racial mixture was thus appropriated by Arab Brazilian elites to incorporate Arabs into the Brazilian national narrative of "racial democracy." This affirmation of racial democracy, for Karam, is not simply an example of being duped but rather of the creative use of language against social exclusion.

Theresa Alfaro-Velcamp's essay, "From 'Baisanos' to Billionaires: Locating Arabs in Mexico," explores Lebanese Mexican identity, demonstrating that discourses on Arabness in Mexico relate to specific historical, economic, and social contexts that have produced a certain ambivalence among Mexicans. Through a reading of popular print media in the form of columns, cartoons, newspaper clippings, and interviews, and through an examination of a cultural community center for Lebanese immigrants (Centro Libanés), Alfaro-Velcamp explores how Arab immigrants construct a unique Lebanese Mexican identity that transforms them into the oxymoron "foreign citizens." She reveals how class conflicts are personified in Lebanese discourses in Mexico, where financially affluent Lebanese groups play up their foreignness, even if they are Mexican-born, as a way to exclude poor and Muslim Arabs from a hegemonic notion of Lebanese identity. Using the concept of "foreign citizenship" to describe relational issues of identity, Alfaro-Velcamp explains how Lebanese groups use their "foreignness" to distinguish themselves from their Mexican counterparts while often facing contradictory receptions including xenophobia because of their wealth. Alfaro-Velcamp tracks these differences, explaining the contrast between elite Lebanese groups, who identify primarily as Lebanese, and poorer Lebanese (Muslims in particular), who tend to identify as Mexican while simultaneously maintaining a strong sense of Lebanese identity.

Christina Civantos's "Ali Bla Bla's Double-Edged Sword: Argentine President Carlos Menem and the Negotiation of Identity" examines representations of the most prominent Arab Argentine, former president Carlos Menem. In the late 1980s, as Menem rose in national politics, anti-Arab sentiment and Orientalist representations rose as well. Civantos's essay inquires into the role of references to an Arab world of turbans, harems, and odalisques, and also a strict, fatalistic, and overpowering Islam within Menem's public presence, both in terms of his reception and the public persona he crafted. Taking into account nineteenth-century Argentine as well as Middle Eastern history and the figure of the Argentine gaucho or cowboy, Civantos examines representations of Menem in print media and popular entertainment to find that, although there is certainly much to criticize in Menem's political record, critiques of his administration invoke Menem's Arab background as though it were the inescapable source of his flaws. An analysis of Menem's public persona reveals that he has responded by, on the one hand, embracing an Orientalist vision of an opulent Arab world and, on the other hand, opening up a space for Argentine religious pluralism. Menem's class, ethnic, and religious self-fashioning, for Civantos, is a double-edged sword: while it exacerbates existing Orientalism, it also expands and opens up conceptions of Argentine identity.

Amira Jarmakani's "They Hate Our Freedom, But We Love Their Belly Dance: The Spectacle of the Shimmy in Contemporary U.S. Culture" approaches the recent surge in the popularity of belly dancing as a counterpoint to the demagoguery of the contemporaneous War on Terror. Jarmakani explores the parallels between the rhetoric of freedom in popular articulations of American belly dancing and the deployment of the concept of freedom in the War on Terror. Popular narratives of American belly dancing, she argues, inadvertently echo the logic used to justify U.S. military action in Iraq and Afghanistan; both focus on individual freedoms at the expense of any sustained consideration of systemic freedoms. Jarmakani also conducts a close reading of "Bellydance Superstars" to unpack how this series of DVDs signifies ideas about American nationalism through its tagline "the pursuit of life, liberty, and dance." Through the cooptation of difference, the championing of free trade, and the promotion of "freedom," belly dance becomes a kinetic embodiment of all these concepts. The popularity of belly dancing, for Jarmakani, allows U.S. audiences to endorse their own pursuit of freedom all the while ignoring their complicity in a global war.

In "From Arab Terrorists to Patriotic Arab Americans: Representational Strategies in Post-9/11 TV Dramas," Evelyn Alsultany examines how writers and producers have attempted to create representational strategies to circumvent accusations of racism and stereotyping in light of criticism by the Council on American-Islamic Relations and other watchdog groups. She identifies a series of strategies deployed by writers and producers of post-9/11 TV dramas when representing Arabs and Muslims as terrorists, such as including a "good Muslim" to "balance" the terrorist representation.

Through an examination of TV dramas that depict Arabs/Muslims as terrorists with a War on Terror framework, such as *24* and *Sleeper Cell,* Alsultany highlights what she calls "simplified complex representations," that is, the creation of apparently complex images that are ultimately predictable and formulaic. "Simplified complex representations" foster the illusion that the United States has entered a "postrace" era. These representational strategies, she argues, perform ideological work by producing a postracial imaginary that facilitates the denial of the severity and persistence of institutionalized racism. She assesses the limited impact of these strategies by examining their reception by TV critics and viewers and demonstrates how TV dramas are important sites in mediating the War on Terror, particularly in keeping viewers living and reliving the War on Terror.

Junaid Rana's "When Pakistanis Became Middle Eastern: Visualizing Racial Targets in the Global War on Terror" examines the construction of a racialized Muslim within post-9/11 U.S. visual culture. Through analyses of the television series *Sleeper Cell* and of the film *Syriana,* Rana notes the existence of a new kind of "ethnographic cinema" that both produces and contains the threatening Muslim figure who occupies either an Arab, African, or South Asian body. Rana argues that *Sleeper Cell* draws on multiple specters in the American imagination, such as race wars, civil rights, multiculturalism, and anti-imperialism that gesture toward fears of terrorism, and that *Syriana* figures Muslims, Arabs, and Pakistanis against the United States despite being praised for its complex rendering of the Muslim world. Rana illustrates how these media representations code Muslims as backward and inherently anti-American, and naturalize the Muslim body as the location of terrorism, despite more complex representations, and therefore advances the Muslim racial formation that collapses the boundaries of race, culture, and religion. Emphasizing visual technologies of racialization, Rana contends that the problem of defining Pakistani immigrants is not so much about the commonalities of Muslim countries and regions but rather about complex migrations, foreign policies, and geopolitical strategies of empire building. Based on a critical analysis of popular media treatment of themes of terror and Islam, his essay demonstrates how the figure of the Muslim is rendered as a geographically and historically legible racial target, which is then deployed to depict Pakistani migrants as potential terrorists.

Sunaina Maira's essay begins the volume's second part, entitled "Diaspora, Transnation, and Translation." Her chapter, "'A Strip, A Land, A Blaze': Arab American Hip-Hop and Transnational Politics," explores the ways in which hip-hop has become a site for constructing an Arab American identity at once political and cultural, national and transnational. Based on interviews with rap artists and the analysis of song lyrics by Excentrik, Iron Sheik, Ragtop, and others, Maira argues that progressive Arab American hip-hop provides an archive of histories of displacement and resistance that helps forge affiliations with other minoritized communities in the United States. At the same time, it challenges the repression of Arab American political movements, while linking the concerns of Arab and Muslim communities to the War on Terror and U.S. policies in the Middle East. Ultimately, in Maira's view, hip-hop forms part of a growing youth subculture that offers a critique of colonialism and racism by resisting Orientalist depictions of Arabs.

In "Muslim Digital Diasporas and the Gay Pornographic Cyber Imaginary," Karim Tartoussieh explores the rise of Arab digital diasporic communities in the United States and the ways in which Muslim Arab Americans use cyber technology. Set against the backdrop of post-9/11, Tartoussieh argues that the Internet allows Muslims in the United States to cope with their sense of alienation by providing platforms through which they can connect with other Muslims in both the diaspora and the homeland. Through an analysis of digital Muslim networking sites—Muslim dating sites, the cyber preaching of Amr Khaled, and online Muslim forums—and cyber representations of male Arab queerness in gay pornography websites, the essay highlights the linkages between transnational digital production, citizenship, and identity formation. Islamic digital networks have helped create a virtual public sphere for the community while also fostering digital citizenship that allows the construction of Muslim American identities without compromising religion. However, not everyone may participate in these communities; queer Arab Americans have been largely excluded. Despite attempts to create queer Arab American online spaces, marginal efforts exist in contrast to the plethora of Internet pornography sites that fetishize imagined Arab bodies, which capitalizes on sexual fantasies that conflate "Muslim" and "terrorist," as well as mark Muslim Arab bodies as signifiers of danger and violence. The juxtaposition of these two digital spaces offers different snapshots of the cyber imaginary, on the one hand illustrating how Muslims are using the Internet to find an acceptable marriage partner and explore their faith, and on the other, exhibiting fetishized forms of how Muslims and Arabs are imagined.

Helle Rytkønen's "Drawing the Line: A Rhetorical Analysis of the Mohammed Cartoons Controversy as It Unfolded in Denmark and the United States" examines the 2006 controversy provoked by Danish newspaper cartoons depicting the Prophet Mohammed as a terrorist. Rytkønen compares the U.S. and Danish media discourses and governments' reactions to this controversy, as well as the meanings that were produced about Muslim identity. According to Rytkønen, the Danish government framed the controversy around a putative Muslim inability to understand free speech, and therefore their inability to assimilate in the West, placing Muslims outside the imagined Danish national community. The U.S. government, in contrast, framed the controversy around the newspaper's lack of responsibility in misusing their right to free speech. Both the U.S. and Danish media broadcast the violent demonstrations that broke out in relation to the cartoons daily, highlighting what was perceived as an overreaction that signified Muslim inability to assimilate. However, many U.S. newspapers refused to reprint the cartoons in order to be religiously sensitive, while European newspapers tended to republish them. Rytkønen demonstrates that the U.S. response to the cartoons does not necessarily reflect greater pluralism as compared to Denmark but rather reflects its concern with its global image in the age of the War on Terror.

Heba El Attar's "*Turcophobia* or *Turcophilia*: Politics of Representing Arabs in Latin America" examines both the dominant representations of Arabs in Latin American literature and Arab-Latin American counter–self-representations. Through a focus on Turcophobia, the fear of the Arab "other," and Turcophilia, the integration of the Arab into a Latin American hybridized identity, El Attar reveals a dynamic tension in discourses that include and exclude Arabs from Latin American national imaginaries. Through an examination of representations of Arabs in Colombian novelist Gabriel García Márquez's *Chronicle of a Death Foretold*, the work of Palestinian-Chilean poet Mahfud Massis, and the Arab-Chilean magazine, *Al-Damir*, El Attar charts a shift from Turcophobia and toward Turcophilia. These representations and counter-representations, for El Attar, show that more complex understandings of Arab identity in Latin America have become possible, ultimately demonstrating Arab immigrants' ability to assert their hyphenated identities and to strengthen intercultural bonds within Latin American society.

In "User-Friendly Islams: Translating Rumi in France and the United States," Ziad Elmarsafy focuses on Rumi, the thirteenth-century mystic thinker and poet from Tajikistan and Turkey, who wrote in Persian and became well-known in the 1960s and 1970s among both poets and readers within Anglophone literary society. Elmarsafy examines how Rumi's poetry has been packaged, marketed, and sold in the United States compared to France. Within the United States, Rumi's popularity depended on de-Islamicizing his identity, whereas in France his popularity was linked to his Muslim identity. In the United States, Rumi is custom-designed to appeal to a New Age audience, constructed as a supranational and non-denominational figure whose message of peace and tolerance feeds spiritually deprived American readers. In France, in contrast, Rumi's work is respected not only for its message of love but also for the Muslim roots of his writing in the Qur'an. This difference in representation derives, for Elmarsafy, from the very different historical relationships to the Middle East of the United States vis-à-vis France.

R. Shareah Taleghani's essay "'Axising' Iran: The Politics of Domestication and Cultural Translation" examines the representation of Iran in the United States through the reception of particular English-language memoirs by Iranian women. Drawing on poststructuralist translation studies, Taleghani demonstrates how memoirs such as *Reading Lolita in Tehran* (2003) and *Lipstick Jihad* (2005) serve as domesticated forms of cultural translation. Framing cultural translation as an ethnographic process, Taleghani notes that the production of Iranian women's memoirs allows Iran to be textually, politically, and culturally appropriated, rendered as coherent and monolithic, even while claiming to combat stereotypes about Iranian life. The narratives often constitute their authors as authoritative subjects, failing to situate the production of these memoirs as part of a market economy that favors the production of particular types of narratives about Iran while ultimately affirming U.S. cultural supremacy. Taleghani links the celebratory but highly problematic reception of these texts to the marginalization of Persian literature in English translation, while also suggesting how alternative forms of translation can function as cultural intervention.

In "'The Uneven Bridge of Translation': Turkey in between East and West," Shouleh Vatanabadi examines the politics of translation in the context of cultural production in modern Turkey. Turkey is approached as a constructed site of a bridge-nation "in-between" the axes of "East" and "West," and is discussed as a case study that highlights the complexities, contradictions, and, above all, the power inequalities inherent in the politics of cultural representation through translation. In the process of constructing a "modern" and "Western" Turkish identity, Vatanabadi contends, the bridge between "East" and "West" was ultimately unidirectional, serving mainly as a crossing into the European "West," while creating a disconnect with the Asian "East." Through a discussion of the work of Nobel Prize–winning author Orhan Pamuk and Elif Shafak, Vatanabadi reveals the asymmetries of cultural exchange and cultural production across the geographies of the Middle East and the United States. Vatanabadi historicizes the Kemalist modernizing project in Turkey as one that strategically translated Western classics into Turkish, and severed its connection to Persian and Arabic in order to purify itself from its Ottoman past, and in order to redefine Turkey within a Western paradigm. In contrast, writing in English by Middle Eastern authors as well as the translation of Turkish literature into English have been limited by an Orientalist framework that has marketed cultural difference where the Turkish authors in cultural translation are simultaneously included and excluded.

This volume attempts to address a lacuna in the scholarly landscape by examining the production and critique of Orientalism from a transnational perspective that complicates the East/West. It also attempts to examine differing and overlapping forms of Orientalism on the North/South axis, all performed within a postcolonial studies-cultural studies approach. By including essays that examine diverse national contexts and their in-betweenness, the volume hopes to illuminate the study of Middle Eastern diasporas within a comparative, relational, and transnational perspective. Cumulatively, the essays point to the complex and ambivalent situation of Arabs/Muslims in the Americas, where they are at once celebrated and demonized, integrated and marginalized. Rather than present a single monolithic voice as embodying a unified and coherent community, the volume orchestrates a polyphony of voices, pointing to the irrevocable heterogeneity of Arab/Muslim communities, in the plural, despite the monologic essentialisms of Islamophobic demogogues. The essays reveal Arab/Muslim identity as multiple and conjunctural, shaped by very diverse situations in North America, South America, and Europe, and in relation to already existing communities and asymmetrical national and transnational formations and ideologies. In the United States, the Middle Eastern diaspora incorporate and transform the nationalist ideologies of "an immigrant nation" and "the melting pot" and "E Pluribus Unum," while also fighting off the rhetoric of a "Christian nation" and the "War on Terror."[62] In Latin America, Arab/Muslims are less haunted by the War on Terror but still bring with them contradictory memories of the Crusades and the Convivencia, the Conquista and Al Andalus, while interacting in the present day with the discourse of "la Raza Cósmica," the stereotype of "el Turco," and the idealizations of "racial democracy." Within this process, the representatives of Arab/Muslim communities, including its scholars and intellectuals, interface with various national ideologies that are conflictual, not only between nations but also within them, where Islamophobia competes with Islamophilia, racism with antiracism, colonialism with anticolonialism.

NOTES

1. On Brazil and Latin America's contradictory Sephardic/Moorish longing and Moorish unconscious, see Ella Shohat's essay in this volume.

2. The CD features belly dance music produced by Marcus Viana and includes the Mouzayek Arab Ensemble and Syrian singer Tony Mouzayek, who resides in Brazil.

3. *El Universal,* cited from www.telenovela-world.com, 6 (accessed October 1, 2010).

4. Information supplied by Brazilian film scholar João Luis Vieira in conversation with Ella Shohat, Rio de Janeiro, spring 2003.

5. Steve Brennan, "Telemundo Revives 'El Clon' for Latino Market," Reuters,

May 12, 2008, http://www.reuters.com/article/idUSN1256382420080512 (accessed May 1, 2012).

6. Ibid. and Elizabeth Barbosa, "The Brazilian Telenovela 'El Clon': An Analysis of Viewer's Online Vicarious and Virtual Learning Experiences," Dissertation, Lynn University, 2005, http://www.floridabrasil.com/brazilian-soup-opera/47.html (accessed May 1, 2012). Also see Meghan Simpson, "Traveling Soap Operas, Brazil to Kyrgyzstan: Meaning-making and Images of the 'Muslim Woman,'" *Journal of International Women's Studies* 11, no. 1 (November 2009): 304–24. http://www.iiav.nl/ezines//IAV_606411/IAV_606411_2009_11_1/Meghan.pdf (accessed May 1, 2012).

7. This argument here on the interconnectedness of regions is premised on the proposal for such modes of cultural analysis in Ella Shohat, ed. *Talking Visions: Multicultural Feminism in a Transnational Age* (Boston and New York: MIT Press and the New Museum, 1998); and Ella Shohat, *Taboo Memories, Diasporic Voices* (Durham: Duke University Press, 2006).

8. Here one could expand the notions of a Black, Red, and White Atlantic to speak of a Brown Atlantic, or Arab/Muslim Atlantic, or Sepharic/Moorish Atlantic, as part of a multiply raced Atlantic, or the Rainbow Atlantic. See Ella Shohat and Robert Stam, *Race in Translation: Culture Wars around the Postcolonial Atlantic* (New York: New York University Press, 2012).

9. On this shared Orientalist intertext but also on the difference in terms of foundational self-definition of Europe against Islam, in contrast to the United States, see Robert Stam and Ella Shohat, *Flagging Patriotism: Crises of Narcissism and Anti-Americanism* (New York: Routledge, 2006).

10. Lauren Russell, "Church Plans Quran-Burning Event," CNN, July 31, 2010, http://www.cnn.com/2010/US/07/29/florida.burn.quran.day/index.html (accessed May 1, 2012).

11. David W. Dunlap, "When an Arab Enclave Thrived Downtown," *New York Times*, August 24, 2010, http://www.nytimes.com/2010/08/25/nyregion/25quarter.html?_r=1&adxnnl=1&adxnnlx=1283773048-Lke2mYrQBSmD747iM9yLEg (accessed May 1, 2012).

12. For a proposal for such methodological investigation as "linked analogies," see Ella Shohat and Robert Stam, "Transnationalizing Comparison: The Uses and Abuses of Cross-Cultural Analogy," *New Literary History* 40, no. 3 (Summer 2009): 473–99; Ella Shohat and Robert Stam, "De-Eurocentrizing Cultural Studies: Some Proposals," in *Internationalizing Cultural Studies: An Anthology*, ed. Ackbar Abbas and John Nguyet Erni (Blackwell Publishing, 2005), 481–98; and Ella Shohat and Robert Stam, *Race in Translation*.

13. On this problem of invisibility and hypervisibility, see Mervat Hatem, "The Invisible American Half: Arab American Hybridity and Feminist Discourses in the 1990s," and on the erasure of the hyphen in the Moroccan-Israeli-American and the making of certain Middle Eastern identities invisible, see Ella Shohat, "Introduction," both in Shohat, ed. *Talking Visions*. For more on representations of Arabs and Muslims in U.S. TV dramas, see Evelyn Alsultany, *Arabs and Muslims in the Media: Race and Representation after 9/11* (New York: NYU Press, 2012).

14. This argument for a relational approach is based on Ella Shohat and Robert Stam, *Unthinking Eurocentrism*, and Ella Shohat's "Introduction" to *Talking Visions*.

15. "Americans' Views of the Islamic World," *Gallup Poll News Service*, February 8, 2006.

16. "Anti-Muslim Sentiment Fairly Commonplace," *Gallup Poll News Service*, August 10, 2006.

17. Anny Bakalian and Mehdi Bozorgmehr, *Backlash 9/11: Middle Eastern and Muslim Americans Respond* (Berkeley: University of California Press, 2009); American-Arab Anti-Discrimination Committee, "Report on Hate Crimes and Discrimination Against Arab Americans: The Post-September 11 Backlash" (Washington, DC: American-Arab Anti-Discrimination Committee Research Institute, 2003). http://www.adc.org/hatecrimes/pdf/2003_report_web.pdf (accessed September 30, 2008). For additional information on hate crimes, the experiences of Arab Americans, and government measures post-9/11, see Arab American Institute, "Healing the Nation: The Arab American Experience after September 11," AAI's first-anniversary report on Profiling and Pride, 2002, http://www.aaiusa.org/issues/1639 (accessed September 30, 2008); and Human Rights Watch, "We Are Not the Enemy: Hate Crimes against Arabs, Muslims, and Those Perceived to be Arab or Muslim after September 11th," *Human Rights Watch Report* 14, no. 6 (G), (November 2002), http://www.hrw.org/reports/2002/usahate/ (accessed September 30, 2008). Also see Louise Cainkar, "The Impact of 9/11 on Muslims and Arabs in the United States," in John Tirman, ed., *The Maze of Fear: Security and Migration after September 11th* (New York: The New Press, Spring 2004).

18. See "Blocking Faith, Freezing Charity," ACLU Report, June 16, 2009, http://www.aclu.org/human-rights/report-blocking-faith-freezing-charity (accessed August 18, 2010), and Louise Cainkar, *Homeland Insecurity: The Arab American and Muslim American Experience after 9/11* (New York: Russell Sage Foundation, 2009).

19. Nadine Naber refers to this trauma as "internment of the psyche"; see Naber, "Rules of Forced Engagement," *Cultural Dynamics* 18, no. 3: 235–65. On return emigration, see Junaid Rana, *Terrifying Muslims: Race and Labor in the South Asian Diaspora* (Durham: Duke University Press, 2011).

20. For more on Holy Land Mania and biblical Orientalism, see Burke O. Long, *Imagining the Holy Land: Maps, Models and Fantasy Travels* (Bloomington: Indiana University Press, 2003); Hilton Obenzinger, *American Palestine: Melville, Twain and the Holy Land Mania* (Princeton University Press, 1999); Melani McAlister, *Epic Encounters: Culture, Media, and U.S. Interests in the Middle East since 1945* (Berkeley: University of California Press, 2001); Alex Lubin, "Locating Palestine in pre-1948 Internationalism," in *Black Routes to Islam,* ed. Manning Marable and Hisham Aidi (Palgrave, 2008); Sherman Jackson, "Black Orientalism: Its Genesis, Aims and Significance for American Islam," in *Black Routes to Islam;* Ella Shohat, "Gender and the Culture of Empire" (1990), republished in *Taboo Memories, Diasporic Voices;* and Shohat, *Israeli Cinema: East/West and the Politics of Representation* (Austin: University of Texas Press, 1989; republished, IB Tauris, 2010).

21. For "Self-Orientalization," see Edward Said, *Orientalism* (New York: Vintage, 1979).

22. Fabricio Soza, "Argentárabe, algo más que una moda," Clarin.com, July 24, 2006, http://www.clarin.com/diario/2006/07/24/conexiones/t-01239538.html (accessed September 30, 2008).

23. See "Havana Habibi" at http://www.youtube.com/watch?v=tKXDBlmuXEA (accessed May 1, 2012).

24. For examples of belly dancing classes see www.odalisca.com and http://www.seleneodalisca.com.ar/. For an example of academic research on Arabs in Argentina, see www.altapolitica.com (accessed May 1, 2012).

25. For more information on these artists, see their websites: Ilham Al-Madfa'i (www.ilhamalmadfai.com), Enrico Macias (http://enrico.macias.free.fr/), Ziad Al Rahbani (www.ziadalrahbani.com), Hamza El Din (www.hamzaeldin.com), Ofra Haza (http://www.haza.co.il/), Hassan Hakmoun (www.hassanhakmoun.com), Cheb Khaled (http://khaled-lesite.artistes.universalmusic.fr/), Natacha Atlas (www.myspace.com/natachaatlasofficial), Alabina (www.alabina.info) (accessed September 30, 2008).

26. Hanine y Son Cubano's Facebook page: http://www.facebook.com/pages/Hanine-Y-son-cubano/17475686963#!/pages/Hanine-Y-son-cubano/17475686963?v=info (accessed September 30, 2008).

27. Louis Ibrahim, "'Hanine y Son Cubano' Enhancing Cultural Dialogue through Music," *The Star*, June 30, 2002, http://www.embacubasiria.com/Jordan/hanine.html (accessed September 30, 2008).

28. The material on Suheir Hammad is taken from Shohat and Stam, *Flagging Patriotism: Crises of Narcissism and Anti-Americanism* (New York: Routledge, 2007). We would like to thank Robert Stam for agreeing to have this shared material used here.

29. Many newspapers have written about Middle Eastern comedians. See, for example, Jodi Wilgoren, "Arab and Muslim Comics Turn Fear into Funny," *New York Times*, September 1, 2002, http://query.nytimes.com/gst/fullpage.html?res=9B05E4D8103FF932A3575AC0A9649C8B63 (accessed May 1, 2012); Jannat Jalil, "Muslim Comedians Laugh at Racism," *BBC News*, June 15, 2004, http://news.bbc.co.uk/2/hi/americas/3796109.stm (accessed May 1, 2012); Roya Heydarpour, "The Comic is Palestinian, the Jokes Bawdy," *New York Times*, November 21, 2006, http://www.nytimes.com/2006/11/21/nyregion/21ink.html?fta=y (accessed May 1, 2012); James Poniewozik, "Stand-Up Diplomacy," *Time*, March 19, 2007; Lorraine Ali, "Mining the Middle East for Laughs," *Newsweek* Web Exclusive, October 18, 2007, http://www.newsweek.com/id/56656 (accessed May 1, 2012); Larry Fine, "New Yorkers Laughing Again after Sept. 11 Trauma," *Yahoo! News, Canada*, July 19, 2002, http://ca.news.yahoo.com/020719/5/nqcj.html (accessed September 15, 2002).

30. In the 1980s and 1990s, Arab cultural representation was few and far between. Alongside such work as Joan Mandell's "Tales from Arab Detroit" (1995), there were a few other notable efforts, such as, the Arab Film Festival (curated by Margaret Penar); Middle Eastern diaspora art curated by Neery Melkonian; the Middle Eastern culture venue at the LA Festival (produced in the early 90s by Peter Sellers, which included a Middle Eastern film series curated by Ella Shohat); events at universities, such as "the Cinema of Displacement" at NYU organized by Ella Shohat, 1994); the screening of Palestinian films at the San Francisco Jewish Film Festival (1989, 1992); photographic exhibition on Yemeni Americans curated by Jonathan Friedlander (1988): and a few panels or individual papers on Middle Eastern diasporic culture at the Society for Cinema Studies, Modern Language Association, and the American Studies Association.

31. Other examples including ArteEast (established in New York in 2003), Alwan for the Arts (established in New York in 1998), and the Levantine Cultural Center (established in Los Angeles in 2001) have drawn engaged audiences for screenings, exhibitions, concerts, and book launches, along with panels, workshops, and public discussions. In Los Angeles, in 1995, *Al Jadid* has focused on reviewing and recording Arab culture and arts, including in diasporic locations. The journal *Mizna*, focusing on Arab American prose, poetry, and art in the United States, was launched in 1999 out of Minneapolis.

32. Along with Middle Eastern film festivals, there has been an increase in series

with a specific national focus: Iranian, Israeli, Palestinian, or Turkish cinemas. Media-related activities have also been giving voice to Arab and Middle Eastern diasporic perspectives. Established in Seattle in 1990, Arab Film Distributors has specialized in distributing Arab and Middle Eastern films.

33. In 2006, the Guggenheim Museum in New York dedicated a retrospective exhibition to the Iraqi-born architect Zaha Hadid, named in *Time Magazine*'s hundredth issue as one of the most influential thinkers in 2010. Iranian American artist Sherene Neshat, similarly, was featured on the cover of the *New Yorker*. Her work, like that of other artists of Middle Eastern origins such as the Palestinian-Lebanese-British Mona Hatoum and Lebanese-Canadian Jamelie Hassan, has been exhibited in galleries and museums such as the National Gallery of Canada, the Massachusetts Museum of Contemporary Art, the Museum of Contemporary Art in Chicago, the Irish Museum of Modern Art, La Fábrica Galería in Madrid, and the 10th Biennale of Sydney. Some of Jamelie Hassan's work has specifically commented on colonialism, Orientalism, American propaganda texts, and Canadian immigration policies.

34. Other examples include Arab Community Center for Economic and Social Services (ACCESS), The Union of Palestinian Women Associations of North America (UPWA), Palestinian American Women's Association (PAWA), Muslim Public Affairs Council (MPAC), the Palestine Office, Sunbula: Arab Feminists for Change, National Council on Arab Americans (NCA), Radical Arab Women's Activist Network (RAWAN), Arab Movement of Women Arising for Justice (AMWAJ), Free Palestine Alliance, Ahbab: The Queer Arab Site, the Gay and Lesbian Arab Society, and Lazeeza for Arab Queer Women. The San Francisco Bay Area Golden Thread Productions has been dedicated to Middle East–related production of theatrical works. Alternative media and cultural organizations, meanwhile, include The Arab American News, Arab Women Active in the Arts and Media (AWAAM), and the Radius of Arab American Writers, Inc. (RAWI). KPFA has given regular space to the program "Voices of the Middle East and North Africa." Radio and TV, such as the Arab Satellite Network, Link TV, and Arab Cable Television, broadcast Arabic programs produced locally in the United States as well as in the Middle East. On the Arabic cable station in New York one can watch Syrian news, Friday Muslim prayer services, and Coptic Egyptian sermons, along with Egyptian films and soap operas. Bridges TV, the first Muslim American English-language cable television channel, premiered in the United States in 2004.

35. Rabab Abdulhadi, Evelyn Alsultany, and Nadine Naber, eds., *Arab and Arab American Feminisms: Gender, Violence, and Belonging* (New York: Syracuse University Press, 2011); Nabeel Abraham and Andrew Shryock, eds., *Arab Detroit: From Margin to Mainstream* (Detroit: Wayne State University Press, 2000); Hishaam Aidi and Manning Marable, eds., *Black Routes to Islam* (New York: Palgrave, 2009); Amal Amireh and Lisa Suhair Majaj, eds., *Etel Adnan: Critical Essays on the Arab-American Writer and Artist* (Jefferson, NC: McFarland, 2002) and *Going Global: The Transnational Reception of Third World Women Writers* (New York: Routledge, 2000); Barbara Aswad, *Family and Gender among American Muslims: Issues Facing Middle Eastern Immigrants and Their Descendants* (Philadelphia: Temple University Press, 1996): Anny Bakalian and Mehdi Bozorgmehr, *Backlash 9/11: Middle Eastern and Muslim Americans Respond* (Berkeley: University of California Press, 2009); Moustafa Bayoumi, *How Does it Feel to be a Problem?* (New York: Penguin Books, 2008); Louise Cainkar, *Homeland Inse-*

curity: *The Arab American Experience after 9/11* (New York: Russell Sage Foundation, 2009): Brian Edwards, *Morocco Bound: Disorienting America's Maghreb, from Casablanca to the Marrakech Express* (Durham: Duke University Press, 2005): Sarah Gualtieri, *Between Arab and White: Race and Ethnicity in the Early Syrian American Diaspora* (Berkeley: University of California Press, 2009): Yvonne Haddad, *Not Quite American? The Shaping of Arab and Muslim Identity in the United States* (Longview, TX: Baylor Press, 2004); Elaine Hagopian, *Civil Rights in Peril: The Targeting of Arabs and Muslims* (London: Pluto Press, 2004); Salah D. Hassan and Marcy Newman, eds., *Arab American Literature,* MELUS 31, no. 4 (2006); Sally Howell, Amaney Jamal, Wayne Baker, Ann Chih Lin, Ronald Stockton, and Andrew Shryock, *Citizenship and Crisis: Arab Detroit after 9/11;* Lutfi Hussein, *The Internet Discourse of Arab-American Groups* (New York: Edwin Mellen Press, 2009); Amira Jarmakani, *Imagining Arab Womanhood: The Cultural Mythology of Veils, Harems and Belly Dancers in the U.S.* (New York: Palgrave, 2008); Mohja Kahf, *Western Representations of the Muslim Woman: From Termagant to Odalisque* (Austin: University of Texas Press, 1999); Pauline Kaldas and Khaled Mattawa, eds., *Dinarazad's Children: An Anthology of Contemporary Arab American Fiction* (University of Arkansas Press, 2nd ed., 2009); Alex Lubin and Alyosha Goldstein, eds., "Settler Colonialism," *South Atlantic Quarterly* 107, no.4 (Fall 2008); Sunaina Maira, *Missing* (Durham: Duke University Press, 2010): Melani McAlister, *Epic Encounters* (Berkeley: University of California Press, 2005); Minoo Moallem, *Between Warrior Brother and Veiled Sister* (Berkeley: University of California Press, 2005); Nadine Naber, *Arab America: Gender, Cultural Politics, and Activism* (New York: New York University Press, 2012); Nadine Naber and Amaney Jamal, eds., *Race and Arab Americans Before and After 9/11: From Invisible Citizens to Visible Subjects* (Syracuse University Press, 2007); Hamid Naficy, *The Making of Exile Cultures: Iranian Television in Los Angeles* (Minneapolis: University of Minnesota Press, 1993); Hamid Naficy, ed., *Home, Exile, Homeland: Film, Media, and the Politics of Place* (New York: Routledge, 1998); Sherene Razack, *Casting Out: The Eviction of Muslims From Western Law and Politics* (Toronto: University of Toronto Press, 2008); Steven Salaita, *Anti-Arab Racism in the USA: Where It Comes From and What It Means for Politics Today* (London: Pluto Press, 2006) and *The Uncultured Wars: Arabs, Muslims, and the Poverty of Liberal Thought* (London: Zed Books, 2008); Michael Suleiman, *Arabs in America: Building a New Future* (Philadelphia: Temple University Press, 1999); Jack Shaheen, *Guilty: Hollywood's Verdict on Arabs after 9/11* (Northampton, MA: Olive Branch Press, 2008); Evelyn Shakir, *Bint Arab: Arab and Arab American Women in the United States* (New York: Praeger Press, 1997).

36. Habeeb Salloum, "Arabs Making Their Mark in Latin America: Generations of Immigrants in Colombia, Venezuela and Mexico," *Al Jadid* 6, no. 30 (Winter 2000), http://www.aljadid.com/essays_and_features/ArabsMakingTheirMarkinLatinAmerica.html (accessed September 30, 2008).

37. Chris Moss, "Latin America's First Mega-Mosque," Islam Online, HispaniceMuslims.com, not dated, http://www.hispanicmuslims.com/articles/other/openseyes.html (accessed May 1, 2012).

38. See http://www.islamerica.org.ar/ and http://www.islamhoy.org/ (accessed May 1, 2012).

39. Rui Ferreira, "Some Cubans are Converting to Islam," *El Nuevo Herald,* 4/18/06, http://www.sunherald.com/mld/miamiherald/news/world/americas/14365407.html (accessed May 1, 2012).

40. See http://www.latinodawah.org/ and http://hispanicmuslims.com.

41. See http://hispanicmuslims.com/articles/. For examples of conversion stories, see http://www.muhajabah.com/my_journey_to_islam/sister_eri.php, http://www.islamonline.net/english/journey/jour34.shtml, http://www.homestead.com/nur/1truth.html, http://www.islamonline.net/english/journey/jour21.shtml (accessed September 30, 2008). Also see "Olé Allah Hisham Aidi Profiles New York's thriving Latino Muslim convert community," *Islam for Today*, n.d., http://www.islamfortoday.com/ole.htm (accessed May 1, 2012).

42. For more on Arabs in Latin America, see John Karam, *Another Arabesque* (Philadelphia: Temple University Press, 2007); Christina Civantos, *Between Argentines and Arabs* (Albany: State University of New York, 2006); Ignacio Klich and Jeffrey Lesser, eds., *Arab and Jewish Immigrants in Latin America* (New York: Routledge, 1998); and Theresa Alfaro-Velcamp, *So Far From Allah, So Close to Mexico* (Austin: University of Texas Press, 2007).

43. See statistics from 2005 from the U.S Department of State—*The International Religious Freedom Report for 2005*, http://www.state.gov/g/drl/rls/irf/2005/c15682.htm (accessed May 1, 2012). Also see Pop. Data—2009 CIA World Factbook and Habeeb Salloum, "Arabs Making Their Mark in Latin America: Generations of Immigrants in Colombia, Venezuela and Mexico," *Al Jadid* 6, no. 30 (Winter 2000), http://www.aljadid.com/essays_and_features/ArabsMakingTheirMarkinLatinAmerica.html (accessed September 30, 2008).

44. http://www.islamicpopulation.com/America/america_general.html (accessed May 1, 2012).

45. Larry Luxner and Douglas Engle, "The Arabs of Brazil," *Saudi Aramco World* 56, no. 5 (September–October 2005): 18–23, http://www.saudiaramcoworld.com/issue/200505/the.arabs.of.brazil.htm (accessed May 1, 2012).

46. Stan Lehman, "Arab Roots Grow Deep in Brazil's Rich Melting Pot," *Washington Post*, July 11, 2005, http://www.washingtontimes.com/news/2005/jul/11/20050711-92503-1255r/ (accessed May 1, 2012). For more on Arabs in Brazil, see John Karam, *Another Arabesque: Syrian-Lebanese Ethnicity in Neoliberal Brazil*.

47. "100 Questions and Answers About Arab Americans," *Detroit Free Press*, http://www.freep.com/legacy/jobspage/arabs/arab1.html (accessed September 30, 2008); Council on American Islamic-Relations, www.cair.com

48. Canada Statistics, http://www.statcan.gc.ca/pub/89-621-x/89-621-x2007009-eng.html (accessed September 30, 2008).

49. For more on mahjar writers, see Jacob Berman's essay in this volume and his book, *American Arabesque: Arabs and Islam in the Nineteenth Century Imaginary* (New York: NYU Press, 2012); Christina Civantos, *Between Argentines and Arabs;* Salma Khadra Jayyuis, *Trends and Movements in Modern Arabic Poetry*, vol. 1 (Belgium: Leiden E. J. Brill Press, 1977); and María del Mar Logroño Narbona, "A Transnational Dialogue from the Arab-Argentine Immigrant Press," *Al-Raida* 24, no. 116–17 (Winter/Spring 2007): 5–9, http://www.iiav.nl/ezines//email/alraida/2007/no116-117.pdf (accessed May 1, 2012). Also see the entry on Mahjar literature in *Encyclopedia of Arabic Literature*, vol. 2 by Julie Scott Meisami and Paul Starkey (New York: Routledge, 1998), 493.

50. Mary Louise Pratt, "Arts of the Contact Zone," *Profession* (New York: MLA), 91:33–40.

51. Ella Shohat and Robert Stam, *Unthinking Eurocentrism*, 2.

52. The argument concerning the complex relations between ethnic studies, area studies, and postcolonial studies is based on Shohat's proposals in her Preface and introductory essay "Gendered Cartographies of Knowledge: Area Studies, Ethnic Studies and Postcolonial Studies," in *Taboo Memories, Diasporic Voices.*

53. Steven Salaita, *Anti-Arab Racism in the U.S.A: Where It Comes From and What It Means for Politics Today* (London: Pluto Press, 2006), *The Holy Land in Transit* (New York: Syracuse University Press, 2006), and *Arab American Literary Fictions, Cultures, and Politics* (New York: Palgrave, 2007); Amaney Jamal and Nadine Naber, eds., *Race and Arab Americans Before and After 9/11: From Invisible Citizens to Visible Subjects* (Syracuse: Syracuse University Press, 2007); Louise Cainkar, *Homeland Insecurity* (New York: Russell Sage, 2009); Sunaina Maira, *Missing* (Durham: Duke University Press, 2010); Moustafa Bayoumi, *How Does It Feel to be a Problem?* (New York: Penguin Books, 2008); Junaid Rana, *Terrifying Muslims: Race and Labor in the South Asian Diaspora* (Durham: Duke, forthcoming, 2011); Detroit Arab Study Team, *Citizenship and Crisis: Arab Detroit after 9/11* (New York: Russell Sage Foundation, 2009).

54. One such exception is Darcy Zabel's edited volume, *Arabs in the Americas: Interdisciplinary Essays on the Arab Diaspora,* which does examine the Arab Diaspora in both North and South America. Darcy Zabel, ed., *Arabs in the Americas: Interdisciplinary Essays on the Arab Diaspora* (New York: Peter Lang, 2006). Also see W. Anderson and R. Lee, eds., *Displacement and Diasporas: Asians in the Americas* (New Jersey: Rutgers University Press, 2005).

55. www.telenovela-world.com (accessed September 30, 2008).

56. Ibid.

57. See Ella Shohat and Robert Stam, *Unthinking Eurocentrism,* 148.

58. http://tripatlas.com/O_Clone (accessed September 30, 2008).

59. Meghan Simpson, "Traveling Soap Operas, Brazil to Kyrgyzstan: Meaning-making and Images of the 'Muslim Woman,'" *Journal of International Women's Studies* 11, no. 1 (November 2009): 304–24, http://www.iiav.nl/ezines//IAV_606411/IAV_606411_2009_11_1/Meghan.pdf (accessed May 1, 2012).

60. This critique that addresses the limits of "positive image" analysis is based on Shohat and Stam's chapter "Stereotype, Realism, and the Struggle Over Representation," in *Unthinking Eurocentrism.* For a related critique of the image of the "good Arab" in Zionist representations, see Shohat's *Israeli Cinema: East/West and the Politics of Representation* (1989, republished by IB Tauris, 2010); and Evelyn Alsultany, *Arabs and Muslims in the Media.*

61. The term *harem structures* is used by Ella Shohat in her essay "Gender and the Culture of Empire" to refer to gendered/sexualized spaces imagined in ways similar to the Orientalist imaginary, even in the absence of harems, and in the contexts where the Orient is not thematized (*Quarterly Review of Film and Video,* Vol. 13, Iss. 1, 1991: 45–84), and also in the chapter "Tropes of Empire" in Shohat and Stam's *Unthinking Eurocentrism.*

62. For more on attempts to incorporate Arabs and Muslims within the imagining of a U.S. American nation, see Evelyn Alsultany, "Selling American Diversity and Muslim American Identity through Non-Profit Advertising Post-9/11," *American Quarterly* 59, no. 3 (September 2007): 593–622.

TWO

The Sephardi-Moorish Atlantic
Between Orientalism and Occidentalism

Ella Shohat

The question of beginnings in relation to Edward Said's book *Orientalism* can be narrated in very diverse ways, leading to a potentially productive question: when and where does Orientalism, and the critique of Orientalism, actually begin? On the occasion of the thirtieth anniversary of Said's book, it is instructive to situate the book in relation to the various geographies, histories, and fields of knowledge in which it is embedded. What are the contexts and intertexts of Said's work? How can we characterize its undergirding conceptual paradigms and disciplinary methodologies? What about the neighboring fields, such as ethnic studies, critical race studies, and cultural studies, which impacted and have been impacted by Said's work— are they relevant to Middle Eastern studies? Since the Saidian critique of Orientalist epistemology has by now been extrapolated to diverse cultural geographies, how can we map these transnational currents in relation to the study of the Middle East and its diasporas? And, finally, what does a book by a diasporic Palestinian in the United States tell us about the kinds of analytical frames and methods of readings that might illuminate what interests us in this volume: how to study transnationally a Middle East that is not merely "over there" but also "back here"?; and how to analyze cultural flows that are neither simply "over there" nor simply "back here"?

Decolonization of Knowledge and the Seismic Shift

The critique of Orientalism forms part of a broader movement of thought that shaped social, cultural, and intellectual life worldwide, to wit, the larger political/epistemological crisis of the postwar period. Although in the long view anticolonial discourse goes back to the early historical resistance to colonialism, its more immediate catalysts lie in a series of events—colonialist violence, the Jewish Holocaust, the postwar disintegration of the European empires, the Third World revolutionary minority movements in the West—events that cumulatively undermined confidence in European modernity and its master narrative of Progress. The diverse decolonizing projects of the period questioned the deeply entrenched hierarchies of race, nation, and gender, which had come to form part of the hegemonic "common sense." The decolonization of the academe, in this sense, constituted a local manifestation of a much larger transformation that Robert Stam and I have called "the postwar seismic shift."[1]

Against this backdrop, Said's book reverberated with the efforts to transform the so-called Other from the object into the subject of history. Within Middle Eastern studies, Said's *Orientalism* was anticipated by such precursors as Anouar Abdel-Malek, Abdul-Latif Tibawi, Maxime Rodinson, and Abdallah Laroui. What could be called "proto-postcolonial" work was also performed by Arab intellectuals, somewhat surprisingly, within French Orientalist studies. In the 1950s, Orientalist academic institutions in France began to recognize the independence struggles in the Arab world, while also absorbing a few Arab intellectuals into their ranks.[2] As insiders/outsiders, French-speaking Arab intellectuals resembled the British-educated "white but not quite" colonial elites, or the English-speaking Arab participants in Near Eastern studies in Britain or Middle Eastern studies in the United States. In 1963, a decade and a half before Said, Anouar Abdel-Malek, published "Orientalism in Crisis" in the journal *Diogenes*.[3] Independence struggles inevitably impacted Oriental studies, Abdel-Malek explained, by turning those who had been "objects of study" into sovereign subjects. For Abdel-Malek, "the hegemonism of possessing minorities, unveiled by Marx and Engels, and the anthropocentrism dismantled by Freud [had been] accompanied by Europocentrism in the area of human and social sciences, and more particularly in those in direct relationship with non-European peoples."[4] A decade later, Abdallah Laroui's *La Crise des Intellectuels Arabes* denounced the Orientalist penchant of "speaking for [Arab] others" and criticized the Orientalists as a bureaucratic caste.[5] These critics no longer saw Orientalism as uniquely the site of productive knowledge but also of unproductive prejudice.

At the same time, Said's text was also informed by the anticolonialist writings of such Caribbean figures as Aimé Césaire, Frantz Fanon, and Roberto Fernandez Retamar. Although Fanon never spoke of "Orientalist discourse," his critique of colonialist imagery provided proleptic examples of what would later be called "anti-Orientalist critique" à la Said. Indeed, in *Culture and Imperialism*, Said's self-declared sequel to *Orientalism*, Said acknowledges some of the key catalytic figures in the postwar shift, especially C. L. R. James and Fanon, thus making explicit the tacit intertext of his earlier book. When Fanon argued that the colonizer "cannot speak of the colonized without having recourse to the bestiary," he called attention to the animalizing trope by which the colonizing imaginary rendered the colonized as beastlike and animalic.[6] Within colonial binarism, as Fanon put it, "the settler makes history; his life is an epoch, an Odyssey, while against him torpid creatures, wasted by fevers, obsessed by ancestral customs, form an almost inorganic background for the innovating dynamism of colonial mercantilism."[7] Here Fanon anticipated Said, Talal Assad, and Johannes Fabian's critique of classical anthropology's projection of the colonized as "allochronically" (Fabian) living in another time, mired in a putatively inert tradition seen as modernity's antithesis.[8] For anticolonialist thinkers such as Fanon, as for postcolonial thinkers later, the colonizer and the colonized are contemporaneous and coeval. Rejecting the "progressive," Eurocentric two-speed paradigm of Progress, anticolonialist thinkers insisted that the colonized do not want to "catch up" with anyone. Although critics such as Fanon and Said have been sometimes reduced to essentialism, they share with poststructuralism an emphasis on the conjunctural, malleable character both of racial categorizations and of communitarian self-definition. Both saw identity as languaged, situated, constructed, projected.

In *Orientalism*, Said deployed Gramsci's idea of hegemony and Foucauldian notions of discourse and the power-knowledge nexus to examine the ways that Western imperial power, in affiliation with colonizing institutions, constructed a stereotypical "Orient." But Orientalism should not be seen in isolation; it forms a kind of subgenre or variant within the larger and more global category of Eurocentrism. As Robert Stam and I have argued in *Unthinking Eurocentrism*, the notion of Eurocentrism signifies the discursive residue of colonialism and its consequence—Western hegemony. Eurocentrism is the discursive precipitate of colonialism, exerting its power even in the absence of colonialism or even of explicitly colonialist discourse. As a discursive substratum, Eurocentrism permeates and organizes contemporary practices and representations. It embeds, takes for granted, and normalizes the uneven power relations generated by colonialism, naturalizing them and rendering them as inevitable and even progressive. Although generated by the colonizing process, Eurocentrism's links to that process are obscured through a kind of buried epistemology. Summing up, "colonialism" refers to the actual historical practices of domination; "colonial discourse" refers to the apologia for these practices; "Orientalism" refers to the discursive dimension of these practices insofar as they have to do with the East/West binary; while "Eurocentrism" refers to the discursive residue of colonialism and neocolonialism globally, in the broadest possible sense.[9] Said locates the beginnings of Orientalism as a field of study and discursive formation in the post-Enlightenment period, a consequence of European imperial intrusions in the Middle East. However, from another perspective, I will suggest later, the formation of Orientalism as a discourse preceded and anticipated Orientalism as a field of study.

The various anticolonialist, antiracist, anti-Orientalist, and anti-Eurocentric trends impacted different disciplines in different ways, leading to interrogations of the axial assumptions of such disciplines as sociology, literature, history, and anthropology. Critical and even insurgent proposals emerged within a whole series of disciplines, expressed in recombinatory coinages such as "revisionist history," "critical law," "radical philosophy," "reflexive anthropology," and "critical pedagogy"—where the qualifiers suggested that a canonical discipline was being reconceptualized from the periphery and from below. The venerable discipline of "English Literature," the disciplinary location of much of Said's work, began to expose the racially tinged assumptions of writers like Faulkner and Conrad, while literary studies began to debate the incorporation into the canon of texts by women, writers of color, and Third World authors. In the 1960s and 1970s many scholars began to rethink their disciplines in terms of the global changes triggered by decolonization and by the struggles of racialized minorities. The thrust was doubly critical, first of the absence of non-European cultural and historical topics, and second of the presence of racist ideology and ethnocentric perspectives.

Said's *Orientalism* was published, then, at a very specific moment in the history of the U.S. academe, when ethnic studies, women's studies, and Third World studies had transformed the intellectual landscape by challenging the epistemological foundations of what constituted a legitimate object of knowledge, as well as the regimes of representation that determined who formed a legitimate subject of inquiry deserving institutional academic space. But these currents triggered a backlash, turning the university into the highly symbolic battleground for the culture wars. Written at the intersection of diverse forms of what Said himself called "adversary scholarship," Said's work further consolidated what came to be the burgeoning fields of (multi)cultural studies and postcolonial studies. Indeed, *Orientalism*, a seminal text for postcolonial theory, was published in a period when terms such as "the Third World" and "neo-colonialism" were in circulation, a decade prior to their eclipse by the term "postcolonial."

The critique of Orientalism, then, exists in relations of partial homology to two multidisciplinary spaces, each with its own specific relation to colonialism. It relates, on the one hand to (1) those academic formations based on geographical regions, that is, the various "area studies," defined as "over there" in relation to the home base of the American academe. And on the other, it relates to (2) the various "ethnic studies," defined as "back here." These two institutional formations have had a very different, and in some ways even opposite, genealogy and drift. While ethnic studies initially emerged out of the bottom-up activism of communities of color, area studies initially arose out of top-down Cold War governmental geopolitical perspectives and needs. Yet both area studies and ethnic studies, despite their distinct beginnings, are shaped by the contexts of colonialism and imperialism. Area studies was formed during the historical lap-dissolve from European (especially British and French) to U.S. hegemony, while ethnic studies was formed in the post–Civil Rights era, when Native Americans, African Americans, and Chicano/as were theorized as "internal colonies." Today the growing fields of Arab American studies and Middle Eastern diasporic studies have emerged against the backdrop of U.S. direct interventionist wars in the Middle East. Arab American studies, as its very name suggests, exists in relation to both ethnic studies and area studies, just as Latino studies as a category of ethnic studies exists in dialogue with Latin American studies as a category of area studies. In this sense Said's *Orientalism* can also be regarded as an Arab American Studies text, not simply because of the author's identity but also because of the book's final chapter that explores the representation of the Middle East in the United States. The purpose of a critical Middle Eastern / Arab diasporic studies project would be to orchestrate a kind of polylogue between diverse area studies, such as Middle Eastern studies and Latin American studies, and diverse ethnic studies, such as Latino studies and Arab American studies. Rather than reproduce "an American" nationalist teleology, Arab American studies, as we shall see, would have to be reconceptualized so as to transcend a nation-state analytical framework.

Imaginary Geographies—The Double Axis

Some neo/conservative scholars, interestingly, do treat both the Middle East and Latin America, but do so through compartmentalized, Eurocentric and Orientalist perspectives. Samuel Huntington's work provides a clear example of these tendencies. Huntington approaches both regions in a Eurocentric way, but with revealing nuances. While his book *The Clash of Civilizations and the Remaking of World Order* is largely set along an East–West axis, his later book *Who Are We?* is largely set along a North–South axis.[10] If one book is premised on the irreconcilable differences between hermetically sealed-off cultures internationally, the other book is premised on the allegedly unbridgeable intranational gap between Anglo-Americans and Latinos. The North-over-South hierarchy developed by Huntington comes with a lofty pedigree that includes some of the most prestigious figures of Continental philosophy. His anti-Latin diatribe takes place against the larger ideological frame of the already well-developed comparisons between South America / North America in general within a discursive apparatus that could be called "Anglo-Saxonism."[11] In *The Philosophy of History* Hegel, for example, posits a contrast between a democratic, prosperous, orderly, and unified Protestant North America, on the one hand, and, on the other, an authoritarian, impoverished, disorderly, and disunited Catholic South America.[12]

Huntington's evolving work, from his binarist vision of "the clash of civilizations" to his fixed notion of "who we are," demonstrates that Eurocentrist/Orientalist discourse is not monolithic; it displays regional variations, even in the work of the same thinker. While in the case of the Middle East, Huntington marshals an essentialist view of a retrograde Islamic East contrasted with the progressive West, in the case of Latin America, he marshals a Hegelian-Weberian-derived view of a retrograde Catholic South contrasted with the dynamic Protestant North, but in both instances the privileged pole retains its "positional superiority." Huntington's work thus merges the two phobic discourses in his "culture clash" paradigm, alternatively demonizing the East (Arabs/Muslims) and the South (Latin Americans and Latinos).

The U.S. Right, meanwhile, has explicitly scrambled the polarities by bringing up the East/South connections in the context of Islamic terrorist threats lurking behind the Mexico border. The vigilante patrols on the southern border have thus thrown a harsh interrogatory spotlight on the brown bodies not only of Latin Americans but also, potentially, on those of Middle Easterners presumably infiltrating from the South. Post-9/11 Islamophobia thus comes to dovetail with pre-9/11 anti-Latin xenophobia. Rightwing rhetoric presents the wall between Mexico and the United States as a doubly necessary rampart not only against the Latin South but also against the Arab/Muslim East. The patronizing view of Latin America as a U.S. "backyard" gets superimposed on the War on Terror to form an overarching narrative of menace; a discursive matrix that significantly does not allude to the northern border of the United States. The Right has also made a Middle East / Latin America link by focusing on the triangular smuggling of arms between Brazil, Argentina, and Paraguay,[13] thus fusing the political "geographical reductionism"[14] inherent in the "banana republic" trope with the topos of Middle Eastern "republics of fear."

The classical paradigms of Orientalism and Eurocentrism are also merged in a manner reminiscent of current anti-immigration discourses in

Europe with regard to the South of the Mediterranean. Yet, from a different perspective, one that focuses on parallel hegemonies and repressions, it could be possible to discern a homology between two literal and figurative "Souths," between the Muslim/Arab Mediterranean as Europe's South, and Latin America as the United States' South.[15] The confident Huntingtonian assertion of "us" versus "them" could easily be contrasted with the postcolonial slogan "we are here because you were there," a reminder of the North or the West's imperial expansions. Europe's anxiety over an Arab/Muslim invasion, not unlike like U.S. anxiety about a Mexican/Latino invasion, is premised on the denial of the historical fluidity of borders and cultures, whether found in the Mediterranean or in the American Southwest.

At the same time, despite shared colonialist and imperialist discourses, there are some differences that separate Europe and the Americas. The question of Orientalism and Eurocentrism shifts its signification depending on whether one is speaking of British and French imperialism in the East, or of the colonial settler-states of the Americas. In the long view, it was the conflicts with Islam, going back to the Crusades, that triggered Europe's self-consciousness as a cultural unit. Following the general process by which virtually all nations historically define themselves "with," "against," and "through" their neighbors, victims, and enemies, official France, for example, historically defined itself against the Muslim world (Charles Martel, the Crusades, *El Cid*), and later against Great Britain, Germany, and now the United States. The dominant United States, meanwhile, defined itself with and against Native Americans internally, and externally against Great Britain (the Revolutionary War), Spain (the Spanish-American War), Germany and Japan (the two world wars), the Soviet Union (the Cold War), and now against Islamic fundamentalism (the War on Terror). While Europe partly emerged as a self-aware continental unity in contradistinction to the Islamic world, the nation-states of the Americas defined themselves not against Islam but against both indigenous peoples and the colonial metropole. While the dominant discourse in the United States inherited many of the Christian prejudices against Muslims, and later the colonialist prejudices against the Arabs / Middle Easterners, the United States, from the outset, also defined itself as a place of religious freedom, open to Jews and Muslims.[16]

Although some Christian Rightists have been trying to rewrite history in order to paint the United States as a "Christian nation" threatened by Islam, the Founding Fathers were secular Deists, for whom "God" was not the Christian God but rather the rational clockmaker Deity of the Enlightenment. Indeed, at the time of the American Revolution, many foreign commentators saw the United States not as religious but as "godless." Under the Constitution, one critic complained, it is possible for "a papist, a Mohamatan, a deist, yea an atheist," to become president of the United States.[17] And roughly a century later, a Spanish newspaper, *El Pensimiento Español,* described the United States as "founded on atheism."[18] The text of the Treaty of Tripoli in 1796, signed by George Washington, pointed to a secular American Republic (Article 11).

> As the government of the United States of America is not in any sense founded on the Christian Religion—as it has in itself no character of enmity against the laws, religion or tranquility of [Muslims] and as the said States never have entered into any war or act of hostility against any Mehomitan nation, it is declared by the parties that no pretext arising from religious opinions shall ever produce an interruption of the harmony existing between the two countries.[19]

The sentiments expressed here, confirmed again when Jefferson approved the treaty in 1806, are remarkable not only for their assertion of the nonreligious character of the United States but also for their lack of hostility to Islam and Muslims. The treaty was signed by John Adams and ratified, moreover, by two-thirds of the Senate.

Huntington-style clash-of-cultures Manichaeism thus represents only one discursive strand within U.S. American thinking. It clearly eschews the Enlightenment-oriented conceptualization of the United States in favor of a line leading from the Salem witch trials to the PATRIOT Act. It forms the antithesis to the poststructuralist approach taken in Said's *Orientalism,* where the deconstruction of the East/West essentialism does not, pace Said's critics, reproduce another essentialism in reverse. Through literal and figurative translations, Said's approach has been extrapolated for diverse regions such as South Asia, the Balkans, and Latin America. In an intertextual process that now comes full circle, Said is impacted by the work of Caribbean / Latin American writers; they, in turn, are impacted by Said. In his book *The History of the Concept of Latin America in the United States,* Brazilian political scientist João Feres Jr., for example, usefully deploys a Saidian prism to anatomize the writings of certain U.S. scholars working in the service of Cold War ideology such as Samuel Huntington and Seymour Martin Lipset, who represent Latin Americans as irrational, passion-driven, pathological, and unproductive, condemned to historical immobility. Within this discourse, to cite Feres, "the Anglo-Saxon Protestant Occident constitutes the beacon of progress and human development, while Catholic Latin America is the prison which maintains its detainees frozen in the feudal past."[20]

Other Latin American studies scholars, such as Walter Mignolo, have pointed out that postcolonial discourse, by concentrating on "Orientalism" as a discursive symptom of later forms of British and French imperialism, forgets that "Orientalism" was itself preceded by "Occidentalism."[21] In *The Idea of Latin America* Mignolo deploys the concept of "Occidentalism" in a sense very different from that of writers such as Ian Buruma and Avishai Margalit, who use it as part of what amounts to a variation on the "reverse racism" argument vis-à-vis Said, in this case a "reverse Orientalism" argument, which suggests that Arab/Muslims have themselves subjected the West to dehumanization and pernicious stereotypes.[22] For Mignolo, in contrast, Occidentalism, as the idea of the West and its ideology of expansionism, refers to the consequences of the European Conquest in the Americas. Mignolo, in the vein of Caribbean and Latin American studies scholars in general, crucially identifies the beginnings of colonial discourse not with the post-Enlightenment era but with Columbus and 1492. In contrast to much of postcolonial studies, including Said's *Orientalism*, the question of "the colonial" as embedded in 1492 requires that one examines continuities and discontinuities between early Iberian expansionism and latter-day nineteenth-century, largely British and French, imperialism.

The Two 1492s—Toward Another Beginning

At the same time, one could slightly amend both Feres and Mignolo, for different but related reasons, having to do with the question: when exactly does Orientalism begin? Feres's identification of the United States as the primal fount of Orientalism runs its own risks, some of which derive from certain omissions within Said's *Orientalism* itself. Feres's emphasis on U.S.-style Monroe Doctrine, Big Stick Diplomacy, and Cold War Orientalism in Latin America forgets the fact that latter-day Orientalism comes superimposed on the preexisting forms of Orientalism—as a branch of colonial Eurocentric discourse—that have shaped Caribbean / Latin American history itself.

Prior to the U.S. orientalizing of Latin America à la Feres, the Spanish and Portuguese had already orientalized, as it were, the indigenous peoples—"los Indios." Columbus, in this perspective, could be regarded as the first Orientalist of the Americas, even in the sense of imagining himself, as his diaries indicate, to be actually *in* the Orient, in the land of the Great Khan. In his fanciful account, the island, supposedly off the shore of India, was peopled with wild flora, fauna, cannibals, and mermaids. In the wake of 1492, Orientalist discourse traveled to the Americas, generating the emergence of Western world order, which in turn created another base from which to disseminate Eurocentric conceptions of the world. Infused and empowered by the Americas' material wealth, Europe subsequently colonized Egypt, Algeria, and the rest of the Middle East and North Africa, subjecting these regions to an old/new kind of Orientalism. Before arriving in the Orient, then, the Orientalist imaginary had arrived in the West Indies. Columbus's spatial disorientation is thus foundational to the narrative of the beginning of Orientalism.

Although Feres assumes Said's genealogy of Orientalist discourse as dating back to latter-day European empires, Orientalist discourse as a mode of colonial/Eurocentric discourse could just as easily be traced back to the early colonization of the Americas. While extending Said's critique of post-Enlightenment Orientalism to clarify U.S. attitudes toward Latin America is certainly productive, in other respects it overlooks the ideological conquest of the Americas generally within Orientalist paradigms. In this sense, Mignolo provides a corrective to both Feres and Said by speaking of Latin America's "double wound," first from Iberian Conquest and second by American imperialism. Yet, while in full agreement with the Latin Americanist take on the beginning of colonial discourse, by the same token, however, one might offer another genealogy that argues that Occidentalism à la Mignolo did not begin simply in one 1492 but rather simultaneously in *two* 1492s. The Conquista was itself already informed by what could be called the "proto-Orientalism" of the Reconquista, which was imbricated in Judeophobia and Islamophobia. Columbus, after all, by travelling west, intended to go to the east and intended to convert the diverse heathens, including Muslims and Jews. Orientalism, in this sense, begins with the very arrival, at the end of the fifteenth century, of Iberian theological vision in the Americas.

If we examine the circulation of tropes and metaphors, as well as the discursive connections and links between the two 1492s, we afford ourselves another way to begin the story of Orientalism. To reflect on these submerged analogies, we need to think back again to the events associated with the cataclysmic moment when the beginning of the conquest of the "new" world converged with the forcing-out of Sephardic Jews and Muslim Moors from Spain. The ground for colonialist racism was prepared by the Inquisition's Limpieza de Sangre (cleansing of blood), by the Edicts of Expulsion against the Jews and Muslims, by the Portuguese exploration of the west coast of Africa, and by the transatlantic slave trade. Forged in the centuries of the Reconquista, fifteenth-century Spain provided a template for the creation of other racial states and for ethnoreligious cleansing. Although the Limpieza de Sangre was formulated in religious terms—by which the "problem" of Jewishness and Muslimness could be remedied by conversion—the metaphor of the "purity of blood" prepared the way for the biological and scientific racism of the nineteenth century. Christian demonology thus set the tone for colonialist racialization. The various "questions"—the Jewish, Muslim, "Indian," Black, and the African questions—have been interwoven for centuries. Their linked trajectories can be traced, as Robert Stam and I argued in *Unthinking Eurocentrism,* back to the events associated with the cataclysmic moment summoned up by the various "1492s"—i.e. the conquest of the "new" world, the expulsion of the Moors, and the Inquisition.

In effect, discourses about Muslims and Jews armed the conquistadors with a ready-made demonizing vision, transferable from the "old" to the "new" world. Amerigo Vespucci's accounts of his own voyages invoked the familiar anti-Jewish and anti-Muslim idiom to characterize the indigenous peoples as infidels and devil worshipers.[23] The conquest of "the Indians" of the Americas, for sixteenth-century Spanish historian Francisco Lopez de Gomara, prolonged the struggle against "the infidels" in the East. In his *Historia General de las Indias* (1552), de Gomara wrote that "the conquest of the Indians began after that of the Moors was completed, so that Spaniards would ever fight the infidels."[24] The Hieronymite friars, for their part, referred to the inhabitants of Hispaniola as "Moors."[25] Shakespeare's Caliban in *The Tempest,* meanwhile, mingled the traits of African Moors and indigenous Americans. Within a phantasmatic resemblance, both the internal non-Christian "enemy" and the external indigenous American and African "savage" are all imagined as "sorcerers," "cannibals," and "blood drinkers." Indigenous deities (for example, the Tupi deity Tupan) and West African orixas (such as Exu) were diabolized to fit into a normatively Manichaean Christian schema. Anti-Semitism or Judeo-phobia, along with anti-infidelism or Islamophobia, provided a conceptual framework projected outward against the indigenous peoples of Africa and the Americas.[26] Occidentalism (in Mingolo's sense), then, does not exist without (proto) Orientalism, just as Orientalism (in Said's sense) does not exist without earlier Occidentalism—both of which are modes of Eurocentric discourse.

Columbus's Atlantic route generated foundational paradoxes that illuminate the formation of both Occidentalism and Orientalism. In the hopes of both material riches and theological expansions in the East, Columbus's voyage moved toward the west, partly to avoid the enemy lands dominated by Muslims.[27] It is often noted that Columbus took with him an interpreter, the converso Luis de Torres, whose knowledge of Semitic languages was to facilitate encounters in the East. Although Arabic was irrelevant in the period of "the Discovery," that language arrived in the Americas with the Arabic-speaking Muslim African slaves, long before the late nineteenth-century Arab immigration from the provinces of the Ottoman Empire.[28] Apart from the innumerable traces of Arabic and Hebrew that have persisted in Portuguese and Spanish till today, the new coinages specific to the Americas were also sometimes borrowed from Arabic. The term for racial miscegenation between white and red in Brazil—"mamelucos"—for example, could be traced back to the Arab/Muslim context of the "Mamluks."[29] Conversos and Moriscos also traveled to the Americas, where Inquisition persisted in places like Mexico (including what is now the southwestern United States) and Brazil. The various routes around the Atlantic were linked in ways that partly mirrored Europe's geopolitical landscape; some Sephardic Jews who escaped from the Inquisition to Holland ended up in the Dutch-dominated territories in the Americas. In 1654, the Sephardic Jews of Pernambuco in north Brazil left with the withdrawing Dutch to New Amsterdam, where they established the first (Portuguese) synagogue in what is now downtown Manhattan. In light of the political battle over the Cordova Islamic Center near Ground Zero, it is also worth noting that the Muslim presence in New York goes back to the very beginnings of colonization. Historian Michael Gomez cites the case of the freeman Antonio the Turk, supposed to have been born in Morocco, who became one of the largest landowners in Manhattan.[30]

The Iberian wrestling with its legacy of "the Orient," associated with Africa and the South, and "the Occident," associated with Europe and the North, persisted in the Americas. In this version, the concept of "Orientalism" functioned as a synonym for the negative view of the Moorish Muslim and Sephardic Jewish "orientalization" of Iberia and consequently of its new territories in the Americas.[31] In this expanding Atlantic space, the ritual legacy of the struggle between Christians and infidels, such as the equestrian combats between Spaniards and Moors, continued to be reenacted in the form of popular spectacles, featured, for example, in Brazilian street festivals on Easter Sunday. "The Christians," in the words of the Brazilian anthropologist Gilberto Freyre, "were always victorious and the Moors routed and punished. And Easter Saturday ended or began with the effigy of Judas being carried through the streets and burned by the urchins in what was evidently a popular expression of religious hatred of the Catholic for the Jew."[32] Jews were viewed, in the words of Freyre, as the "secret agent of Orientalism."[33] Thus, before the contemporary Eurocentric erasure, as it were, of the hyphen in the "Judeo-Islamic" and the insertion of the hyphen in the "Judeo-Christian," the "Jew" and "the Muslim," or "the Sephardi" and "the Moor," or "the Morisco" and "the converso" were articulated within the same conceptual space, as one allegorical unit. To speak of the Muslim Moor is therefore also to invoke the Sephardi Jew and vice versa. As a form of Iberian anxiety about its Arabization/Judaization, "Orientalism" was thus carried over to the Americas, where it participated in the shaping of emerging regional and national identities.

Yet, if Iberia witnessed centuries of an ideology that justified the cleansing of the "Orientalized" Moorish/Sephardic past, Latin America, as a complex site of global cultural encounters and of ambivalence toward the colonial metropole, has also witnessed a certain nostalgia for that "Oriental" past. The tropical imaginary has partly been shaped by what could be called "the Moorish unconscious" of Latin America, where denial and desire of that forgotten origin have simultaneously coexisted. The mundane pride of some families in their Moorish "Morisco" or Sephardi "converso" lineage has been expressed in popular tales and registered in the various Latin American texts. From José Martí's exhortation "Seamos Moros!" to Carlos Fuentes's celebration of Mexico's "buried mirror" the question of the Moor never stopped haunting, even if only on the margins, the Latin American imaginary.[34] In his theorization of Brazilian identity, Freyre gives great weight to the Moorish/Sephardic cultural history of Portugal as actively shaping Brazilian customs and practices. In the early colonial era, Brazilian people maintained Moorish/Sephardic traditions such as the covering of women attending church, or the preference to sit on rugs with legs crossed, and they deployed various Moorish architectural structures and artistic design, including glazed tiling, checkered windowpanes, and so forth.[35] But with the programmatic adoption of Occidental-European customs that were institutionalized with Brazil's independence in 1822 began a detachment from the Moorish/Sephardic heritage.[36]

For Freyre, the Europeanization—another word for modernization—of Brazil came through the triumph of "the Occidental" over "the Oriental."[37] The Brazilian Occidentalization project meant a self de-Orientalization that is a cleansing of the Sephardic/Moorish traces from the veins of Latin America. Within a certain romanticism of search for lost origins, Freyre, however, developed an argument for a genealogy of Brazilian national character whose positive traits of cultural flexibility, plasticity, and adoptability were largely traced back to Moorish/Sephardic Portugal.[38] He also emphatically stresses the Moorish/Sephardic blood of the Portuguese that reveals a hybridity running through the veins of the colonizers even prior to their mixing with indigenous Tupis and enslaved West Africans. Setting aside Freyre's culturalist-essentialist assumptions, his act of theorizing Brazilian identity in relation to Moorish/Sephardic heritage sheds significant light on the linked cultural histories of the two 1492s. Despite the project of de-Orientalizing Ibero-American blood and culture, it can be argued that the Moor (here also standing in for the Sephardi) never fully disappeared from Latin America, whether as a specter or figure of desire. Even if often only remaining in the shadow, the figure of the Moor has been revisited for the purpose of self-conceptualization in some Latin American texts. The highlighting of an "oriental" genealogy in such texts stands in glaring contrast to the Reconquista/Conquista de-orientalizing project; it turns the Moor into a kind of a return-of-the-repressed figure.

Orientalism as an ideological discourse, one could thus argue, preceded Orientalism as a field of study that emerges with the post-Enlightenment and the colonization of the Middle East / North Africa. While Said's *Orientalism* inaugurated a critique of the imaginary of the Orient in European thought, particularly British and French, in another perspective, Orientalism is embedded in both the Reconquista and the Conquista. Colonial discourse in relation to the Americas, then, did not simply take in latter-day French or British or North American Orientalist discourse but rather was *constituted* by it. Occidentalism—in Mignolo's sense—does not exist without Orientalism, just as Orientalism—in Said's sense—does not exist without Occidentalism. Orientalism and Occidentalism (Mignolo), meanwhile, can both be seen as branches of Eurocentric epistemology; as such they are intimately connected, mutually constitutive within the same historical moment. The concept of the "Moorish unconscious" of Latin America thus helps us chart another route for tracing the genealogies of both Orientalism and Occidentalism. In this sense, one could speak, in tandem with the by-now-familiar "Black Atlantic," and of the less familiar "Red Atlantic" and "White Atlantic," of a "Brown Atlantic" or "Arab/Muslim Atlantic" or "Sephardi/Moorish Atlantic" as part of a multiply-raced "Rainbow Atlantic."[39] The history of the traffic of Orientalist ideas, thus, is not merely longer but also more multifaceted and multidirectional than might at first appear.

From Diaspora to Diasporic Readings

The last chapter of Said's book focuses on "Orientalism Now." And thirty years later, the era of transnational flows and the ongoing diasporization of Middle Eastern peoples pose a challenge to notions of reified cartographies and isolated regional units. But what analytical frameworks are available for studying these cross-border movements between regions? Can Middle Eastern studies be rethought as a more inclusive and fluid space in ways that expand the boundaries of what constitutes a legitimate object of inquiry within current area studies? And how can such a reconceptualization bypass the notion of the Middle East as a fixed sign with quarantined boundaries between East and West?—a notion that was one of the objects of Said's critique. And where do American studies, ethnic studies, and Latin American studies fit into this picture? Are there discursive spaces of mutual illuminations?

Situating the critique of Orientalism in relation to multiple geographies necessarily challenges the boundaries separating ethnic studies, presumed to study those within the nation-state "over here," and area studies, particularly the designation of study according to national or regional boundaries such as Middle Eastern studies, Latin American studies, Asian studies, and African studies. Conceptualized around demarcated regions of specialization, Middle Eastern/North African studies has traditionally tended to ignore diasporic Middle Eastern communities around the world, focusing solely on the bounded "insides" of the region. In this sense both area studies and ethnic studies marginalize Middle Eastern Americans by positioning them as "foreigners" to be studied merely "over there," denying their entry into a scholarly framework of race and ethnicity in the Americas. In Latin America, meanwhile, ethnic studies does not exist as an institutional or curricular formation, while Latin American area studies is often conceived in terms of the nation-states of South and Central America as well as the Caribbean. In those sites, the predominant paradigm for discussing ethnicity is the racial/chromatic triad—Indigenous Red, European White, and African Black ancestries—a formulation that excludes Asians generally and Arabs specifically.

Thus diasporic Arab/Muslim communities inevitably intersect not only with other diasporas—and in the Americas only the indigenous peoples did *not* come from transoceanic diasporas—but also with preexisting discourses and ideologies. In Brazil, the Arab community (which is predominantly Christian) enters into a national field defined by particular discourses, notably the "fable of the three races" (roughly, Red, Black, and White) and the discourse of "mesticagem" (miscegenation). While the Arab diaspora fits rather uneasily into the three-races triad, it does fit easily into the discourse of miscegenation—the constantly reiterated nostrum that "we are all mixed"—including because the Middle East itself is *already* miscegenated. In the United States, meanwhile, the Arab/Muslim community intersects with a different set of discourses, notably the discourses of American pluralism, as well as the "immigrant nation" and "we are all immigrants" narrative, while also tiptoeing along the razor's edge of the tense ambiguities of the white/black binary. All of that has become further complicated, however, by the social fallout of 9/11 and the War on Terror.

The external emphasis of area studies and the internal focus of ethnic studies, in their different ways, have historically discouraged scholarly frameworks that depart from the "terra firma" of regions to highlight diasporic in-betweenness. Mutually exclusive frameworks impede the study of the co-implicatedness of regions, for example, of America in the Middle East and the Middle East in America. Nonetheless, there is an increasing visibility of cross-border analyses in publications, conferences, and course offerings.

Post-9/11, associations such as the Modern Language Association, the Society for Cinema and Media Studies, and the American Studies Association have all witnessed an increase in panels on Middle East–related themes. American studies and ethnic studies departments (such as the University of Michigan, Ann Arbor, and San Francisco State University) have developed an Arab American and Muslim diasporas curriculum; while some women's, gender, and sexuality studies programs have offered courses within transnational, postcolonial cultural studies perspectives on the Middle East. Such perspectives have also been addressed in such books as Amal Amireh and Lisa Suhair Majaj's *Going Global,* Minoo Moallem's *Between Warrior Brother and Veiled Sister,* and Shouleh Vatanabadi and Mohammad Mehdi Khorrami's *Another Sea, Another Shore;* as well as in various articles published in such journals as *Third Text, Diaspora: A Journal of Transnational Studies, Middle East Critique, Arab Studies Journal, Interventions: International Journal of Postcolonial Studies, The Middle East Journal of Culture and Communication, Journal of Middle East Women's Studies, Meridians: Feminism, Race, Transnationalism, MERIP (Middle East Research and Information Project),* and *Journal of Palestine Studies*—to give just a few examples.

Said's work is frequently referenced within the related fields of postcolonial and cultural studies, academic domains where "culture" is viewed as embedded in the political realm but not reducible to it. In *Orientalism,* Said analyzed texts and discourses in ways that emphasized the constitutive power of culture but which still went beyond any essentialist cultural*ism,* that is, the tendency to reduce complex social phenomena to a monolithic and unchanging cultural essence, deployed as an all-purpose explanatory mechanism. Without completely abandoning the textual analysis inherited from literary studies, Said thus operated within the anticulturalist and antiessentialist assumptions that have marked the field of cultural studies, associated with the Birmingham school, for whom "culture" was not unified but rather a contested, heteroglossic, and dissensual arena.

Needless to say, the impact of Said's work on postcolonial/cultural studies is distinct from its impact on Middle Eastern studies. Meanwhile, the scholarly work performed in-between these academic spaces, such as it is, exists on the margins of both spaces, with relatively little dialogue between the two. The reasons for this lack of dialogue have to do less with political positions, perhaps, than with methodological and theoretical perspectives. Assumed within postcolonial / cultural studies are the various structuralist and poststructuralist "turns": the linguistic turn (Saussure), the discursive turn (Bakhtin and Foucault), and the cultural turn (Jameson). Within Middle Eastern studies, the critique of Said as a deficient political scientist or historian or anthropologist, however valid from specific disciplinary perspectives, on another level sidesteps the book's main concern with the problem of representation, in terms of rhetoric, figures of speech, narrative structure, and discursive formation.

Within a cultural studies / postcolonial studies perspective, Said called attention to the ways regions and communities are figured, sequenced, narrated, and represented through an often unacknowledged set of axiomatic doxa and grids. Said's method entails the simultaneous constitution and reading of a discursive corpus—in this case the Orientalist corpus. Surely, it is legitimate to point out that Orientalist discourse is not homogeneous, that it manifests historical specificities with national variants, and that not all Orientalists are the same. At the same time, Said's critical reading of a discourse remains productive, precisely because the reading discerns, beyond the "trees" of the differences from text to text and nation to nation, the "forest" of the discourse, exposing recurrent leitmotifs manifest across styles, genres, and historical contexts. Whatever the pitfalls of poststructuralist protocols of reading, and critics are certainly right to point them out, such readings can illuminate dimensions that other grids might miss.

It is thus not a coincidence that Said's work has constantly been referenced in literature, film/media, and cultural studies, precisely because his method of textual and discourse analysis reverberates with familiar methodological premises in those fields. Within Middle Eastern studies these fields of investigation have often been seen through the prism of a rather gendered tropology of soft and hard knowledges. The heated debates over Said's *Orientalism* have focused on hard knowledge, that is, ideology and politics. It is as if the study of the politics of culture is viewed as marginal to the "real" debate over Orientalism, that is, the ideological-political debate. But Said's critique bears precisely on the inextricable nexus between the supposedly "hard" institutional power and the supposedly "soft" power of culture. Said's political critique, therefore, cannot be detached from his cultural critique. Indeed, the assumption that politics and culture are thoroughly imbricated forms the cornerstone of that post-Marxist field called "cultural studies" as a field that deployed Gramsci to reconfigure the base/superstructure relation, within an intellectual paradigm where culture and politics are mutually constituted, in and through each other.

The interdisciplinary space of cultural politics, arguably the scholarly genre within which Said's book was written, offers opportunities for an expanded notion of Middle Eastern studies as including the Americas. Increasingly, a vibrant and growing field of scholarship has taken on board such questions as the new technologies that instantaneously link the globe and the back-and-forth movements across borders of commodities and communities. Such work addresses neo-Orientalism not only in relation to the

Middle East per se but also **in** and **around** it; for example, through work on the transnational reception of Middle Eastern literature, cinema, music, and visual arts, and its impact on the "self-orientalizing" of Middle Eastern cultural production; on the politics of translation of novels and memoirs within gendered Orientalist paradigms; on globalized digital technologies as actively mediating and shaping identities beyond national boundaries. Taken as an ensemble, such work analyzes cultural formations and practices as at once national and transnational, local and global.

The methodological/theoretical challenge is to approach the different regions through a lens of both identity and alterity, continuity and discontinuity, convergence and divergence. The intersectionality of regions and cartographies of knowledge allow us to redraw static maps of scholarly terrain, stretching and broadening the field. The study of cross-border movements through interarea studies approaches deterritorializes regions as stable objects of study, and offers new angles on the ongoing critique of the essentialist fixity of East-versus-West and North-versus-South. By discussing Arab-America in conjunction with the Middle Eastern diaspora in Latin America as well, we further broaden the scope of the discussion. We can approach transnationalism, meanwhile, not only in terms of the circulation of people across borders but also of the circulation of cultural products and ideas. We can thus demonstrate the links between discourses about Middle Eastern diaspora in Latin America and the Caribbean and those in North America, even if each nation-state possesses its own specificity.

The nexus of "culture" and "politics," in sum, is foundational not only for discussing postcolonial Middle Eastern diasporic cultures but also for reading a critical text such as *Orientalism*. To situate the text one must articulate the issue of Arab American diaspora—the case of Edward Said—while also, more importantly, moving toward the notion of a diasporic critique as a method of reading. Although the field of Orientalism and its critique are associated with specific geographies, they can also be seen as part of a multidirectional flow connected to cross-border circuitries. The decolonization of knowledge as articulated in *Orientalism* thus begins by situating the text within multiple points of entry and departure, not all of them explicitly articulated within the text itself. Such a relational diasporic reading forges reciprocally haunting connections between divergent yet historically linked colonized zones, in order to demonstrate the potentialities of cross-border mutual illuminations. It is not, ultimately, a question of migratory demographics, of merely following a population from its originary base into new geographical zones. Rather, it is a question of taking seriously what could be called the "diasporic turn," of thinking of all regions, including the Middle East / North Africa itself, in a profoundly diasporic manner, where each geography constitutes not a point of origin or final destination but rather one terminal in a transnational network.

NOTES

*A shorter earlier version of this essay, entitled "On the Margins of Middle Eastern Studies: Situating Said's Orientalism," was presented at the plenary session of the Middle East Studies Association, as "Celebrating the Thirtieth Anniversary of *Orientalism:* Critiques and New Insights" (Washington, DC, November 24, 2008), which was organized and moderated by MESA president Mervat Hatem, and published in *Review of Middle Eastern Studies,* 43:1 (Summer 2009). Part of the research here was made possible thanks to a research/lectureship Fulbright award, The University of São Paulo, spring 2010.

1. On the notion of "the Seismic Shift" in the decolonization of knowledge, see Ella Shohat and Robert Stam, *Race in Translation: Culture Wars around the Postcolonial Atlantic* (New York: New York University Press, 2012); for a related argument see Howard Winant, *The World Is a Ghetto: Race and Democracy since World War II* (New York: Basic Books, 2001) on what he termed "the post-war break."

2. See Thomas Brisson, *Les Intellectuels Arabes en France* (Paris: La Dispute, 2008).

3. Anouar Abdel-Malek, "Orientalism in Crisis," in *Diogenes,* no. 44 (Winter 1963).

4. Quotation from Anouar Abdel-Malek's "Orientalism in Crisis" is taken from Alexander Lyon Macfie, ed., *Orientalism: A Reader* (New York: NYU Press, 2000), 51.

5. See Abdallah Laroui, *La Crise des Intellectuels Arabes: Traditionalisme ou Historicisme* (Paris: Francois Maspero, 1974).

6. See Ella Shohat, "Post-Fanon and the Colonial: A Situational Diagnosis," in *Taboo Memories, Diasporic Voices* (Durham: Duke University Press, 2006), 250–89.

7. Frantz Fanon, *The Wretched of the Earth* (New York: Grove Press, 1964), 210.

8. Talal Asad, "The Concept of Cultural Translation in British Social Anthropology," in James Clifford and George Marcus, eds., *Writing Culture* (Berkeley: University of California Press, 1986), 141–64; Edward Said, "Representing the Colonized: Anthropology's Interlocutors," *Critical Inquiry* 15, no. 2 (Winter 1989): 205–25; and Johannes Fabian, *Time and the Other* (New York: Columbia University Press, 2002).

9. The definitions and distinctions here are taken from Shohat and Stam, *Unthinking Eurocentrism* (New York: Routledge, 1994), 14–32.

10. Samuel Huntington, *The Clash of Civilizations and the Remaking of World Order* (New York: Simon and Schuster, 1998); *Who Are We? The Challenges to American National Identity* (New York: Simon and Schuster, 2004).

11. Robert Stam and I have suggested using the term *Anglo-Saxonism* for this specific ideological discourse, traced back to Hegel and Weber, which argues for a superiority of the Anglo-Saxon Protestant North over the Latin Catholic South. See our section "Family Feud" in *Flagging Patriotism* (New York: Routledge, 2007); and also "Between Anglo-Saxonism and Latinism," in Stam and Shohat's *Race in Translation.*

12. See G. W. F. Hegel, *The Philosophy of History* (New York: Prometheus Books, 1991).

13. For a political analysis of the triangle, see Paul Amar's *The Security Archipelago: "Human Security States," Sexuality Politics, and the End of Neoliberalism,* Social Text Book Series, forthcoming in 2012 from Duke University Press.

14. On the notion of "geographical reductionism," see Shohat and Stam, *Unthinking Eurocentrism*, 148.

15. For further elaboration on this point see, Stam and Shohat, *Race in Translation*; see also Hisham Aidi, "The Interference of al-Andalus: Spain, Islam, and the West," in "Edward Said: A Memorial Issue," ed. Patrick Deer, Gyan Prakash, and Ella Shohat, *Social Text* 87 (Summer 2006): 67–88.

16. For further elaboration on these parallels and differences between the United States and Europe, see Stam and Shohat, *Flagging Patriotism: Crises of Narcissism and Anti-Americanism* (2007).

17. Cited in Eric Foner, *The Story of American Freedom* (New York: Norton, 1998), 27.

18. *El Pensimiento Español*, September 1862.

19. Quoted in Barry Rubin and Judith Colp Rubin, *Hating America* (Oxford: Oxford University Press, 2004), 48.

20. João Feres Jr., *A Historia do Conceito de "Latin America" nos Estados Unidos* (São Paulo: Edusc, 2005), 129.

21. See Walter D. Mignolo, *The Idea of Latin America* (Malden, MA: Blackwell Publishing, 2005); in *Unthinking Eurocentrism* (1994), Robert Stam and I advanced a parallel critique of postcolonial theory, which focused on the "colonial" as beginning with the heights of the nineteenth-century imperial expansionism, of British and French imperialism, while tending to ignore 1492.

22. Ian Buruma and Avishai Margalit, *Occidentalism: A Short History of Anti-Westernism* (London: Atlantic Books, 2004). See also James Carrier, *Occidentalism: Images of the West* (Oxford: Calrendon Press, 1995).

23. See Jan Carew, *Fulcrums of Change* (Trenton: Africa World Press, 1988).

24. Barbara Fuchs, *Mimesis and Empire: The New World Islam, and European Identities* (Cambridge: Cambridge University Press, 2001), 228. Also quoted in Anouar Majid, *We Are All Moors* (Minneapolis: University of Minnesota Press, 2009), 10.

25. Luis Weckmann, *La Herencia medieval de México*, quoted in Tomás Lozano, *Cantemos al alba: Origins of Songs, Sounds, and Liturgical Drama of Hispanic New Mexico*, ed. and trans. Rima Montaya (Albuquerque: University of New Mexico Press, 2007), 316.

26. This argument here about the discursive links between the two 1492s is based on a series of my related publications on the quincentenary, see Ella Shohat, "Rethinking Jews and Muslims: Quincentennial Reflections," *Middle East Report*, September–October 1992, 25–29; "Staging the Quincentenary: The Middle East and the Americas," *Third Text* (London), Special issue on "The Wake of Utopia," 21 (Winter 1992–93): 95–105; "Columbus, Palestine, and Arab-Jews: Toward a Relational Approach to Community Identity," in *Cultural Readings of Imperialism*, Keith Ausell Pearson, Benita Parry, and Judith Squires, eds. (London: Lawrence & Wishart in association with New Formations, 1997), 88–105; "Taboo Memories, Diasporic Visions: Columbus, Palestine and Arab-Jews," in *Performing Hybridity*, ed. May Joseph and Jennifer Fink (Minneapolis: University of Minnesota Press, 1999), 131–56 (also reproduced in *Taboo Memories, Diasporic Voices*, 2006); and Shohat and Stam's chapter "Formations of Colonialist Discourse," in *Unthinking Eurocentrism*. Hisham Aidi and Anouar Majid, both Moroccan Americans, have also called attention to the issue of Arab/Muslim's links to the Americas. See Hishaam Aidi, "Let Us Be Moors: Islam, Race and 'Connected Histories,'" *Middle East Report*, no. 229 (2003); and Anouar Majid, *We Are All Moors*.

27. In one of his key letters, Christopher Columbus wrote to the Spanish queen: "Your Highness completed the wars against the Moors, after having chased all the Jews and sent me to the said region of India, in order to convert the people there to our holy faith." See Shohat, "Taboo Memories, Diasporic Visions: Columbus, Palestine, and Arab-Jews" (1992–93 and 2006).

28. On Arabic and Muslim slaves, see João Reis, *Slave Rebellion in Brazil* (Baltimore: Johns Hopkins University Press, 1993); and Michael Gomez, *Black Crescent: The Experience and Legacy of African Muslims in the Americas* (New York: Cambridge University Press, 2005).

29. Miguel Nimer, *Influências Orientais Na Língua Portuguesa* (São Paulo: Editora Universidade de São Paulo, 2005).

30. See Michael Gomez, *Black Crescent,* 75.

31. See Gilberto Freyre, chapter 9, "Orient and Occident," *The Mansions and the Shanties* (New York: Knopf, 1963).

32. Freyre, *The Mansions and the Shanties,* 297.

33. Ibid.

34. José Martí, "España en Melilla," in *Cuba: Letras,* vol. 2 (Havana: Edición Tropico, 1938); Carlos Fuentes, *The Buried Mirror* (New York: Houghton Mifflin, 1992). For a historical overview of José Martí and Latin American references to the Moor, see Hishaam Aidi, "Let Us Be Moors: Islam, Race, and Connected Histories"; "The Interference of al-Andalus: Spain, Islam, and the West"; and "A Moorish Atlantic" (unpublished paper sent by Aidi to the author), which stresses the connected histories between the Muslim world and Latin America. While the term "the Moorish Atlantic" tends to refer to the Moroccan coast of the Atlantic, I use the phrase to highlight not only the positive cross-Atlantic historical, discursive, and cultural links between "the Orient" and "the Occident," but also the anxieties that such links provoked. I am also suggesting that this Muslim space must be viewed as always already Sephardic as well, within shared cultural geographies that are part and parcel of the Americas. As already explored in "Staging the Quincentenary," "Taboo Memories, Diasporic Visions," and in *Unthinking Eurocentrism,* the cross-Atlantic Sephardi/Moorish space inaugurated with the **two** 1492s carried over the ocean hegemonic Iberian discourses about Muslims and Jews. In short, I am interested here in the ambivalences that the Moor/the Sephardi, as Janus faced figure, has provoked in the Americas in ways that disturb any facile schism of orient/occident, and north/south.

35. See Freyre, *The Masters and the Slaves,* especially the chapter "The Portuguese Colonizer," originally published in Portuguese in 1933.

36. See Freyre, chapter 9, *The Mansions and the Shanties.*

37. Ibid.

38. See Freyre, *The Masters and the Slaves.*

39. The notion of a multiply raced Atlantic, i.e., "the Rainbow Atlantic," is taken from my work with Robert Stam, from our forthcoming book, *Race in Translation.*

*Nation, Culture,
& Representation*

THREE

Mahjar Legacies
A Reinterpretation

Jacob Berman

> One day, at the office of an Arabic newspaper in New York, I met a man who spoke Arabic with a soft unfamiliar accent, and I was curious to know where he was from. His reply was more interesting than his speech. It was even surprising. For seldom does one see in the Syrian Colony of New York a man from the Yaman; and as I was on the eve of my departure for Arabia, I availed myself of the opportunity of adding something to my little store of knowledge.
>
> —Ameen Rihani, *Arabian Peak and Desert*[1]

In the opening lines of his 1930 Arabian travel narrative, Ameen Rihani locates himself with an Orientalist contradiction. Positioned within the "Syrian Colony of New York" and with access to its modes of modern print culture, the Lebanese émigré author nevertheless seeks "knowledge" from a provincial Arabian stranger before setting out on his Oriental tour. Rihani published *Arabian Peak and Desert* in both English and Arabic. The book was part of his advocacy for a pan-Arab state that resembled, in structure, the United States.[2] "I admit, however, that the complete success of Pan-Arabism—Arabia under one ruler—is not expected at the present or in the near future," Rihani explained in his standard 1920s and 1930s English-language lecture on pan-Arabism. "But the success of an Arab confederation, following the pattern, more or less, of the United States of America, is not far off."[3] Despite his use of the language of "Western" reform, Rihani is no simple Orientalist.

Presenting himself as a local Arab colonist in America, and a cosmopolitan American stranger in Arabia, Rihani troubles any stable notion of center and margin. The fascination the metropolitan intellectual Rihani has with the vernacular authenticity and authority of the "man from the Yaman" suggests that Syria, the Arabian Peninsula, and America act for him as complex and shifting loci of cultural identification. Part of a larger transnational Arab literary renaissance known as *al-nahda* (النهضة),[4] Rihani was familiar with Orientalist conceits about the East, as well as eager to show his mastery of Western literary forms. Yet, despite his claims to be a translator between East and West, Rihani's writings do not synthesize the standard oppositions distinguishing Orient from Occident. Rihani's repeated use of inversion and reversal demonstrates that he is far more interested in the representative power of contradiction. Though the American version of the *nahda* intellectual has often been accused of playing to the master discourse's essentialist tropes of Oriental identity, Rihani disrupts essentialism by presenting Arabness as several different things simultaneously. In Rihani's oeuvre, figurative Arab-ness replaces religious, tribal, and national allegiances.

Rihani immigrated with his uncle to New York City from Mount Lebanon in 1888, at the age of twelve. Raised as a Maronite Christian, Rihani was typical of the pioneer generation of Arab immigrants to the Americas in both religious and regional affiliation. The community Rihani describes in his reference to the "Syrian Colony of New York" would come to be known as the *mahjar*, a word derived from the Arabic word for migration (*hejira*, هِجْرة). This community also produced the most popular-selling English-language writer of Arab descent to ever be published, Khalil Gibran. Gibran, who was born in 1883 in the Lebanese town of B'Sharri, immigrated with his mother to Boston's South End in 1895. Like Rihani, Gibran was raised a Maronite Christian. Along with several other Lebanese émigré intellectuals from what was then Greater Syria, Rihani and Gibran formed a literary club in the United States called the *Rubiyat al-Qalam*, or Pen League. Though the name *mahjar* came to identify all Arab immigrants to the Americas in the period between 1880 and 1924, it was a self-identifying term circulated by the active Syrian press and adopted with particular zeal by Syrian/Lebanese émigré elites such as Rihani and Gibran.

The bulk of the first Arab émigrés to the Americas were not intellectuals but rather predominantly Christian peasants from the Ottoman-administered Mount Lebanon area. Whether they came from Lebanon or "the Yaman," these first Arab migrants to America were motivated largely by economic opportunity. Most of them worked as pack-peddlers. Many of the migrants from Greater Syria intended to return home to their native villages after a period of work. Those that did established what Akram Khater describes as the modern Lebanese middle class.[5] Others, however, never went back to the Mountain, and still others did return, only to make the trip once again to the Americas. By the 1920s a thriving Syrian press in America, with newspapers written in both English and Arabic, had been established. In addition, a network of peddling-supply distributors, stretching from Louisiana to North Dakota, had been in place since the turn of the century.

Despite the existence of these elements of a particularized ethnic community, historians of Arab immigration in America have argued, with rare exceptions, that the *mahjar* generation was remarkably successful in their effort to integrate into an unhyphenated American culture.[6] Furthermore, these historical accounts implicate *mahjar* writings in many of the same practices of Arab erasure that critics such as Nadine Naber have identified as emanating from U.S. popular culture and contributing to contemporary Arab American invisibility.[7] Chronicles of the *mahjar* generation largely emphasize the immigrants' rapid Americanization, and critics of *mahjar* literature emphasize the émigrés' ethos of deracination. Given this critical reception of the *mahjar*, the pioneer period of Arab immigration to the United States would seem to have a bearing on issues such as the absence of Arab American as a category on the census and the almost complete absence of Arab American writers in contemporary anthologies of American literature.[8] Is the lack of ethnic and cultural specificity in current U.S. representations of Arab identity the legacy of white Orientalist representation or of early Arab American self-representation? How do both discourses contribute to the current invisibility of Arab American as a category of American-ness?

In the pages that follow I will examine how the *mahjar* writers Ameen Rihani and Khalil Gibran conceptualized Arab, as well as Arab American, identity in their literature. Beginning by looking closely at representations of American Arab-ness proffered by popular writers of European descent, the essay will place *mahjar* identity politics within the larger context of U.S. immigration discourse. Rihani and Gibran both migrated to America at the beginning of the golden age of immigration in the 1880s and 1890s. They also witnessed, at first hand, the advent of the exclusionary immigration laws that would bring that golden age to an end with the 1924 Johnson-Reed quota system. Both Rihani's and Gibran's identity construction is infused with the representational politics of this historical context. The confrontation between constituent discourses of ethnic particularity and a national discourse of assimilation, however, produces different results in their respective representations of Arab-ness.

For example, Rihani's self-identification at the beginning of *Arabian Peak and Desert* as simultaneously a colonist and an immigrant, a native and a foreigner, an Orientalist traveler and an Oriental challenges the essentialist logic underpinning the criteria for U.S. citizenship that emerged after 1924. On the other hand, Rihani often framed the argument for Arab independence from postwar European mandates in the very essentialist language that dominated the discourse on U.S. immigration and which his own enunciations of multiple identities seemed to contradict. Reading *mahjar* writing in the context of the dominant culture's definitions of Arab-ness allows us to analyze the dialectic between minority narratives of self-identification and national narratives of assimilation. Ultimately this moment of *mahjar* ethnic self-reckoning has a salient legacy for current conceptualizations of Arab American identity, a point I will bring home by looking at Rihani's relationship to contemporary Arab American writing.

The Street Arab

Rihani's identification of an Arab stranger amid the "Arab" strangers of the "Syrian Colony of New York" delineates the contextual (and at times elective) nature of Arab identity in the Syrian/Lebanese *mahjar*. It also dramatizes a confrontation between a nineteenth-century American discourse on Arabs and the early twentieth-century literary enunciation of an Arab American identity. In her work on Arab racial identity and classification Lisa Suhair Majaj asserts,

> In addition to using Christian identity to assert their intrinsic affinity to white American society, Arab-American authors also made strategic use of the "exoticism" of their Holy Land origin. In doing so, they drew on the overlapping paradigms of racial essentialism, assimilation and cultural pluralism that structured cultural interaction in the American context. While the essentialism that viewed races and ethnic groups as totally distinct set Arabs apart from European Americans it also allowed them to assert their "uniqueness" (transposed onto a cultural and spiritual plane) as exotic emissaries from the Holy Land.[9]

Majaj identifies the dovetailing of turn-of-the-century American racial politics and *mahjar* identity politics. The double strategy these *mahjar* authors employed meant emphasizing both their similarity with European America and their difference as exotic Arabs. Arabs, in other words, were able to culturally assimilate to white-ness and retain their essential ethnic distinction. Arab American literary enunciation in the *mahjar* period captures the struggle between avowal and disavowal that is part of the birth pangs of all ethnic American literary traditions. However, Arab American literature does not hold the place in the canon occupied by other ethnic literary traditions that began in the early twentieth century. Because of this absence, the particularity of the image of the Arab in the context of American assimilation discourse bears scrutiny. The most pertinent image of the Arab circulating during the *mahjar* period of immigration was the street Arab.

Made popular by writers such as Horatio Alger Jr., the street Arab character appeared in American cultural consciousness around the 1850s. The street Arab was both a new urban problem to be solved and a link to the grander American narrative of immigration, one that normalized European nativity in New World space through references to biblical covenant, biblical geography, and biblical ancestors.[10] In this ur-story of becoming American, the Arab was a transitional node that was simultaneously privileged and in need of eradication. In Alger's 1871 *Tattered Tom; or, The Story of a Street Arab*, the street Arab also appears as a primitive type in a Protestant-inspired narrative of missionary redemption. Describing Tom, Alger writes,

> Arab as she was, she had been impressed by the kindness of Captain Barnes, and she felt that she should like to please him. Still, there was a fascination in the wild independence of her street life which was likely for some time to interfere with her enjoyment of the usages of a more civilized state. There was little prospect of her taming down into an average girl all at once. The change must come slowly.[11]

The polarities of "wild independence" and civilization that Alger's narrative erects makes it clear that as Tom moves from the figurative position of Arab and into the position of "average" American girl, she plays out a capitalist allegory of social progress. In Alger's formula the street Arab is a protean version of the Protestant American entrepreneur. But the visible markings of Arab ethnicity itself are erased once the waif makes the transition into the mainstream of American citizenry. Operating as fetish, the image of the street Arab represented both cultural difference, through metonymic signifiers such as unclean faces and itinerant sleeping arrangements, and the fantasy of eradicating that difference through cultural assimilation.

Given the instructive Protestant redemption scenario attached to the character, the street Arab was also instrumentalized in the rhetoric of U.S. urban reform movements. In the decade after the publication of Alger's children's series on Tattered Tom, a Danish immigrant journalist named Jacob Riis took his camera into New York City's most infamous slums, the Five Points, and captured the figure of the street Arab in a series of photographs that were meant not to inspire confidence in the democratic promise of America's capitalist system but rather to haunt the social conscience of America's democratic audience. The images Riis published, in a book entitled *How the Other Half Lives* (1890), present the American public with a view into the harsh living conditions of the United States' new class of immigrants. As with Alger's street urchin though, the term *Arab,* for Riis, operates as a marker of symbolic foreignness. Because it is found in an immigrant child this foreignness has the potential to be erased if the urchin can be "redeemed" by the "civilized state." Riis writes of the street Arab,

> His sturdy independence, love of freedom and absolute self-reliance, together with his rude sense of justice that enables him to govern his little community, not always in accordance with municipal or city ordinances, but often a good deal closer to the saving line of "doing to others as one would be done by"—these are strong handles by which to catch the boy and make him useful. Successful bankers, clergymen, and lawyers all over the country, statesmen in some instances of national repute, bear evidence in their lives to the potency of such missionary efforts.[12]

Riis marks the link between "Arab" and American identity by commenting on the street Arab's "sturdy independence," "love of freedom," "self-reliance" and biblical code of ethics. Because these character traits are shared by both "Arabs" and "Americans," the street Arab is ripe for missionary conversion. Indeed, with the benefit of these "missionary efforts," Riis promises the street Arab will become a productive member of the nation's body politic. Unlike Tom in Alger's *Story of a Street Arab,* the tenement children who stared back at the viewer through the sepia glow of Riis's photographs could not have their racial and social alterity cleansed away by a bath, and it would take at least a generation for their ethnic identities to be integrated into the phantasm of American citizenship. However, as Italians replaced the Irish and as the Chinese replaced the Italians in Five Points' ghetto streets, each ethnic group moved out of the position of social marginalization, of Arab foreignness, and, like Tom, eventually toward entrance into America's "civilized state." By and large, Arab-ness in nineteenth-century America was a typology that individuals could become and un-become. But whatever mobility figurative Arab-ness provided to individuals, the trope of the Arab remained unchanged.

The Alger narrative of becoming American is particularly relevant to the way the trope of the Arab operates in the nineteenth century. In discussing the second-generation Arab Americans' attitude toward their pioneer Syrian immigrant parents, Alixa Naff writes, "Most of them conceive of that period in Horatio Alger terms in which poor illiterate immigrants, with little or no English, succeeded by ingenuity and hard work. References to Horatio Alger are, of course apt."[13] The "apt" references to Alger indicate the degree to

Fig. 3.1. Image from Jacob Riis's *How the Other Half Lives* (1890), the Street Arab section. The caption beneath the picture reads, "Didn't Live Nowhere."

which the *mahjar* generation has been historicized as integrating themselves into the American mainstream through the formula made familiar in figures such as Tattered Tom—figures whose ethnic identities are shed as they climb the social ladder. The success of this integration, whether real or imagined, is a testament to the power of nineteenth-century discourses on the Arab and the influence of those discourses not only on early twentieth-century Arab American self-representation but also on subsequent histories of the period. Naff makes the claim that if the political and economic events of post–World War II had not reactivated Arab immigration, "Syrian-Americans might have assimilated themselves out of existence."[14] By looking more closely at the conceptualization of Arab-ness provided by writers such as Gibran and Rihani in the context of current definitions of the Arab, however, this putative legacy of *mahjar* self-erasure appears ripe for reinterpretation.

Canonizing Gibran

Though not a single anthology of American literature includes any mention of the *mahjar* writers, Khalil Gibran remains one of the most recognizable names in American literary history.[15] An advocate of Americanization and of preserving Arab heritage, Gibran initially published prolifically in both English- and Arabic-language presses in America. With the publication of *The Prophet* in 1923, however, he moved steadily away from specific articulations of Arab identity, as well as Arab American identity politics, and toward self-representation as an abstracted Oriental writer. Gibran's self-representation capitalized on the increasing popularity of exotic themes in the United States in a period marked by a modern literary revolution.[16] A book review from the *New York Times* on June 10, 1934, highlights Gibran's reception as an "Eastern" mystic who appealed to Bohemian artistic sensibilities.

> [Gibran evinces] an unworldliness reminding one of Guatama and the philosophers of the Upanishads; there is a lyric manner and picturesqueness that recalls the best of the old Hebrew prophets; . . . there is an epigrammatic pithiness of utterance that makes many of Gibran's saying not unworthy to be placed side by side with those of older sages of the Orient.[17]

India, the Old Testament, and a generalized Orient are all mentioned in relation to Gibran, but Arab-ness is absent. It is no coincidence that *The Prophet* received increased attention and a surge in sales during the 1960s, another period in which Bohemian-minded U.S. citizens were turning to an abstracted East for lessons on spirituality. The appearance of Gibran's most popular book as a decontextualized spiritual guide in a 2005 movie about Johnny Cash, *Walk the Line,* reprises the role that the writer has occupied in American cultural consciousness since the book's publication. As critic Geoffrey Nash puts it, "Absent from Khalil Jibran's later discourse are not merely concrete social situations and categorizable psychological processes, but the Arab identity which was at least to be found in his early Arabic writings."[18]

Despite his visibility, to accept Gibran as representative of *mahjar* literature's overall characteristics is a mistake. Gibran's English-language writings are mostly devoid of the struggles between modernity and tradition, East and West, authority and free choice that are prevalent in the writings of his contemporary turn-of-the-twentieth-century Arab and Arab American colleagues, colleagues far less recognizable to an American audience then and now.[19] Instead of articulating national, racial, or ethnic particularities, Gibran's work from *The Prophet* onward focuses on human universals. With the publication of *The Prophet,* Suheil Bushrui argues, "the simplicity of Gibran's language had . . . become the most striking feature of his writing."[20] This simple language had none of the markings of ethnicity that characterized the dialect renderings of other American immigrant writers, most notably contemporary European Jews such as Abraham Cahan.[21] Gibran's use of a simple, universal language presents a version of oriental identity that aims toward a synthesis of Eastern and Western identity but ultimately is not demonstrably different than an Orientalist representation.

Given Gibran's adoption of what Nash has called the "acculturated Oriental code" recognizable to Western readers, it is not difficult to deduce why he has found a place in the American popular cultural imaginary, if not the American literary canon. Gibran's deracinated self-representation as a conglomerate Oriental prophet figure was readily integrated into an Orientalist tradition in American literature, one that it mimicked in many ways. However, though Gibran's writings are popular with American audiences they are ignored by anthologies of American literature. The reason for Gibran's absence in the canon of accepted American ethnic writing is that he is perceived by editors to not properly convey an ethnic experience. Because of its abstract representation of Oriental identity, Gibran's writings do not adequately comply with the paradigm of inclusion required for entrance into the pluralistic pantheon masquerading as America's multicultural canon.[22] The sacrifice of vernacular specificity and ethnic consciousness in Gibran's writing has resulted in sacrificing a place in American literature's ethnic canon.

The figure of the Arab, as fashioned by American Orientalism, as utilized by a writer such as Gibran, and as historicized by chroniclers of the *mahjar*, is a transition point rather than an identity to be articulated, developed, and defended. Even when resistance to assimilation is noted in historical chronicles of the *mahjar* it is dismissed as a doomed endeavor. Writing about the pioneer pack peddlers, Naff comments,

> In their trade, the unavoidable contacts with American society broke down resistance to learning by interacting with and imitating many aspects of American life. Any barrier that Syrian leaders would later erect against the tide of Americanization would be built on the quicksands of the peddling experience. (199)

In formulations such as these, Americanization becomes a fait accompli, and a hegemonic reading of Arab absence in U.S. culture is produced out of the convergence between the master discourse of American assimilation and the minor histories of Arab immigration.

While Gibran tried to capitalize on the exotic purchase of his Eastern origin by representing himself to his Western readers in roles fashioned for him by Orientalist discourses, most pioneer-generation immigrants resisted these American definitions of their identity. In his book *Inventing Home*, Akram Khater challenges the emphasis in *mahjar* histories on the making of "new man" Americans out of Syrian/Lebanese immigrants. Khater argues that "large numbers of immigrants rejected 'America' as an idea and reality" (15). Instead of assimilation these immigrants preferred a complex process of "mixing and matching what they brought with them and what they saw in the streets and homes of America" (15). Though these immigrants were often forced to internalize the dichotomy of the "traditional" and the "modern" that they encountered in American culture and through the diverse institutions that tried to "reform" their practices of child-rearing or marriage, most pioneers interpreted themselves as "modern." Khater's emphasis on a transnational understanding of the Syrian/Lebanese *mahjar* leads him to deprivilege the U.S. context. He concludes that "what we see among the immigrant communities in the Americas is the rise of a class whose members tried to distinguish themselves as different (culturally and socially) from middle-class America as well as from peasant Lebanon" (91).

Khater's analysis is valuable not only in its emphasis on the émigré as well as the immigrant but also because it suggests that the first Arab immigrants to the United States did not see themselves as "Orientals" in the way that American discourse had fashioned the term. Whether they assimilated to the dominant culture and thus erased their "Oriental" cultural features or whether they reinterpreted their cultural practices as modern in the face of Orientalist views, the *mahjar* generation was keen to transition out of the "Arab" identity provided by American literature. In creating a new identity for themselves, however, these Syrian/Lebanese émigrés left the image of the Arab essentially unchanged. In a sense Akram discusses the Syrian/Lebanese yin to Gibran's universalist yang. The two forms of self-representation combine to instantiate an image of the Arab largely shaped by nineteenth-century Orientalist conceits.

But if Gibran represents the willingness of some *mahjar* writers to strategically adapt Oriental codes of self-representation, Rihani's writings resist these codes through sophisticated strategies of figurative self-representation. In both his fictional novel *The Book of Khalid* (1911) and his semifictional travel writings Rihani fashions a persona that literally inhabits the codes of nineteenth-century Orientalism in order to revise them. Often read as a deracinated attempt at Western assimilation, Rihani's writings are in fact, I would argue, an attempt to establish models of citizenship that are not nation based and models of ethnicity that resist tropological closure. Rihani's negotiations with the tropes of Oriental identity offer an example of thinking not past ethnicity but rather through the self-making romantic possibilities of tropic representation. Khalid, the hero of Rihani's only novel, *The Book of Khalid* (1911), begins as a capitalist pack-peddler, becomes a bohemian ladies' man, and tries out anarchism, Marxism, and pan-Arabism before eventually ending as a wandering prophet in the desert. Viewed through Rihani and not Gibran, the legacy of Arab American writing in American literature looks quite different. In Rihani, kitsch representation is replaced with ludic representation. The first repeats tropes to establish the essential character of a specific group, the second stretches tropes past their logical limit, revealing essentialism as a ridiculous premise.

A return to Rihani's 1930 *Arabian Peak and Desert* travel narrative will help elucidate his playful approach to questions of self-representation and identity.

> Although a Syrian by birth, an American by naturalization, I am in my blood an Arab; and although Christianity is the religion of my inheritance, I am also of the faith of the great poets and philosophers—Al-Ghazzaly, Al-Farid and Abu'l-Ala—as well as the young Arabs of today who are working for union and independence, and seeking to reinvest their country with its former prestige and power . . . "Who upholds Arabia, upholds Al-Islam."[23]

Rihani's self-presentation (to Imam Yahya, to the reader) resists the closure of essentialism while still relying on essentialist tropes of Arab-ness. Rihani does not synthesize Arab and American, Islamic and Christian, traditional and modern. He presents them as unreconciled constituent pieces of his contradictory identity. It is, of course, ludicrous for Rihani to be simultaneously all of the things he presents himself as—but that is precisely my point.

In the process of identifying himself to Imam Yahya, the ruler of Yemen, as "Arab in blood," "American by naturalization," and "Syrian by birth," Rihani recreates the shifting loci of identity that I introduced in this essay's first page. It is an identity built in constellations, where constituent pieces orbit around one another rather than eclipsing one another. The bridge Rihani constructs across potential boundaries of religious, ethnic, and national difference is figurative—his Arab "blood." Rather than interpret this reference to "blood" strictly as an essentialist mode of identity politics born out of a particular historical moment, I want to suggest that Rihani offers us an opportunity to think about contemporary Arab American identity formation rhizomatically. Rihani, in this latter read, offers Arab-ness as a labile territorial assemblage—a form of becoming that allows us to, in the words of Deleuze and Guattari, "grasp the trace of creation in the created" nature of all self-identification.[24] Arab-ness here is presented as a performative modality, rather than an essential identity.

Rihani's Contemporary Legacy

In his emphasis on the contextual value of the term *Arab* and the possibility for it to be multiple things to different people, Rihani articulates a form of identity politics that resonates with contemporary Arab American writing. Just as current Arab American writers insist on their ability to inhabit what are seen as competing cultural identities, Rihani's conceptualization of Arab identity refuses either/or dichotomies. Rihani's refusal to distill Arab-ness to one thing or another presents an alternative vision of global networks of belonging, one that is suspicious of ossification and sensitive to flux. The eminent contemporary poet and scholar of Arab American culture Lisa Suhair Majaj offers a vision of Arab American identity formation that is equally suspicious of either/or formulations.

> But the ArabAmerican woman has news.
> She knows who she is, and its not what you think.
> When she wears hiking boots and jeans
> she's just as authentic
> as her sister in the embroidered dress.
> When she walks up a mountain, her identity goes up with her
> and comes back down again.
>
> Besides, she's learned a secret.
> Two cultures can be lighter than one
> if the space between them
> the space they open up—
> is fluid, like a stream of light,
> or wind between two open hands,
> or the future, which knows how to change.[25]

By focusing on an Arab American woman's choice of clothes, Majaj implicitly challenges a metonymic sign of culture that, depending on context, either reifies authenticity or signifies oppression. Instead of weighing in on whether the Arab woman in traditional clothes is the victim of patriarchy or the reservoir of heritage, Majaj announces the connection between the "sister in the embroidered dress" and the woman in the jeans and hiking boots. Like Rihani before her, Majaj rejects the either/or of the Arab and American binary, opting instead to explore "the space between," where she displays her cultural negative capability. Rihani claims the traditionalist al-Ghazzali and the voices of pan-Arab modern reform in the same breath. Majaj implicitly connects women in a traditional Arab village with women in a Western metropolitan culture. In Imam Yahya, the ruler of a conservative Zaidi-controlled Al-Yaman, Rihani faced a man whose notion of fealty could aptly be described as quite similar to the "with us or against us" mentality pervading much of U.S. political discourse since 9/11. As in Rihani's response to Imam Yahya's questioning of his identity (and by extension his loyalty), Majaj's statement is a statement of simultaneous contestation and reconciliation.

Today's Arab American writers are a diverse and multifaceted group, but the thrust of their articulations about the state of Arab American writing suggests that to be Arab in America is not a transitional node anymore but rather a home worth fighting for with words. The influence of the *mahjar* in their writings is fugitive at best. When *mahjar* literature is acknowledged, it is often marked as a beginning point but rarely as an impetus to explore what it has meant historically to be Arab in the "American" context.

In 2008, *PMLA* devoted an issue to the subject of the current state of Arab American writing, entitled "Writing While Arab."[26] The one author who focused on the mahjar, the poet Iman Meshal, revisited Khalil Gibran's legacy in her article "Eliminating Diasporic Identities." The thrust of Meshal's argument, that Gibran should not be forced to be representative of anything beyond his own art, is convincing and eloquent. Meshal identifies the "ready-made identities circulating through cultural and institutional discourse" as a burden on the diasporic writer.[27] In the case of Gibran, this burden produced a literature that met a Western audience's kitsch expectations and an identity that was largely formed by his perception of those expectations. But, as I have been suggesting, Rihani had a very different approach to the expectations that he be representative. In Rihani, diasporic identity does not lead him to present Arab-ness as either an Orientalist essential or a Western mimicry. Instead, Rihani uses the oppositions of diasporic affiliation to present an identity that is fueled by unsynthesized contradictions. In Rihani, Arab-ness is figurative and thus open to but never closed by interpretation.

NOTES

1. Ameen Rihani, *Arabian Peak and Desert: Travels in Al-Yaman* (London: Constable, 1930), 1.

2. For Rihani's pan-Arabism see Geoffrey Nash, *The Arab Writer in English: Arab Themes in a Metropolitan Language, 1908–1951* (Portland, OR: Sussex Academic Press, 1998).

3. Ameen Rihani Papers, Library of Congress Manuscript Division, "Pan-Arab Lecture," Box 4, Folder 5, 45.

4. The critical literature on the *nahda* is extensive, but a good place to start is Hisham Sharabi, *Neopatriarchy: A Theory of Distorted Change in Arab Society* (London: Oxford University Press, 1988).

5. Akram Khater, *Inventing Home: Emigration, Gender, and the Middle Class in Lebanon 1870–1920* (Berkeley: University of California Press, 2001).

6. On the *mahjar* see Alixa Naff, *Becoming American: The Early Arab Immigrant Experience* (Carbondale: Southern Illinois Press, 1985). For an account of Arab Ameri-

can presence in America that looks beyond the pioneer generation see Gregory Orfalea, *The Arab Americans: A History* (Northampton, MA: Olive Branch Press, 2006). For an analysis of Syrian immigration to South America during the same pioneer period (1880–1924) see Christina Civantos, *Between Argentines and Arabs: Argentine Orientalism, Arab Immigrants, and the Writing of Identity* (Albany: SUNY Press, 2006), and John Tofik Karam, *Another Arabesque: Syrian-Lebanese Ethnicity in Neoliberal Brazil* (Philadelphia: Temple University Press, 2007). For earlier, informative edited collections of accounts of early Arab immigration to America see Eric Hooglund, ed., *Crossing the Waters: Arabic-Speaking Immigrants to the United States before 1940* (Washington, DC: Smithsonian Institution Press, 1987); Nabeel Abraham and Sameer Y. Abraham, eds., *Arabs in the New World: Studies in Arab American Communities* (Detroit: Wayne State University Center for Urban Ethnic Studies, 1983); Elaine C. Hagopian and Ann Paden, eds., *The Arab Americans: Studies in Assimilation* (Wilamette, IL: Medina University Press International, 1969). For the seminal account of the Syrian presence in America see Philip K. Hitti, *The Syrians in America* (New York: George Doran, 1924). The assimilation argument is a consistent strain in Naff; Hagopian and Paden; Hooglund; and Abraham and Abraham.

7. Nadine Naber, "Ambiguous Insiders: An Investigation of Arab-American Invisibility," in *Ethics and Racial Studies* 23, no. 1 (January 2000): 37–61.

8. The most recent *Norton Anthology of American Literature* (6th ed., 2003), edited by Nina Baym, has no Arab American writers represented in any of its five volumes. *The Heath Anthology of American Literature* has one Arab American writer represented, the poet Naomi Shihab Nye, who has been featured since the influential 1990 volume. Even recent American literature anthologies specifically geared toward "multicultural" approaches to American literature ignore Arab American writing. For example, A. Robert Lee's *Multicultural American Literature* (Jackson: University of Mississippi Press, 2003) focuses on black, Native, Latino, and Asian American fictions, thus reproducing the usual canon of American ethnicity.

9. Lisa Suhair Majaj, "Arab-Americans and the Meaning of Race," *Postcolonial Theory and the United States,* ed. Amritjit Singh and Peter Schmidt (Jackson: University of Mississippi Press, 2000), 329.

10. For a cogent and compelling theorization of the discourse of America as Near East see Hilton Obenzinger, *American Palestine: Melville, Twain and Holy Land Mania* (Princeton: Princeton University Press, 1999).

11. Horatio Alger Jr., *Tattered Tom: Or, The Story of a Street Arab* (Boston: Loring, 1871), 104.

12. Jacob Riis, *How the Other Half Lives* (New York: Charles Scribner and Sons, 1890), 68.

13. Alixa Naff, 161.

14. Ibid., 330.

15. This of course excludes those dedicated expressly to Arab American writing such as Gregory Orfalea and Sahrif Elmusa, eds., *Grape Leaves: A Century of Arab American Poetry* (Boston: Interlink, 1999).

16. For more on the increased interest in exotic material during the first decades of the twentieth century see Christine Stansell, *American Moderns: Bohemian New York and the Creation of a New Century* (New York: Holt, 2001).

17. Suheil Bushrui and John Munroe, eds., *Kahlil Gibran: Essays and Introductions* (Beirut: Rihani House, 1970), 179.

18. Nash, 44.

19. See M. M. Badawi, "Perennial Themes in Modern Arab Literature," *British Journal of Middle East Studies* 20 (1993): 3–19.

20. Suheil Bushrui, *Kahlil Gibran of Lebanon* (Gerrards' Cross, Buckinghamshire: Colin Smyhe Limited, 1987), 68.

21. "There is a streak of sadness in the blood of my race," the character David Levinsky announces in the first pages of Abraham Cahan's seminal novel of Jewish immigration to America, "very likely it is of Oriental origin." Because of writers such as Cahan, the figure of the Jew in American literary representation transitioned out of Oriental identity and into an ethnic American niche. Abraham Cahan, *The Rise of David Levinsky* (1917; New York: Penguin, 1993), 4.

22. For ethnic canon formation see David Palumbo-Liu, ed., *The Ethnic Canon* (Minneapolis: University of Minnesota Press, 1995). Palumbo-Liu argues that the inclusion of ethnic writers in the canon is too often dictated by diversity management strategies that reproduce dominant structures of cultural belonging, structures that are often productive pluralism models disguised as multiculturalism.

23. Rihani, 95.

24. Gilles Deleuze and Felix Guattari, *A Thousand Plateaus: Capitalism and Schizophrenia,* trans. Brian Massumi (Minneapolis: University of Minnesota Press, 1987), 337.

25. "The Arab-American Woman Reads Poetry," in Susan Muaddi Durraj, ed., *Scheherazade's Legacy: Arab and Arab American Women on Writing* (Westport, CT: Praeger, 2004), 33.

26. PMLA, "Writing While Arab" (October 2008).

27. Iman Meshal, "Eliminating Diasporic Identities," in *PMLA* 123, no. 5 (October 2008): 1581–89.

FOUR

Turcos in the Mix
Corrupting Arabs in Brazil's Racial Democracy

John Tofik Karam

Turco (Turk) has served as a general designation for "Middle Easterner" in Brazil for more than a century. Coined by late nineteenth-century Brazilian elites to denigrate Syrian and Lebanese immigrants as economic pariahs, the term of difference today continues to attribute an alleged shrewdness to Brazilians of Middle Eastern origin. This was the case in a São Paulo city government corruption scandal in 1999 and 2000. Though few Arab Brazilian politicians were implicated, *turcos* came to stand for corruption in media coverage. "We have seen voracious Arabs commanding the money-laundering schemes," observed a well-known pundit in the *Estado de S. Paulo* newspaper, "the whole band of *turcos* . . . eating *esfihas* ["Middle Eastern" meat pies] and baba ghanoush and transforming São Paulo into a cavern of Ali Baba."[1]

In responding to such representations of Arabness, politicians and everyday citizens of Syrian-Lebanese descent strove to distance themselves from the drama of corruption. Some political leaders carried out the second annual commemoration of Lebanese independence day in São Paulo's city council, using it as a way to praise their ostensible *mescla* (mix) in Brazil. Other citizens placed blame on those leaders, finding such media coverage neither racist nor discriminatory. This essay endeavors to show that these two responses to the representation of putative Arab corruption each reflect Brazilian nationalist ideology. In claiming mixture or nondiscrimination, Arab Brazilian politicians and laypersons have reproduced nationalist notions of "mixture" (*mestiçagem*) and "racial democracy" (*democracia racial*) in Brazil.

Conventionally speaking, these ideas were first celebrated by the highly influential Brazilian writer and essayist Gilberto Freyre (1900–1987).² Constructing a past shared by lighter male masters and darker female slaves on colonial plantations in his masterpiece *Casa grande e senzala,* Freyre claimed that miscegenation among Indians, Africans, and Portuguese created a mixed society that "balanced racial antagonisms."³ Though such a mythical narrative has served as a lightning rod of Brazilian nationalism in the twentieth and early twenty-first century, scholars have long documented racism and racial inequalities in Brazil.⁴ In exploring how Middle Eastern descendants confirm this nationalist ideology, however, my aim is *not* to portray Arab Brazilians as the bearers of some sort of false consciousness. Rather, I contend that their discourses of mixture and nondiscrimination point to an Arab formation that must be understood vis-à-vis Brazil. In privileging this national context, my essay serves as an initial step to outline the contours of this particular arabesque today in the Americas.⁵

Creating Turco *Difference*

Mostly departing from present-day Syria and Lebanon, Middle Eastern immigrants to Brazil numbered 140,464 from 1880 to 1969.⁶ Until World War I, they carried travel papers issued by the Ottoman Empire and hence were labeled *turcos* by Brazilian elites and masses. In the Amazon, so-called Turks came to dominate the grain and rubber trades.⁷ Likewise in the state of São Paulo, they attained a predominant position in the textile market. As early as 1893, Middle Easterners made up 90 percent of the "mascates" (peddlers) in the São Paulo city almanac.⁸ In these circumstances, the *turco* term of difference came to attribute a shrewd commercial acumen to so-named subjects. As the famous poet Carlos Drummond de Andrade rhymed in the first half of the twentieth century, "The *turcos* [Turks] were born to sell / colorful knickknacks in canisters / door-to-door. / . . . If they open the canister, who resists / the impulse to buy? / It's cheap! Cheap! Buy now! / Pay later! But buy!"⁹

Early twentieth-century Brazilian business and state elites, however, endeavored to attract cheap rural labor and *embranquecer* (whiten) the nation. During the Getúlio Vargas regime in the early 1930s, an immigration quota system was created in order to favor European immigrants with alleged agricultural skills. The place of Middle Easterners here was clear, as presciently pointed out by a convener of the 1926 National Society of Agriculture meeting: "We should also do everything to make difficult the immigration of Syrian elements which, far from benefiting agriculture, parasitically exploit it in the profession of false businessmen."¹⁰ This view was propagated by Herbet Levy, a federal deputy and the owner of the *Gazeta Mercantil* newspaper. Levy wrote that "the type of immigration required by the country's needs is that of agricultural workers and the Syrians are not classified in this category," being rather "dedicated to commerce and speculative activities." He specified that "Syrians are not present" among the 700,000 agricultural laborers in São Paulo.[11] Middle Easterners were thus marginalized in Brazilian immigration policy.

At the same time, national cultural production, such as the aforementioned celebration of Brazil's racial "mixture" in Gilberto Freyre's *Casa grande e senzala* (1933), strove to obscure these forms of exclusion. Beholden to racist policies and racially mixed claims, state elites scrutinized immigrants' "miscegenation" through their marital practices. Although earlier works found Middle Easterners' mixed rates "reasonable,"[12] later publications questioned such "optimistic" findings. One particularly harsh critic alleged that "Syrian immigrants" were marrying the "Brazilian children of Syrians" and thus were erroneously categorized as "mixed."[13] "Although in social circles they have become intimate with the rest of the population," another ethnologist qualified, "their [marital] ties almost always proceed within their own colony." He added that "*Syrios*" prefer São Paulo residents of the "ancestry of their own origin."[14] A sociologist concluded that only future studies would discern whether "Syrians" tended toward endogamy, "with possible consequences, favorable or not, for the *Pátria*."[15] Middle Easterners were questioned in the seemingly "mixed" Brazilian nation.

Historically constructed as shrewd traders who failed to labor in agriculture and miscegenate in nuptials, Syrian-Lebanese nonetheless followed a distinct trajectory from petty commerce to industrial and liberal professional pursuits in World War II times and beyond.[16] Such upward mobility foregrounded their entrance into politics. From 1945 to 1966, forty-one "distinct politicians of Syrian-Lebanese origin" from São Paulo exercised eighty-eight mandates in municipal, state, and federal arenas.[17] Most striking in 1962 and 1966, Syrian-Lebanese garnered 10 percent and 17 percent of the total number of state and federal deputies, respectively, elected in São Paulo.[18] Such an "over-representation" of Middle Easterners in midcentury politics continued through two decades of military rule and the return of democracy in the late twentieth century.[19]

Paulo Salim Maluf has served as the most infamous, if enigmatic, Arab politician during this time. Born to wealthy Lebanese parents in São Paulo, Maluf gained political clout through a friendship struck with General Costa e Silva in horse-racing clubs during the 1950s. As chief of state in the early years of the dictatorship (1967–69), General Costa e Silva appointed the young Maluf mayor of São Paulo. In the next three decades, Maluf embarked on a career as a resourceful—some would say sly—politician. He won special infamy in the race for the São Paulo governorship in 1978. At the time, the leadership of Arena, the political party of the dictatorship, sought to pass him over as its candidate. Meanwhile, Maluf personally visited the majority of the eight hundred Arena delegates who would choose the party candidate. "On the day of the convention," relates the journalist Maurício Puls, "Maluf greeted all the delegates of Arena by name. . . . he knew their city and wives' and children's names," too.[20] In late 1978, Maluf was made governor by the São Paulo legislative assembly.

Still today, Maluf has garnered much support among those who identify with his brand of populism, *malufismo*. A common saying among his detractors (and even some followers) is that Maluf *rouba mas faz* (steals but gets things done). Yet Puls remembers that the expression *rouba mas faz* was originally coined in reference to Adhemar de Barros, a prominent figure in the country's first redemocratization process (1945–64), used in his dispute with Jânio Quadros for the São Paulo governorship in 1954. While Barros was characterized by the popular mantra *rouba mas faz*, Quadros won the election based on his promise to *varrer* (sweep out) corruption.[21] Historically, Maluf's image as a wily politician had been inherited from *adhemarismo*, Adhemar de Barros's style of populism in midcentury Brazilian politics.

Corrupting Arabness

In 1999 and 2000, these dynamics gained a novel force in the so-called *máfia das propinas* (mafia of kickbacks), implicating past and present São Paulo city governments. In exchange for legislative deference to the mayor, city councilors were given the power to appoint directors of local administrative units of the municipality (called regional administrations, or ARs). In the cases investigated, handpicked cronies bribed constituencies by bypassing or providing government laws or services. The kickbacks collected from different groups—namely, street vendors and commercial enterprises—were then rerouted back to city councilors who voted in accordance with the mayor and rightist establishment.[22] This quid pro quo provided the mayor with a council majority and councilors with administrative machinery to cull election support and forward self-interests. Once ensuring political success, this institutionalization of personal connections increasingly has been labeled "corruption" by the press.

The mafia of kickbacks began when a street vendor denounced a Lebanese Brazilian politician in early 1999, which then turned into a drama of governance in newspaper articles and television reports through the year

2000. Exerting influence over the administrative unit of Sé in downtown São Paulo (AR-Sé), city councilman Hanna Garib (Brazilian Progressive Party, PPB) allegedly ordered the murder of the street vendor who had made the damning accusations. Garib had a lot at stake. He took bribes from street vendors in exchange for de facto permission to remain stationary on sidewalks and streets. Ironically, Garib also received payments from commercial establishments to remove the area's street vendors. The extortion scheme netted millions for Garib and other councilmen, but investigations were cut short by the rightist establishment, allowing the conviction of only three councilmen: Vicente Viscome, José Izar, and Hanna Garib. Only Izar and Garib had been ethnically marked by corruption in media headlines.

Suspicions haunted the Brazilian Progressive Party (PPB) at city hall. In fact, eighteen of the thirty city councilors who supported the mayor in exchange for control of the city's administrative units stemmed from the PPB. Even its "godfather," Paulo Maluf, had been implicated when accusations of corruption reached his handpicked successor, Mayor Celso Pitta (1996–2000). As a onetime *apadrinhado* (political godchild), Pitta was elected mayor in 1996 with Maluf's support.[23] At the time, PPB's godfather promised in newspapers, on television, and in radio broadcasts, "If Pitta is not a good mayor, never again vote for me." Not surprisingly, the bills proposed to continue formal investigations of the mayor's office (and to impeach Pitta) were defeated by rightist city councilors.

Figures in the mafia of kickbacks were depicted not only as dishonest politicians but also as corrupt Arabs in 1999 and 2000. This representation of Arab corruption was realized via innuendoes about the popular Brazilian "Arab" fast-food restaurant Habib's, as well as "Arab food," such as tabouleh (a salad with parsley, tomato, and bulgur wheat), *kibe* (ground meat with bulgur wheat), baba ghanoush (eggplant pâté with garlic and sesame-seed paste), and even *esfihas* (meat pies).[24] One political pundit awarded "prizes" to the most unpopular figures in São Paulo, serving up the "Habib's prize" to Paulo Maluf. In early 1999, he wrote:

> The Habib's Prize goes to doctor (doctor of what, eh?) Baulo Baluf [*sic*]. After one of those years in which the mayor's order turned into a *pita azeda* [bitter pita bread; a reference to Celso Pitta] and the fight that was to be tabouleh turned into raw *kibe,* all that's lacking the illustrious citizen is to open up a *cadeia* [double meaning of chain or prison] (no pun intended) of Arab food and give license to his charms to make all his opponents get cancer.[25]

As corruption was associated with Middle Eastern foods, including pita bread, tabouleh, and *kibe,* Paulo Maluf was mocked for his support of Celso

Pitta's city government, which plunged São Paulo into one of its worst corruption scandals ever.

Within the next few months in 1999, another social commentator levied similar criticism of several figures involved in the mafia of kickbacks. Taking the form of a "Dear Gabby" column, a perhaps fictitious reader fretted:

> WELL DONE
>
> My last votes went to Maluf, Pitta, Garib and Viscome. Will I eternally burn in the fires of hell, or will I be deserving of some divine clemency? Do I have some chance of being forgiven? How?
> —Fried *Kibe* in Boiling Oil

In "response," the political satirist wrote:

> DEAR SENHORA HABIB'S,
>
> I fear that you will suffer the same punishment as other São Paulo city residents who committed the same sin: being condemned to live in an ugly, dirty, and wicked city.[26]

Although two non-Arab politicians implicated in the corruption scandal were mentioned (Celso Pitta, a self-identified black Brazilian,[27] and Vicente Viscome, of Italian descent), the discourse on Middle Eastern food ("fried *kibe*") and the reference to the Habib's fast-food chain colored corruption with the ethnicity of Paulo Maluf and Hanna Garib. Political corruption was conflated not with blackness or Italianness but with Arabness in São Paulo.

The media, however, was not the sole source of criticism. In June 2000, the Union of Bank Clerks organized a protest in which members distributed three thousand *esfihas* (Middle Eastern meat pies) in front of the city council chambers. Angered by the failure to impeach Paulo Maluf's handpicked successor, Celso Pitta, protestors expressed indignation by modifying a colloquial expression, *Vai acabar em pizza*—literally, "It will end in pizza," meaning, "Nothing will come of it." In the words of one organizer, since the protest was *em homenagem aos árabes e libaneses* (in dedication to Arabs and Lebanese), the scandal would end not in "pizza" but in an *esfiha* (meat pie).[28] Covering the event, the journalist related:

> Instead of pizza, one group of fifty bank clerks, dressed as Arabs, gave *esfiha* meat pies to the people passing in front of City Hall in protest of the rejection of Mayor Celso Pitta's impeachment trial. The president of the Union of Bank Clerks . . . said that the switch of pizza for *esfiha* was motivated by the fact that "the godfather of Pitta, Paulo Maluf, is of Lebanese origin."[29]

Covering their heads with kaffiyehs (Arab scarves) and promising that a belly dancer would come on the scene, union members overlooked the backgrounds of other politicians implicated in the scandal and embodied Arabness as the canker of corruption in city government.

Curiously, the most cutting criticisms of Middle Eastern politicians stemmed from left-of-center media elites who identified themselves as "Lebanese descendants." José Simão, famous for writing a daily column in *Folha de S. Paulo,* was relentless in his witty and sometimes cryptic discourse on the corruption of fellow *turcos*. Satirizing the insignia of Paulo Maluf's PPB, Simão once wrote, "Since I am Lebanese, I can say that PPB means *Propinas Pros Brimos*. Hahaha!"[30] Roughly translated, *"Propinas Pros Primos"* means "Kickbacks for `Cousins." Simão played on native Arabic speakers' difficulty in pronouncing the *p* in *primo* (cousin), enunciating it as a *b*—hence *brimo,* or "cousin." Simão also quipped in other articles that Paulo Maluf would take advantage of his time in the limelight to write and release an autobiography titled *Minha Vida É uma Esfirra Aberta* (My Life Is an Open Meat Pie).[31] Satirizing Arabic language and food, this self-identified Lebanese journalist highlighted the corrupt character of Middle Eastern ethnicity in national presses.

Hanna Garib was mocked in equally creative ways. In the excerpt that follows, Simão commented on how Garib's forced departure from the political arena led to his replacement by another politician, Wadih Helou, who coincidentally also was Middle Eastern.

> Attention! It's the Turco-Circuit in Sampa [São Paulo]. "Cash Garib" leaves and his replacement is Wadih Helou? One *turco* leaves and another enters? As a reader friend of mine says: "They switched a *kibe* for an *esfiha*? It's like an all-you-can eat meal at Habib's! Ha ha ha! It [the corruption scandal] ended in *esfiha,* and not in pizza!"[32]

Using Middle Eastern food and the popular ethnonym of *turcos,* the Lebanese commentator outlined the corrupt contours of Hanna Garib and even his replacement, Wadih Helou (who had nothing to do with this corruption scandal itself).

Arnaldo Jabor, another well-known pundit who writes in the *Folha de S. Paulo* and makes brief appearances on the Globo television network,[33] accentuated the alleged Arabness of corruption and the servile role of blackness. He surmised that the mafia of kickbacks under the administration of Celso Pitta, São Paulo's first black mayor, was orchestrated by Paulo Maluf and other *turcos*. Satirizing Middle Eastern politicians as a "mafia of baba ghanoush eaters with sesame dripping from their chins," he joked that the black mayor "will turn into *kibe* in the hands of the *turcos*." Celso Pitta was a *negro de ganho* (black servant) "put in his place" by Maluf and the Conexão Esfiha (meat-pie connection), who reaped lucrative profits from the kickback scheme.[34] The blackness of Celso Pitta was referenced insofar as it came to symbolize his subservient position in relation to shrewder *turcos*. While blacks were servants, Jabor insinuated, Arabs were the masters in the "Casa Grande" of corruption.[35] As the blackness of Pitta was depicted as fulfilling a subordinate role in nefarious governmental dealings, the Arabness of Garib, Maluf, and others was conflated with corruption itself.

Commemorating Lebanon's Independence Day in Brazil

The second-generation Lebanese councilwoman Myryam Athie gained a significant presence in this media coverage. Serving as the chief officer in a special investigatory committee, she represented the key vote sparing Pitta (and their political godfather) from prolonged investigations. In the aftermath of the premature "archiving" of one proceeding held against the mayor, Athie had gained notoriety as an accomplice of the status quo. Alleging that there was not sufficient evidence against the mayor and the city council, she had been colored by corruption in media coverage, even once admitting, "I . . . felt like a criminal stamped on all the newspapers."[36] Like many colleagues, Athie left Maluf's PPB in late 1999 for the right-of-center Party of the Brazilian Democratic Movement (PMDB). It was also Athie who sponsored the *sessão solene* (ceremonial session) in honor of November 22, Lebanon's independence day. First held in 1999, the Commemorative Day of Lebanese Independence was held again in 2000, soon after the incumbent city councilor had won the municipal election.

Held in the "Salão Nobre" (Noble Ballroom) on the eighth floor of the city council chambers in downtown São Paulo, the event welcomed attendees with champagne glasses decorated with the national symbol of Lebanon, the cedar tree, as well as small pins in the shape of Lebanon and also decorated with its flag. Like the sparkling bubbles from the champagne and the shine from the lapel pins, the eighth floor glowed with men dressed in sleek suits sporting gold watches and women adorned in fine dresses and jewelry.

In attendance were several notables of the Lebanese and Syrian communities, including religious figures, state congressmen, diplomats (from Middle Eastern and European countries), and mostly second- or third-generation subjects from about fifty Arab cultural and political associations in São Paulo. Their names were announced and "registered" for the public record. This roll call of important individuals and entities lasted for fifteen minutes at the beginning of the ceremony. A handful of telegrams and letters from "illustrious figures" were read aloud and greeted with applause. Congratulating both the city councilor on her initiative and honored guests of the Lebanese community on their independence day, a federal deputy and governor not in attendance stressed that they "pride[d] themselves in being of Lebanese descent." As Lebanese names were outlined in media headlines of corruption, the ceremonial session's participants embraced their ethnic appellation with overt pride.

After the Lebanese and Brazilian national anthems were played, the master of ceremonies invited councilwoman Athie to take the podium for the next ten minutes. First, she thanked the audience for participating in the commemoration of Lebanon's national day of independence, promulgated on November 22, 1943. She declared that "the tribute we carry out today is directed toward some Lebanese descendants who distinguished themselves in São Paulo and Brazil." Whether peddlers or physicians, businessmen or judges, artists or sportsmen, Athie continued, descendants "distinguished" themselves in all professions. "The presence of Lebanon," she concluded with a sound bite, "is a constant in this [Brazilian] nation that has so caringly received us." In this light, the celebration of Lebanese independence day in São Paulo concerned not only "Lebanon" but also Lebanese in the Brazilian nation.

Athie stressed the strong presence of "Lebanese descendants" in the Brazilian state. In fact, two influential federal statesmen of Lebanese descent were seated next to her at the head table. In deference to Michel Temer, then the president of the federal Chamber of Deputies, she smiled and noted that a *filho de libaneses* (a son of Lebanese [immigrants]) held the third most powerful post in Brazil. Temer, who also belongs to the PMDB, smiled as his ethnic persona was extolled. Athie next turned to admonish the senator from Rio Grande do Sul, Pedro Simon, a presidential hopeful in the 2002 elections. While press coverage pinpointed Arabs as corrupt politicians in São Paulo, their ethnicity was exalted via the presence of Brazilian federal congressmen in this ostensible celebration of Lebanon's independence.

After the consul of Lebanon in São Paulo hailed the Lebanese contribution to Brazil, fifteen Lebanese Brazilians (fourteen men and one woman) were individually called to the front of the Salão Nobre. Only two were naturalized citizens, the majority being either *filhos* (sons) or *netos* (grandsons) of immigrants. Proudly calling out each name, the master of ceremonies first read a short biography of the venerated guest, highlighting a long list of economic positions or political posts once achieved or currently held in Brazil (never Lebanon). Awarded a plaque in the shape of Lebanon's national territory adorned with its flag (a cedar tree with one white and two red stripes), honorees posed for pictures as the audience applauded. Thanking parents, families, and the city councilwoman, each honored guest expressed pride not only in Lebanese "roots," "origins," "blood," or "descent," but also in "being Brazilian" and "living in the Brazilian nation." Recurrent references made to Brazil were not "out of place" in what was a Lebanese independence day celebration. After all, ethnic elites were praised for their economic and political achievements not in the Lebanese homeland but in Brazil.

The emphasis on the Lebanese presence in Brazil became more pronounced in the speeches of the federal congressmen at the end of the ceremony. For his part, Senator Pedro Simon took the podium abdicated by the master of ceremonies. Using all of the eloquence and ardor for which he is notorious, Simon addressed the audience for more than ten minutes. In one of his lyrical flashes, Simon announced that "there are folks who think that the Brazilian people . . . it has even appeared in the headlines . . . [are] a people atavistically turned toward corruption." Referring to the São Paulo City Council corruption scandal, the senator gave a non sequitur response. "Brazil," he stressed, is "a great people," because it *fez a mescla* (made the mix) of "white, black, Indian, Caboclo ["mixed" Indian], Portuguese, Italian, German, Arab, [and] Lebanese" peoples.[37] He continued, "We integrated ourselves into what we can call the Brazilian race. It's within this Brazilian race . . . that we look to the Lebanese people as one of those who contributed the most." Simon thus distanced Lebanese from the spectacle of corruption and reinserted them in the nationalist discourse of race mixture, despite the fact that this language was used in the past for the very purpose of marginalizing Arabs in Brazil.

Reproducing the Brazilian Nationalist Narrative, Arab-Style

Such an invocation was repeated in media coverage of the Lebanese independence day commemoration. In addition to ethnic and neighborhood newspapers,[38] the event appeared on the fourth-largest television network in Brazil, the Rede Bandeirantes. Not coincidentally, its second-generation Lebanese Brazilian founder was posthumously honored by the councilwoman for his "pioneering work" in national media development. Having invited his daughter to accept the honor and award, Athie was able to arrange for mainstream television coverage. During the ceremony, cameramen had taped sound bites and elegant poses that aired on November 23, 2000, in a four-minute segment on the Bandeirantes's midnight news show.

Opening with footage of religious, diplomatic, and national figures in posh poses, the narrator recounted that the "São Paulo City Council paid homage to Lebanese and descendants who distinguished themselves in Brazil." The male voice specified that the founder of the Bandeirantes radio and television network was one of the awardees. The program cut to a shot of the eldest daughter, who stated that her father, "being a person who dedicated his whole life to the integration between races in Brazil, [was] a man of [television and] radio. The prize is for this reason." Quickly proceeding to images of Pedro Simon and Michel Temer, the two federal statesmen in attendance, the narrator recounted that both had been honored at the event as well. Simon said, "Lebanese descendants [*pause*]. They have a very significant characteristic. They integrate themselves in Brazil. They identify themselves with Brazil. They adore Brazil." After Arabs were inserted and extolled within the Brazilian nationalist ideology of racial mixture and democracy, the narrator then concluded that "the author of the bill that honors the Lebanese is City Councilwoman Myryam Athie." Athie smiled and stated, "Lebanon contributed much to the formation of Brazil. . . . Lebanon exported great personalities to this country." Historically viewed as "not mixing" and today depicted as corrupt subjects in the public sphere, Arabs sought to represent themselves in ethnic glory in the allegedly "racially mixed" Brazilian nation.

Yet, this did not offset the frustration felt by everyday Arab Brazilians. Colleagues emphasized how the corruption scandal *sujou* (dirtied) or *envergonhou* (shamed) the name of the *colônia* (community). Márcia, a sculptor, reflected on the difficulty of picking up the newspaper when the corruption scandal broke in the press because "there would appear the name, you would see all these Arab last names, all of them appearing as corrupt." Middle Eastern names, reflected Wlademir, an engineer, simply stood out in newsprint. Summarizing what many descendants felt, a businessman declared:

> I'm annoyed in knowing that there are so many Arabs in politics . . . making trouble. Stealing, appearing in the newspaper . . . with names in the newspaper associated with the scandal, with stealing. So Arabs, sometimes they pick up the connotation of being clever . . . meaning, there are so many Arabs in politics that they're making a curse. We are even at times afraid to elect one more Arab so that he doesn't do anything wrong, because he dirties the name of the *colônia*.

Disturbed at witnessing the name of their community dragged into the scandal, ordinary Arabs reproduced the image of a putatively "Arab" corruption in Brazilian politics. Hassan, a medical doctor, proclaimed, "All of this [dirt on the Arab name] is Maluf's fault!" Employing the exact same words, Wlademir remarked, "*Tudo isso é culpa do Maluf.*" In parallel fashion, several observers placed blame on Hanna Garib and his well-known ego. Other citizens expressed sympathy and even pity for Myryam Athie, who was embroiled in the controversy as well. Such sentiments were reiterated by conservative and progressive-minded ethnics alike who were frustrated with the seeming corruption of Arab political leadership.

In so doing, these ordinary citizens did not consider the press coverage as *preconceitouso* (prejudiced) or *racista* (racist). In fact, the only two subjects who denounced the media representations of "Arab" corruption as "prejudiced" were right-of-center politicians who were implicated by it. In contrast, for the majority of laypersons, the scandal and its coverage generated *constrangimento* (strained discomfort). Ricardo, an architect, commented, "We feel a certain *constrangimento*. Nowadays when you speak of Arabs, they're viewed with a certain mistrust." Such wariness associated with Arabs, however, was understood by Wlademir as "not prejudice, but jealousy, envy, making fun of guys." This "jealousy" or "envy," he explained, was invoked when colleagues jested about his corrupt *patrícios* (countrymen). Reminding them that Brazilians of various backgrounds were involved, Wlademir said that his response was, "Shit! What about your [countrymen]?" Middle Easterners' emphasis on the nondiscriminatory character of press coverage confirmed the idea of racial democracy in Brazil.

Not surprisingly, everyday Arab Brazilians expressed a similar language about the *turco* label, mentioned at the very beginning of this essay. When I asked about the term's meaning, colleagues reflected that, although *turco* was employed in a prejudiced way in the past, it is used in an innocuous manner in the present. "There were a lot of people who used it as a pejorative term before," said Said, a physician, "but today, I don't see much of this." Likewise, a retired schoolteacher, Roberto, reflected that when "the Arab peoples came to Brazil, it was the Ottoman Turks who dominated the region. So immigrants had Turkish passports and were called *turcos*. It was pejorative, but now it's affectionate [*afetivo*]." Generally, professionals today have thus stressed the nondiscriminatory character of the *turco* category. In the words of a medical doctor, Sarkis, "the Brazilian has a caring way to call you 'turco.' It's a form of caring, typically Brazilian . . . that does not have a racist connotation or a discriminatory connotation. It is not prejudicial." Similarly pointing out that *turco* is not discriminatory, Dr. Arap stressed that "prejudice here in Brazil is a really light thing." A business administrator, Jorge, stressed that *turco* should not be seen as "prejudicial" because "all the races are equal" in Brazil. In responding to this term of difference or media coverage of a putatively "Arab" corruption, everyday Arab elites bear the imprint of the Brazilian "myth" of *democracia racial*.

Such understandings dispel the notion of a singular way to confront what many would consider anti-Arab discrimination. By framing Arab Brazilian politics in relation to Brazilian nationalist ideology, this essay has aimed to show that Arabs in the "other Americas" do not enact a kind of politics that would be readily embraced by their counterparts in the United States. Instead of denouncing stereotypical images of "Arab" corruption (ironically authored by many Arab journalists), Arab politicians celebrated their "mixture" in Brazilian society, and laypersons disavowed the discrimination evident in news reportage of a corruption scandal. These distinct responses should be first situated in relation to the ways that such discourses were used to marginalize Arabs in Brazil during the first half of the twentieth century. Most important, Arabs' own articulation of Brazilian nationalist discourses must be viewed as disrupting the dichotomy that frequently frames "Arabness" in relation to the "U.S. American" (politics, multiculturalism, foreign policy, and so on). The currency of what I have elsewhere called "another arabesque,"[39] or another Arab formation that circulates in the Americas, lies in destabilizing conventional approaches to Arabness in the modern world ecumene.

NOTES

This essay is based on research supported by a Fulbright-Hays Doctoral Dissertation Award in 2000–2001. The earliest version was presented at Syracuse University in 2002 and was awarded a student paper prize by the Association for Political and Legal Anthropology in the same year. It was published in *PoLAR: Political and Legal Anthropology Review* a year later. I thank Annelise Riles, Harry West, and two anonymous reviewers for crucial suggestions and many words of encouragement. A different version of this essay appears in my book *Another Arabesque: Syrian-Lebanese Ethnicity in Neoliberal Brazil* (Philadelphia: Temple University Press, 2007). I am also grateful to Jeff Lesser for his pathbreaking work on ethnicity in Brazil. See Jeffrey Lesser, "(Re)Creating Ethnicity: Middle Eastern Immigration to Brazil," *Americas* 53, no. 1, 1996: 45–65; "'Jews Are Turks Who Sell on Credit': Elite Images of Arabs and Jews in Brazil," *Arab and Jewish Immigrants in Latin America: Images and Realities,* ed. Ignácio Klich and Jeffrey Lesser, London: Frank Cass, 1996: 38–56; and *Negotiating National Identity: Immigrants, Minorities, and the Struggle for Ethnicity in Brazil.* Durham: Duke University Press, 1999.

1. Arnaldo Jabor, "Pitta ficou com os lábios roxos e a boca seca," *Folha de S. Paulo,* March 21, 2000.

2. Let it be noted that the actual term *racial democracy* was not coined by Freyre, though he was the first to celebrate Brazil's alleged "racial harmony." See Antônio Sérgio Alfredo Guimarães, "Racial Democracy," In *Imagining Brazil,* ed. Jessé Souza and Valter Sinder. New York: Lexington Books, 2005: 119–40.

3. Gilberto Freyre, *Casa grande e senzala.* Rio de Janeiro: José Olympio Editora, 1977 (1933).

4. Fernando Henrique Cardoso and Octávio Ianni, *Côr e mobilidade social em*

Florianopolis. São Paulo: Companhia Editora Nacional, 1960; Carlos Hasenbalg, *Discriminação e desigualdades racias no Brasil*. Rio de Janeiro: Graal, 1979; Charles Wagley, ed. *Race and Class in Rural Brazil*. Paris: United Nations Educational, Scientific and Cultural Organization, 1952.

5. See Karam, 2007.

6. Immigration museums, news articles, and Arab Brazilians themselves estimate that there are between six and eight million Middle Eastern immigrants and descendants in present-day Brazil. Yet such inflated calculations, I tend to think, have more to do with the marked visibility of Arab descendants in Brazilian society, politics, and economy.

7. Barbara Weinstein, *The Amazon Rubber Boom*. Cambridge: Harvard University Press, 1983 and Emil Farhat, *Dinheiro na estrada: Uma saga de imigrantes*. São Paulo: T. A. Queiroz, 1987.

8. Charles Knowlton, *Sírios e libaneses em São Paulo*. São Paulo: Editora Anhembi, 1961: 117; Oswaldo Truzzi, *Patrícios: Sírios e libaneses em São Paulo*. São Paulo: Editora Hucitec, 1997: 49.

9. André Castanheira Gattaz, "História oral da imigração libanesa para o Brasil—1880–2000." Ph.D. diss., Universidade de São Paulo, 2001: 15.

10. Sociedade Nacional de Agricultura, *Immigração: Inquérito promovido pela Sociedade Nacional de Agricultura*. Rio de Janeiro: Villani e Barbero, 1926: 359.

11. Amarilio Junior, *As vantagens da imigração syria no Brasil*. Rio de Janeiro, 1935: 39, 41–2.

12. Alfredo Ellis Jr., *Populações paulistas*. São Paulo: Companhia Editora Nacional, 1934: 197–211; Oliveira Viana, *Raça e assimilação*. São Paulo: Companhia Editora Nacional, 1932: 120–22

13. Levy as cited in Junior 1935: 40.

14. Rafael Paula Souza, "Contribuição i ethnologia paulista," *Revistado Arquivo Municipal* 3, no. 3 (1937): 93–105, 101–2.

15. Oscar Egidio de Araújo, "Enquistamentos étnicos," *Revista do Arquivo Municipal* 6, no. 65 (1940): 227–46.

16. John Tofik Karam, "A Cultural Politics of Entrepreneurship in Nation-Making: Phoenicians, Turks, and the Arab Commercial Essence in Brazil," *Journal of Latin American Anthropology* 9, no. 2 (2004): 319–51.

17. Oswaldo Truzzi, "Sírios e libaneses em São Paulo: A anatomia da sobre-representação." In *Imigração e política em São Paulo*, ed. Boris Fausto, São Paulo: Editora IDESP/Sumaré, 1995: 27–69.

18. Curiously, this Arab presence in mid-twentieth-century Brazilian politics was reiterated by a political pundit nearly fifty years later in the newspaper *Folha de S. Paulo*. In 1999, Ricardo Ricupero recalled that in 1961 or 1962, he had "heard from the late Emílio Carlos [Kryillos, an Arab politician] that there were more than fifty members of what he called the 'block of the United Arab Republic' in the [Brazilian] National Congress," Ricardo Ricupero, "Patrícios, mascates, e deputados," *Folha de S. Paulo*, August 29, 1999. Acclaiming the political ascent of Syrian Lebanese *patrícios* (countrymen), Ricupero's comments came at a fortuitous time. On the same day, the newspaper ran articles on a "mafia" popularly associated with Arabs: Otavio Cabral, "Escândalos perseguem vereadores pela cidade"; "Vereadores paulistanos são vistos com desconfiança após escândalos"; and "Desgaste não evita nova candidatura," all in *Folha de S. Paulo*, August 29, 1999. Constructed in early twentieth-century Brazil,

Arabs' reputation for economic cleverness was increasingly conflated with political corruption in the late 1990s.

19. Many attest to the rightist political tendency of the *colônia*. I discerned that Syrian Lebanese politicians garner diverse affiliations on the right and left, though rightist elements seem to be most successful in culling the community's electoral and financial support.

20. Maurício Puls, *Folha Explica: O Malufismo*. São Paulo: Folha de São Paulo, 2000: 33.

21. The symbol of Jânio Quadros's campaign was the *vassourinha* (little broom). He would use it to "sweep out" the corruption supposedly endemic to the political establishment in São Paulo. Although Quadros won the election and served his term, he was stripped of political rights with the onset of the military dictatorship in 1964.

22. In the words of the principal investigator on the city council, the *máfia de propinas* permitted councilpersons to "suggest the name of a political client who he want[ed] to see appointed and, in exchange, take on the responsibility of 'supporting' the mayor, 'approving' the bills that are addressed to the legislative [body]." Interestingly, Cardozo received the most votes of any city council candidate in the 2000 municipal elections. He has since become a federal deputy (after his victory in the 2002 round of elections). See José Eduardo Cardozo, *A máfia das propinas: Investigando a corrupção em São Paulo*. São Paulo: Editora Fundação Perseu Abramo, 2000.

23. Let me add that for a time in the press, political cartoons satirized Maluf, a *turco*, as the "father" of Pitta, a black Brazilian.

24. Marketed as a *franquia de comida árabe*, the Arab food franchise Habib's, as well as the growing popularity of "Middle Eastern cuisine," is discussed elsewhere (Karam 2007). Suffice it to say that the actual label *árabe* (Arab) is used when referring to what would be called "Middle Eastern" cuisine in the United States. The ubiquitous presence of *comida árabe* in the present-day Brazilian market may explain why food—and not other markers of ethnicity, such as clothes or language—was used to associate Arabness with corruption.

25. Bustavo Ioschpe, "Aos vencedores as batatas: Os piores de 1998," *Folha de S. Paulo,* January 11, 1999.

26. Barbara Gancia, "BEM FEITO," *Folha de S. Paulo,* April 25, 1999.

27. Early in his political career, Pitta refused to identify as black (perhaps due to his disaffection for the black movement on the left). But he later assumed his blackness as his administration drew increased criticism.

28. Another political commentator employed the wordplay on the pizza expression in relation to Maluf, remarking that, "though everything here ends in pizza, the senhor . . . of this (mis)governed municipality will be the indigestible and authoritarian *kibe*": Celso Luiz Prudente, "Casa Grande x Senzala," *Folha de S. Paulo,* September 13, 2000.

29. "Protesto troca pizza por esfiha," *O Estado de S. Paulo,* June 21, 2000.

30. José Simão, "Ueba! Melô a CPI e fiquemos sem Grana Garib!" *Folha de S. Paulo,* June 11, 1999.

31. José Simão, "Buemba! Buemba! Na Globo abunda Pita," *Folha de S. Paulo,* March 16, 2000.

32. At the time, Garib had already left the city council (attempting to escape scrutiny) and taken his place in the São Paulo State Assembly, to which he had been elected in 2000. Hence, Wadih Helou substituted Garib in the State Assembly: José Simão, "Grana Garib! Turcocircuito em Sampa!" *Folha de S. Paulo,* July 1, 1999.

33. An accomplished writer and public figure, Jabor appears weekly on Globo's eight o'clock nightly news program. He has also participated in cable-television programs, such as *Manhattan Connection,* aired on a Globo-related television station. He is widely watched by middle and upper classes.

34. Arnaldo Jabor, "Temos de beber desta lama luminosa e vital," *Folha de S. Paulo,* April 4, 2000; Jabor, "Corrupção global vai do angu até o FBI," *Folha de S. Paulo,* May 2, 2000.

35. Such metaphors of racial and ethnic difference underlie Prudente's article mentioned earlier. "Casa Grande x Senzala," *Folha de S. Paulo,* September 13, 2000.

36. "Mudança de discurso," *Folha de S. Paulo,* February 3, 1999.

37. Interestingly, Jews were not present in this "mix." Also important to note was Simon's differentiation between Arabs and Lebanese, despite Athie's use of both labels.

38. See: "A data celebrada na Câmara Municipal de São Paulo" and "Palavras de Myryam Athie," *Chams* 10, no. 100 (January 2001); "Câmara Municipal de São Paulo homenageia descendentes libaneses: A vereadora Myryam Athiê organiza e discursa para 300 convidados," *Carta do Libano* 6, no. 55 (November 2000). "Líbano, 57 anos de Independência," *Jornal do Brás,* November 25–December 15, 2000.

39. See Karam, 2007.

FIVE

From "*Baisanos*" to Billionaires
Locating Arabs in Mexico

Theresa Alfaro-Velcamp

In a popular U.S. newspaper column called "¡Ask a Mexican!" a reader wrote the following to columnist Gustavo Arellano in April 2009.

> Dear Mexican: First of all, don't think that I'm a self-loathing Mexican. . . . For some strange reason, I have developed an intense fascination with—you might say love for—Arab culture, language, cuisine, etc. especially Lebanese, Syrian, Jordanian, Palestinian and Iraqi, and I don't even have a drop of Arab blood in me. . . . Do you think I could be of Lebanese ancestry and not know it? . . . Would a DNA test tell me what my ancestry is, and could it turn up libaneses in my family tree? Let me know. [Signed] Wannabe Arab, a.k.a. El Libanés

Gustavo Arellano responded:

> Dear Wab: . . . Your chances that the *sangre* [blood] of the Levant courses through your veins are more likely than *gabachos* [literally French person, white person] may think. As you noted, Lebanese migrated to Mexico throughout the 20th century and contributed to the *patria* [homeland] in both positive (tacos al pastor, Salma Hayek) and negative (billionaire Carlos Slim Helú).[1]

Although Arellano's column targets audiences in the United States, his reader alludes to the popular interest and acknowledgment of Arabs in Mexico. As the reader signs his letter, he interchanges "Arab" and "Lebanese" illustrating the slippage of ethnic categories used in Mexico. Mexico offers several discourses on Arabness, and each has its own historical, economic, and social context, producing a certain ambivalence among Mexicans.[2] Popular Mexican discourses employ Arabness, although a predominantly "Lebanese" Mexican discourse has emerged.

The Transformation of an Arab Discourse

In Mexican popular culture, Arabness has often been tied to a stereotyped *turco* (Turk), a term dating back to the end of the nineteenth century and referring to subjects of the Ottoman Empire who immigrated to Mexico. The *turcos* have sometimes been portrayed as taking advantage of Mexicans in commercial dealings, and the stereotype endures. In an episode of a Mexican contemporary *telenovela* (soap opera), for example, the heroine whispers to her friends as they leave an Arab merchant's apartment, "The Turk is cheap."[3] The Arab merchant has a large hooked nose and sports a comical, bushy mustache with the ends twisted up. While this character is not particularly important to the story line, his appearance underscores the *turco* stereotype as he tries to swindle these Mexican women.

The term *árabe* also appears in popular Mexican discourse. Early in the twentieth century, for example, a headline in the Mexican newspaper, *El Universal*, read, "A young girl of a humble origins killed an Arab who wanted to rape her."[4] According to the article, María Rosario Ortega, the young girl from Guadalajara, Jalisco, was at home alone when the *árabe* came to her house. He had come earlier, requesting payment for some clothes she had purchased, but she had lacked sufficient money to pay him. On return, the Arab merchant reportedly tried to rape María Rosario. María Rosario grabbed a shaving blade and stabbed him. The *árabe*, Salomé Bernabé, died. Yet, at the end of the article, the author notes that Bernabé was Ukrainian.[5] The linking of Arabs and Ukrainians, not to mention Turks, illustrates a conflation of immigrant merchants, while also indicating the general application of the term *árabes* to all immigrants who sold clothes in the early twentieth century.[6] The popular idea and its representations in print media, that foreigners and merchants might take advantage of and even rape Mexicans, highlights the discursive association of Arabs (as *turcos*) with commercial cunning at the expense of Mexicans.

Popular Mexican discourses of Arabness further developed in the 1940s with the production of two films about Arab peddlers, *El baisano Jalil* and *El barchante Neguib*.[7] *El Baisano Jalil*'s title uses a dialectic version of the word *paisano*, or countryman, because many Arab immigrants have been known to mispronounce the letter *p* as *b*, since the Arabic language does not have comparable phoneme for the letter *p*. The film *El baisano Jalil* tells the story of a courtship between Jalil Farad's son and the daughter of an aristocratic Mexican family that has fallen on hard times. Although the film is a comedy about family relationships, it portrays the Farads as honest and hardworking as compared to their Mexican aristocratic counterparts who are reduced to depending on Jalil Farad's resources. Among the film's many themes, *El baisano Jalil* reflects the ambivalence that Mexicans share about the economic prowess of Arab immigrants and the influence of the descendants of Arab immigrants.

Ambivalence about the economic position of Arabs in Mexico endures. The newspaper *El Reforma* ran a cartoon showing the contemporary billionaire Carlos Slim Helú in a boxing ring clearly squashing his opponent.[8] The title "Billion Dollar Baby" refers to the 2004 film *Million Dollar Baby* in which a young female boxer enters the male world of boxing, momentarily finds success, and eventually succumbs to tragedy. In the cartoon, the ring ropes are telephone lines representing Slim Helú's control of Teléfonos de México (TelMex) of which he holds a major share. One question that often arises in connection with Carlos Slim Helú is, How did he gain such wealth in Mexico, a country known for poverty? This question prompts a broader social question: What does such wealth imply in a country that grapples with grave economic inequality? Websites hosted by Mexican left-wing newspapers such as *La Jornada* suggest that Slim Helú's wealth derives from overpriced landline and cellular phone services. Others hint that the selling of TelMex by former president Carlos Salinas de Gortari (1988–94) at an undervalued price in 1990 enabled Slim Helú to dramatically increase his wealth. After years of negative speculation and commentaries, Slim Helú has recently come forward about his commitment to philanthropic work.[9] One of his longest-standing commitments has been to the Lebanese community in Mexico and more specifically to the *Centro Libanés,* Lebanese Center.

Slim Helú and his family are splashed on the *Centro Libanés* website as both exemplary Lebanese Mexicans and also generous donors to the centers. There are ten Lebanese Centers throughout Mexico with the original center founded in 1959. The centers have been instrumental in the shaping of a "Lebaneseness" discourse in Mexico. Lebaneseness has become imbued with a sense of cultural superiority, largely derived from claims to a Phoenician past and to Christian roots. What is perhaps the most distinctive aspect of the construction "Arabness" in the Mexican context has to do with this notion of Lebaneseness. Although the present-day Arab community in Mexico is composed primarily of second- and third-generation Arabs who can trace their roots to Arabic-speaking nation-states, there is a strong cultural identification with Lebanon. A hegemonic Lebanese discourse has emerged whereby publications of the *Centro Libanés* assert a relationship between

Lebanese Mexicans and Lebanon, deploying images and rhetoric that register a deep cultural connection. The idea of a broadly shared Lebaneseness among elites of Arab descent, as pushed by the *Centro Libanés*, possesses the attributes of hegemony, going largely unchallenged by Mexicans and Lebanese Mexicans alike.[10]

The identity of Arabs in Mexico must be viewed in the context of identity discourse in Mexico. The dominant Mexican discourse embraces an interethnic past through the idea of *mestizaje*, the mixing of primarily Spanish/Europeans with indigenous peoples. *Mestizaje* and its power, as extolled by José Vasconcelos, secretary of public education (1921–24) and author of the idea of the "cosmic race," have long given a voice to the importance of the mixing of races. However, beneath this stated discourse, Mexican intellectuals have long favored the European influences in Mexican society. The ability of the Lebanese Centers to draw on European connections—French and Christian connections in particular—has therefore furthered its objective of exclusiveness. The fluidity of Mexican identity—*mexicanidad*—has also allowed ethnic definitions to shift over time. Ethnic categories for those of Arabic-speaking backgrounds began with *turcos,* then *árabes* (Arabs), evolved into *Sirio-Libaneses* (Syro-Lebanese), and ultimately became Lebanese. This trajectory is not entirely linear but nevertheless indicates how the use of ethnic categories has changed with geopolitical events in the Middle East and elsewhere in the Americas.[11] For instance, during the early twentieth century, people from the Ottoman Empire sometimes self-identified as Arabs (*árabes*) when they were from modern-day Lebanon.[12] Moreover, the ability to produce Lebaneseness as part of a distinctly Mexican discourse relates to the concept of the "foreign citizens" in Mexico, which encompasses the process by which immigrants and their descendants retain aspects of their foreign identity while simultaneously becoming Mexican citizens.

Immigrants, Mestizaje, and Mexicanidad

Immigrants from the complex region of the Middle East found a dynamic national discourse in Mexico that could simultaneously accommodate, tolerate, and integrate difference, and also suppress, disregard, and obscure it. Since the Mexican Revolution (Civil War, 1910–20), *mexicanidad* (Mexicanness) has drawn upon *indigenismo* and Europeanness.[13] According to José Vasconcelos, the best of Spanish and Indian cultures would create a new hybrid race.[14] Yet, this was no egalitarian mixture: Spanish or European blood and cultural leadership helped the racially mixed *mestizo* to "improve." Therefore, the notion of *mestizo* implied the loss of specific group characteristics. It aimed to temper the influence of foreigners and the visibility of the indigenous, and to narrowly define *mexicanidad*. Despite the intellectuals' and state's attempt to construct a monolithic Mexican, Mexico has become a multiethnic society, with multiple ways of being Mexican. The flexibility of Mexicanness—who can belong to the Mexican nation—enables these "once" Arab immigrants to, as citizens, perpetuate Lebaneseness in Mexican society and attain influence.

Perhaps one key to the flexibility of Arab immigrants is their willingness to participate in Mexico's nationalism. As historian Arthur Schmidt notes, "For decades following the Mexican Revolution, indigenismo and economic development served as powerful hegemonic symbols for Mexico's national identity, for the image of a homeland that would provide for all Mexicans."[15] By linking commercial enterprises in urban centers with the sale and distribution of goods among remote and rural populations, Arab immigrants found opportunities to connect to the European and indigenous elements of Mexican society. In part, and as economic actors, Arabs obtained both inclusion and exclusivity through their commercial occupations (although not without protest and controversy). The ability to leverage Mexican nationalism in the name of economic development, in turn, has created a place for Arab immigrants and their descendants.

Producing Foreign Citizens

Second- and third-generation descendants from the Middle East, such as the children of Carlos Slim Helú, have both acculturated into the dominant Mexican culture and maintained elements of their Lebanese ethnicity by drawing on a tradition of foreign merchants in Mexico.[16] This tradition enabled Arab immigrants and their children to define themselves as "foreign citizens," or citizens who, while being legally and nationally Mexican, draw upon an ancestral root to better define their identity. As foreign citizens, a term that I use to describe these relational uses of identity, they use their "foreignness" to distinguish themselves as superior to their Mexican counterparts while often facing contradictory receptions, including xenophobia, because of their wealth.[17] These foreign citizens are Mexicans of Lebanese descent, who refer to themselves as "Lebanese" in some instances and "Mexican" in others, depending on the context. The notion that citizenship can be granted to a foreigner on the promise that he or she brings skills and capital is not uncommon. In Mexico, the ability to declare foreignness helps explain the elite's sense of entitlement and distance from poor fellow countrymen. While to rise within the system requires Mexicanness, once a person has reached economic elite status, he or she may claim foreign roots to explain (and perhaps justify) success. Therefore, immigrants from the Middle East have used their claims both to Mexican citizenship and to foreignness in order to move up the socioeconomic ladder, enjoying a privileged position as foreign citizens.

The first generation of Arab immigrants often downplayed cultural differences to better acculturate into Mexican society. However, by the second and third generation, with economic ascendancy, some Arabs were able to create a new Lebanese Mexican identity. By contrast, Arab immigrants who were not economically successful tended to more fully acculturate into Mexican society because they often did not have the time or resources to participate in Arab (and later Lebanese) community activities. Foreign citizenship is also closely linked to the importance of European discourses in Mexico. For instance, one possible explanation for why Arab immigrants chose a Lebanese identity and not an Arab one could be that Mexican society has tended to be more accepting of those immigrants with European and Christian backgrounds. The Maronites' close linkages with French culture probably encouraged some Arab immigrants to draw on this more compatible Christian background. In addition, the building of a Mexican nation-state in the twentieth century motivated many of the successful immigrants to unite and perpetuate the elements of their foreignness that gained them such wealth and recalled European cultures and traditions.[18]

Constructing Lebanese Mexican Identity

As the Mexican nation-state prioritized development, the Lebanese have viewed themselves as economic role models for Mexicans. They have often asserted that their Phoenician ancestry has given them enterprising talents to make profits in commercial enterprises and to distinguish themselves in Mexico. According to Carmen Mercedes Páez Oropeza's 120 interviews in the 1980s with Lebanese immigrants and their descendants, interviewees projected a self-image of being more responsible, harder working, and more capable of maintaining stable homes than Mexicans.[19] Only two Lebanese admitted that they lacked economic resources. Other members of the Lebanese community described these two individuals as less wealthy, less competitive, less intelligent, and lazier than typical Lebanese.[20] It is no surprise, therefore, that the *Centro Libanés* has tended to function as an elite social club that advocates Lebanese cultural superiority and business acumen.

Affiliated with the *Centro Libanés* is a youth organization called the Unión Nacional de Jóvenes Mexicanos de Ascendencia Libanesa (JOMALI).

JOMALI, founded in 1983, holds annual conventions for Lebanese descendants throughout Mexico, creates awareness of Lebanese culture, and provides a means for social networking.[21] While it has not been explicitly stated in its promotional literature, JOMALI also serves as a place for future spouses to meet and perpetuate what it means to be Lebanese Mexican.

Although both JOMALI and the *Centro Libanés* are active Lebanese ethnic organizations in Mexico, they are not especially visible to the average Mexican and exclude those outside of Lebanese circles. Specifically, the Lebanese discourse does not address Arabs who did not become wealthy, Arabs that never advanced beyond peddling, and Arabs that married into the Mexican middle and lower classes. Rather, some poor and middle-class Arab immigrants tended not to maintain their immigrant identities because survival demanded greater acculturation into Mexican society.[22] Therefore, many second- and third-generation descendants of Arabs now feel little or no connection to the Middle East.[23] And these marginalized Arabs are not included in the Lebanese discourse.

Since the Lebanese Mexicans who affiliate with the *Centro Libanés* and JOMALI tend to accentuate their Christianity to demonstrate their Mexicanness, they do not reflect the historical, socioeconomic, or religious diversity of Arab immigrants in Mexico. As one Lebanese immigrant living in Mexico City in 1999 stated, "Most of [those at the Centro Libanés] . . . were racist against Muslims." He felt that the *Centro* was composed of Maronite Lebanese "who measure people by their wealth, who are very arrogant against Mexicans. They felt superior to Mexicans." He continued, "You can't compare these Lebanese with the Lebanese in Lebanon."[24] The Lebanese discourse is thus unique to Mexico and tends to distinguish Lebanese Mexicans from affiliation with Islam.

Locating a Muslim Mexican Discourse

Questions often arise about the Muslims in Mexico and the ability to trace Islamic roots to the early Spanish conquerors. It is probable that some of the early explorers to the Americas were Muslims, guised as newly converted Christians (*conversos*).[25] However, the strongest evidence of a Muslim presence emerged with late nineteenth-century emigration from the Ottoman Empire and the area that composed Greater Syria. Many of these Muslim immigrants settled in northern Mexico, especially in the Laguna area of the states of Coahuila and Durango, where they probably enjoyed more religious tolerance and social networks extending to the north.[26] Members of the first generation of Muslims in the Laguna area appear to have retained many elements of their Lebanese culture as well as their Islamic faith.[27] Their descendants form a small, informal community of Muslims in Torreón who participate in worship at a mosque that is located in the Colonia of Nueva Los Angeles in Torreón, Coahuila. In 1993, the mosque received official status from the Mexican government as a religious association.[28] Most of the first generation of Muslims know Arabic and can read the Qu'ran, a skill that has been lost, for the most part, by the second generation. Most members of the community, however, are familiar with the Qur'an in translation. The community still prepares and eats Arabic food weekly.

Despite their Muslim Lebanese backgrounds, most of the children of the immigrants identify themselves as Mexican. They are clearly proud of their Lebanese heritage, but their homes and hearts are in Mexico, and they are not part of the *Centro Libanés*. The fact that one second-generation Muslim described himself as feeling more "Arab" than Mexican or Muslim can perhaps be explained by the more recent politicization of the Arab world. The Muslims in Torreón cannot be described as *fanáticos* (fundamentalists). Rather, they see themselves as spiritual people who accept interfaith marriages and are open to the changes taking place in their community. As first-generation Muslims, they have inherited a version of Shi'ite Islam that they learned from their parents. Although the Torreón community does not engage in a Lebanese discourse such as those of the *Centro Libanés* in Mexico City, both groups are careful not to conflate being Arab and Muslim. This is also the case with the practicing Muslims in Mexico City.

Beyond the small community in Torreón, Mark (Omar) Weston plays a strong leadership role in the Centro Cultural Islámico de México (CCIM), formerly the Muslim Center de México. In Mexico City, the community used to pray in Colonia del Valle, a middle-class residential area. The prayer service that I attended in 1999 was clearly male-dominated, with some eighty to one hundred men of all nationalities attending. Employees of the Embassies of Algeria, Egypt, Indonesia, Iran, Iraq, Malaysia, Morocco, Pakistan, Palestine, Tunis, Turkey, and Saudi Arabia in Mexico worked with the CCIM on various occasions. In 2003, CCIM purchased lakefront property around Lake Tequesquitengo in the Mexican state of Morelos for *Dar as-Salam* (abode or house of peace) to teach Mexican converts about Islam.[29] According to Omar Weston, "the place is called Teques Inn and is for Halal and cultural tourism and events." When I inquired about the CCIM in 2009, I was told that it has been reduced to a website, event organization, and publicity campaigns.[30] The CCIM has remained very active in the propagation of Islam to the general Mexican population.[31] There are also other small Islamic groups, such as the *Centro Salafi de México*[32] and the Sufi Jalveti Herrahi Order[33] that focus on exposing Mexicans to a wide range of interpretations of Islam. Overall, neither the Muslims nor the *Centro Libanés* explicitly link Arabness and Islam in Mexican society.

Glimpses of Arabness in Mexico

Exploring Arabness in Mexico requires not only examining relationships of power between Mexicans and the *Centro Libanés* but also exploring what discourses exist and what messages these discourses do and do not include. Although this essay has focused on a few examples of popular discourses surrounding Arabness in order to explore the discursive construction of Lebanese Mexican identity, how Arab immigrants and their history have been written into Mexican national history has not been addressed. In the last two decades, scholars have begun to identify ethnic and immigrant groups (outside of the Spanish and French) in Mexican historiography, but the Mexican metadiscourse[34] does not yet reflect popular discourse on Arabs and Arabness. Therefore, columns, cartoons, newspaper clippings, and interviews become a means to extrapolate the role of Arabs in Mexican society. However, these provide merely glimpses of particular moments and neither a complete reflection of Mexico nor of all Mexicans.

Last, the *Centro Libanés* continues to dominate the discourse of Lebanese identity in Mexico. Its website proudly displays both a statue of a nineteenth-century emigrant that the *Centro Libanés* has given to Lebanon and one given to the state of Veracruz (symbolizing the emigrant route), as well as a plaque in its lobby with a renowned saying. Quoting Mexican President Adolfo López Mateos (1958–64), the plaque reads, "The one who does not have a Lebanese friend needs to look for one!"[35] If sayings and images are the content of discourse, then the place of Arabs—from *baisanos* in the 1940s to billionaires in 2009—remains ambivalent within Mexicans' vision of *mexicanidad*.

NOTES

I thank Sherene Sekaily for encouraging this project and Amanda Angel, LeiLani Nishime, Kim Hester-Williams, Chingling Wo, and Robert McLaughlin for reading early versions of the paper. Evelyn Alsultany and Ella Shohat offered invaluable feedback—thank you. The anonymous reviewers also provided instructive guidance. Finally, thanks to Teresa Garza, Bill Taylor, and Karin Taylor for bringing the *New Yorker* article to my attention.

1. Gustavo Arellano, "¡Ask a Mexican! From Puebla to Palestine," *OC Weekly*, April 23, 2009.
2. As Pierre Bourdieu explains, discourses help produce messages both by the

speaker and for the recipient: "What circulates on the linguistic market is not 'language' as such, but rather discourses that are stylistically marked both in their production, in so far as each speaker fashions an idiolect from the common language, and in their reception, in so far as each recipient helps to *produce* the message which he perceives and appreciates by bringing to it everything that makes up his singular and collective experience." Pierre Bourdieu, *Language and Symbolic Power*, ed. John B. Thompson, trans. Gino Raymond and Matthew Adamson (Cambridge: Harvard University Press, 1995), 39, 64.

3. *El privilegio de amar, Televisa* (July 27, 1998–February 26, 1999).

4. *El Universal* (September 23, 1923).

5. Unfortunately, more information on this incident in historical records has not been located.

6. The *El Universal* article reads: "Árabes casi siempre que se dedican a vender ropa en abonos" (September 23, 1923). For an interesting discussion of the Ukrainian diaspora, see Orest Subtelny, *Ukraine: A History*, 2nd ed. (Toronto: University of Toronto Press, 1988, 1994). See chapters 27 and 28.

7. Gregorio Wallerstein produced the films that were directed by the Mexican actor Joaquín Pardavé, who also played the protagonists. Josefina Estrada, *Joaquín Pardavé: El señor del espectáculo*, vol. 2 (Mexico City: Editorial Clío, Libros y Videos, 1996), 35–36. Joaquín Pardavé (1900–1955) acted in seven films in 1942 and four films in 1945. Paulo Antonio Paranaguá, *Mexican Cinema*, trans. Ana M. López (London: British Film Institute, IMCINE, and CONACULTA, 1995), 292.

8. See http://pacocalderon.net/uploads/photos/1779.jpg (accessed June 1, 2009). As of March 2012, Carlos Slim Helú and his family were worth $69 billion and ranked number one on the "The World's Billionaires" by *Forbes*'s magazine. http://www.forbes.com/billionaires (accessed April 15, 2012). He was also ranked number 23 of the most powerful people in the world. http://www.forbes.com/profile/carlos-slim-helu (accessed April 15, 2012).

9. Elisabeth Malkin, "New Commitment to Charity by Mexican Phone Tycoon," *New York Times* (June 28, 2007), C1, C13.

10. As Jean Comaroff and John Comaroff theorize, "We take hegemony to refer to that order of signs and practices, relations and distinctions, images and epistemologies—drawn from a historically situated cultural field—that come to be taken-for-granted as the natural and received shape of the world and everything that inhibits it. Hegemony homogenizes, ideology articulates." Jean Comaroff and John Comaroff, *Of Revelation and Revolution*, Volume 1: *Christianity, Colonialism, and Consciousness in South Africa* (Chicago: University of Chicago Press, 1991), 23–24.

11. Although there is scholarship on Sephardic Jews in Mexico, there has been little synthetic work to explain their history as part of the broader Arab presence in Mexico.

12. Theresa Alfaro-Velcamp, *So Far from Allah, So Close to Mexico: Middle Eastern Immigrants in Modern Mexico* (Austin: University of Texas Press, 2007).

13. "Indigenismo," writes Susanna Rostas, "as an official policy, aimed to encourage those indigenous activities and attitudes that would best engender a sense of Mexican nationalism. It targeted for eradication certain practices, such as languages and others related to other core aspects of indigenous culture (such as medicine or agricultural techniques), in the interests of turning Mexico's indigenous people into mestizos and establishing Mexico as a nation." In "Performing 'Mexicanidad': Popular 'Indigenismo' in Mexico City," *Encuentros Antropológicos: Power, Identity and Mobility in Mexican*

Society, ed. Valentina Napolitano and Xochitl Leyva Solano (London: University of London, Institute of Latin American Studies, 1998), 56, 60–61.

14. He wrote, "The advantage of our tradition is that it has greater facility of sympathy towards strangers. This implies that our civilization, with all defects, may be the chosen one to assimilate and to transform mankind into a new type; that within our civilization, the warp, the multiple and rich plasma of future humanity is thus being prepared." José Vasconcelos, *The Cosmic Race / La raza cósmica: Misión de la raza iberoamericana,* trans. Didier T. Jaen (Baltimore: Johns Hopkins University Press, 1925, 1979), 17.

15. Arthur Schmidt, "Mexicans, Migrants, and Indigenous Peoples: The Work of Manuel Gamio in the United States, 1925–1927," in *Strange Pilgrimages: Exile, Travel, and National Identity in Latin America, 1800–1990s,* ed. Ingrid E. Fey and Karen Racine (Wilmington: Scholarly Resources, 2000), 174.

16. For Lebanese ethnicity, see Luz María Martínez Montiel and Araceli Reynoso Medina, "Inmigración europea y asiática, siglos XIX y XX," *Simbiosis de culturas: Los inmigrantes y su cultura en México,* ed. Guillermo Bonfil Batalla (Mexico City: Fondo de Cultura Económica, 1993), 317. For the role of foreign merchants, see D. A. Brading, *Miners and Merchants in Bourbon Mexico, 1763–1810* (London: Cambridge University Press, 1971). See also Louisa Schell Hoberman, *Mexico's Merchant Elite, 1590–1660: Silver, State, and Society* (Durham: Duke University Press, 1991).

17. Martínez Montiel and Reynoso Medina, "Inmigración europea y asiática" (Mexico City: Fondo de Cultura Económica, 1993), 273.

18. In looking at North American and European democracies, Bonnie Honig suggests that foreignness can be relational and fungible, in that it reflects the values of the society. In particular, Honig examines the role of the capitalist foreigner, who although "depicted as someone who is interested in material things, . . . quickly turns from someone who has something to offer us into someone who only wants to take things from us." This transition from an inquisitive immigrant into a self-serving materialist resonates with popular Mexican reflections on the role of Arab immigrants in their country. Although Honig's analysis is limited to liberal democracies, her use of foreignness and the notion that foreigners enable regimes to import needed skills and talents from the outside can be applied to the case of Mexico. Bonnie Honig, *Democracy and the Foreigner* (Princeton: Princeton University Press, 2001), 12, 80 n15.

19. Ibid., 200.

20. Carmen Páez Oropeza, *Los Libaneses en México: Asimilación de un grupo étnico* (Mexico City: Instituto Nacional de Antropología e Historia, 1984), 166.

21. See http://www.jomali.com (accessed April 15, 2012).

22. Luis Alfonso Ramírez contends that Lebanese identity matters only as a secondary cultural characteristic for middle-class Mexicans, whereas the elite accentuate it. Luis Alfonso Ramírez, *Secretos de familia: Libaneses y élites empresariales en Yucatán* (Mexico City: Consejo Nacional para la Cultura y las Artes, 1994), 198.

23. David Nicholls, in studying Middle Easterners in the Caribbean, quotes a Lebanese businessman who commented, "There is a terrifying division within the community on a class basis," and a young Syrian woman who observed, "Certain families living in the Belmont area [of Trinidad] have gained little recognition and acceptance from the [Levantine] community at large." David Nicholls, *Haiti in Caribbean Context: Ethnicity, Economy, and Revolt* (New York: St. Martin's, 1985), 161.

24. Interview conducted by author with anonymous interviewee, April 1999, Mexico City.

25. However, evidence of descendants of these early immigrants practicing their faith into the twentieth century has not been found. According to colonial Latin American historian Amanda Patricia Angel, the terms "*moriscos, mulatos* and *conversos*" are often used interchangeably in colonial documents. These documents, however, are not clear as to whether these individuals were indeed Moors practicing Islam. See Amanda Patricia Angel, "Spanish Women in the New World: The Transmission of a Model Polity to New Spain: 1521–1570" (Ph.D. diss., University of California, Davis, 1997).

26. In addition to the north of Mexico, many Muslim Lebanese went to the center of the country, Mexico City, which had 24 percent of the Muslim immigrant population. Mexico City, as many capital cities, has served as a transitional location for immigrants to make contact with fellow countrymen. The National Registry of Foreigners, Migration (1926–50). *Archivo General de la Nación,* Mexico City.

27. Theresa Alfaro-Velcamp, "Mexican Muslims in the Twentieth Century: Challenging Stereotypes and Negotiating Space," *Muslims in the West: Sojourners to Citizens,* ed. Yvonne Haddad (New York: Oxford University Press, 2002), 278–92.

28. A plaque in the lobby of the mosque notes, "Comunidad Islámica de la Laguna" on June 15, 1993.

29. For an interesting ethnographic account of living with Mexican Muslim converts, see Mark Lindley Highfield, "Mission and Modernity in Morelos: The Problem of a Combined Hotel and Prayer Hall for the Muslims of Mexico," paper prepared for the Annual Conference of the Association of Social Anthropologists of the UK and Commonwealth, Thinking through Tourism (London, April 10–13, 2007).

30. Email communications with Omar (Mark) Weston, September 21, 2009.

31. Although the CCIM website does not explicitly indicate which branch of Islam, CCIM followers are predominantly Sunni Muslims.

32. See http://www.islammexico.net (accessed April 15, 2012).

33. See http://www.sufimexico.com (accessed April 7, 2009).

34. Roger Bartra, *The Cage of Melancholy: Identity and Metamorphosis in the Mexican Character,* trans. Christopher J. Hall (New Brunswick: Rutgers University Press, 1992).

35. See http://www.centrolibanes.org.mx (accessed April 15, 2012).

SIX

Ali Bla Bla's Double-Edged Sword
Argentine President Carlos Menem and the Negotiation of Identity

Christina Civantos

In November 2001, while former Argentine president Carlos Menem was under house arrest in relation to an illegal arms deal investigation, the Argentine soccer legend Diego Maradona came to visit him wearing a black turban.[1] How can we begin to understand Maradona's flamboyant gesture of support for the tarnished Menem? More broadly, what role do references to the Arab world—an Arab world of turbans, harems, and odalisques, but also strict, fatalistic, and overpowering Islam—play in Menem's public presence, in both his reception and the persona he has crafted? In order to answer this question one needs to begin by reaching back into nineteenth-century Argentine as well as Middle Eastern history. On the one hand, in the 1840s Argentine intellectuals began using images of the Orient in their attempts to define or decry the current cultural and political situation of Argentina; on the other hand, only two decades later Arabic-speaking immigrants began to relocate from provinces of the Ottoman Empire to Argentina.[2]

"The Orient" and the Construction of Argentina

Various nineteenth-century Argentine writers used negative portrayals of Arabs in order to oppose the dictatorship of Juan Manuel de Rosas. Some of these authors connected representations of savage Arab rulers and soldiers to the Argentine dictator and his support system of *caudillos* (local leaders or warlords) and their militias made up of gauchos (the *mestizo* cowboys of Argentina). Others directly described Rosas as a lascivious and authoritarian yet effeminate sultan with an attending harem. In all cases, the Argentine intellectuals drew from European Orientalism in their attempt to resist and reject the Rosas regime. Among these writers, Domingo F. Sarmiento stands out because of the connection he makes between Arabs and gauchos, and because of his ambivalence toward both Arabs and gauchos: he uses these figures to disparage Rosas and also to define Argentina in the wake of political independence from Spain.[3]

During the 1910s and 1920s, most Argentine Orientalist literature, and particularly that of the elite, was written as part of the Latin American symbolist movement known as *modernismo* and often participated in the intellectual current known as *hispanismo*. These texts, with their heavy literary ornamentation, often used portrayals of an exotic East to subtly protest the new Argentine reality: a large, urban working-class immigrant population with more interest in wealth and industry than in arts and letters. While the early twentieth century saw a burgeoning of Orientalist images in Argentine literature, it also saw a rise in anti-immigrant and anti-Semitic (targeting both Jews and Arabs) sentiment and official policies. Among the writers of this period, Leopoldo Lugones stands out because of his use of an unusually positive depiction of the Arab to establish the gaucho as a national icon.

Sarmiento and Lugones were both tied to key elements of Argentine cultural history and specifically of Argentine Orientalism: relations with Spain, immigration, and the figure of the gaucho. A part of Spanish culture that was intensely debated from the eighteenth through twentieth centuries is the legacy of the almost nine hundred years of Muslim presence in the Iberian Peninsula and the process of the Spanish *Reconquista*. The debate was basically between two intellectual camps in Spain: those who saw the expulsion of Jews and Muslims and the Inquisition as the cause of Spain's decline, and those who saw the Jews and Muslims as a negative influence on Spain that needed to be eliminated. The Orientalisms of *criollo* Argentines (Argentines of Spanish descent)[4] have been shaped to a great extent by contemporaneous relationships to Spain and these two opposing interpretations of the Arab presence in Spain. First, in the 1800's, with political independence from the Spanish empire, the founding fathers of Argentina actively rejected Spain. Although Spanish Romantics, inspired by the history and culture of the Moors of Granada, drew Argentines (such as Sarmiento) to Arab Spain, at the same time, Sarmiento and other liberals of the Generation of 1837 blamed the political turmoil of mid-1800's Argentina on having been colonized by Spain, which they generally saw as a backward, not truly European or "civilized" country. Later, in the early twentieth century, Argentine intellectuals participating in the *hispanismo* movement sought to revalorize Hispano-America's Spanish heritage as a way to define a national culture in the face of massive immigration. In looking to the Spanish roots of Argentina to try to delineate a 'national soul,' Lugones focused on the Arabs of Spain and granted the Moorish element of Spanish cultural history a positive and primary position that went beyond even that of the Spanish thinkers of his time.

With regard to immigration, Sarmiento was among the many mid-nineteenth-century Argentine statesmen who believed that Argentine progress depended upon populating the country with Europeans. In the mid 1800's the Argentine provinces began programs of promotion and active recruitment of European, and particularly Northern European, immigrants. On the one hand, the ruling class wanted a workforce to make Argentina's vast territory agriculturally productive; on the other hand, they believed that through immigration the remaining indigenous peoples would be absorbed into the "whiter" national body and the *mestizos* and *criollos* would be counterbalanced with "superior" Northern European stock. The Argentine immigration project, however, did not turn out as its promoters had hoped. Rather than Northern European immigrants, it was mostly Italians and Spaniards, and in lesser numbers Arabs and Eastern European Jews, who arrived; rather than work in agriculture, most immigrants became part of urban life.

By the late 1800's the Argentine elite's disappointment in the outcome of the immigration project had turned into anti-immigrant sentiment. Immigrants' involvement in labor organizing as well as the rise of a *nouveau riche* immigrant class, created within the elite a fear about foreignness and nostalgia for pre-immigrant Argentina: a vision of traditional values and rural *criollo* life. At the turn of the century, cultural nationalism and anti-immigrant sentiment were strong and on the rise among the upper classes. By the mid-1930's nationalism had become a major political movement characterized by authoritarianism and xenophobia. From the 1910s through the 1930s and beyond, Semitic immigrants—whether Christian Arabs, Eastern European Jews, Muslim Arabs, or Arab Jews—were targeted as the most undesirable of immigrants. Within this anti-immigrant climate, representations of the *turco* (that is, the Arab emigré from the Ottoman empire) began to appear in Argentine literary and popular culture. In general terms, Arabs and Jews were seen as not only culturally, but also biologically, different—so different that they could not be assimilated into Argentine culture.

Who were the so-called *turcos* that were part of the immigrant ranks against whom nationalists reacted? In the 1860's a flow of Arab immigrants began to arrive in the Americas. They left their homes due to various political, economic, religious, and cultural factors, most of them linked to the crisis that arose in the Ottoman empire in the mid-1800's and culminated in the empire's dissolution after World War I. Most of these immigrants came from what was then the province of Greater Syria under Ottoman rule (what are today Syria, Lebanon, Palestine/Israel, and parts of Jordan). In Argentina in particular, between 1887 and 1913, amid the flood of European immigrants, approximately 131,000 Arabs arrived. The numbers of Arab immigrants peaked between 1904 and 1913, and then went down because of World War I, which created both difficulties in travel and the hope of Arab political independence. In the 1930s to 1950s there was a smaller wave that included mostly Palestinians. Later the Lebanese civil war resulted in an influx of Lebanese in the 1980's. The majority of the Arabic-speaking immigrants to Argentina were Christians (of various sects), but all of them, in the eyes of Euro-Argentines, were associated with Islam. Today, Arabs make up the third or fourth largest immigrant group in Argentina.[5]

Since the vast majority of the first Arab immigrants to Argentina came from the Ottoman Empire, they were called *turcos*, "Turks," a term that ironically identifies them with their colonizers. To this day *turco* usually carries a derogatory connotation linked to the anti-Semitism of the first half of the twentieth century and to a second wave of anti-Arab sentiment that arose at the end of the 1980s. The term originally conjured up the image of the bedraggled, yet crafty *mercachifle* (peddler) who traveled the countryside or the urban center of Buenos Aires selling his or her wares. With time, other stereotyped figures—the cunning arms dealer or the corrupt, powerful sheik—joined the wily *mercachifle* in Argentine public perception of the *turco*.

As elsewhere in the Americas, the Arabic speakers who arrived at the turn of the century usually started out as itinerant salesmen and then set up shops for the sale of cloth, notions, and housewares. Though many Arab Argentines are still small business owners, a number have also became major industrialists or key figures in regional politics. This can be seen in the case of Carlos Menem, the son of Syrian Muslim immigrants, who rose from local Peronist politics in the agricultural region of La Rioja to become president of Argentina from 1989 to 1999. Although a good number of Arab Argentines have enjoyed political and economic success, or precisely because of this success, anti-Arab sentiment resurfaced in the 1980s, albeit in more subtle forms.[6]

The (Arab) Gaucho and Argentine Identity

Various Arab Argentine writers have responded in different ways to Argentine representations of the Orient and the Arab immigrant. A particularly interesting manifestation of this response, and one in which Carlos Menem plays a part, revolves around the figure of the Arab gaucho—first formulated by none other than Sarmiento and Lugones. In order to understand the significance of the figure of the Arab gaucho, we must first consider that the history of the gaucho as a social group has long been disputed. The debates surrounding the gaucho were most active during the period of heightened cultural nationalism from the late 1800's through the early 1900's. Slatta explains that the proponents of theories about the social origins of the gaucho can be divided into two broad groups: the Hispanists and the Americanists. The Hispanists point to an Andalusian or Arab source for the horse-centered culture of the gauchos.[7] In contrast, the Americanists either see the gaucho as a *criollo,* frontier phenomenon, as derived from nomadic native cultures, or as the product of *mestizaje*—of the mixture of Spanish and indigenous elements.[8] Furthermore, Shumway notes that to this day debate surrounds both the etymology of the word *gaucho* and to whom exactly it refers.[9]

The ambiguities surrounding the origins and very name of the gaucho allowed the gaucho to be recodified while continuing to function as a key cultural sign in Argentina. Initially, Argentine liberals, looking to Europe for cultural orientation, maintained that these mixed-race cattle hands were uneducated masses that were influenced and controlled, to negative ends, by *caudillos.* But eventually, nationalists and populists romanticized the gaucho, exalting him as the authentic Argentine, "the true *criollo.*"[10] The gaucho came to embody the virtues of the Argentine spirit and it was not long before immigrants, seeking to negotiate around conceptions of *criollo* authenticity, began to participate in the strategic use of the gaucho. Thus, the ruling class's desire for a narrative of the nation that could be adapted to different historical moments (as circumstances, and elite needs, changed) as well as marginalized immigrants' need for a point of insertion into the Argentine narrative have both been met by the gaucho. Even now that gaucho culture has essentially disappeared, the gaucho continues to function as a potent national symbol.

Two of the key texts in the symbology of the gaucho were written by Sarmiento and Lugones and both make heavy use of Orientalist imagery and direct comparisons between Arabs (elided with Berbers) and gauchos. Sarmiento's *Facundo o Civilización y barbarie* (*Facundo or Civilization and Barbarism*), the cornerstone of Argentine and even Latin American literature, was published in 1845 as an attack on the Rosas dictatorship of the period. The text is a Romantic biography of Juan Facundo Quiroga, the *caudillo* of La Rioja province of the 1820s and 1830s who, with his gaucho militia, was Rosas's main supporter in the interior. What is particularly striking about *Facundo* is that in depicting what Sarmiento saw as the clash between elements of civilization (Buenos Aires, the urban, and the European) and barbarism (the interior, the indigenous, and to a large extent the mixed-race gaucho), Sarmiento repeatedly makes references to "the Arab" and "the Orient"—a stylized or stereotyped version of West Asia and North Africa. Furthermore, Sarmiento's images of the Orient and the Arab are as ambivalent and contradictory as his attitudes toward Argentine barbarism—in fact, these Orientalist references are deeply intertwined with his attitudes toward the "barbarism" of Argentina. In *Facundo* and also a travel essay about his experiences in Algeria (in *Viajes por Europa, África y América* [*Travels in Europe, Africa, and America*]), Sarmiento likens gauchos to Arabs, engages in opposition to, as well as identification with, the Arab gaucho, and struggles to comprehend his gaucho Other, and his gaucho Self, through his Orientalism. That is, he uses the figure of the Arab as a graspable counterpart to the gaucho, and thus formulates a national identity that navigates between embracing civilization and embracing, and controlling, the gaucho.

The figure of the Arab gaucho is also crucial to Lugones's essay "El payador." In 1916 Lugones, a central figure of Argentine *modernismo* and an influence upon the avant-garde, published this extensive essay that revalorizes the figure of the gaucho. The essay praises the gaucho as a mediator, or translator, between civilization and barbarism. By this point in Argentine history, rather than the immigrants being the element of civilization that would tame "barbarian" gaucho culture, the gaucho was invoked as the true Argentine who had tamed the pampas. Lugones arrives at his formulation of the gaucho as cultural translator through a rhetoric of comparisons with and references to the Arab component of Spanish culture. This rhetoric is a reflection of the conceptual model of cultural mediation and of contact with the Other that is most common in the Hispanic tradition: *moros y cristianos*. In Lugones's formulation, Moors and Christians are at times at odds but also closely connected socially and biologically. Lugones uses the *moro* to make the conflict-ridden gaucho an Argentine icon, and one that represents pre-immigration Argentina.

In the 1960s and 1980s the Arab Argentines Ibrahim Hallar and Juan Yaser wrote essays that utilize Sarmiento's and Lugones's links between Arabs and gauchos in order to create a deep connection between the Arab immigrant and Argentina. In this way, these Arab Argentines turned the gesture of rejection of the immigrant—that is, the elevation of the gaucho to national hero, as well as a particular form of Orientalism, into an entry point for the Arab immigrant into Argentine subjecthood. In a further manipulation of the figures of the gaucho and the Arab, one of Argentina's most prominent descendants of Arab immigrants, Carlos Menem, also crafted an Arab gaucho, not in a textual assertion of identity, but in the creation of his own public image. In the 1970s Menem consciously crafted his public image as a populist to invoke that of the famous *caudillo* of La Rioja's gaucho militias, Juan Facundo Quiroga, and then beginning in the late 1980s he rounded out his emerging neo-liberal persona of affluence and flashy fun through Arab dance and festivities.

During the first two decades of his political career, Menem, who was born and raised in La Rioja, consciously cultivated identification between himself and Quiroga, the traditional Riojan icon of populism. During the 1970s and 1980s, as governor of La Rioja, Menem dressed and wore his hair like the local *caudillo*.[11] He often wore the regional poncho associated with gauchos and always sported the long hair and bushy sideburns (see figs. 6.1 and 6.2) that portraits of Quiroga (see fig. 6.3) have made part of the popular imaginary, and that Sarmiento linked to brash populism. Another manifestation of Menem's homage to Facundo Quiroga is the name he gave his first son: Carlos Facundo. In an essay on Menem's image, the group known as Colectivo Situaciones points out that during the 1970's Menem, along with Perón, represented the continuity between the *caudillos* of Northern Argentina, and in particular Facundo Quiroga, and contemporary Peronist populism. Menem's wild sideburns were a key element in this representation of traditional rural Argentine values and the power of the common people. I would add that Menem invoked the nineteenth-century populist leader of La Rioja, not only to play up and strengthen Menem's own populist politics, but also, to attempt to establish a *criollo* identity—to downplay his *turco* lineage and highlight his "authentically" Argentine attributes.

Menem's invocation of Facundo Quiroga may in fact have its roots in Sarmiento's description of Quiroga as a sort of Arab gaucho. According to Gabriela Cerruti, Menem's personal copy of Sarmiento's *Facundo* has particular passages underlined: those that point to Quiroga's supreme power over La Rioja and his political charisma, along with those in which Sarmiento describes Quiroga with Orientalist references.[12] Sarmiento describes Quiroga with references to Tamerlane, the prophet Muhammad, Muhammad Ali (Ottoman governor of Egypt), and *The 1001 Arabian Nights*. Ironically, Menem's imitation of Quiroga allowed the Arab Argentine to emphasize his participation in the nationalist tradition that Quiroga represents.

Orientalizing President Menem

In spite of Menem's attempts to play up his *criollo* identity, albeit through Sarmiento's Orientalist description of the *criollo* that Menem took as his model, the Argentine populace never lost sight of Menem's Arab origins.

Fig. 6.1. Menem in 1973 while governor of La Rioja. (From Wikipedia, http://en.wikipedia.org/wiki/File:Carlos_Menem_1973.jpg, accessed May 1, 2012).

Fig. 6.2. Menem wearing a poncho as he campaigns for the presidency on the streets of Buenos Aires in 1989. (From "Variaciones Sobre Menem" in ExArgentina, March 2003, http://www.exargentina/_es/_04/variationen.html, accessed May 1, 2012).

Fig. 6.3. Juan Facundo Quiroga, famous caudillo of La Rioja. From Wikipedia, http://www.en.wikipedia.org/wiki/File:Facundo_Quiroga.jpg (accessed May 1, 2012).

Beginning in 1988, when Menem campaigned for the presidential nomination of the Peronist *Justicialista* party and then won the nomination in July of that year, latent anti-Arab bigotry rose to the surface and continued to be palpable throughout his two terms as president and beyond. While some manifestations of this second wave of anti-Arab sentiment explicitly refer to Menem, all of them are implicitly linked to Menem as the catalyst of this second wave and as the most prominent Arab Argentine. Furthermore, they all reflect as well as shape Euro-Argentine attitudes toward Argentines of Arab descent and toward the Middle East in general. The use of the term *turco* is emblematic of the intertwined nature of representations of Menem and the Syro-Lebanese at large. Though Argentines may refer to any descendent of Arab immigrants as *el turco,* the Argentine public regularly refers to Menem as *el Turco.*

Soon after Menem's nomination as presidential candidate, the popular Argentine magazine *Humor* (*Hum®*), a magazine of social and political satire that ran from the 1970's through the 90's, began having fun with the regional origins to which the term *turco* refers and the religion with which it is associated. In the late 80's and early 90's, the magazine's treatment of Menem alternated between digs at his politics and public appearances, jabs at his outdated sideburns and his Riojan accent, spoofs of the stereotypical *"turco"* pronunciation of Spanish (primarily the substitution of the sound "p" with "b," an accent which Menem does *not* have), and references to Islam and the Arab world (see figs. 6.4–6.7). Analogous references to other ethnic or religious backgrounds are not to be found in the magazine. Thus, from the start of his role in national politics, Menem's background was given disproportionate significance and was deemed humorous.

With time, in *Humor* and elsewhere, Menem's faults were linked to his

Fig. 6.4. An issue of *Humor* included these mock pages from the Argentine newspaper *Página/12*. The spread plays with the name of Menem's political ally, the Argentine trade union leader Lorenzo Miguel, Orientalist visions of Lawrence of Arabia (in Spanish, Lorenzo de Arabia), and Menem's Arab origins. Leaving aside T. E. Lawrence's British nationality and Miguel's Spanish parentage, the item turns Menem and Miguel into caricatured versions of Lawrence of Arabia and his camel. The entire item also pokes fun at the typical Arabic speaker's accent; for example, *página* becomes *bágina*.

Págína/12

Organo Oficial de la Brensa — Beronista • Edición 1989 - Año Uno de Menem Bresidente

Ejemblar de regalo bara el bueblo

Economía

UN EXITO: BLAN "NORTEÑO" Y SALARIAZO

El clima de felicidad y brosperidad que se extiende bor el baís, tiende a hacerse insobortable. El bueblo está tan contento que ya de asco y rebulsión.

No es bara menos, baisano. Los blanes de reactivación económica, la continua inversión de cabitales foráneos y la abertura de nuevas fuentes de trabajo están asombrando a los baíses vecinos, al mundo entero y a sus alrededores. Con los fuertes lazos comerciales y culturales que Menem ha establecido, el bueblo entero está unido y grita de corazón: "¡Más inversión, más inversión!". Los aviones de Aerolíneas Arabergentinas —la embresa otra vez nacionalizada y arrebatada a la SAS— no dan abasto bara trasbortar a miles de comerciantes libaneses, kuwaitíes, sirios y sauditas que traen sus alforjas rebletas e instalan fábricas de alfajores, almohadones, berfumes de almizcle, almijaras y alfombras con arabescos.

¡Qué lejos quedaron aquellos días en que se engañaba al bueblo diciendole que se levantarían las bersianas de las fábricas! Ahora sí que las bersianas están levantadas. El Blan "Norteño", al contrario del "Austral", es un símbolo de federalismo. Borque La Rioja está al norte, no como antes cuando la cabital del baís tiraba ba'l sur.

Ni qué hablar de los efectos del "Salariazo" dishuesto por el combañero Menem. Con el 300% de aumento de sueldos, la gente ya no sabe en qué gastar los maravedíes. Es más: el baís está absorbiendo la fuerte corriente de inmigrantes de los baises árabes, que vienen a "hacer la turca". Rechazados y marginados bor Alemania, Francia e Inglaterra —esos baises del brimer mundo que bor olvidar al tercero están terminando con el segundo— millones de trabajadores llegan a la Argentina; y los bocos que no son absorbidos bor las embresas brivadas tienen lugar en la administración bública, que ha incrementado su bersonal en un 200%.

¡La Argentina Botencia no se detiene! ¡Estamos bersuadidos!

La columna del Bresidente

BOLARIZAR NO ES AL BEDO

Bor: Carlos Saúl Menem

Yo, que brimero bolaricé al bueblo de La Yioja, y que desbués ayibé al gobierno yeventando con votos beronistas las urnas, estoy bersuadido de que en este baís bolarizar no es al bedo. La bolarización buso en las últimas elecciones las cosas en su lugar. A mí, en la bresidencia, y a Angeloz en su casa. Esto, combañeros, es bueno, bara nosotros y bara el país. Borque vamos a ver, ¿quiénes le temían a la bolarización? Los yadicales, bor subuesto, y los liberales, borque tenían miedo de berder. Y como berdieron, queda claro que la bolarización bolítica ha sido algo bueno, sobre todo bara nosotros. La bolarización nos hemos sacado de encima a todos los bolíticos de obosición y el bueblo ha recuberado su soberanía. La blataforma beronista que yo imbulso bretende ahora hacer de la bolarización la solución ideal y esbecífica de los broblemas brincibales de la Argentina. Debemos bolarizar más, mucho más. ¿Bor qué? Bor lo siguiente: la bola-

Fig. 6.5. Another issue of *Humor* contains mock pages from the Argentine newspaper *Página/12* in the form of an oversized two-leaf insert. In this insert, every mock article is marked with a crescent moon and star as a symbol of Islam, conveying the idea and/or fomenting the fear that Menem is Islamicizing Argentina.

Bágina 12

BANORAMA CULTURAL

◆ Albargatas sí

La albargata, bilar de la cultura beronista, es una brenda de vestir abta tanto bara el hombre de cambo como bara el viandante urbano. Este ventajoso calzado, conveniente bor su bajo brecio, se ha convertido, además, con el gobierno del bresidente Menem, en un toque de brestigio. A tal bunto, que hoy se las bonen bor igual el intelectual del bar La Baz, el obrero laborioso, la baica de los barrios bravos y las bibas de Belgrano. Un banquete, el estreno de una belícula o un bartido de basket-ball son ocasiones brobicias bara lucir un bonito bar de albargatas. Confeccionadas con buenas lonetas y berfectas suelas de cáñamo, las albargatas argentinas no son ya el emblema de la bobreza y el hambre sino el símbolo de un baís nuevo y bujante.

◆ Libros ahora

debe trabajar en tareas beligrosas, insalubres, y bor muy boca blata. Una brueba más de que el desarrollo y el bienestar de Euroba es, brioritariamente, bara los eurobeos, que así discriminan entre rébrobos y elegidos. Un libro esbectacular, no se lo bierda.

◆ Saer en Barís

El director de Relaciones Culturales de la Cancillería, Julio Bárbaro, acaba de nombrar como agregado cultural de la Embajada Argentina en Barís al escritor Juan José Saer, hombre de brobada ascendencia turca y que vive en Francia desde hace bastante tiem-

◆ El insbector Biglia

Se ha sabido que el gobierno estudia la bosibilidad de distinguir bróximamente a otro escritor. Se trata de Ricardo Biglia, autor de "Resbiración artificial" y "Brisión berbetua", quien sería nombrado — como lo fue Borges en años basados— Insbector de Mercados Municibales.

◆ Se acabó la censura: Dalmiro Sáenz ya buede volver a bublicar

La besada herencia de la censura a Dalmiro Sáenz imbuesta por el gobierno anterior ha sido resuelta bor el bresidente Menem. Así que el autor del célebre éxito "Las boludas" buede volver a bublicar en nuestros baís. Dalmiro Sáenz se abresta, en consecuencia, a entregar a la imbrenta una novela en dos volúmenes, otro desafío —debe bensarse— al budor hibócrita. El primer volumen lleva bor título "La boronga". El segundo, bara no ser menos, "La bija". El bresentador de televisión Gerardo Sofovich se abresuró a declarar que no biensa invitar a Dalmiro a su brograma.

◆ Fue bremiada en Braga la última belícula de Bino

Fig. 6.6. From the third page of *Humor*'s mock *Página/12* spread seen in figure 6.5, this cartoon represents the *turco mercachifle*. Though benign in comparison with other visual and literary representations of the Arab immigrant peddler, this drawing highlights the Syro-Lebanese peddler's ignorance with a sign in which he spells *peines* (combs) and *peinetas* (ornamental hair combs) as *beines* and *beinetas*. Presented within this spread, the cartoon associates Menem with this laughable figure.

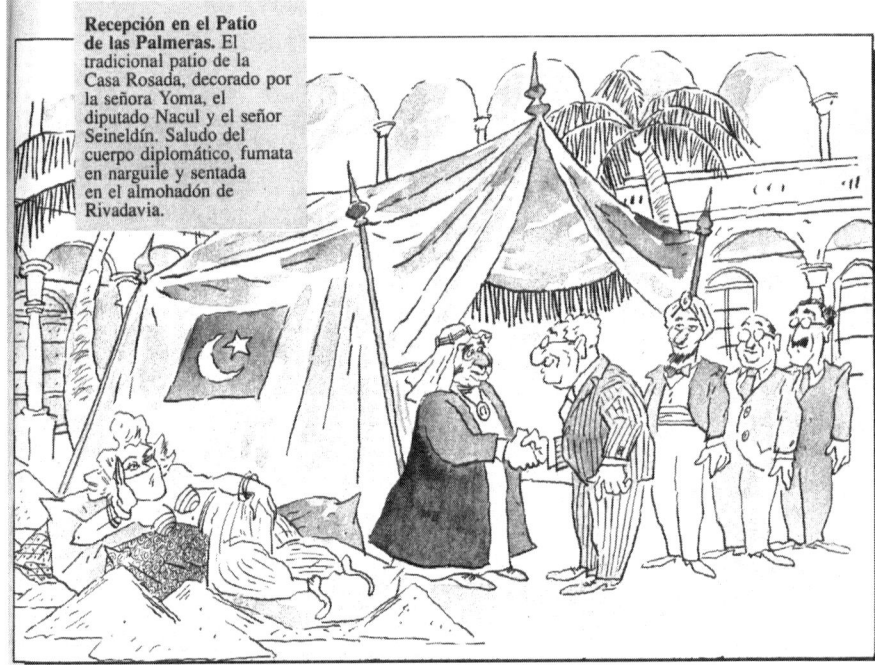

Fig. 6.7. *Humor*'s coverage of Menem's upcoming assumption of the presidency included this depiction of the reception at the presidencial residence (*La Casa Rosada*). The text explains that Menem's then-wife, Zulema Yoma (a Muslim Argentine of Syrian parents whom Menem met in Damascus), and two other (in)famous Arab Argentines had decorated La Casa Rosada for the event, and presents Menem and Yoma, in Oriental garb, greeting guests.

ethno-religious origins. Unfortunately, Menem's administration gave credence to some of the *turco* stereotypes common in Argentina. To begin with, once he became president he shed (in practice, though not in rhetoric) his Peronist politics. Though elected on a populist platform, taking on a country in the midst of economic trouble, he quickly shifted to neo-liberalism and instituted free-market policies and large-scale privatization. For many the shift created the general impression that he failed to keep his promises. In addition, the Menem government's policies are seen as a major contributor to Argentina's most recent major economic crisis (1999–2002). Menem was also criticized for pardoning the leaders of the military dictatorship that controlled Argentina from 1976 to 1983. Moreover, suspicions of corruption and cases against Menem's associates during his terms later turned into various different judicial cases brought against Menem himself for different forms of dishonesty or misdeed.[13]

Given Menem's track record, and Euro-Argentines' already well-established Orientalism, from the middle of his first term as president through the years immediately following his second term there was a steady crop of criticisms of Menem that had a distinctly Orientalist flavor. The use of references to the Arab world, Islam, and Arab ethnicity to characterize and criticize Menem creates and upholds simplistic, fixed conceptions of Arab and Muslim cultures as well as the identities of Argentines of Arab descent. Rather than recognize the complexities of both Arabo-Islamic societies and ethnically diverse Argentina, that is, the multiplicity and change-ability of identities, these representations of Menem operate within—and impose upon those represented—rigid, oversimplified, and often ahistorical paradigms of individual identity and social systems.

In a later example from *Humor,* the magazine began to use the term *turco,* with the ambiguity of its general and its particular (i.e. in reference to Menem) senses, to create an authorial persona for pieces in the publication. Using the Argentine slang version of "el *turco* boludo" (equivalent to "the *turco* ass") and Arabizing it with the attached article "el," the magazine created a fictional thirteenth-century thinker named "Bolud el-Kotur." Various pieces in the magazine were signed with the name Bolud el-Kotur, a figure representing mock Eastern wisdom.

In a similar vein, a popular theater show that satirized Menem represented him wearing Arab garb and was entitled *Lo que el Turco se llevó.* This title is a play on the Spanish version of the title *Gone with the Wind* (*Lo que el viento se llevó,* literally: what the wind [or the *turco*] took with it). A mix of comedy and Las Vegas-style revue, *Lo Que El Turco Se Llevó* was a huge success in 1999 and 2000 in Buenos Aires and Mar del Plata. Through political jokes, impressions, and the sex appeal of women dancers, the show carried out a review of sorts of the ten years of Menem's administration that had just passed.

The Orientalist take on Menem has been just as rampant in more serious forms of cultural expression. In the 1990's, no doubt inspired by the Menem administration, a particular genre of popular non-fiction blossomed in Argentina: book-length exposes written by journalists. Many of the best-selling volumes were about Menem. These include titles such as *La traición de Alí-Babá* (Ali Baba's betrayal) and *La carpa de Alí-Babá* (Ali Baba's tent) which invoke the famous story "Ali Baba and the 40 Thieves" from *The 1001 Arabian Nights.* Other books, *El jefe, vida y obra de Carlos Saúl Menem* (The chieftain [or boss], the life and work of Carlos Saúl Menem), *Pizza con champán: crónica de la fiesta menemista* (Pizza with champagne: chronicle of the Menemist feast [or party]), and *El harén: Menem, Zulema, Seineldín, Los árabes y el poder político en la Argentina* (The harem: Menem,

Zulema, Seineldín, the Arabs and political power in Argentina) use the trope of the harem, other cultural practices associated with Arabs, and a narrow and simplistic conception of Islam to criticize Menem, his family, and his allies.

Norma Morandini's *El harén* is particularly noteworthy because of its popularity (the first edition appeared in November 1998 and the *fourth* only one month later) and its contradictory content. Although the author's stated intention is to counteract the prejudice surrounding Arab Argentines and particularly Menem, she resorts to the most stereotyped images of Arabs and Muslims. At times it seems as if Morandini is using the mystique of the Orient evoked by her sensationalist title, and also the back cover blurb, to draw in readers, only to then undermine their essentialist notions. Nonetheless, overall she reproduces rigid and racist constructions of 'Oriental' identity. For instance, when Morandini explains why she chose to focus on Carlos Menem, Menem's ex-wife Zulema Yoma (also of Syrian Muslim descent), and Mohammad Alí Seineldín,[14] she states: "The three of them believe that life follows infallibly an indelible path: destiny, the strongest concept within Islam, to which they must submit themselves with patience and resignation."[15] Thus, she reduces all three to one cultural logic and one set of religious beliefs that she refers to as Islam. In doing so, she adheres to a deterministic and formulaic view of Islam in which anyone born Muslim is a resigned believer in destiny and there is no awareness of the religion as interwoven with other cultural systems. At other points, Morandini refers to Menem's Arab background by saying that he belongs to a "culture of vengeance" and "that culture in which the word is used more as a seduction, poetry, a caress to the ears, with no commitment to the content."[16] After pages of recourse to essentialized conceptions of Arab Argentines' heritage, Morandini actually connects Menem to the political trajectory showcased by Sarmiento in the figure of Facundo Quiroga. Yet in spite of this final twist, the overwhelmingly deterministic view put forth in the majority of the text establishes that Morandini is against preconceptions and prejudice, but very much upholds the idea of essences, of certain religious and cultural roots that persevere in overpowering all others.

As Hortiguera points out, many of the works within this genre of exposés that includes Morandini's *El harén* blur the separation between fiction and non-fiction to such an extent that they call into question the definition of the real.[17] Nonetheless, by using these references to the Arab world and Islam to understand the reality of Menem, these texts reduce Menem to stereotypes associated with his cultural origins (ignoring his Argentine context) and thus present a very incomplete picture of both those origins and contemporary Argentina.

Embracing The 1001 Arabian Nights *while Establishing Religious Pluralism*

Although there certainly is plenty to criticize in Menem's political record, critiques of his administration, such as those in mass-circulation political satire (*Humor*), theatrical entertainment (*Lo que el Turco se llevó*), and popular nonfiction (*El harén*), invoke Menem's Arab background as though it were the inescapable source of his flaws. These examples from Argentine popular and print cultures give a sense of the late twentieth century and early twenty-first century climate of Orientalist attitudes that surrounds Argentines of Arab descent in general, and Menem in particular. Menem has responded to this web of essentialist images of the Middle East by, on the one hand, embracing the *1001 Arabian Nights* version of the Arab world and, on the other hand, opening up a space for Argentine religious plurality while at the same time eschewing personal questions of religion. He has opted to play the part of the Arab of lavish festivities, a role very much in tune with his turn toward neo-liberal politics, while simultaneously creating a space for Islam (and potentially other creeds) in Argentina and distancing himself from a Muslim identity.

Menem, who converted to Catholicism in the 1960's, has insisted on his identity as a Roman Catholic, that is, his adherence to the religion of standard, traditional Argentineness. At the same time, he has publicly displayed his non-normative ethnic identity as part of a general transformation of his public image. When Menem discarded his populist politics he phased out the gaucho image anchored by Facundo Quiroga and cultivated a cosmopolitan, and at times Arab ethnic, persona. Colectivo Situaciones comments upon Menem's transition away from the side-burned provincial *caudillo* look noting that it began during his first presidential campaign (1988–89), in which Menem, "an empty actor pulled between two scripts," is marked by "the anachronism of his sideburns." During the campaign and early in his first term, photographs of Menem that appeared in the press show him still cultivating the Facundo look and gathering with humble working class Argentines. In the days immediately following his election to the presidency, as Argentine businesspeople were turning to Menem for a solution to the economic crisis, newspaper photos already showed another version of Menem: wearing a stylish, tailored suit with his sideburns present, yet trimmed down. As his sideburns slowly disappeared and his hairstyle became shorter, other images of Menem began to proliferate: Menem with beautiful women, with expensive cars, with business executives.

As part of this transition from "down home" looks and values to chic, well-groomed, neo-liberal affluence, another image of Menem began to appear: Menem, not as the poor, dissheveled, yet crafty *turco mercachifle*, but as a flamboyant, fun-loving Arab à la *1001 Arabian Nights*. Joining the trend toward merging politics and television that began in the United States and Europe decades before, since the beginning of his presidencies Menem has made several appearances on televised variety and talk shows, demonstrating his flair for the playful improvisation and sound bite opinions of televised entertainment.[18] This interest in television appearances began at the start of his first presidency with a display of Arab flamboyance in which the gaucho look of the traditional Argentine *caudillo* was nowhere to be seen. After being elected president in May of 1989, in August of that year Menem kicked off his presidency by appearing on the variety show *Almorzando con Mirtha Legrand* (Lunch with Mirtha Legrand), where he appeared dancing to Arabic music with a scantily clad, curvaceous belly-dancer (see fig. 6.8).[19] While one could interpret this enactment of Arabness on Argentine television as a gutsy assertion of a more positive ethnic identity, the version of the Arab that it showcased simply reiterated *The 1001 Arabian Nights* images of opulent decadence that were already in heavy circulation in Argentina. Perhaps in order to move away from the images of corruption and abuse of power (the figures of the drug and weapons trafficker and the tribal chieftan) Menem opted for a dance performance. Yet, in doing so rather than pointing to the complexities, the multiple interlocking facets, of Arab culture and the immigrant experience, Menem fueled one of the existing paradigms for understanding the Arab world: that of exotic, erotic debauchery made popular in Europe and beyond through the translation of the tales of *The 1001 Arabian Nights*.

In addition to Menem's televised presidential belly dance, press coverage of Menem has often included details and images of his attendance at Arab festivities. In news articles and television features on events ranging from his birthday celebration to an homage paid to him by a Syro-Lebanese Muslim association, details of Arab food and odalisques abound. In fact, in April 2004 this type of coverage caused problems for Menem with regards to one of the judicial cases brought against him. When Federal Judge Norberto Oyarbide had called for Menem's extradition from Chile as part of an investigation of Menem's purported failure to declare a Swiss bank account while president, Menem had claimed that he was unable to travel because of a fractured arm. Soon after, though, images of Menem dancing away with an odalisque at a Syro-Lebanese community party in Chile appeared on Chilean television. Considering this proof that Menem did not suffer from any health problems that impaired his mobility, and further proof of Menem's intention to evade the investigation, Oyarbide issued an international arrest warrant for Menem. As Menem's camp continued to insist that his arm was in a cast, the image of extravagant Arab revelry joined together with the stereotype of deviousness and cunning.[20]

Though many aspects of Menem's political record are reprehensible and

Fig. 6.8. Menem dances with odalisque on the Mirtha Legrand show in 1989 (From "La Odalisca que se suicidió había bailado para Menem," 24CON, October 2009, http://24con.infunews.com/conurbana/nota/28975-La-odalisca-que-se%C2%AOsuicid%C3%B3-hab%C3%ADa-bailado-para-Menem/, accessed May 1, 2012).

elements of his public life laughable, his attempt to create a space for non-*criollos* and particularly non-Catholics in Argentina is noteworthy, particularly given the Argentine context of intertwined cultural nationalism and Orientalism. Menem's public persona has shifted from gaucho-type *caudillo* to urbanite with Arab flair; however, this assertion of an Arab Argentine identity in an inhospitable cultural climate is a very limited intervention. Menem's negotiation of the tensions surrounding Arab Argentines ultimately serves to further entrench one or more particular stereotype. In contrast, Menem's interventions in the realm of religious identity, though not without paradox, are much more powerful. Arguably the one true accomplishment of Menem's political career has been the constitutional reform regarding the eligibility requirements for the presidency. Until 1994 in order to become president of Argentina one had to be Catholic. Menem was eligible because he had converted to Catholicism early in his career. Once he became president, he promoted the reform of the constitution that removed religion from the requirements for candidacy and from the presidential oath.[21]

Despite the change in presidential eligibility requirements—or perhaps in an effort to downplay his connection to this change—Menem often disavows ever having been anything other than Catholic (although his oldest son was openly Muslim and this son's funeral rites and burial were Islamic[22]). In a 1999 television interview a reporter asked Menem, "You were never Muslim?" Menem answered, "No, I have always been an Apostolic Riojan—I mean, Roman—Catholic [*No, siempre fui católico, apostólico, riojano . . . digo, romano*]."[23] Menem's transposition of the rhyming words "riojano" and "romano" was seen as a comical blunder in the midst of the disavowal of something that was already public knowledge. But the verbal switch, whether conscious or not, points to Menem's understanding (or projection) of his Argentine identity. What makes him *católico* [*Catholic, but also: true, proper*]—that is, a legitimate and authentic Argentine—is not being Roman Catholic, but rather, being Riojan. In one sense, he is Riojan by virtue of having been born and raised in La Rioja, and, in another sense, by defining himself according to the models created by Sarmiento, (representations of) Facundo Quiroga, Lugones, and others.

Curiously, the *romano/riojano* interview took place while workers were rushing to finish a mosque in the Palermo neighborhood of Buenos Aires, reportedly so that Menem could preside over the inauguration before the end of his presidency. In December 1995 the Menem government had donated a large tract of unused land in Palermo to the Saudi Arabian embassy. There the embassy built the largest mosque and Islamic center of Latin America, despite criticisms that expressed concerns about urban planning and questioned why Argentina gave the land as a gift, particularly to the Saudi Embassy and a specific religious group. Though the criticisms were certainly well-founded, one wonders whether they would have been raised if a European embassy were building a Catholic church and school. When the Palermo mosque was inaugurated in September 2000, Menem, who had recently left office, served as unofficial host. Not surprisingly, press coverage of this event blended different archives of Orientalist imagery and described the inauguration as a scene out of *The 1001 Arabian Nights*.[24] Criticisms of the land gift and Orientalist framing of the opening notwithstanding, the Palermo mosque has certainly made Islam very visible in Argentina, similar to what occurred with the funeral and burial of Carlitos Menem Jr. (Menem's son). In March of 1995, after the tragic death of the president's son, Muslim rites were displayed on Argentine television and radio.[25] Thus, through intentional and circumstantial avenues, Menem has profoundly affected Argentina's relationship to religion, and in particular to Islam. Not necessarily foreign, Islam can now be recognized as part of Argentine terrain.

In the wake of the series of books critiquing Menem that carried titles referring to Ali Baba—of forty thieves and "open sesame" fame—two readers of Argentina's leading newspaper, *La Nación,* wrote letters to the editor correcting and modifying the use of the name Ali Baba to refer to Menem. The first letter-writer points out that Argentines were conflating Ali Baba and the thieves, when, in fact, in the story from *The 1001 Arabian Nights* Ali Baba is an honorable person, not part of the band of thieves.[26] Another letter writer also seeks to protect the honest Ali Baba of literature from confusion with the thieves, and from comparisons with "some politician of ours," and to this end he proposes "for ours" the name of "Alí bla bla which would adapt itself better to the circumstances and in this way we can catalog him within the literature of the River Plate."[27] This "bla bla" points to the empty, filler words that accompany the different versions of the suspect public figure, of the protean politician. But read in another way, this discussion of the figure of Ali Baba demonstrates the workings of Orientalism: the extent to which Menem and others are subject to the (mis)interpretations of literary legends. Given the history of Orientalism, Arab Argentines cannot speak unproblematically; they are prone to replay the "bla bla bla" of empty conventional representations. Yet, even still, the second letter, rather than reject Menem as a foreign element, unequivocally claims him as genuinely Argentine, as "our own," as part of local tradition—a new conception of tradition and authenticity.

Menem's negotiation of the tensions around Arabs in relation to the intersection of religious, nationalist, ethnic, and racial discourses in Argentina is a double-edged sword: while it exacerbates existing problems, it also creates a new opening. Menem's public persona simultaneously demonstrates auto-Orientalism—the assumption of an Orientalism-informed ethnic identity—and establishes the beginnings of a more nuanced, plural, and inclusive conception of Argentine-ness.

NOTES

1. Menem was suspected of having consented to illegal arms sales from 1991 to 1995 to Croatia and Ecuador, in defiance of UN weapons embargoes. In 2001, Menem spent five months under house arrest during investigation of the allegations. In August 2003, the judge dropped the charges. However, Menem is still under investigation for his role in the 1995 Río Tercero explosion which has been linked to the arms scandal.

2. I use more or less interchangeably the terms *Arab* and *Syro-Lebanese,* to refer to Arabic-speaking immigrants, primarily from the Ottoman province of Greater Syria. Argentines began to commonly use the term *Syro-Lebanese* in the 1920's, however it does not recognize Palestinian Argentines or the small number of North African immigrants (see Ignacio Klich, "Árabes, judíos y árabes judíos en la Argentina de la primera mitad del novecientos," *Estudios interdisciplinarios de América Latina y el Caribe* 6, no. 2 [1995]: 109–43). When wishing to highlight Euro-Argentine perspectives on Arab Argentines, I also use the term *turco*—which Argentines generally use pejoratively.

3. Sarmiento was a prominent Argentine statesman (including a term as president), educator, and prolific author.

4. The term *criollo* (from the same root as *Creole,* though with different racial connotations) refers to descendants of Spanish colonizers. The term *criollo* has a particular valence in Latin American cultural history where the "criollo" is first at odds with the colonial Spanish administration and then with immigrants. I use the broader term *Euro-Argentine* in order to also include turn-of-the-century immigrants from Europe and their descendants.

5. Precise statistics on how many Syro-Lebanese emigrated are difficult to establish because of illegal departures, non-standardized or inaccurate terms used to record origins at arrival points, and return migration. Estimates indicate that between 1875 and 1914 there were more than a million émigrés from the Ottoman Empire that arrived in the Americas. Within Argentina, both Arabs and Jews have claimed the place of third largest immigrant group. This ambiguity is no surprise given the absence

of exact statistics as well as the ways in which the religious, ethnic, geographic, and linguistic identities of Arabs and Jews are intertwined.

On the migration of Arabic-speakers to Argentina, and their communities there, see Sélim Abou, *Liban déraciné: Immigrés dans l'autre Amérique*, 1978; Lilia Ana Bertoni, "De Turquía a Buenos Aires. Una colectividad nueva a fines del siglo XIX," *Estudios Migratorios Latinoamericanos* 9, no. 26 (1994): 67–94; Jorge Bestene, "La inmigración Sirio-Libanesa en la Argentina, una aproximación," *Estudios Migratorios Latinoamericanos* 3, no. 9 (1988): 239–68; Michael Humphrey, "Ethnic History, Nationalism, and Transnationalism in Argentine Arab and Jewish Cultures," in Klich and Lesser, *Arab and Jewish Immigrants in Latin America, Images and Realities* (1998): 167–88; 'Abd al-Wahid Ikmir, *al-'Arab fi al-Arjantin: al-Nushu' wal-Tatawwur*, 2000; Gladys Jozami, "La identidad nacional de los llamados turcos en la Argentina," *Temas de África y Asia* 2 (1993): 189–204; Klich, Michel Nancy and Elisabeth Picard, eds. *Les Arabes du Levant en Argentine*, 1998; Marta H. Saleh de Canuto and Susana Budeguer, *El aporte de los sirios y libaneses a* Tucumán, 1979; Alberto Tasso, "Aventura, trabajo, y poder--sirios y libaneses en Santiago del Estero 1880–1980," 1988; Estela Valverde, "Integration and Identity in Argentina: The Lebanese of Tucumán," in *The Lebanese in the World: A Century of Emigration*, edited by Albert Hourani and Nadim Shehadi (1992), 313–37; and María ElenaVela Ríos and Roberto Caimi, "The Arabs in Tucumán, Argentina," in *Asiatic Migrations in Latin America*, ed. Luz María Montiel (1988), 125–46. On the textual dialogue between Arab Argentines and Euro-Argentines, including elaboration on Sarmiento, Lugones, and Morandini, see Christina Civantos, *Between Argentines and Arabs: Argentine Orientalism, Arab Immigrants, and the Writing of Identity* (2006).

6. For more on anti-Arab sentiment since the 1980's, see Klich, "Árabes, judíos y árabes judíos" 141–42; Jozami, "La identidad nacional de los llamados turcos en la Argentina," 190–91; and Pedro Brieger, "Latin Islam since 11 Septemberm," *ISIM Newsletter*, International Institute for the Study of Islam in the Modern World, 11 (December 2002): 8.

Anti-Arab sentiment has also taken the form of violent acts specifically targeting Argentine Muslims. Two different mosques in Argentina have been attacked with explosives, in June 1986 and in January 2001. Most recently, in an act that has been seen as part of the aftermath of the September 11, 2001 attacks in the United States, in July 2002 tombs were desecrated in a Muslim cemetery in Buenos Aires. The Muslim community of Argentina mostly saw it as an act of discrimination. However, the Buenos Aires police did not classify the incident as a hate crime nor investigate it as such. For more on these incidents see Brieger.

7. Richard Slatta, *Gauchos and the Vanishing Frontier* (1983), 7.

8. Ibid., 7–8.

9. Nicolas Shumway, *The Invention of Argentina* (1991), 12, 69.

10. On Argentine elites' repositioning of the gaucho, see Josefina Ludmer, *El género gauchesco, Un tratado sobre la patria*, 1988.

11. Menem first held the governorship of La Rioja from 1973 to 1976. After the military dictatorship and its Dirty War (1976–83), during which Menem spent five years in prison, Menem was governor again from 1987 to 1989.

12. Gabriela Cerruti, *El jefe* (1993), 15–17.

13. Menem is also censured for his apparent obstruction of justice in relation to the AMIA bombing. In July 1994, during Menem's presidency, a major Jewish Argentine

cultural center in Buenos Aires, the Asociación Mutual Israelita Argentina (AMIA), was bombed. The bombing resulted in 86 deaths and at least 120 wounded. The investigation into the bombing has been marked by scandal and has still not led to any convictions. Argentine investigators' efforts at prosecuting the Iranian government officials it says organized the attack have been thwarted by a lack of international cooperation. In addition, Menem is suspected of having undermined the prosecution. A defector from Iran's intelligence agency has accused Menem of having purposely hindered the official investigation. On the international hindrances to the investigation and Menem's role, see Larry Rohter, "Argentines Criticize Investigation of '94 Attack," *New York Times,* 19 July 2004, late ed.: A6; See also "Caso AMIA: acusaron a iraníes, sirios y libaneses, pero nadie probó nada," *Agence France Presse—Spanish,* 16 July 2004.

14. Seineldín is a retired Argentine army colonel who, after being born into a Druze family and converting to conservative Catholicism, was jailed for leading a right-wing uprising within the military.

15. Norma Morandini, *El harén* (1998), 13.

16. Ibid., 224 and 213, respectively.

17. For more on this genre of "journalistic research," see Hugo Hortiguera, "De la investigación periodística al *potin*: El relato documental argentino de fin de siglo," CiberLetras 9 (July 2003) and LucianaVázquez, *La novela de Menem. Ensayo sobre la década incorregible,* 2000. Though both authors analyze the rhetoric of these exposés on Menem, neither notes the Orientalism that operates in a number of the texts.

18. For more on this topic, see Adriana Schettini, *Ver para creer. Televisión y política en la Argentina de los 90,* 2000 and Victor Hugo Ghitta, "Atraído hasta el fin por la luz de la TV: La visita de Menem a 'Sábado bus'," *La Nacion On-Line,* 10 June 2001, http://www.lanacion.com.ar/311577 (accessed July 24, 2002).

19. Due to the economic crisis, president Alfonsín left office six months early and thus Menem assumed the presidency early.

20. See Nueva orden de captura contra Menem," *La Nacion On-Line,* 27 April 2004, http://www.lanacion.com.ar/596087 (accessed January 16, 2007).

21. For more details, see Pedro Brieger, "Latin Islam since 11 September," Newsletter, International Institute for the Study of Islam in the Modern World (December, 2002), 8.

22. Gladys Jozami, "The Manifestation of Islam in Argentina," *The Americas,* 53, no. 1 (1996).

23. Verónica Bonacchi, "Menem y Quintero," *La Nacion On-Line,* 24 January1999, http://www.lanacion.com.ar/99/01/24/s05.htm (accessed 6 June 2001).

24. Cynthia Palacios, "Fiesta religiosa en Palermo," *La Nacion On-Line,* 26 September 2000, http://www.lanacion.com.ar/34495 (accessed January 16, 2007).

25. Jozami, "The Manifestation of Islam in Argentina."

26. Diego Martínez Estrada, "Defensa de Alí Babá," *La Nacion On-Line,* 22 July 2002, http://www.lanacion.com.ar/415686 (accessed 16 January 2007).

27. Juan Contarino, "Alí bla bla," *La Nacion On-Line,* 24 July 2002, http://www.lanacion.com.ar/416232 (accessed 16 January 2007).

SEVEN

They Hate Our Freedom, But We Love Their Belly Dance
The Spectacle of the Shimmy in Contemporary U.S. Culture

Amira Jarmakani

> The spectacle is the existing order's uninterrupted discourse about itself, its laudatory monologue.
>
> —Guy Debord

At a nearby Moroccan, Turkish, Lebanese, Greek, or Mediterranean restaurant, belly dancers contribute to the general ambiance of the dining experience. In the local gym, belly dancing classes have been added to the menu of New Age exercise options, guaranteed to tone women's bodies in addition to improving their body image. In the 2001 advertising scheme for Camel cigarettes, a silhouette of a belly dancer was employed to signify the "carnivale" aspect of what Camel called the "7 pleasures of the exotic," while live belly dancers were hired to perform at the 700 parties, which were staged to promote the new line of "exotic" cigarettes. In the bonus features section of comedienne Margaret Cho's 2005 video, *Assassin,* one can find "Margaret Cho's belly dance," a noncomedic segment in which the irreverent, spunky, and controversial comedienne discusses the revolutionary potential of belly dancing as a means through which women can "define [their] own standard of beauty." Taken together, these widely varied examples of how belly dancing is threaded through the U.S. cultural milieu certainly testify to the predominance of belly dance as a popular U.S. cultural form. As such, the figure of the belly dancer in U.S. popular culture lends itself to a consideration of the ways in which this dance form can speak to such a multivalent group of audiences. The more interesting question, however, emerges out of an exploration of the timeliness of these varied appropriations of the dance form. Representations of the belly dance as a popular new exercise form or cabaret-style performance are usually depoliticized and abstracted from the realities of contemporary U.S. involvement in the Middle East. However, I argue that there is an indirect conceptual link between the renewed interest in and marketing of belly dancing in the United States and the War on Terror claim that the United States is bringing freedom and democracy to the Middle East. In fact, the contemporary popularity of belly dancing in the United States reveals the irony of the fact that the commodified Middle Eastern cultural form of the belly dance is appropriated to advocate for female liberation in the United States at the same time that the U.S. state mobilizes the assumption of female oppression in the Middle East to justify military action. Exploring this irony, American belly dancing can serve as a concrete example of the way that "liberty, freedom, and democracy have been turned into powerful rhetorical instruments justifying globalization and empire."[1] The rhetoric of freedom, then, does not only function in the realm of politics; its echoes and reverberations can be heard and felt throughout the cultural fabric of U.S. popular culture.

A Concise History of American Belly Dancing

As is evident from the examples with which I begin this essay, belly dancing has a wide range of manifestations in U.S. popular culture, which speaks to its rich history in the United States. Contrary to various narratives that consistently cast belly dancing as an authentic and unmediated example of Middle Eastern culture, American belly dancing is a "new dance genre"[2] insofar as it combines a set of folk dances originating from various regions in the Middle East with multiple influences, including Orientalist representations and dance movements from other regions and cultures. While it has been influenced by "native" dancers, for example, both from Middle Eastern immigrant communities in the United States and from Algerian and Syrian dancers brought to perform at the 1893 Chicago World's Fair, their performances have also shifted to adapt to U.S. demands, such as in amusement parks and Middle Eastern restaurants, both of which I discuss below.

Popular (and nontechnical) representations of belly dance have influenced the overall genre, both those from Hollywood films[3] and those from Egyptian films, which apparently influenced well-known U.S. performers and instructors like Jamila Salimpour and Morocco.[4] Adding to the mix of elements that characterize American belly dancing are also professional

U.S. and European dancers from the early twentieth century, who created interpretive dances based on inspiration from an imagined East.[5] As the last example implies, Orientalist notions of the "East" often resulted in a "choreographic pastiche" of "movements and elements from Egypt, Persia, India, Java, Bali, and the Far East."[6] This spirit of cultural and stylistic fusion still exists in American belly dancing today, as can be seen in the popularity of forms such as American Tribal Belly Dance[7] and Gothic Belly Dance.[8] More recent adaptations of belly dancing have recast it in the mold of the exercise industry, itself an appropriation of some popular feminist interpretations of the dance in the 1960s and 1970s. In this combination of examples, one can notice at least three overlapping, and sometimes conflicting, ideas about belly dancing that have shaped the American interpretation of it. Below, I trace some key sites in the historic formation of belly dancing as a new dance genre, focusing on its presentation as exotic spectacle, on its consumerist successes in the United States, and on its construction as a liberatory, female-centered dance, touted for its contributions to the empowerment of women.

Historically, the power to consume the belly dance, or to render the belly dance into consumerist spectacle, has also been linked to the project of colonialism. Perhaps one of the best examples comes from the Orientalist travel writer Gustave Flaubert, whose famous encounter with Kuchuk Hanem solidified the link between belly dancing and prostitution in the popular European imagination.[9] Colonialist expectations that the "East" was replete with countless manifestations of erotic sensuality in many ways created the conditions for the very performances that were assumed to be indigenous. The colonial cabarets, which boasted belly dance performances, in the first half of the twentieth century were predicated on such Orientalist expectations and assumptions. These venues were clear displays of colonialist power. They represent the ability of French and British colonial forces to create a bounded space in which colonized women performed for the scopic pleasure of colonizing men. Moreover, it named that performance as natural and indigenous to the region, thereby theoretically eclipsing the impact of colonial power to construct the scene. While the overt power dynamic of the colonial context does not determine contemporary belly dance performances in the United States, the legacy of staging belly dancers' sexuality for the scopic pleasure of the audience undoubtedly tinges popular perceptions of the dance today. Contemporary restaurant performances, for example, can be understood as an extension of the performances that took place within colonial cabarets in the early 1900s, as can the exhibitions at world's fairs and amusement parks in the turn-of-the-century United States.

World's fairs, and particularly the 1893 Chicago World's Fair, are influential sites in the larger history of belly dancing in the United States.[10] While they are not necessarily the original locations in which the dance was introduced in the United States, the success of belly dance exhibits helped to popularize and disseminate it to mainstream audiences. The general structure of world's fairs, moreover, replicates that of colonial cabarets in that native performers were staged as a strange and exotic exhibit catering to the expectations of the white U.S. audience that came to watch. What that audience perceived as a shocking, lascivious dance (particularly because it demonstrated freedom of movement in the hips and abdominal region of a woman's body in an era in which elite U.S. women wore corsets) then made its way into a series of performance styles, including vaudeville, burlesque, and striptease.[11] While its eventual incorporation into striptease (during the Jazz Era) certainly explains its lingering association with erotic dance in the contemporary context (an association that most belly dance practitioners reject), it also highlights a particular framing of the dance in the U.S. context, one that casts it as an exotic spectacle. For example, in the transition from burlesque to striptease, Robert Allen argues that the belly dance form played a role in disempowering performers, since it helped to transition the performers into eroticized, nonspeaking objects for scopic consumption.[12] Likewise, cabaret also began in the late nineteenth century as a countercultural form that offered a forum for satirical commentary on the ruling order. However, by the 1920s, also like burlesque, the cabaret form gave way, in some instances, to the strip club genre, an association that has persevered, thanks to films like *Cabaret* and popular representations of the entertainment form.[13] The perceptions of belly dancing that enabled it to play these kinds of roles persist in many contemporary iterations of it, including in Middle Eastern–themed restaurants, which lure customers with belly dancing performances.

Alongside the history of belly dance as Orientalist spectacle staged for mainstream audiences, and reinforcing patriarchal notions of female sexuality, is its enduring commercial success. The performance of belly dancing in the United States can be consistently tied to its history of cooptation in the interests of consumerism, since the belly dance concessions have been credited with saving the 1893 Chicago World's Fair from financial demise.[14] Its subsequent adoption into the entertainment amusement parks in the early twentieth century further attests to its framing as a lucrative commodity. Indeed, while many popular histories of belly dancing in the United States (on popular belly dance websites and recent how-to belly dance books) skip from the 1893 Chicago World's Fair directly to its revival in the 1960s and 1970s, belly dancing was alive and well in U.S. popular culture during the interim years. As mentioned above, in the 1920s and 1930s popular perceptions of it as a lascivious dance were incorporated into the performance of striptease, an incorporation no doubt aimed at increasing the commercial success of striptease. Moreover, in the realm of representation, and particularly Hollywood films, belly dancing (often combined with harem structures) also sometimes made an appearance[15] and served in this way as a referential marker to earlier appropriations of belly dancing that used it as a means of drawing consumer interest (i.e., at world's fairs and amusement parks). Contemporary iterations of this kind of appropriation manifest in Middle Eastern restaurants that feature belly dancing performances in order to draw customers, and in the marketing of belly dancing as a trendy new exercise.

Despite the best efforts of some belly dance practitioners in the United States, who want to emphasize the cultural and folkloric origins of "oriental dance,"[16] the wider context of belly dancing in the United States is influenced by the legacies of colonialism and consumer exploitation, both of which cannot be extricated from a contemporary understanding of it. At the same time, one cannot ignore interpretations of the dance in the American belly dance community that seek to present it within its own cultural context. In this endeavor, U.S. dancers have benefited from the knowledge and instruction that have come out of immigrant communities in the United States. As Andrea Deagon has pointed out, the search for history and cultural awareness is a "strong thread" among "oriental dancers,"[17] who sometimes utilize trade magazines such as *Habibi* and *Arabesque* to access cultural and historical information. Indeed, one intervention in the colonialist and consumerist framings of belly dance in the United States could come from the acknowledgment that, in the Middle East and elsewhere, belly dancing (*raqs sharqi*) is often performed at informal—"amateur"[18]—settings, such as at weddings or at intimate gatherings of family and friends.

The final thread in the history of belly dance in the United States actually reclaims and builds on the notion of it as a form of expression that women perform in community with one another, and frames it as a liberating dance form that celebrates (rather than exploits) female sexuality. This resurgence of popular interest in learning how to belly dance intersected in some ways with the women's liberation movement in the 1960s and 1970s, insofar as it emphasized belly dancing as a form of empowerment for women and as a vehicle for reclaiming women's inherent power. In this respect, it echoes both essentialist forms of feminism (some narratives even claim that belly dancing is a link to long-lost matriarchal cultures[19]) and some aspects of liberal feminism. Much like the critiques of liberal feminism and "second wave" feminism, which note the movement's focus on middle- and upper-class white women's issues, the 1960s and 1970s interest in belly dancing was also largely a white women's movement, centered on universalizing notions of freedom and empowerment.[20]

In this brief history of belly dancing in the United States, I have focused on three main orientations toward belly dance—the cabaret style and its intersections with colonialism, its imbrication in consumerist projects, and its appropriation into women's empowerment movements. Though I have separated out these threads for the purposes of clarity, I want to emphasize that they do not operate independently of one another but rather as overlapping discourses that often coexist simultaneously in the same context. For example, many women who learned to belly dance during the 1960s and 1970s resurgence (as well as contemporarily) have earned money by performing "belly grams," short belly dance performances "sent" as a gift to someone, usually on a special occasion. Though most belly dancers would likely reject any association between "belly grams" and individualized strip performances, customers likely do make such associations, highlighting the interweaving of the colonialist cabaret legacy, the commercialization of the belly dancing form, and the seemingly contradictory notion of it as a form of women's empowerment, all in one example.

Dancing to the Goddess Within

The contemporary popularity of belly dancing recombines elements of its historical legacy by marketing it as a way for women to empower themselves. While belly dancing remains popular in the standard venues of restaurant performances and specialized belly dance classes, it has also "emerged as one of the hot new workout trends in recent years, according to the American Council on Exercise."[21] Indeed, the exercise industry has capitalized on the growing success of belly dance classes, by emphasizing the theme of women's empowerment through "embracing femininity."[22] As one fitness belly dance instructor explains, "Women can get together and work on their bodies and it's women supporting women. It lets us appreciate our bodies and ourselves for who we are as women instead of trying to live up to some stereotype."[23] A *Time* magazine article about the phenomenon puts it a bit more bluntly: "To understand why belly dancing is enjoying such popularity today, it's important to set aside certain preconceptions. Banish the image of nubile harem girls undulating under an Arabian moon for the amusement of sheiks. Envision instead women of expanding waistlines and advancing ages finding their inner goddess under fluorescent lights at the local Y."[24] From these reports, it would appear that the lingering cabaret and striptease stereotypes of belly dancing as an erotic dance have been replaced with its incorporation into what might be loosely termed a "New Age" movement. In this formulation, the purpose of belly dancing is to help women search within themselves, revalue their femininity, and, in the process, develop a "'stronger sense of self,' even if that self doesn't look like Shakira."[25]

In these examples, Orientalist notions about the Middle East (through the belly dance form) uniquely combine with U.S. conceptions of individuality and self-reliance to produce abstract and decontextualized conceptions of spirituality. The perception of belly dancing as essentially feminine and sensual couples with a vague Orientalist notion of the generalized East as inherently more spiritual. For example, a 2001 news article about the popularity of belly dancing quotes a student explaining, "You know, it's ultra-feminine, it's an opportunity to live that goddess that everybody has inside them."[26] Here, the invocation of a "goddess that everybody has inside them" both references an abstract notion of spirituality and suggests that one need only look inside herself to find it. In a recent article in the *New York Times*, another belly dance student builds on this point, clarifying the dance's exotic appeal: "It touches the inner goddess of every woman, which is something you don't let out because you're too civilized."[27] In a classic Orientalist formulation, the implication here is that belly dancing, as a (Middle) Eastern dance form, can help dancers reconnect with their primordial nature since their own cultures have become too "civilized" to maintain such base connections. Importantly, in the U.S. landscape of belly dancing, these Orientalist notions of spirituality ultimately operate as a vehicle for self-transformation, as related to mainstream body image ideals. As one belly dance practitioner claims on a popular U.S. belly dance website, "We gain a more loving and intimate relationship with our bodies and with our sensuality. And yes, after overcoming social taboos and identifying with a strong female archetype, we gain greater self-esteem."[28] Women are encouraged to strive toward a transformation of their own self-esteem, which, they are assured, they can gain by embracing their own femininity.

Like elements of the 1970s feminist reclamation of belly dancing, these constructions of belly dancing borrow from essentialist iterations of feminist thought, which privilege femininity (as naturally connected to womanhood) as a means of speaking back to patriarchy. To combat the popular idea that "belly dance [is] objectifying and exploiting the female body . . . in a part of the world where women's rights [are] held in little regard," one belly dance practitioner claims that belly dancing is, instead, "part of a new feminist revolution which [she calls] the Bellybutton Revolution."[29] The potential problem with such a revolution, however, is that it is consistently oriented toward the individual female subject—to bring out the "goddess within." The implicit message is that the problem lies within women themselves, who simply need to reconnect with the power of their own femininity in order to combat patriarchal oppression. Taken to its extreme, this kind of interpretation of feminism can actually undermine the larger project of working toward gender justice by making it seem as if the "revolution" is under way, or even achieved, despite the lack of widespread systemic change.

A (further) watered-down version of this idea of feminism is also readily incorporated into mainstream popular culture. One example is in the popular HBO TV series *Sex and the City*, which capitalized generally on the theme of female empowerment, though its main characters remain thoroughly invested in classic patriarchal structures. Not surprisingly, the show incorporates the "New Age" understanding of belly dancing discussed above, therefore demonstrating its ready appropriation into popular mainstream venues. In the fourth episode ("Boy, Girl, Boy, Girl") of season three, *Sex and the City* characters Carrie and Miranda sign up for a "Goddess Workout" class so that Miranda can find her "inner goddess" and get in touch with her "feminine side." While she ultimately decides it is not for her, the incorporation of this particular iteration of belly dancing into such a popular show illuminates common U.S. engagements with belly dancing that promulgate individualized notions of female empowerment, which are abstracted from larger sociopolitical realities.

In her discussion of "spiritual belly dance," Donnalee Dox describes this type of New Age phenomenon, putting it in the context of goddess imagery and adulation. She explains that, within this genre, "the goddess . . . is conceived as an image of an eternal, universal spirit operating outside a worldview structured by hierarchy, patriarchy, or conflict."[30] The transformation advocated within this framework is therefore one that seeks to transcend oppressive realities by simply not addressing them. In this formulation, to be free from systemic oppression (like patriarchal body image ideals) is to operate on a spiritual plane, disconnected from material realities. The goddess framework tends to decontextualize and dehistoricize in an effort to achieve universality, abstracted from the realities of hierarchy and patriarchy. However, universality is an unmarked category already coded by unspoken hierarchies. The appeal to universality, in this context, then, actually reinscribes the power of unmarked hierarchies. Further, it promotes an abstract and ungrounded conception of freedom, which loses its ability to signify something meaningful.

The power of the goddess framework, contributing greatly to its marketability, is its appeal to the exotic; it signals that it offers a completely different way of conceptualizing the body outside of Western traditions. Perhaps this is why various conceptions of "New Age" spirituality are sometimes conflated in belly dancing venues and products. For example, Suhaila Salimpour has produced a "fitness fusion" DVD, in which she combines belly dance and yoga moves in an overall workout.[31] The justification for a belly dance/yoga "fusion" could easily be attributed to the fact that both strengthen abdominal, "core" muscles and therefore complement one another nicely. However, advocates of such fusion often go one step further, connecting them on a philosophical plane. Z-Helene Christopher, for example, explains, "In its profoundest sense, to really Belly Dance one has to know oneself. To this extent, Belly Dancing has certain elements in common with the Eastern spiritual practices of Zen Buddhism and Yoga."[32] Another belly dance practitioner puts it this way: "Another reason people may be attracted to both Belly dance and Yoga is the release from typical Western thinking. Both Belly dance and Yoga originated in ancient times and on different continents/subcontinents."[33] In both of these statements, the most salient connection between the two traditions seems to be their "Eastern" geography and their association with "ancient" traditions. The desire and struggle to "really . . . know oneself," however, could just as easily be associated with typical American ideals of self-reliance. Dox concludes that "the power of a concept of the Goddess" is that "it provides imagery that can be adapted and shaped to match an individual's own life experience."[34] Indeed, such a focus on individuality belies the foundation of U.S. ideals that inform American belly dancing and fitness fusion. Though U.S. appropriations of belly dancing and yoga present themselves as practices that counter Western philosophical traditions by contradicting the notion of a mind/body split and by celebrating the power of the female body, they often participate in the discourses of universality and individuality that are actually embedded in very "American" notions of liberal-democratic freedoms. Along the way, they therefore circumvent the possibility of a committed and contextualized engagement with the political and philosophical concerns undergirding ongoing war and conflict and, ultimately, with the notion of freedom.

Such an abstract and idealized notion of freedom, moreover, extends to other various expressions of belly dancing, including in a surprise "special feature" of comedienne Margaret Cho's DVD (based on a comic show), entitled *Assassin*. Cho presents an interesting case in that she is an outspoken critic of U.S. foreign policy, and, further, *Assassin* is unapologetically and critically focused, in part, on exposing the hypocrisies of the War on Terror. Nevertheless, in the extra features section of the DVD, she promulgates a stunningly mainstream and uncritical argument about belly dancing. Posing with her belly dance instructor, Cho sings the praises of the belly dance form because of its presumed ability to help women revalue the female body as necessarily fleshy and curvy. Ironically, Cho credits belly dancing with the ability to help women love and accept their bodies no matter what size they are in a DVD in which she has neglected to comment on her own apparent substantial weight loss. By failing to comment on her weight loss, when in previous performances she had incorporated her body size into the routine, she participates in normalizing a thin body ideal. It becomes a standard to achieve, which can then go unmarked and which therefore deserves no comment. Regardless of this seeming contradiction, Cho sums up her appreciation of belly dancing thusly: "We are allowing ourselves to define our own standard of beauty, which is a revolutionary idea. If we could impress this on other women, we could all be free."[35] Like essentializing notions of finding one's inner goddess, Cho means that women could be free from their own negative body image. While she speaks to the "revolutionary" possibility of women "defining [their] own standard of beauty," the visual example she gives actually reinforces mainstream beauty ideals. Immediately after issuing this statement, for example, Cho dons a cabaret-style belly dance outfit (characteristic of colonialist and patriarchal interpretations of the dance) and demonstrates her newfound freedom. In one fell swoop, Cho manages to both unreflexively appropriate another cultural form for her own purposes (an act that is, admittedly, not inconsistent with her style of comedy) and to deploy the concept of freedom in a way that ultimately undermines its potential power and that ironically parallels the rhetoric of the U.S. War on Terror that she opposes.

If the Cho example reveals the ironies of popular engagements with belly dance, it also demonstrates some of its nuances and complexities. The fact is that, to some extent at least, belly dancing does offer a challenge to mainstream body ideals in the United States by requiring a certain amount of flesh and fat in order to maximize some of the key moves of the dance form. In this respect, it certainly does intersect with the feminist goals of questioning and intervening in constricting body-image ideals, and popular belly dance websites are full of women testifying to its success in empowering them. My aim is not to undermine these realities and uses of belly dancing, but rather to complicate them. Consider, for example, Andrea Deagon's explanation of the relationship between belly dancing and feminist thought: "It is my own feeling that belly dance as performance is subversive. It allows women to seem to conform to patriarchal expectations while at the same time challenging them through powerful self-expression. But the problem with subversive intent and seeming conformity is that they play across a dangerous edge."[36]

In this article, I focus on the dangerous side of the edge to look at the parallels between the rhetoric of freedom in popular articulations of American belly dancing and the deployment of the concept of freedom in the War on Terror. Popular narratives of American belly dancing, I argue, (re)produce an inadvertent echo of the logic used to justify U.S. military action in Iraq and Afghanistan; both focus on individual freedoms (where, in some cases, the "individual" is actually a corporation) at the expense of any sustained consideration of systemic freedoms.

Life, Liberty, and the Pursuit of Dance—
The "Bellydance Superstars"

Perhaps the best example of the inadvertent echo at work is the multimedia and multivenue production of the "Bellydance Superstars," a group that tours nationally and internationally staging belly dance shows that incorporate a number of different styles. Their performance has had wide popular appeal and crossover into a large range of materials, such as CD compilations of the dancers' favorite music and a documentary entitled *American Bellydancer: Life, Liberty, and the Pursuit of Dance*. While the Bellydance Superstars do have some overlap with the larger American belly dance community, they are not entirely representative of that community. Instead, they represent a clear, if extreme, example of the consumerist legacy of American belly dancing, a fact evinced by creator Miles Copeland's statement that he "sees it as a marketing tool to sell things to women."[37] In their advertised goal to "take this ancient art form into the mainstream," the Bellydance Superstars' marketing materials demonstrate interesting intersections of classic orientalism with founding U.S. ideologies (i.e., life, liberty, and the pursuit of happiness), which parallel official U.S. rhetoric about bringing freedom and democracy to Iraq and Afghanistan through military action.

In fact, such a condescending framework, in which military action is essentially cast as a civilizing mission, reflects Copeland's own construction of the Bellydance Superstars extravaganza: "As Islamic Fundamentalism came to the U.S. mainland and the Pentagon bombed its way back into Afghanistan and Iraq, Copeland began to see his belly dancers as a healing force, wooing Americans to Arabic culture and exploring a new, feminised version of belly dancing to Islamic cultures that could do with some female emancipation."[38] The implication that American belly dancers could introduce a "new, feminised" version of the dance to the Middle East is laughable in its condescension, not to mention its ignorance about belly dancing itself, but the broader suggestion of the connection between the War on Terror and the popularity of belly dance in the United States lays the groundwork for a comparison between the two. In what follows, I first situate the Bellydance Superstars within the larger history of American belly dancing, tying it to the legacies of consumerist and colonialist orientations, and then examine their deployment of "liberty" and "freedom" in promotional materials, noting the echoes with discursive constructions of the War on Terror.

The Bellydance Superstars show is, in many ways, a quintessential consumerist spectacle, or, as their advertising materials announce, it is "an exciting, exotic, and mysterious spectacle." The title of the 2006 touring show,

"Raqs Carnivale," demonstrates the fact that it is situated squarely within a tradition of consumerism in relation to belly dancing in the United States. While the term *raqs* (meaning "dance" in Arabic) is a gesture to the Arabic term (*raqs sharqi*) for belly dance, the word *carnivale* indicates that the dance has historically been incorporated into U.S. venues for its marketability as an exotic or lascivious spectacle to be taken in. Perhaps unknowingly, the name for the Bellydance Superstars 2006 show also echoes the 2001 advertising scheme of Camel cigarettes, entitled "7 pleasures of the exotic," in which one of the seven "pleasures," named "carnivale," was represented by the silhouette of a belly dancer. Finally, it references colonial cabaret performances and contemporary American restaurant performances, which are often loyal to the cabaret style.

Despite its clear relationship to the commodified legacy of Little Egypt and her moneymaking prowess at the amusement parks and fairs since the 1893 Exposition, however, advertisements for the Bellydance Superstars stress their sensual (but, they qualify, not sexual) revaluing of the "feminine spirit." A promotion sent to women's studies professors asking them to send their students to the show proclaims that "bellydancing was created for women by women, and is very empowering" and that the "feminine and sensual dance art celebrates all women and has helped elevate bellydancing as a new fitness craze." Here, the promoters borrow from contemporary belly dance discourses, which seek to capitalize on the notion that the belly dance, as a particularly female dance form, can empower women and combat negative body image.[39]

However, this appeal is easily revealed as simply one more selling point for that "exotic" and "mysterious" spectacle, which works to conceal the economic goal that fuels its production. While belly dancing is often marketed in the United States as a means of reconnecting with a natural and sensual femininity, unmediated by modern forms of alienation from one's own body, its presentation as spectacle achieves just the opposite. As Guy Debord argues, "In societies where modern conditions of production prevail, all of life presents itself as an intense accumulation of *spectacles*. Everything that was directly lived has moved away into a representation."[40] The belly dance performance is the perfect example of an entertainment form that produces a sense of distance and alienation in the audience while presenting itself as immediately accessible and lived. It achieves this, in part, through its manipulation of spatial and temporal realities. Advertisements for it highlight its status as an "ancient" dance form that hails from distant and exotic lands, while inviting the audience to directly experience that which is imagined to be distant, both spatially and temporally, from contemporary U.S. society.

Underlying the capitalist form of production that determines the U.S.

belly dance performance is a notion of time as linear, continuous, and consumable, able to be broken down into discrete units of labor and production. Conversely, the popular U.S. narrative about this "ancient" dance form depends on a notion of time as frozen and/or cyclical, in which only "natural" rhythms prevail (e.g., the rhythms of the seasons, or of childbirth, as belly dance is sometimes lauded as an ancient childbirth ritual). In fact, the ability of belly dance to deliver this lost conception of time is one of its primary selling points; the advertisement for the Bellydance Superstars promises that the performers "exhibit an intoxicating spectacle that transports the audience to a distant time and place." Time here is effectively transformed into both a place that one might visit and a good for sale. Such a notion of an ancient temporality could only be commodified in a world that has, as Debord insists, "oriented itself toward the sale of . . . blocks of time."[41] The real commodity, then, is not necessarily an escape to the exoticized Middle East but rather an escape from the demands and concerns of contemporary capitalist society.

The Superstars promotion collapses geographical space by conflating disparate cultures and by incorporating multiple distinct genres and styles into one, undifferentiated performance. "Raqs Carnivale" is advertised as a "great cultural show—incorporating everything from Arab and Turkish cultures to African, Egyptian, Hispanic, Caribbean, and American cultures!" (In this construction, Egypt is somehow neither Arab nor African, perhaps because of the spectacular legacy that ancient Egypt enjoys in the U.S. popular imagination.) Indeed, one discovers that such wide geographical expanses collapse in on themselves because of the liberal appropriation of disassociated, and often stereotypical, cultural elements. Again, the promotion proclaims, "Not only do they incorporate Yoga into every move they make, but the show also incorporates backflips, dreadlocks, stilts, hula skirts, feathered headpieces, big chunky jewelry and tattoos; Samba, contemporary rap, hip-hop, flamenco, tribal and Middle Eastern music." The incommensurability of this dizzying list of items and styles notwithstanding, the cornucopia of popular multicultural markers demonstrates the perception of belly dancing as representative of generalized notions of exoticism and culture, which can be combined with or exchanged for other generalized and decontextualized markers, like "hula skirts," "yoga," or "dreadlocks," all of which are "aestheticized . . . as if they could be separated from history."[42] In this way, cultural differences are, as Lisa Lowe says, "aestheticized" in their increased commodification, but they are also anesthetized since their abstraction from temporal and spatial realities flattens them into common goods for sale rather than elements of living cultures.

As consumerist spectacle, then, the belly dance performance in this context is demonstrative of a neocolonial capitalist formation. It has reduced lived cultures to commodified symbolic elements of these cultures (e.g., "feathered headpieces" and "big chunky jewelry"), and it has collapsed any notion of the historical and geographical distance that separates these elements in their contexualized form. The radical collapse and erasure of geographical distance that is enacted by such cultural appropriations and substitutions, however, is recovered in the mechanics of spectacle itself, which enacts an alienating distance while proclaiming its unmediated accessibility. It reconstructs collapsed distance in the space between the audience viewers and the performance as a "spectacular separation."[43] It therefore demonstrates a particular kind of alienation—if not from one's own labor, then from lived culture—perpetuated by capitalist modes of production. The spatial and temporal modalities of people in particular historical and geographical contexts are transformed, in the belly dance spectacle, into the spatiotemporality of things (hula skirts, dreadlocks) in abstraction.

The brilliant trick of this form of alienation is, of course, the illusion it presents of offering unmediated access to lived culture. In the case of belly dance appropriations and performances in the United States, they are often packaged and sold in terms of a particular rhetoric of freedom. Belly dance in this form claims to represent a freedom to travel through time and space, and to sample any number of exotic cultures, or, for U.S. women, it is marketed as a means through which to gain freedom from negative body image. In the "pursuit of dance" represented by the Bellydance Superstars, these freedoms actually resemble U.S. political discourses about freedom, a fact that is especially highlighted in their DVD *American Bellydancer.*

Belly Dancing as a "Mascot" of Freedom

The Bellydance Superstars package, complete with a traveling show, a CD of performers' favorite dance songs, instructional DVDs, and a documentary DVD about the formation of the troupe, is the creation of mastermind Miles Copeland. Copeland, who is perhaps best known for devising the collaboration between Sting and Cheb Mami that resulted in the hit song "Desert Rose," sees belly dancing as the perfect vehicle for diversifying marketing opportunities at a moment in which CD sales are undeniably on the decline. While he is clearly interested in expanding on the wild success that Sting enjoyed when he incorporated North African Arabic music into his song (the name of the first troupe Copeland assembled was the Desert

Roses), Copeland sees belly dancing as a way of creatively responding to market forces and shifting into a different phase of music production and marketing. His idea, based on the success of Riverdance, is to produce a set of materials (mostly CDs and DVDs) that are, in essence, promoted and sold by a set of performers (the Desert Roses and the Bellydance Superstars) who market materials by performing in multiple venues both nationally and internationally.

One of the most interesting products in the Bellydance Superstars package is the documentary *American Bellydancer: The Pursuit of Life, Liberty, and Dance,* which offers a "behind the scenes" exposé of the inception of the troupe. The documentary chronicles the search for the Bellydance Superstars performers, follows them on their first unofficial tour performing at Lollapalooza, and features interviews with prominent members of the American belly dance community, such as Tamalyn Dallal, Morocco, and Suhaila Salimpour (daughter of Jamila Salimpour). Perhaps the most revealing detail in the entire film, however, is in the subtitle itself. The film is clearly interested in demonstrating the American-ness of this particular iteration of belly dancing, and in associating the dance with widely recognizable icons of U.S. culture. The front cover of the DVD, for example, features an image of a belly dancer superimposed over the image of the Statue of Liberty. The subtitle cements such associations by proclaiming American belly dancing as "the pursuit of life, liberty, and dance," thereby tying the film to some of the founding ideals of the nation. Such heavy-handed references to freedom and liberty, however, go farther to demonstrate the imbrication of the Bellydance Superstars project in neoliberal ideals of individual entrepreneurial freedoms and the principles of free trade.

In fact, the grounding of the film and the Bellydance Superstars project in the rhetoric of freedom connects it also to universalized claims to freedoms, individualism, and objective and rational truths. The invocation of "life, liberty, and the pursuit of happiness" enacted by the subtitle of the *American Bellydancer* DVD situates the film within a discourse of rights that emphasizes neutrality and universality as supreme goals. Presumably, one is meant to understand belly dancing—or the Bellydance Superstars—as purveyors of these rights and freedoms through the "pursuit of life, liberty, and dance." The framework of classical liberalism, which serves as the paradigm for the founding U.S. ideals of freedom and liberty, situates the notions of equality and rights as universal and neutral terms. They are presented as abstract concepts that apply to all citizens regardless of distinctions such as race, class, sex, and gender. In other words, the discourse of rights does not claim to register human differences according to which people of color and white women have historically been denied the "inalienable rights" of "life,

Fig. 7.1. DVD cover, *American Bellydancer*, Ark 21, 2005.

liberty, and the pursuit of happiness." Scholars in the fields of ethnic studies, queer studies, and women's and gender studies have demonstrated, following this contradiction, that the category of the universal, neutral citizen has actually functioned as an unmarked white, male, propertied, heterosexual citizen. Since this discourse of rights has grounded itself in a universal claim while simultaneously functioning in exclusionary ways, it has led Shannon Winnubst to describe it as a dehistoricizing and disembodying type of discourse.[44] In other words, it presents itself as a principle that is utterly transcendent of the particularities of historical contexts or the materiality of the body. Returning to the tension that propels my argument here: How, then, has belly dancing—an undeniably bodily dance form that is associated with ethnicized and exoticized different bodies—come to be so closely associated with the universalized ideals of freedom and liberty?

An analysis of the *American Bellydancer* DVD offers two possible rationales for the marriage of belly dancing and freedom. The first is quite particular to the Bellydance Superstars project itself and its benevolent patriarch, Miles Copeland. The DVD claims to give voice to the belly dancers themselves, even those who display differing views of the dance form than those Copeland espouses; one example is the famous instructor and dancer Morocco, who has critiqued Orientalist interpretations of the dance form.[45] Nevertheless, the entire project is contained within the framework of white, hegemonic masculinity, which sees the potential for profit in marketing the performance of scantily clad hypersexualized women. Copeland casts himself as sympathetic and benevolent in his apparent respect for the dance form, and in the fact that he supposedly capitulates to the expertise of belly dance instructors in choosing dancers for the troupe. This suggestion of his respect, however, is not corroborated by the discrepancy in the footage of the Bellydance Superstars auditions, during which Copeland chooses a dancer because he quite insistently approves of her "look," despite the fact that the lead dancer complains that she clearly has no formal dance training.

It is quite possible, then, that Copeland's unmarked, universalized status helps to usher in the "American Bellydancer" as a tokenized, sexualized, and scopophilic symbol. Despite Copeland's claims that he does not "consider [belly dancing] erotic at all,"[46] his presentation of the Bellydance Superstars suggests otherwise. His protestations about the eroticism of the dance actually function to locate the Bellydance Superstars squarely within an already existing lucrative market among female consumers. He says, "Well, I mean, if you think a beautiful woman is erotic then it's erotic . . . but I think what it is more is women being comfortable with themselves and their own sexuality, as opposed to being there to show off their tits to a man."[47] Here, he taps directly into the rhetoric of mainstream consumerist discourses used to sell belly dancing to women. The fact that Copeland spent part of his childhood in the Middle East because his father was a member of the OSS (the progenitor of the CIA) only solidifies the surface claim of his benevolent patriarchy (the film implies that living in the Middle East engendered a sympathetic interest in it), while demonstrating an underlying relationship of domination and surveillance with the region. Given these details, the dance is revealed here as a vehicle for the exercise of white, male, heterosexual, American freedom (e.g., the freedom to enjoy the scopic pleasure of belly dance performances), or, again, an abstract freedom for women to find their inner feminine selves, rather than a means to freedom in and of itself.

Miles Copeland and the Bellydance Superstars are only one example of a U.S. engagement with belly dancing; the American belly dance movement is full of women who reject the benevolent patriarch model and are drawn to the dance precisely for its women-centered qualities. In addition, as I have demonstrated elsewhere, the concept of liberation is quite central to the project of American belly dancing, especially since the codification of the movement in the 1970s.[48] As evidenced by the seamless incorporation of belly dancing into the self-help genre in the United States, the emphasis here is on individualism; members of the American belly dance movement applaud the capacity of belly dance to help women cultivate a sense of inner freedom. Instructor Tamalyn Dallal demonstrates such a position when she explains on the *American Bellydancer* DVD that "so much of our oppression comes from ourselves,"[49] following her comment about the detriment of plastic surgery and body image ideals to women's sense of self in the United States. In this way, she advances an understanding of liberation that is incapable of accounting for the way in which individual rights and freedoms can be impacted or curtailed by larger social systems, such as patriarchy or racism. Further, the idea of belly dancing as a tool that U.S. American women can use to shed the trappings of their own civilization and reconnect with their primordial, "goddess" selves mimics a liberal multiculturalist stance, in which "multiculturalism" means appropriating and commodifying ethnic difference. Conceiving of difference in this way offers a paradigm for understanding how belly dancing, which is tied in the U.S. popular imagination to the baseness of the body and associated with categories of ethnic difference that are clearly marked, can be so easily appropriated as a symbol of freedom. Whether it is the American belly dancer oriented toward its self-help qualities or the white male entrepreneur of the belly dancing industry, the abstract and universalized individual commodifies belly dancing as difference and simultaneously disavows the social, political, and historical contexts in which it has functioned.

The most alarming implication of such co-optation of belly-dance-as-difference is the way in which belly dancing seems to have become, in the words of prominent member of the American belly dance community Suhaila Salimpour, a "mascot for freedom."[50] Both the liberal feminist appropriation of the dance in the 1970s as a way of celebrating the supposed universal origins of matriarchy and the contemporary iteration of the dance as a vehicle for liberating women from negative body image work to advance notions of freedom that fail to recognize, much less advocate for, a notion of freedom beyond individualism, commodification, and entrepreneurial opportunities. In other words, belly dance seems to have become a symbol of freedom insofar as it is aligned with the ideals of universal (read white, male, elite) rights, the co-optation of difference, and the championing of free trade as a greater global good. Like Copeland's suggestion that American belly dancing could function as a "healing force," in part by bringing a "new feminised" version of the dance to "Islamic cultures that could do with some female emancipation," this conception of belly dancing reconfigures it as a U.S. American product, which can be sold back to the culture(s) from which it was taken under the guise of helping those cultures become more liberated.

The suggestion of belly dancing as the mascot for a revised version of a civilizing mission skates along a thin edge of converging with U.S. political discourse about the War on Terror. The concepts of freedom and liberty, as circulated in the political rhetoric of the Bush administration, assumed an abstract idealism, presented as the grand and benevolent goal of U.S. military action in Iraq and Afghanistan. However, the freedoms actually brought to the region have been those benefiting goods, trade, and multinational corporations, rather than people. Indeed, the Bush administration measured the delivery of freedom to Iraqi people with announcements such as the one Paul Bremer gave on September 19, 2003, when he ordered the elimination of trade barriers, privatization of public services, and an open door for foreign companies to benefit from the rebuilding effort in Iraq.[51] Despite this grand, idealistic claim, as is clear from ongoing reports of death and strife, Iraqi people are hardly enjoying the rights and privileges that go along with freedom, even several years later.

Such a Janus-faced deployment of freedom is not limited to U.S. involvement in Iraq; rather it has become, in the words of David Harvey, "hegemonic as a mode of discourse . . . to the point where it has become incorporated into the common-sense way many of us interpret, live in, and understand the world."[52] The concept of freedom is here revealed to mean the freedom to co-opt exoticized cultural elements for profit; to mean the freedom to appropriate a Middle Eastern cultural dance form to perpetuate U.S. liberal feminist goals; and to mean the freedom to co-opt these same liberal feminist goals (i.e., the promise to introduce "women's rights" in Iraq and Afghanistan) to justify U.S. military action. Here, the popularity of belly dancing enables U.S. audiences to engage with the rhetoric of freedom while sublimating the painful realities of ongoing war.

In the wake of 9/11, belly dancing came to more explicitly form part of an imperialism-through-freedom discourse, which represented the events of September 11 as a symbol of shock, surprise, and rupture rather than a tragic continuation of hostilities that are coterminous with a tense political relationship between the United States and the Middle East since at least the 1970s. In the logic of imperialism-through-freedom, the Arab and Muslim world is home to a set of oppressive, fundamentalist, and irrational regimes and organizations who "hate freedom," one is led to believe, simply because they "hate our way of life." Such a tautological argument both erases the historical context out of which the events of September 11, 2001, emerged and also occludes a historicized and contextualized understanding of the concept of freedom. In the middle of the *American Bellydancer* DVD, the image of the destroyed Twin Towers of the World Trade Center in New York City is deployed in order to make an argument about the alignment of American belly dancing with freedom. Lest viewers feel concern that belly dancing would be associated with the negative press heaped on all things Middle Eastern, the World Trade Center image is followed by a reassuring statement from Suhaila Salimpour that her classes "tripled" in size immediately following 9/11. Despite the somewhat overbearing message promulgated by the producers of the DVD that American belly dancing is on the right side of freedom, the underlying capitalist lesson is hard to miss. Belly dancing as a symbol of individualistic liberation (inner freedom) and free market enterprise (the right to appropriate cultural difference for one's own capital gain) is indeed a "mascot" of freedom, whereby freedom is understood as the rhetorical device through which a late capitalist version of imperialism is deployed.

From the Bellydance Superstars to Margaret Cho's belly dance, belly dancing as a consumer product has also been used as a vehicle for achieving individualized freedom, illustrating the way in which the concepts of freedom and liberation gleam with the manufactured veneer of consumerism. Though they present themselves discursively as abstract, universalized ideals, they function within a framework of neoliberal imperialism that gives them the unmistakable glint of commodification. In the midst of a historicopolitical context that seems to have swallowed the narrative of Manichaean inevitabilities, such as good/evil, with us / against us, and terrorism/democracy, offered up by the Bush administration at the inception of the War on Terror, the very notions of freedom and liberation seem to have fallen prey to the same kind of either/or logic. They simultaneously inhabit a space of abstract idealism while functioning within the specific contexts of neoliberalism and militarism. As deployed in the commodification of belly dance in the United States, these concepts are clearly in conversation with the political realities of the U.S. relationship to the Middle East. The deafening narrative of terrorism, as an irrational, premodern, and indigenous aspect of Arab and Muslim cultures and regions, produces an inadvertent echo, demonstrated by the belly dance as liberation narrative, in which the abstracted concepts of freedom and liberation turn back on themselves to promote the freedom of goods in the midst of increasingly restrictive and limiting realities for people.

NOTES

1. Stephen John Hartnett and Laura Ann Stengrim, *Globalization and Empire: The U.S. Invasion of Iraq, Free Markets, and the Twilight of Democracy* (Tuscaloosa: University of Alabama Press, 2006), 5.

2. Anthony Shay, *Dancing Across Borders: The American Fascination with Exotic Dance Forms* (Jefferson, NC: McFarland, 2008), 128.

3. For more on this, see Ella Shohat, "Gender and the Culture of Empire," *Quarterly Review of Film and Video* 131 (Spring 1991): 1–2, republished in her *Taboo Memories, Diasporic Voices* (Durham: Duke University Press, 2006), 48–50.

4. Ibid., 141–42.

5. An example of the latter is Ruth St. Denis, whom I discuss in *Imagining Arab Womanhood* (New York: Palgrave Macmillan, 2008). See also Amy Koritz, "Dancing the Orient for England: Maud Allan's *The Vision of Salome*," in *Meaning in Motion: New Cultural Studies in Dance*, ed. Jane Desmond (Durham: Duke University Press, 1997), and Nancy Lee Ruyter, "La Meri and Middle Eastern Dance," *Belly Dance*, ed. Anthony Shay and Barbara Sellers-Young (Costa Mesa, CA: 2005), 207–20.

6. Shay, 129.

7. Barbara Sellers-Young, "Body, Image, Identity: American Tribal Belly Dance," *Belly Dance*, ed. Anthony Shay and Barbara Sellers-Young (Costa Mesa, CA: Mazda, 2005), 277–303.

8. http://www.gothicbellydance.com.

9. Edward Said, *Orientalism* (New York: Vintage, 1979), 186–87.

10. Amira Jarmakani, *Imagining Arab Womanhood* (New York: Palgrave Macmillan, 2008).

11. Ella Shohat, "American Orientalism," *Suitcase* 2, no. 1–2 (1997).

12. Robert Allen, *Horrible Prettiness* (Chapel Hill: University of North Carolina Press, 1991).

13. Lisa Appignanesi, *The Cabaret* (New Haven: Yale University Press, 2004).

14. Donna Carlton, *Looking for Little Egypt* (Bloomington, IN: IDD Books, 1994), 24; Curtis Hinsley, "The World as Marketplace: Commodification of the Exotic at the World's Columbian Exposition, Chicago 1893," *Exhibiting Cultures: The Poetics and*

Politics, ed. Ivan Karp and Steven D. Lavine (Washington, DC: Smithsonian Institution Press, 1991), 344–65.

15. Ella Shohat and Robert Stam, *Unthinking Eurocentrism: Multiculturalism and the Media* (New York: Routledge, 1994).

16. The term *oriental dance*, or the French *danse orientale*, is the preferred term of many American belly dancers, since it is a translation of the Arabic term *raqs sharqi*. The term *belly dance* likely is an English translation of the French *danse du ventre*, which was the name given the belly dance exhibitions at the 1889 (Paris) and 1893 (Chicago) World's Fairs.

17. Andrea Deagon, "Dance of the Seven Veils: The Revision of Revelation in the Oriental Dance Community," *Belly Dance*, ed. Anthony Shay and Barbara Sellers-Young (Costa Mesa, CA: Mazda, 2005), 269.

18. Najwa Adra, "Belly Dance: An Urban Folk Genre," *Belly Dance*, ed. Anthony Shay and Barbara Sellers-Young (Costa Mesa, CA: Mazda, 2005), 29.

19. Zarifa Aradoon, *Origins and Philosophy of Danse Orientale* (Stanford, CA: Dream Place Publications, 1979); Rosina-Fawzia al-Rawi, *Grandmother's Secrets: The Ancient Rituals and Healing Power of Belly Dancing*, trans. by Monique Arav (New York: Interlink, 1999).

20. Amira Jarmakani, "Belly Dancing for Liberation," *Arabs in the Americas: Interdisciplinary Essays on the Arab Diaspora*, ed. Darcy Zabel (New York: Peter Lang Press, 2006), 145–68.

21. Stephanie Smith, "Belly Dancing: Swivel Your Way to Fitness," CNN.com, June 13, 2003. www.cnn.com/2003/HEALTH/diet.fitness/06/13/bellydancing/index.html (accessed December 15, 2009).

22. Mike Camunas, "Belly Dance Workout," *St. Petersburg Times*, July 19, 2009. www.lexisnexis.com/ (accessed December 15, 2009).

23. Ibid.

24. Michele Orecklin, "Shakin' All Over," *Time*, October 20, 2002. www.time.com/time/magazine/article/0,9171,366315,00.html (accessed December 15, 2009).

25. Ibid.

26. Frank Gardner, "Belly Dancing Goes Global," *BBC News*, June 6, 2001. news.bbc.co.uk/2/low/middle_east/1373029.stm (accessed December 15, 2009).

27. Joseph Berger, "Inner Goddesses, Come Out and Dance," *New York Times*, August 3, 2008. www.lexisnexis.com/ (accessed December 15, 2009).

28. Yasmina Ramzy, "Where Is the Goddess in a Vertical Drop and a Shimmie? Or How Can the Practice of Bellydance Lead the Dancer to a State of Grace or Enlightenment?" April 1, 2009. www.gildedserpent.com/cms/2009/04/01/yasgoddessinshimmie/ (accessed December 8, 2009).

29. Yasmina Ramzy, "Feminism and Bellydance," October 19, 2009. www.gildedserpent.com/cms/2009/10/19/yasminarspeech/ (accessed December 8, 2009).

30. Donnalee Dox, "Spiritual Belly Dance," *Belly Dance: Orientalism, Transnationalism and Harem Fantasy*, ed. Anthony Shay and Barbara Sellers-Young (Costa Mesa, CA: Mazda, 2005), 310.

31. *Bellydance for Beginners with Suhaila: Fitness Fusion—4 volume gift set (Buns, Jazz, Pilates, Yoga)*, DVD. San Francisco: Cerebellum Corporation, 2005.

32. Z-Helene Christopher, "Zen, Yoga, and the Art of Belly Dance." www.zhelene.com/Zen.html (accessed December 15, 2009).

33. Narah, "Connections: Yoga and Belly Dance," www.gildedserpent.com/art46/narahyogabd.htm (accessed December 8, 2009).

34. Dox, "Spiritual Belly Dance," 317.

35. *Assassin,* produced by Paul Colichman and Eric Feldman and directed by Kerry Asmussem and Konda Mason. 90 min. Koch Vision, 2005. DVD.

36. Andrea Deagon, "Feminism and Belly Dance." www.tribalbellydance.org/articles/feminism.html (accessed December 15, 2009).

37. Andrew Billen, "My New Tool for World Domination: Riverdance . . . with Bare Midriffs," June 21, 2005. www.timesonline.co.uk/tol/life_and_style/article535451.ece. (accessed December 15, 2009).

38. Ibid.

39. See my article "Belly Dancing for Liberation" for a critique of such a notion of empowerment, which, I argue, keeps women focused on liberation from their own negative body image rather than larger patriarchal structures.

40. Guy Debord, *Society of the Spectacle* (Detroit: Black and Red, 1983), 1.

41. Ibid., 152.

42. Lisa Lowe, *Immigrant Acts* (Durham: Duke University Press, 1996), 9.

43. Debord, *Society of the Spectacle,* 167.

44. Shannon Winnubst, *Queering Freedom* (Bloomington: Indiana University Press, 2006), 9–10.

45. http://www.casbahdance.org/DANCECOMMUNITY.htm.

46. Billen, "My New Tool for World Domination."

47. Ibid.

48. Again, see "Belly Dancing for Liberation" for my development of this argument.

49. *American Bellydancer,* produced by Miles Copeland and directed by Jonathan Brandeis, 100 min. Ark 21, 2005, DVD.

50. Ibid.

51. David Harvey, *A Short History of Neoliberalism* (Cambridge: Oxford University Press, 2005), 6.

52. Ibid., 3.

EIGHT

From Arab Terrorists to Patriotic Arab Americans
Representational Strategies in Post-9/11 TV Dramas

Evelyn Alsultany

In 2004, the Council on American-Islamic Relations (CAIR) accused the TV drama *24* of perpetuating stereotypes of Arabs and Muslims.[1] CAIR objected to the persistent portrayal of Arabs and Muslims in the context of terrorism, stating that "repeated association of acts of terrorism with Islam will only serve to increase anti-Muslim prejudice."[2] CAIR's critics have retorted that programs like *24* are cutting edge, reflecting one of the most pressing social and political issues of the moment, the War on Terror. Some critics further contend that CAIR is trying to deflect the reality of Muslim terrorism by confining television writers to politically correct themes.[3]

The writers and producers of *24* have responded to CAIR's concerns in a number of ways. For one, the show often includes sympathetic portrayals of Arabs and Muslims, in which they are the "good guys" or in some way on the side of the United States. Representatives of *24* state that the show has "made a concerted effort to show ethnic, religious and political groups as multidimensional, and political issues are debated from multiple viewpoints."[4] The villains on the eight seasons of *24* are Russians, Germans, Latinos, Arabs/Muslims, Euro-Americans, Africans, and even the fictional president of the United States. Rotating the identity of the "bad guy" is one of the many strategies used by TV dramas to avoid reproducing the Arab/Muslim terrorist stereotype.[5] The show's responsiveness to such criticism even extended to creating a public service announcement (PSA) that was broadcast in February 2005, during one of the program's commercial breaks. The PSA featured the lead actor, Kiefer Sutherland, staring deadpan into the camera, reminding viewers that "the American Muslim community stands firmly beside their fellow Americans in denouncing and resisting all forms of terrorism" and urging us to "please bear that in mind" while watching the program.[6]

After September 11, 2001, a number of TV dramas were created with the War on Terror as their central theme. Dramas such as *24* (2001–2011), *Threat Matrix* (2003–4), *The Grid* (2004), *Sleeper Cell* (2005–6), and *The Wanted* (2009) depict U.S. government agencies and officials heroically working to make the nation safe by battling terrorism.[7] A prominent feature of these television shows is Arab and Muslim characters, most of whom are portrayed as grave threats to U.S. national security. But in response to increased popular awareness of ethnic stereotyping and the active monitoring of Arab and Muslim watchdog groups, television writers have had to adjust their storylines to avoid blatant, crude stereotyping.

This essay surveys the strategies writers and producers of TV dramas have utilized when representing Arab and Muslim characters and then examines the reception of some of these strategies among a few ideologically diverse film/TV critics and viewers. I create a list of representational strategies that can be identified in TV dramas in order to point to how schematized these strategies have become and also in order to discuss the ideological work performed by these representational strategies through what I am calling "simplified complex representations," the appearance of seemingly complex images that are in fact quite predictable and formulaic. Simplified complex representations are strategies used by television producers, writers, and directors to give the impression that the representations they are producing are complex. I argue that simplified complex representations are the representational mode of the so-called post-race era, signifying a new era of racial representation. These representations appear to challenge or complicate former stereotypes and contribute to a multicultural post-race illusion. Yet at the same time, most of the programs that employ these strategies promote logics that legitimate racist policies and practices.

It is important to note that some of these representational strategies appeared before September 11, when several Hollywood films contained noticeably more "complex" portrayals of Arabs and Muslims: for example, a plotline giving the terrorist character a backstory, or another including a "good" Arab in the storyline.[8] These films, produced in the late 1990s, were exceptions in a history of representing Arabs and Muslims predominantly as belly dancers, oppressed veiled women, oil sheiks, and terrorists.[9] But it was only after 9/11 that more diverse representations proliferated and became standardized. These new representational strategies seek to make the point that not all Arabs are terrorists, and not all terrorists are Arabs. But they remain wedded to a script that represents Arabs and Muslims only in the context of terrorism.

Strategy One: Inserting Patriotic Arab or Muslim Americans

Writers of television and film have increasingly created "positive" Arab and Muslim characters to show that they are sensitive to negative stereotyping. Such characters usually take the form of a patriotic Arab or Muslim American who assists the U.S. government in its fight against Arab/Muslim terrorism, either as a government agent or as a civilian. Some examples of this strategy include Mohammad "Mo" Hassain, an Arab American Muslim character who is part of the USA Homeland Security Force on the show *Threat Matrix;* Nadia Yassir, in season six of *24*, a dedicated member of the Counter Terrorist Unit;[10] and in *Sleeper Cell,* the lead African American character, Darwyn Al-Sayeed, a "good" Muslim who is an undercover FBI agent who proclaims to his colleagues that terrorists have nothing to do with his faith and cautions them not to confuse the two.[11] Islam is sometimes portrayed as inspiring U.S. patriotism rather than terrorism.[12] Despite inserting a patriotic Arab or Muslim American or a "good" Arab/Muslim as a strategy to circumvent stereotyping, the reference point for Arabs and Muslim identities remains terrorism.

Strategy Two: Sympathizing with the Plight of Arab Americans Post-9/11

Multiple stories appeared with Arab and Muslim Americans as unjust victims of post-9/11 hate crimes. The viewer is nearly always positioned to sympathize with their plight. In an episode of *24* during season four, two Arab American brothers express that they are tired of being unjustly blamed for the terrorist attacks and insist on helping to fight terrorism alongside Jack Bauer, the lead character who saves the United States from danger each season.[13] In an episode of *The Practice,* the government detains an innocent Arab American without due process or explanation and an attorney steps in to defend his rights.[14] On *7th Heaven,* Ruthie's Muslim friend, Yasmine, is harassed on her way to school, prompting the Camden family and larger neighborhood to stand together to fight discrimination.[15] This emphasis on victimization and sympathy challenges long-standing representations that

Fig. 8.1. Strategies 1 and 6, promotional photo of the cast of *24*, season 4, Fox Network. Marisol Nichols, who plays Counter Terrorism Unit agent Nadia Yasir, is pictured on the far right (strategy 1, Inserting patriotic Arab or Muslim Americans). The multicultural cast includes African American president Wayne Palmer, played by D. B. Woodside (strategy 6, Projecting a multicultural U.S. society).

have inspired a lack of sympathy and even a sense of celebration when the Arab/Muslim character is killed.

Strategy Three: Challenging the Arab/Muslim Conflation with Diverse Muslim Identities

Sleeper Cell prides itself on being unique among TV dramas that deal with the topic of terrorism because of its diverse cast of Muslim terrorists. *Sleeper Cell* challenges the common conflation of Arab and Muslim identities, but it does not challenge the ways in which religion has operated as a proxy for race or the racialization of Islam. While the ringleader of the sleeper cell, Faris al-Farik, is an Arab, the other members of this Los Angeles sleeper cell are not: they are Bosnian, French, Euro-American, Western European, and Latino; one character is a gay Iraqi-Brit. Portraying diverse sleeper cell members strategically challenges how Arab and Muslim identities are often conflated by government discourses and media representations by demonstrating that all Arabs are not Muslim, and all Muslims are not Arab, and, furthermore, that not all Arabs/Muslims are heterosexual. However, the involvement of the gay

Iraqi-British character, Salim, in terrorism stems from profound self-hatred. Terrorism and Islam are linked to a repressed sexuality, and Islam is figured as repressive in contrast to a free United States. In this "free" United States, Salim has sex with men in the men's locker room at the gym and seeks to rehabilitate himself by embracing rigid Islam and vowing to take down "the infidels." Salim reinforces what Jasbir Puar refers to as Orientalist fantasies of repressed Muslim sexuality through which properly queered subjects are produced and incorporated into contemporary forms of U.S. nationalism. Puar writes that through such discourses, "the proper modern gay or lesbian Muslim subject is foreclosed, while the terrorist is forever queer, improperly sexual" (14).[16] In other words, Salim as a queer Muslim terrorist constructs a properly queered subject in opposition: a queer American patriot who establishes homonormativity alongside heteronormativity.

In addition, the program highlights a struggle within Islam over who will define the religion, thus demonstrating that not all Muslims advocate terrorism. The TV drama represents an ideological struggle within Islam by focusing on the dynamics and debates internal to the Muslim community. This is done by contrasting Muslim characters with different positions and identities and by exploring religious debates that take place in the mosque, demonstrating that Islam is not a monolithic faith but a dynamic one. On the one hand, through representing diverse Arab and Muslim identities, Arab and Muslim identities are delinked, and an argument against racial profiling is advanced based on its ineffectiveness, since anyone could be Muslim. Furthermore, this strategy also shifts Islam from nation-based to international. On the other hand, according to *Sleeper Cell*'s tagline, not only could anyone be Muslim, but also anyone could be a terrorist—"friends, neighbors, coworkers, husbands." Terrorism, according to *Sleeper Cell,* is caused by disaffected non-Arabs who turn to fundamentalist Islam, and Arabs who embrace fundamentalist ideologies—all of whom spew nonsensical rhetoric about U.S. imperialism and the oppression of Palestinians and Iraqis. Consistent with what Mahmood Mamdani calls "culture talk"—the perspective that terrorism can be explained by examining Arab or Muslim "culture"— the notion that Muslims have a monopoly on terrorism is not challenged in the series, nor is the notion that Muslim identity is the "real" problem.[17]

Strategy Four: Flipping the Enemy

While *Sleeper Cell* fails to challenge the popular assumption that Muslims have a monopoly on terrorism, other TV dramas represent multiple terrorist identities. "Flipping the enemy" involves leading the viewer to believe that

Fig. 8.2. Strategy 3, Challenging the Arab/Muslim conflation and representing diverse Muslim identities. DVD cover of *Sleeper Cell,* Showtime, 2005.

Muslim terrorists are *obviously* plotting to destroy the United States and later revealing that the Muslim terrorists are merely pawns for Euro-American or European terrorists. The identity of the enemy is thus flipped: viewers discover that the terrorist is not Arab or Muslim, or they find that the Arab or Muslim terrorist is part of a larger network of international terrorists. On *24,* Bauer spends the first half of season two tracking down a Middle Eastern terrorist cell, ultimately subverting a nuclear attack. In the second half of the season, we discover that European and Euro-American businessmen are behind the attack, goading the United States into declaring a war on the Middle East in order to benefit from the increase in oil prices. Related to this subversion of expectations, *24* does not glorify the United States; in numer-

From Arab Terrorists to Patriotic Arab Americans / 159

Fig. 8.3. Strategy 4, Flipping the enemy. During season 5 of *24*, Gregory Itzen plays U.S. president Charles Logan who is conspiring with the terrorists. Promotional photo, Fox Network.

ous ways the show dismantles the notion that the United States is perfect and the rest of the world flawed. FBI and CIA agents are incompetent or conspiring with the terrorists. The terrorists (Arab and Muslim alike) are portrayed as very intelligent. Flipping the enemy demonstrates that terrorism is not an Arab or Muslim monopoly.

Strategy Five: Humanizing Terrorist Characters

Most Arab and Muslim terrorists in film or on television before 9/11 were stock terrorist villains, one-dimensional bad guys who were presumably bad because of their ethnic background or religious beliefs.[18] In contrast, post-9/11 terrorist characters are humanized in a variety of ways. We see them in a family context, as loving fathers and husbands; we come to learn their backstories and glimpse moments that have brought them to the precipice of terror. Season four of *24* introduced viewers to a Middle Eastern family for the first time on U.S. network television (in a recurring role for the whole season as opposed to a one-time appearance). At first, they seem like an "ordinary" family preparing breakfast—mother, father, and a teenage son. It is soon revealed, however, that they are a sleeper cell family. In the episodes that follow, each family member's relationship to terrorism is explored. The father is willing to kill his wife and son in order to complete his mission; the mother reconsiders her involvement with terrorism only to protect her son; and the teenage son, raised in the United States, cares about humanity, preventing him from being a terrorist. This strategy—humanizing the terrorists by focusing on their interpersonal relationships, motives, and backstories—is also central to *Sleeper Cell*. Each sleeper cell member has his or her own motivation for joining the cell: from rebelling against a leftist liberal parent (who is a professor at the University of California at Berkeley) to seeking revenge on the United States for the death of family members (one character's husband was killed by U.S. forces in Iraq). Adding multiple dimensions to the formerly one-dimensional bad guy has become increasingly common since 9/11.

Strategy Six: Projecting a Multicultural U.S. Society

Projecting a multicultural U.S. society is another strategy to circumvent accusations of racism while representing Arabs and Muslims as terrorists. In *Sleeper Cell*, the terrorists are of diverse ethnic backgrounds, and Darwyn, the African American FBI agent, is in an interracial relationship with a white woman. For several seasons of *24*, the U.S. president was African American, his press secretary Asian American; the Counter Terrorist Unit is equally diverse, peppered with Latinos and African Americans throughout the show's eight seasons. The sum total of the casting decisions creates the impression of a United States in which multiculturalism abounds. The projected society is one in which people of different racial backgrounds work together, and racism is socially unacceptable.

Strategy Seven: Fictionalizing the Middle Eastern or Muslim Country

It has become increasingly common for the country of the terrorist characters in the storyline to go unnamed. This strategy rests on the assumption that leaving the nationality of the villain open eliminates the potential for offensiveness; if no specific country or ethnicity is named then there is less reason for any particular group to be offended by the portrayal. In season four of *24*, the terrorist family is from an unnamed Middle Eastern country, possibly Turkey; it is, we assume, intentionally left ambiguous. In *The West Wing*, the fictional country "Qumar" is a source of terrorist plots; in season eight of *24*, it is "Kamistan." (This is also done with other ethnic groups. For example in season seven of *24*, the African country "Sangala" is an important source of terrorism.) Fictionalizing the country of the terrorist can give a show more latitude in creating salacious story lines that might be criticized if identified with an actual country. Viewers, however, are well aware that the fictionalized country is supposed to be Arab or Muslim. Fictionalizing Arab and Muslim countries adds to the conflation and generalization of Arab and Muslim identities by implying that terrorism originates from a fictional country that could be any of a number of Arab/Muslim countries. The specificity of the context becomes irrelevant. These fictionalized countries operate as allegories—standing in as doubles for the "real"—insofar as they illustrate how the sites in which the United States is waging a War on Terror (Iraq and Afghanistan) often operate as abstract or even fictional locations for viewers.

Fictional Latin America, with locations such as San Pasquale in *Commander in Chief* (2005), Tecala in *Proof of Life* (2000), and Curaguay in *The A-Team* (1983–86), has been a staple of Hollywood and mainstream television for decades. Similarly, "Fictional Arabia" is not a new representational strategy; rather it is a strategy that is making a comeback. Hollywood films have often portrayed a fictionalized Middle East. *Harum Scarum* (1965) with Elvis Presley, for example, takes place in "Abulstan" and "Lunacan." The Disney film *Aladdin* (1992) takes place in "Agrabah." It was originally going to be set in Baghdad, but because of the Gulf War, the location was changed to avoid associating this fairy tale with war. These films sought to create an imaginary fantastical and exoticized East through fictionalized locations. However, it has become common in filmmaking to portray actual locations in order to create presumably realistic depictions of current and historical events. What has changed with this representational strategy is that filmmakers conflate their methods, seeking to create "realistic" storylines in fictionalized locations.

Responding to Simplified Complex Representations

These seven representational modes I have found are not exhaustive, nor are they all new since 9/11. Rather, these strategies collectively outline some of

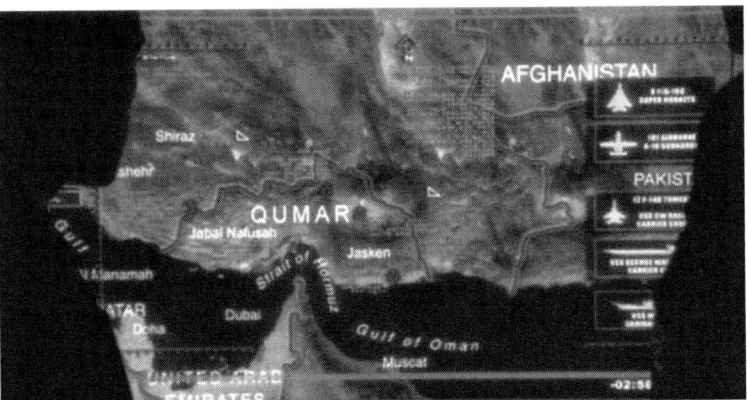

Fig. 8.4. Strategy 7: Fictionalizing the Middle Eastern or Muslim country. A map of Qumar, *The West Wing*, Season 4, NBC, 2002–3.

the ways in which writers and producers of television (and film) have sought to improve representations of Arabs (and other racial and ethnic groups). These strategies are an astounding shift in the mass entertainment landscape. They present an important departure from stereotypes into more challenging stories and characters. This new breed of terrorism programs reflects a growing sensitivity to the negative impact of stereotyping. These new representational strategies seek to make the point—indeed often with strenuous effort—that not all Arabs are terrorists and not all terrorists are Arabs. However, more diverse representations do not in themselves solve the problem of stereotyping. As Ella Shohat, Robert Stam, Herman Gray, and other media studies scholars have shown, focusing on whether or not a particular image is good or bad does not necessarily address the complexity of representation.[19] Rather, it is important to examine the ideological work performed by images and storylines. What ideological work do these representational strategies perform? And to what extent do these representational strategies influence viewer responses to these TV dramas?

The range of critiques offered by film and television critics tends to fall along ideological lines. Yet, surprisingly, the differentiation is not that drastic. Taking *Sleeper Cell* as a case study of viewer responses, we find that political conservatives, or those on the right, tend toward harsh criticism of these representational strategies claiming that they prioritize political correctness over an accurate portrayal of the very real Arab/Muslim threat to U.S. national security. Political liberals, or those on the left, tend to acknowledge *Sleeper Cell*'s attempt to offer alternative representations of Muslims but nevertheless criticize it for being pedantic. Both sets of responses demonstrate the limited impact of these representational strategies and how—despite their efforts at complexity—they devolve toward a problematic simplicity.

Conservative writer Dorothy Rabinowitz, in her review of *Sleeper Cell* for the *Wall Street Journal,* states:

> SHOWTIME'S "Sleeper Cell" won't make viewers particularly happy, its intention being, evidently, to teach rather than to delight—a worthy enterprise in this case, and one, it turns out that's also highly compelling most of the time. The 10-part series . . . is clearly meant to represent varying aspects of Muslim society—in particular attitudes towards terrorism. A huge order, that, with a didactic streak more than a little evident in this story of a sleeper cell penetrated by Darwyn (Michael Ealy), an FBI agent and devout black American Muslim—the voice here of Muslims opposed to Islamic extremists.
>
> Its strains and balancing efforts aside, it is soon obvious that there's much in this story about the day-to-day planning and training for a terror strike that should enthrall—and chill—audiences.[20]

Rabinowitz describes *Sleeper Cell*'s teaching mission and its intention to give voice to "Muslim opposed to Islamic extremists" as efforts that will not please viewers. What will please viewers, she goes on to say, are the parts of the show that portray views that "are common in numerous quarters of the radical Islamic world"—in other words, its portrayal of the Muslim threat to U.S. national security.

Film critic and conservative political commentator Michael Medved writes for FOX News: "The problem, it seems to me, in a lot of these new films, is not that they humanized terrorists, that's good dramatically, the problem is that they're sympathetic to terrorists, that they erase the distinction between terrorists and those who are fighting terrorism and that's a terrible thing."[21] Medved is concerned that these post-9/11 representational strategies run the risk of encouraging viewers to sympathize with the terrorists. Medved contends that there is a moral difference between those who kill innocent people and those who kill the killers of innocent people and states that should be accurately reflected in films, revealing his investments in narratives of U.S. exceptionalism. Many right-wing film/TV critics tend to criticize writers and producers of film and television who have utilized these strategies for being overly concerned with political correctness at the expense of confusing the "good" and "bad" guys.

The criticism of liberal writers tends to focus on how the educational thrust of *Sleeper Cell* compromises its entertainment quality. A reviewer for *The Village Voice,* Joy Press, writes:

> Sleeper Cell moves way too slowly to get anyone's pulse racing—except maybe the Arab American community, which will almost certainly protest, despite the writers' awkward attempts to give equal screen time to "good" and "bad" Muslims.... Not only does Sleeper Cell fan free-form paranoia about Arabs, foreigners, and loners (hey, maybe that next-door neighbor with the funny accent is a terrorist after all!), but it plants the idea that the people meant to be protecting us from amorphous terror might be as inept as Inspector Clouseau—or even former FEMA chief Michael Brown. What could be scarier than that?[22]

This reviewer conflates Arabs and Muslims, despite *Sleeper Cell*'s efforts to challenge the Arab/Muslim conflation, and criticizes the TV drama for fueling the public's fears about sleeper cells and inept government officials. While conservative perspectives tend to praise TV dramas such as *Sleeper Cell* for instilling fear in the U.S. public (though they are critical of portrayals of the U.S. government as inept), liberal perspectives tend to be critical of fearmongering.

The show's attempt to challenge the Arab/Muslim/Sikh conflation does not go unnoticed by Gillian Flynn, though she finds plenty of other faults with the show. She writes for *Entertainment Weekly*:

> Strange that only four years after we were forced to add phrases like sleeper cell to our vocabulary so much of a series about terrorists on American soil can feel cliché. Showtime's nine-part *Sleeper Cell*, about a small group of Muslim extremists and the undercover agent who's infiltrated their band, has every feature that every movie involving post-9/11 terrorism seems to deem essential. The optimistically named agent Darwyn al-Sayeed (Michael Ealy) is himself a Muslim, leading to the obligatory declaration that the extremists are distorting the word of the Koran. "These guys have nothing to do with my faith," he proclaims. At various points, the terrorists decry football and American arrogance, a trait highlighted in one scene in which some frat types harass a Sikh, mistaking him for an Arab, and allowing Mr. Survival of the Fittest to explain to them-and-us-the differences between the cultures. These are all certainly important points, but Sleeper makes them artlessly—yet with a confounding confidence that it's teaching us something new.... We know it, we've heard it, find a slicker approach.[23]

Some liberal television critics, in other words, claim that the pedantic quality of these representational strategies compromises the entertainment value.

John Leonard writes for *New York* magazine, "*Sleeper Cell* tries laudably to entertain us and to complicate us simultaneously. But we also experience the Stockholm syndrome in reverse. The more time we spend with these people, the less we care about them."[24] And Joan Juliet Buck writes for *Vogue*, "The earnest realism of *Sleeper Cell* adds up to an exploitative and inept piece of garbage."[25]

In contrast to television critics who acknowledge and criticize these representational strategies, many viewer posts on the Internet tend to praise *Sleeper Cell* for educating the public—not on the diversity of Muslims but on the ongoing Arab/Muslim terrorist threat to national security. Not surprisingly, there are a wide array of viewer responses on Internet forums devoted to television shows. Some (e.g., tampafilmfan.com) are run by individuals, and others (e.g., tvsquad.com) are run by corporations, such as AOL or News Corporation. These websites allow everyone and anyone to be a critic and to anonymously "talk back"—consistent with the new culture of viewer feedback initiated by major networks, such as CNN, that has shifted its news format to invite and include viewer perspectives. Some viewer posts focus on whether *24* or *Sleeper Cell* is more entertaining, others discuss the "hotness" of the actors; still others say what they would like to see happen in the storyline—who will fall in love, who will be avenged, and so on. My focus here is on a particular strain of responses—those that focus on the realism of the show and reflect a collapsed distinction between television and politics. Unlike responses from film and television critics, viewer posts to the Internet represent an unstable archive, as they are often anonymous and the source cannot be verified. Nonetheless, they provide a partial view of responses to these TV dramas. These online postings are fragments of larger sentiments, operating like eavesdropping on conversations for which the larger context is absent. Nonetheless, I examine a sampling of online forums devoted to *Sleeper Cell* as cultural texts that provides a glimpse into how TV dramas that standardize these representational strategies were received by viewers.

A recurring theme in viewer comments is *Sleeper Cell*'s realism, its presumed "realistic" portrayal of the War on Terror and the Muslim threat to U.S. national security. One viewer, Mike Rankin, writes:

> I loved it for being fearlessly honest when it comes to the true face of our real enemies—not turning them into generic, PC comicbook [*sic*] versions of themselves. . . . Unlike most political thrillers from Hollywood, the bad guys didn't turn out to be the American military or the military-industrial complex or the oil companies or our own corrupt politicians. The enemy was the enemy, from start to finish—Islamic extremists who would be happy to see our entire civilization turned to dust.[26]

Rankin is discussing the "flipping the enemy" strategy and is indirectly critiquing *24* (and a smattering of Hollywood films) for portraying Americans as complicit in terrorism. He articulates a preference for *Sleeper Cell* over other TV dramas because Muslims are the sole enemy; no others are implicated along the way; no one else in order to diffuse the potency of an Arab/Muslim threat. This post reflects how TV dramas can be used to make claims to "truth" and "realness"—and how viewers can use them to confirm their own suspicions about what is real. The emphasis here is not on an appreciation for representing diverse Muslims but rather on educating the public on the War on Terror and Arab/Muslim terrorist threat. This viewer seeks programming that affirms an "us" and a "them" and appreciates a drama that reinscribes conceptions of the domestic and foreign wherein the foreign is signified as a threat.

Similar commentary is made by a poster who identifies himself as a military officer:

> I am an NCO in the United States Army. After four over seas tours in the last four and a half years I was beginning to get a little tired of my job. Then *Sleeper Cell* fell into my lap. It truly reminded me why I do what I do every day. I Sit and watch the tv and hear all the negative stuff the media puts out and I get very discouraged. I am out here everyday watching along with my brothers and sisters in arms as we rebuild a torn country. I see us out there working with the MUSLIM society giving entire cities electricity for the first time ever, giving school supplies and clothing to kids, watching as grown Iraqi men break down and cry because we put a new roof on his adobe house and many other things that never make the news. I know this is a fictional story but it is so real to life that it made me get right back in the fight and remember why I am over here doing what I do. I beg Showtime to continue this show if for nothing else but to make America aware of the real terror that faces our blessed nation. Plus it make for one hell of a pass time. BRING THE SHOW BACK SHOWTIME!!! SGT SIEBRASSE BALAD IRAQ[27] [sic]

The military officer acknowledges that *Sleeper Cell* is fictional yet insists that it is realistic to the extent that it inspires him to continue participating in the War on Terror. Drawing on dominant discourses from the Bush administration, Sergeant Siebrasse articulates the benevolent role of the United States during the War on Terror. According to him, "the Muslim" is either a terrorist or a victim in need of rescue by the United States.

Other viewers have also emphasized the realism of this educational drama on the War on Terror and expressed disappointment that the show was not renewed for a third season.

> I am so upset that they have totally taken off *Sleeper Cell*. . . . We should fight for this show to be put back on, it is the world we live in today with these sleeper cells living among us they would just soon chop our heads off. These are doctors, teachers, nanny's so this show is so important to know the knowledge of these TERRORIST living among us and our children. So for them to take off a show full of info. is down right stupid. Instead they want to put on filth, yea don't educate us any on the TERRORIST who want us all dead.[28] [*sic*]

This Internet poster, Isebella, discusses *Sleeper Cell* as if there is no distinction between the show and the War on Terror itself. The people she refers to as terrorists living among us, nannies and teachers, are the covers of two of the show's characters. TV dramas about the War on Terror often come to stand in for non-fictional accounts of the War on Terror.

Surprisingly, many post-9/11 TV dramas with the War on Terror as their central theme did not succeed past a season or two, and some did not last longer than a few episodes. Why did they fail to capture audiences given the ripped-from-the-headlines relevance of these plots and ability to capitalize on post-9/11 fear? *The Wanted*, meant to be a documentary version of *24*, with CIA agents investigating and combating terrorism, lasted for only two episodes. It was attacked by TV critics for promoting questionable journalistic standards and by viewers for being contrived, empty propaganda. In contrast, *Sleeper Cell* was often criticized for being preachy and for trying to teach rather than entertain.[29] The only show that succeeded for multiple seasons was *24*; it was applauded for the ticking time bomb scenario that defines the show and keeps viewers on the edge of their seats. One of the keys to its success, at least as evidenced by the fan forums, is an apparent absence of pedagogy. It seems that viewers and critics alike criticize shows with an educational thrust. However, the "education" that is the focus of criticism is the diverse portrayals of Arab and Muslim identities, as opposed to the presumed "education" on the "reality" of the Arab/Muslim threat.

Some viewers reject the paranoid message of *Sleeper Cell*. One viewer, "Trent B.," fed up with fearmongering, posted the following to metacritic. com (a division of CBS Interactive).

> More mindless neocon propaganda vomited onto our screens. This country is going to collapse into a police state if people are actually believing this garbage. Fellow citizens, start questioning your govern-

ment for God's sake! They're taking away our liberties and expanding federal police control over states and cities. Terrorists don't have any power over us—in fact they have less power to threaten us than street criminals. It's all a facade, and the Feds are using it to grab more control over our lives.[30]

Not all Internet posters accept *Sleeper Cell*'s message about an impending terrorist attack; not all accept its claims to realism. Some explicitly reject the message about the perpetual threat of terrorism and criticize TV dramas for capitalizing on post-9/11 fear needed to support the U.S. government's War on Terror. Nonetheless, the vast majority of posts engage in the TV drama as a stand-in for the actual War on Terror.

One poster's comments elide the War on Terror and the 1995 Oklahoma City bombing perpetrated by Timothy McVeigh and Terry Nichols.

> Having lived in OKC at the time of the Murrah bombing and being a federal government employee, I have an intense interest in terrorism issues. I believe the time will come when the world will finally understand that the OKC bombing was conducted by middle-eastern terrorists using sleeper cells to accomplish the mission while employing "lily white" accomplices, Tim McVeigh and Terry Nichols. There was so much covered up by the FBI, and ordered by higher government officials. Records have been destroyed and evidence has been withheld.[31] [*sic*]

For this viewer, Sue Barnham, *Sleeper Cell* is not only a lens through which to understand the War on Terror but also a lens through which to reevaluate earlier instances of terrorism. Comments from TV critics on the right and from many viewer posts reflect an investment in protecting the domestic from a foreign threat. This particular Internet poster "flips the enemy" in reverse: rather than revealing that there are white accomplices to Arab/Muslim terrorism, she asserts that there are Middle Eastern terrorists behind the Oklahoma City bombing. This poster insists on the unique connection between terrorism and Arab and Muslim identities.

Television critics also comment on the realism of the show and participate in blurring the boundaries between the War on Terror waged by the U.S. government and its representations on fictional dramatic television. Dan Iverson writes for IGN Entertainment (a division of News Corporation) that *Sleeper Cell*

> never sides with the radical Muslims, and it never makes you feel like what they are doing is justified, but what it does is gives you a

window into their culture and the terrorists' perversion of their religion in order to see what would drive people to do what they are doing. For this reason alone, *Sleeper Cell* should have a larger American audience—as we are waging war with this same enemy, and yet we know nothing about them or the religion that fuels their hatred for us. If more television programs were to responsibly give this type of attention to their radical fundamentalist enemies we might not be so ignorant of current events.[32]

Like many posters, Iverson laments the perceived "ignorance" of his fellow Americans. The pessimistic vision of his country, however, is less startling than the faith he has in fictional television: equivalent to news education, bettering our understanding of an entire religion and group of people.

Comments in Internet forums devoted to TV dramas tend to slide between discussing the TV drama and discussing the War on Terror, or terrorism more broadly. Film critic Michael Medved need not be concerned that humanizing the terrorists will make viewers sympathize with them. Despite the range of representational strategies identified above, viewer responses suggest that for most the dominant message remains the same: the United States is at war against terrorism because Arabs and Muslims are a threat.

Reliving the War on Terror

There is a tension between writers' and producers' intentions, on the one hand, and critics' and viewers' responses, on the other. Writers and producers create multiple representational strategies to circumvent accusations of racism and to maintain the largest viewership possible. Yet, most critics dismiss such strategies for being too politically correct, preachy, or artless, and many viewers take away the message that Arabs/Muslims are a threat to U.S. national security despite the multiple representational strategies that would seem to counter that hypothesis. Despite efforts to convey that all Arabs and Muslims are not terrorists, viewer and critic responses demonstrate that the impact of these representational strategies is limited. Viewers do not comment on how they have come to understand the diversity of Arab and Muslim identities. Ultimately, these representational strategies pay lip service to racism. For all their innovations, these programs remain wedded to a script that represents Arabs and Muslims only in the context of terrorism and therefore do not effectively challenge the stereotypical representations of Arabs and Muslims.

Stuart Hall has claimed that even liberal writers and producers of media with the best of intentions who seek to subvert racial hierarchies may inadvertently participate in inferential racism, that is "apparently naturalized representations of events and situations relating to race, whether 'factual' or 'fictional,' which have racist premises and propositions inscribed in them as a set of unquestioned assumptions."[33] The persistent unquestioned assumption in these TV dramas is that Arabs and Muslims are terrorists, despite efforts to create a wider range of Arab and Muslim characters. Efforts to create complex characters and storylines are in fact quite simple in that they are predictable, what I call "simplified complex representations." Simplified complex representations refers to representational strategies that produce the illusion of complexity and sensitivity while continuing to perpetuate stereotypes. It refers to how attempts to make representations complex are simplified, to the predictable strategies that will be used if the plot involves an Arab or Muslim terrorist, and to a new standard alternative to the stock ethnic villains of the past.

The primary objective of commercial television networks is not education, social justice, or social change. Rather, the goal is financial, to keep as many viewers watching for as long as possible. Television must therefore strike a balance between keeping its products as engaging as possible and not offending potential viewers. Writers thus seem to be constrained and influenced by two factors: viewers have been primed to assume that Arabs/Muslims are terrorists, and therefore writers create what viewers expect and what will sell; at the same time, some viewers are particularly sensitive and fed up with stereotypes, and therefore writers must create a more diverse world of characters. The results are some modifications to avoid being offensive while perpetuating core stereotypes that continue to have cultural capital.[34] Post-9/11 television is testimony to the fact that the stereotypes that held sway for much of the twentieth century are no longer socially acceptable—at least in their most blatant forms. But this does not mean that such stereotypes (and viewers' taste for them) have actually gone away; they have only become covert. Simplified complex representational strategies reflect the commodification of the civil rights and multiculturalist movements. The commodification of multiculturalism, while reflecting the sensibilities of some viewers, is submerged under the more prominent consumable message that Arabs and Muslims pose a threat to American life and freedom.

Under the guise of complexity, these representational strategies construct a binary between "good" and "bad" Arabs and Muslims, reinforcing a narrow conception of what constitutes a "good" Arab or Muslim. As Mamdani has written, the public debate post-9/11 has involved a discourse about "good" and "bad" Muslims, and all Muslims are assumed to be bad until they perform and prove their allegiance to the U.S. nation.[35] In TV dramas, we see this framework playing out through defining "bad" Arabs or Muslims as the terrorists and "good" Arabs or Muslims as those helping the U.S. government fight terrorism. Despite the shift away from the more blatant stereotypes of previous decades, Arab and Muslim identities are still understood and evaluated primarily in relation to terrorism. This context overpowers the strategies. Representations of Arab and Muslim identities in contexts that have nothing to do with terrorism remain strikingly unusual in the U.S. commercial media.[36] Arab and Muslim identities are rehabilitated as legitimate through rigid notions of either patriotism or victimization.

I agree with Herman Gray who has argued that representations of the black middle-class family (*The Jeffersons* [1975–85], *The Cosby Show* [1984–92], *Moesha* [1996–2001], *The Bernie Mac Show* [2001–6], etc.) have contributed to the illusion of racial equality in the United States.[37] Gray acknowledges *The Cosby Show* for successfully recoding blackness away from images of the welfare queen and drug dealer. He simultaneously notes that it participated in rearticulating a new and more enlightened form of racism and contributed to an illusion of "feel-good multiculturalism and racial cooperation" (449).[38] Similarly, I am arguing that these strategies used in representing Arab and Muslim Americans after 9/11 create a postrace illusion that can absolve viewers from confronting the persistence of institutionalized racism. Furthermore, I am arguing that modes of vilifying "the enemy" during national crisis have changed. Whereas in the past, it was common to vilify an entire people during times of national crisis, the current representational mode involves simultaneously vilifying and affirming the identity of the perceived enemy as a sign of U.S. progress during times of crisis. This new representational mode characterizes the so-called postrace era.

Inserting a patriotic Arab or Muslim American or fictionalizing Middle Eastern countries are ineffectual devices if Arab and Muslim identities continue to be portrayed through a narrow lens of "good" or "bad" in the fight against terrorism. Casting actors of color to give the impression of a postrace society propagates the comforting notion of an enlightened society that has resolved all of its racial problems. While these representational strategies that challenge the stereotyping of Arabs and Muslims were being broadcast, circulated, and consumed, real Arabs and Muslims were being detained, deported, held without due process, and tortured. Certainly not all Arabs and Muslims were subject to post-9/11 harassment. Nonetheless, what I am arguing is that simplified complex representations—a new representational mode collectively constructed by these multiple representational strategies—perform the ideological work of producing a postrace moment in which denying the severity of the persistence of institutionalized racism becomes possible. These TV dramas produce reassurance that racial sensitivity is the norm in U.S. society while simultaneously perpetuating the dominant perception of Arabs and Muslims as threats to U.S. national security.

The television landscape shifted on 9/11 as the Arab/Muslim threat to U.S. national security took center stage. The storylines in TV dramas, such as *24* and *Sleeper Cell*, reinforce the government's need for a War on Terror; these shows have, in numerous guises, replayed the tragedy of 9/11 weekly to U.S. audiences, keeping the trauma fresh in the collective memory. These cultural productions, despite employing a range of strategies to avoid reproducing stereotypes, offer a very specific story that keeps viewer-citizens living and reliving the War on Terror. As Willis writes:

> America lives its history as a cultural production. The post-9/11 era, as one defined by individual uncertainty in the face of an over-certain but often mistaken and repressive state, has seen a tremendous burgeoning of cultural forms meant to explain and manage the crisis. Daily life in America is articulated across an array of competing popular fictions.[39]

TV dramas are cultural forms that participate in explaining and managing the War on Terror. There is a fundamental contradiction between representational strategies that project an enlightened, postracial culture yet maintain the relevance of the threat. So long as Arabs and Muslims are represented primarily in the context of terrorism, our current crop of representational strategies—for all their apparent innovations—will have a minimal impact on viewers' perceptions of Arabs and Muslims and, far worse, will perpetuate a simplistic vision of good and evil under the guise of complexity and sensitivity.

What is most strongly conveyed by these post-9/11 TV dramas is that Arabs and Muslims pose a threat to U.S. peace and security. The articulated fear, similar to that during the Cold War, is that the enemy is among "us," so that we must live in a state of constant fear and vigilance. According to Douglas L. Howard, "For all we know, our neighborhoods, our businesses, and our highways have been or are being targeted even as we speak, but we are (and we must feel) powerless to protect ourselves from what we cannot see and what we do not know. . . . *24*, in all its violent glory, makes us believe that, if the terrorists are out here, something, everything, in fact, is being done to stop them and to keep us safe."[40] Above all, what is depicted though these TV dramas is a nation in perpetual danger. Audiences relive the War on Terror and the Arab/Muslim threat despite a few good Arabs or Muslims appearing in the storyline. As Melani McAlister has written, "The continuing sense of threat provides support for the power of the state, but it also provides the groundwork for securing 'the nation' as a cultural and social entity. The 'imagined community' of the nation finds continuing rearticulation in the rhetoric of danger."[41] A moment of "crisis" is used to cast Arabs, Arab Americans, Muslims, and Muslim Americans as threats to the nation. Arabs and Muslims become the contemporary racialized enemy through which the nation defines its identity and legitimates the abuse of state power. However, at this historical moment, this is accomplished not through demonizing an entire people but rather through projecting seemingly nuanced representations of Arabs and Muslims, sympathy for the unjust treatment of Arab and Muslim Americans post-9/11, and a diverse and inclusive U.S. society.

NOTES

This essay is an excerpt from Evelyn Alsultany, *Arabs and Muslims in the Media: Race and Representation after 9/11* (New York: New York University Press, 2012).

1. "Fox TV Accused of Stereotyping American Muslims," Reuters, January 13, 2005. http://www.freerepublic.com/focus/f-news/1320357/posts (accessed April 28, 2012).

2. "24" Under Fire from Muslim Groups, *BBC News*, January 19, 2007. http://news.bbc.co.uk/2/hi/entertainment/6280315.stm (accessed April 28, 2012). CAIR has also created an advertising campaign to counteract negative stereotypes. For an analysis of their ad campaign, see Evelyn Alsultany, "Selling American Diversity and Muslim American Identity through Non-Profit Advertising Post-9/11," *American Quarterly* 59, no. 3 (September 2007): 593–622.

3. Critics of CAIR include www.jihadwatch.org and www.frontpagemag.com.

4. "24 comes under Muslim fire," *Northern Territory News* (Australia), January 29, 2007, 23.

5. I use *Arab/Muslim* not to denote that these identities are one and the same, but rather to point to how Arab and Muslim identities are portrayed as conflated.

6. In the public service announcement, Kiefer Sutherland states: "Hi. My name is Kiefer Sutherland and I play counter-terrorist agent Jack Bauer on Fox's *24*. I would like to take a moment to talk to you about something that I think is very important. Now, while terrorism is obviously one of the most critical challenges facing our nation and the world, it is important to recognize that the American Muslim community stands firmly beside their fellow Americans in denouncing and resisting all forms of terrorism. So in watching *24*, please, bear that in mind." Broadcast on FOX on Monday, February 7, 2005.

7. *24*, FOX, Nov. 2001–2010; *Threat Matrix*, ABC, Sept. 2003–Jan. 2004; *The Grid*, TNT, July–August 2004; *Sleeper Cell*, Showtime, Dec. 2005–Dec. 2006; and *The Wanted*, NBC, July 2009.

8. I am referring to *The Siege* (1998) and *Three Kings* (1999).

9. For a history of Arab stereotypes, see Jack G. Shaheen, *Reel Bad Arabs: How Hollywood Vilifies a People* (Northampton, MA: Interlink Publishing Group, 2001).

10. *Threat Matrix*, ABC, September 18, 2003–January 29, 2004; *24*, Season 6, FOX. January 14–May 21, 2007.

11. *Sleeper Cell*, Season 1, Episode 1, "Al-Fatiha," Showtime, December 4, 2005.

12. Waleed Mahdi argues that Islam is portrayed as inspiring U.S. patriotism in Hollywood films post-9/11, for example in the film *Traitor* (2008). Waleed Mahdi, "US vs. Arab/Muslim Trauma Unpacked: An Analysis of the Challenging Mode of Depiction in *Traitor*," paper presented at the Middle East Studies Association Conference, 2009.

13. *24*, Season 4, FOX, March 14, 2005.

14. "Inter Arma Silent Leges." *The Practice*. Season 6, Episode 9. ABC. December 9, 2001. For an analysis of this episode and representations of Arab Americans as victims of post-9/11 hate crimes on TV dramas, see Evelyn Alsultany, "The Primetime Plight of Arab-Muslim-Americans after 9/11: Configurations of Race and Nation in TV Dramas," *Race and Arab Americans Before and After September 11th: From Invisible Citizens to Visible Subjects*, ed. Nadine Naber and Amaney Jamal (Syracuse: Syracuse University Press: 2007), 204–28.

15. "Suspicion." *7th Heaven*. Season 6, Episode 12. WB. January 21, 2002.

16. Jasbir Puar, *Terrorist Assemblages: Homonationalism in Queer Times* (Durham: Duke University Press, 2007).

17. See Mahmood Mamdani, *Good Muslim, Bad Muslim: America, the Cold War, and the Roots of Terror* (New York: Pantheon Books, 2004).

18. See Jack G. Shaheen, *Reel Bad Arabs: How Hollywood Vilifies a People*. (Northampton, MA: Interlink Publishing Group, 2001).

19. See Ella Shohat and Robert Stam, *Unthinking Eurocentrism: Multiculturalism and the Media* (New York: Routledge, 1994), and Herman Gray, *Watching Race: Television and the Struggle for Blackness* (Minneapolis: University of Minnesota Press, 1995).

20. Dorothy Rabinowitz in the *Wall Street Journal*, December 2, 2005, W.8.

21. "Tickets to Terror," *FOX*, January 4, 2006.

22. Joy Press, "There Goes the Neighborhood: A Suburban Miniseries Drops in on the Terrorists Next Door," *Village Voice*, November 21, 2005. http://www.villagevoice.com/screens/0547,tv1,70218,28.html (accessed April 28, 2012).

23. Gillian Flynn, *Entertainment Weekly*, no. 852 (December 2, 2005): 67.

24. John Leonard, *New York* 38, no. 43 (December 5, 2005): 90.

25. Joan Juliet Buck, *Vogue* 195, no.12 (December 2005): 254.

26. Comment by Mike Rankin, March 25, 2007, Tampa Film Fan Blog, http://tampafilmfan.com/blog/2007/03/23/tv-miniseries-reviewsleeper-cellamerican-terror/ (accessed January 11, 2008).

27. Comment by SGT SIEBRASSSE—August 7, 2007, http://tampafilmfan.com/blog/2007/03/23/tv-miniseries-reviewsleeper-cellamerican-terror/ (accessed January 11, 2008).

28. Comment by Isebella—November 4, 2007. http://tampafilmfan.com/blog/2007/03/23/tv-miniseries-reviewsleeper-cellamerican-terror/ (accessed January 11, 2008).

29. For commentary on *The Wanted*, see David Zurawik, "The Wanted: NBC News Show an Embarrassment," *Baltimore Sun blog*, July 21, 2009, http://weblogs.baltimoresun.com/entertainment/zontv/2009/07/the_wanted_nbc_news_terrorism.html; Brian Lowry, "The Wanted," *Variety*, July 20, 2009, http://www.variety.com/review/VE1117940697.html?categoryid=32&cs=1; and viewer comments on The Internet Movie Database, http://www.imdb.com/title/tt1468817/usercomments (accessed March 12, 2010).

30. http://www.metacritic.com/tv/shows/sleepercell (April 28, 2012).

31. Comment by Sue Barnham—December 31, 2006. http://www.tvsquad.com/2006/12/13/sleeper-cell-faith/ (accessed April 28, 2012).

32. Dan Iverson, "Sleeper Cell: American Terror Review," January 26, 2007. http://tv.ign.com/articles/758/758753p1.html (accessed April 28, 2012).

33. Stuart Hall, "Racist Ideologies and the Media," *Media Studies: A Reader,* 2nd ed., Paul Marris and Sue Thornham, eds. (New York: NYU Press, 2000), 273.

34. My use of "cultural capital" comes from Pierre Bourdieu, *The Field of Cultural Production* (New York: Columbia University Press, 1993).

35. Mahmood Mamdani, *Good Muslim, Bad Muslim.*

36. Even recent films with positive representation of Arabs and Muslim characters, such as *The Visitor* (2007) and *Sorry, Haters* (2005) are framed in the context of 9/11. *Little Mosque on the Prairie* (2007–2012), a sitcom on the Canadian Broadcasting Corporation, has not crossed over into the United States.

37. For more on media representations of African Americans, see, for example, Herman Gray, *Watching Race;* Christine Acham, *Revolution Televised: Prime Time and the Struggle for Black Power* (Minneapolis: University of Minnesota Press, 2004); and Darnell M. Hunt, *Channeling Blackness: Studies on Television and Race in America* (New York: Oxford University Press, 2004). Also see Donald Bogle, *Coons, Mulattoes, Mammies and Bucks: An Interpretive History of Blacks in American Films* (New York: Continuum International Publishing Group, 1994).

38. Herman Gray, "The Politics of Representation on Network Television," in *Media and Cultural Studies: Keyworks,* ed. Meenakshi Gigi Durham and Douglas Kellner (Oxford: Blackwell Publishers, 2001), 439–61.

39. Susan Willis, *Portents of the Real: A Primer for Post-9/11 America* (New York: Verso, 2005), 4–5.

40. Douglas L. Howard, "'You're Going to Tell Me Everything You Know:' Torture and Morality in FOX's 24," in *Reading 24: TV Against the Clock,* ed. Steven Peacock (New York: I. B. Tauris, 2007), 142.

41. Melani McAlister, *Epic Encounters: Culture, Media, and U.S. Interests in the Middle East, 1945–2000* (Berkeley: University of California Press, 2001), 6.

NINE

When Pakistanis Became Middle Eastern
Visualizing Racial Targets in the Global War on Terror

Junaid Rana

This essay examines the incorporation of Muslim identities into the U.S. racial formation through the recent War on Terror campaign that has collapsed the boundaries of race, culture, and religion. The history of these categories of race-making are particularly vexing in the case of U.S. populations of Middle Eastern and South Asian descent, broadly racialized as "Muslims." Used by the media, academics, and activists, the unwieldy categories of "Muslim," "Arab," and "South Asian" are collapsed to describe populations targeted for racial discrimination, violent hate crimes, and state policing. Although there is a slow awareness emerging of the differences in these categories, the process of merging them into the racialized figure of the Muslim is far more prevalent. As an example of this making of a Muslim racial formation in the United States, I argue that Pakistani migrants are simultaneously understood through the geographies of South Asia and the Middle East in the rubrics of U.S. popular culture that construct Muslims as Arabs and desis in a contiguous spatial and imagined history.

Pakistanis in the United States, like many immigrants of the post-1965 wave, are a transnational population[1] with a particular socioeconomic makeup and history. The visible demographic of South Asians in the United States, most of which are Indian in origin, are the professional, educated classes drawn to the service economy of the United States after the 1965 shift in immigration law that specifically sought to generate this type of technically skilled migration, referred to as "brain drain." With family reunification in the 1990s, this largely middle-class population began to dramatically shift in character to include the lower middle class and working classes.² In the case of Pakistan, gender roles, differences in education, and access to resources meant that working-class migrations were initially largely male. Starting in the 1980s many of these working-class men eventually obtained sponsorship for their extended families or practiced the recent variant of maintaining a transnational family through seasonal migration. In this latter kinship arrangement families are divided between home and host country, and sometimes scattered in multiple countries, in which transnational migrants work for extended periods of time and return to their nuclear families during vacations or seasonal intervals.

Although the Pakistani immigrant population in the United States is generally understood as originating in South Asia, from the perspective of religious and social identity they are considered to be from the Muslim world. In the North American vernacular the category "Middle East" spans from North Africa across to West Asia. Pakistan, although historically and culturally closely tied to South Asia as part of the Indian subcontinent, is often viewed as part of a larger Muslim world that is conflated with the Middle East. That the Middle East is most often synonymous with countries identified as ethnically Arab has not effectively prevented the slippage of Pakistan into the geographic category of the Middle East. As a conflict region, the Middle East is constructed on one end through the uncertain fate of Palestine and extends as far as Central and South Asia. In the recent framing of the Central Asian countries in the post–Cold War era, and the recurring shadow of the colonial Great Game, the geopolitical importance of the oil- and gas-rich terrains of these former Soviet republics overlaps with the notorious juggernaut of Afghanistan.³ At the other end of this expanded region is the porous border shared between Afghanistan and Pakistan that serves as the front line for the global War on Terror against the nebulous, nonnational, stateless political movements of Al Qaeda and the Taliban.⁴

As terms of comparison, desi, Arab, and Muslim are important elements constitutive of a post-9/11 Muslim racial formation. Although these terms have their own histories and particular valences, the populations they refer to are often conflated in popular culture to connote particular meanings attached to notions of terrorism and immigration—rationales that are placed within the context of post-9/11 explanations of global conflict and violence. As a fictional interpretation of the racialized Muslim that flourishes in the production houses of Hollywood and across the globe, one version of this explanatory narrative posits that the global economy and historical circumstances have victimized working-class labor migrants into anti-American terrorism, while more disturbing variants blame multiculturalism, upward mobility, and the access to resources for immigrants. Such popular culture narratives are based on assumptions mired in the confines of U.S. empire and the claims to a twenty-first-century benevolent imperialism. Following the colonial dictum of the white man's burden, these narratives are rearticulated to impose a sexual economy that claims white men must save Muslim women from Muslim men.[5] In the context of the War on Terror, Muslim women are cast as burqa-clad, isolated, and suffering the violent patriarchy of Islam, who must rely on colonial narratives of rescue.[6]

Representing Targets: Imagining the Racialized Muslim

The incorporation of the figure of the Muslim into the U.S. racial formation involves hierarchies and assumptions of a domestic racial order that proliferates in global and transnational formations. To imagine this multiracial figure of the Muslim, the concept of race and its cloaked relation to Islam is summoned in relation to the racial legacy of U.S. nation statecraft that places subjugation and conquest at the heart of American history.[7] The expansion of U.S. racial logics to Muslim populations presents distinct challenges to theories of race and racism that include articulating anti-Muslim racism at the nexus of culture, religion, and race; the role of imperial racism; and the expansion of the global racial system.[8]

Invoking a race war with Islam from the Crusades and the Inquisition to the buttressing of the anti-immigrant notion of Fortress Europe,[9] and to current U.S. imperial wars in the Middle East and projects of settler colonialism in places such as Palestine,[10] the U.S. racial formation reflexively expands into the global racial system through a multi-pronged philosophy of modern racism of the twenty-first century. This is to say that the system of racial domination in the United States is not isolated to the domestic social structure but relies on a complex relationship to migration, transnationalism, and globalization, which is more formally a global racial system. As a system of violent domination, older forms of racism that rely on mass extermination and genocide are juxtaposed with the late twentieth-century forms of political racism based in the context of U.S. foreign policies of abandonment and dispossession, and the cultural racism of inherent cultural essences as an explanation of broad social and cultural differences. What unites this social formation is a global racial system that incorporates the Muslim figure into a broad framework of American empire that through its chameleon-like nature is able to conceal elements of domination in plain sight.[11] To shore up these policies domestically through popular consent, imperial spectacles became a part of constructing a shared enemy by making them visible, while concealing covert forms of state power in the name of national security.¹² These forms of spectacle and secrecy ultimately serve as state-sanctioned domination through racial demonology and the domestication of foreign policy.¹³

In what follows I will examine the construction of the racialized Muslim in the context of imperial spectacles through what Fatimah Rony has called *ethnographic cinema*. Rony argues that ethnographic cinema is an important technology and social practice from which categories such as "race and gender are visualized as natural categories . . . [at] the intersection between anthropology, popular culture, and the construction of nation and empire."¹⁴ Ethnography and cinema in this argument share the legacy of attempting to capture cultural essences through positivist evidence such as cultural and religious practice, social and kinship networks, food, dress, social institutions, and other objects of the ethnographic gaze. For Rony, ethnographic cinema includes "'art,' scientific research films, educational films used in schools, colonial propaganda films, and commercial entertainment films."¹⁵ In this sense ethnographic cinema is a racial and cultural archive of visual representations that in the context of the post-9/11 era conjures racial threats out of Muslim populations. Visual culture and media, whether based in fact or fiction, imagine an enemy target out of the figure of the racialized Muslim that potentially poses a danger to U.S. state security.

By specifically examining the constructions of the racialized Muslim in the television miniseries *Sleeper Cell* and the Hollywood film *Syriana*, I argue that both are elements of an ethnographic cinema that index the global War on Terror through the terms of U.S. racial formation and a broadly constructed global racial system. By rearticulating U.S. cultural histories with references to militant Black nationalism, multiculturalism, the politics of racial casting¹⁶ and racial passing, the use of racialized geographies, and references to class warfare, both examples contribute to the logics and rationales that imagine Muslims and Islam as threatening. In particular, the recent configuration of this Muslim racial formation is based in U.S. imperial geographies that span from the Middle East to South Asia to incorporate populations from Pakistan and Afghanistan. Producing targets through the many facets of the War on Terror is a generative process. Such ideological production of the racialized Muslim takes place through the technologies of image-making and race-making in post-9/11 ethnographic cinema that establish interpretive frameworks to comprehend targets and racialized bodies. The anatomy of this racialized body is foremost read as a threatening Muslim figure, and when read in relation to transnational labor migration it is imbued with the narrative of class conflict. This latter narrative, coupled with the ideologies of an abstracted Islam, stem from explanations that posit the iconic dilemma of an international working class that opposes the elite interests of upward mobility, and even notions of the middle class, because of the inability to obtain the resources needed to escape a deprived class position.

Visual Partitions: From Palestine to Pakistan in the Multiracial Imagination

In the midst of the post-9/11 boom in terrorism-themed films, documentaries, and television shows, the critically acclaimed Showtime Series *Sleeper Cell* (2005) drew on a number of social issues emanating from the post–Civil Rights era to evoke the twenty-first-century Age of Terror. In the setting of race- and class-divided Los Angeles, an urban metropolis rife with plots and plans to subdue late modern ideas of progress, the series follows the dilemmas of a Muslim FBI agent planted in a terrorist sleeper cell. His objective is to go undercover and infiltrate the group by gaining their trust, determine their membership, find out the means and intended sites of terrorist activity, and ultimately to foil their plans. In the opening scenes of the first season, viewers are introduced to the African American Muslim inmate who is the prison librarian and contact to civilian sleeper cells. Played by Albert P. Hall, an actor who appeared in major war cinema from *Apocalypse Now* (1979) to the television series *24* (season three, 2004), he also acted in two other highly significant roles that represent African American Islam, the first as Elijah Muhammad in the film *Ali* (2001) and the more significant role of Baines in the Spike Lee film *Malcolm X* (1992). In this second role, Hall played the character of a Black inmate who introduces the then Malcolm Little to the teachings of the Nation of Islam—functioning as a sort of prison intellectual and conveyer of religious knowledge. The similarity of this role in *Malcolm X* to Hall's role in *Sleeper Cell* is striking, not only the development of a stock character by a single actor but the ideological shift represented through both of these portrayals. In little over a decade, the use of film-as-history in this prison intellectual character functions to mark the transition in American Islam from the fear of Malcolm X's Black nationalism to the dangers of contemporary post-9/11 multicultural Islam.

The transition to the post-9/11 version of American Islam is represented as nonthreatening at the superficial level but is a threat that can at any moment surface through an unassuming network of underground sleeper cells. The themes connected in these two characters and historical moments are the militant antiracism and anti-imperialism of the Nation of Islam, and the notion of militant terrorism assumed as part of strands of Islamic fundamentalism within contemporary American Islam. In other words, diversity breeds an anti-Americanism that has long been present in American Muslims, whether black Islam or immigrant Islam. The characters portrayed by Hall are significant in that they raise multiple specters in the American imagination—race wars, liberation and civil rights, multiculturalism, and anti-imperialism—that are all read as potential terrorism in this series. In the context of the rise of the Nation of Islam in the civil rights era in the United States, Islam is a militant form of liberation; in the context of post-9/11 America, Islam implies the racial, religious, and social threat of terrorism.[17]

The *Sleeper Cell* series is careful to parse this narrative by depicting mainstream Islam set against the dangers of radical Islam. The characters in the sleeper cell of both seasons are mostly new converts or recent reverts that are overtly subjects of some form of abjection. In the first season they are a Bosnian Muslim who suffers through the genocidal Balkan war and seeks revenge against a U.S. government that failed to save his family because of their religion; a French convert to Islam who wishes to prove his devotion to his estranged Moroccan girlfriend; and a white American convert who is apparently rebelling against his mother who is a feminist professor at Berkeley. These characters set the stage for multicultural failure and terrorist redemption. In the second season, the new cast is joined by a woman convert from Western Europe who is a rape survivor; a Latino Muslim who is an ex-gang member; and an Iraqi brought up in the United Kingdom by a wealthy family, who is struggling with his homosexuality and diverts his stigma toward the war in Iraq. The new cast raises the bar of the multiracial threat of Islam through a pantheon of nonnormative characters. Because of these depictions, the show is lauded for its diverse characters, even though these figures are well-worn threats and dangers imagined through the logic of race and sex panics. Depending on narratives of anger and rebellion, these explanations offer pseudopsychological frames based on interpreting Islam through a model of sexual repression and unresolved rage. Within this quasi-Freudian frame, these archetypes offer easily intelligible answers to terrorist intention, while blaming the edifice of liberal multiculturalism that unleashes diversity and the injury of systemic domination. All the while, the main character played by Michael Ealy, the undercover FBI agent Darwyn al-Sayeed, is a second-generation African American Muslim who has embraced orthodox Sunni Islam and has parted from the radical view of his father who is a member of the Nation of Islam. As the heroic mediator of the show, and the multicultural and multiracial cast of characters, Darwyn represents the hope for American Islam that serves the security interests of the U.S. government to save human lives, while grappling with his faith and the misinterpretations of it by his coworkers in the FBI.[18]

The dynamic of historical evocation through stock characters and actor

Fig. 9.1. Film still of Farik leading prayer in safe-house scene of *Sleeper Cell*, Season 1, Showtime, 2005.

filmography is manipulated throughout the *Sleeper Cell* series. Later in the pilot episode entitled "Al-Fatiha" (after the first chapter of the Quran meaning "The Opening"), viewers are introduced to another character, Faris al-Farik. Darwyn is sent by the jail librarian to a synagogue to meet Farik, the leader of the sleeper cell, and uses the purportedly ideal cover of an American Jew. In this capacity he acts like the model citizen, even coaching a Little League baseball team in his spare time. Dressed in fashionable suits, Farik runs a private security agency perfect for the penetration of potential enemy targets—in this case locations that the sleeper cell will use as sites of mass destruction. After an initial heated encounter in the synagogue between Farik and Darwyn, the two meet at a donut shop where they discuss their roles in the cell. The encounter is opened with a discussion of racial appearance and stereotype.

> DARWYN: Shouldn't you be eating a bagel.
> FARIK: Most people from the Middle East look alike, sometimes even to each other. I've passed as Persian, Turkish, Coptic Christian, as well as Sephardic Jew. Don't African Americans have a long history of trying to pass for white?
> DARWYN: I don't.

Starting as a cultural stereotype of Jewish food, the bagel is then transitioned into a comparison of racial assimilability and dissimulation of the Arab and

Muslim body, and the desire of racial passing for African Americans. In the logic of the show this is the quintessential act of members of a sleeper cell—the ability to embed oneself in an unsuspecting community. Here passing is a form of dissimulation in which race is mobilized for an ambiguous racial figure. Indeed, Arabs have often been cast as racially unclear with a fraught relationship to whiteness.[19] The character Farik, supposedly with an origin in Saudi Arabia, is played by Oded Fehr, an Israeli actor known for his portrayal of Ardeth Bay in *The Mummy* (1999) and *The Mummy Returns* (2001)—another pseudo-Arab character represented through the symbols of ancient Egypt and Islam, and perhaps a stock character of what Sunaina Maira calls "racialized Arab-face"[20] to depict racial impersonation. Second, this question of passing relays racial authenticity not so much to the matter of cultural authenticity—in other words, how culturally black, Jewish, or Muslim one is—but to cultural intention. That is, identity is a practice not just an appearance. In the allegorical context of the show, this idea shifts the idea of racial visibility to a broad set of traits, from phenotype and appearance, to cultural practices and social kinship networks, and to reimagining racial targets of surveillance, regulation, and policing.

The notion of actor choice and casting options is only partly at dispute here. More accurately, it is how unacknowledged histories are embedded in these choices to further reinscribe political and social conflict. For example, the accuracy of Fehr's depiction of a Saudi Arab in the character of Farik is not so much in question, although to most Arabic speakers he clearly has an unusual accent, but rather the history and calculated grammar that is evoked by an Israeli portraying an Arab terrorist. Racial passing and ambiguity is triply played upon in the above dialogue in which an Israeli actor is portraying an Arab Muslim who is impersonating a Jew. The choice of actor is telling in terms of the meaning of the embedded histories of social and cultural interaction. Not any actor can play this character; it is a culmination of choices based on the production and direction of the series as it overlaps with the written script and the performance of the chosen actor. In this sense historical interpretation is both hidden and in plain sight—much like a sleeper cell. The most immediate historical reference is to the Israeli-Palestinian conflict, which in this twist of actor choice in depicting a historical region renders the Arab as a dangerous, rational, and calculating menace to modern secular society. And although such conflicts are discussed throughout the series, the framing of the debates justifies imperial violence against unjustified terrorist responses, creating a simplistic and narrow description. The centrality of the question of Palestinian self-autonomy and Israeli colonial occupation is given scant space in the show; instead the conflict is itself found in the body of Farik/Fehr that is resolved in irrational violence. This is not to say that

Israel and Palestine are given equal space in this genealogy of Hollywood history that draws on the portrayal of Orientalist fear and the stock character of the evil Arab.[21] The narrative of Islamic terrorism inevitably falls into a dyad in which the Israeli state is an innocent entity, associated with democracy, secularism, and rationality, while Palestinians are tied to Muslims as Islamic radicals and terrorists, and are seen as reactionary, emotional, calculated, and violent. The apparent symbolism of Palestine recasts conflict, struggle, and autonomy into the perils and threats of violence, immorality, death, and terrorism. Palestine is an embedded symbol of terror in the complex associations that figure Islam and Muslims into a racial formation.

In recent 9/11-themed film and television, this mechanism of portraying Middle Eastern and Muslim stock characters also relates to a second partition—that of India and Pakistan. A number of Indian-origin actors portray various Muslim characters and, interestingly, Latino characters, thus continuing with a phenotypic racism that relies on the notion of Muslim as brown-skinned. Arab, Iranian, and South Asian Americans are often cast to portray Latina/os, and vice versa signifying a similar displacement or in-between-ness in the U.S. racial formation. For example, in the Showtime series *The L Word* Latinas are cast with mixed-race actors Sarah Shahi, who is of Iranian and Spanish descent and plays an Arab woman in the second season of *Sleeper Cell*, and Janina Gavankar, who is of Indian and Dutch descent. The broad notion of Islamic terrorists as brown-skinned is perpetuated in casting male actors as well. For example, Kal Penn plays Ahmed Amar in *24* (season six, 2007); Ajay Naidu is Rakim Ali in *The West Wing* (season three, "Isaac and Ishmael," 2001); and Naveen Andrews portrays the Iraqi torture agent Sayid Jarrah on *Lost*. That they are non-Muslim is only part of the casting choices displayed in the rationale, but it's more the case that terrorists have a certain look. The profile conflates those hailing from India in origin to a broad geography of the Islamic world most readily combined with the abstracted Middle East. The casting of these actors in a wide spectrum of identities, from Pakistani and Indian to Muslim, Hindu, and Sikh, follows an idea of the uniform appearance of South Asian Americans that are stereotyped based on cultural attributes that vary depending on the ethnic, national, and religious community. As an example of racial dissimulation such casting reifies performances of racial passing as Muslim, Arab, Middle Eastern, or simply Islamic terrorist, thus articulating these assumed identities as authentic. In addition, many of these actors have a diasporic personal history that reinforces notions that they are conversant in multiple social milieus and can temper their portrayals for maximum audience consumption. In other words, diasporic portrayals that often have multiple inflections of an assumed place and location come to represent the authentic immigrant. Thus, in what Shohat and Stam refer to as "the racial politics of casting,"[22] the use of South Asians in this example is not so much about the ability to portray complex characters with multiple temperaments, but to portray multiple racial and ethnic groups that fit stock stereotypes of broad and vast groups and populations to affirm racialized ideas of culture, comportment, and bodily ascription. In producing the illusion of a "reality effect" in realist depictions that use actors to convey racial authenticity,[23] stock characters and portrayals of 9/11-themed material are part of a didactic exercise in profiling the racialized Muslim.

In the post-9/11 era the ability to play a Muslim in Hollywood goes beyond South Asia and is part of a broader geography of the Middle East where "the Muslim" is read as hailing from North Africa, the Arab Gulf, Iran, and as far as Pakistan. These geographies marked by the historical divides of two mid-twentieth-century partitions, between Israel and Palestine, and India and Pakistan, allow popular culture to interchangeably depict them through the figure of the racialized Muslim. The Muslim racial formation conflates Arab and South Asian such that actors can play a broad spectrum of roles and representations. These underlying histories to the narrative plots based in domestic terror schemes in the United States represent the scope of the Muslim Middle East. Racial ambiguity and dissimulation are devices from which to racialize cultural, societal, and historical difference from the perspective of American imperial interests that requires a visible target—that of the racialized Muslim.

The Pakistani Labor Migrant in the Global Racial System

In the otherwise laudable 2005 film *Syriana,* directed by Stephen Gaghan, the Middle East is a place where Muslims of different backgrounds, whether Arab, Iranian, or Pakistani, coalesce into a unitary racial figure.[24] The world of Muslims in the narrative of the film is driven by oil, drugs, arms, labor, Islam, terror, and capital, in which the extremes of wealth and poverty are made apparent through competing geopolitical interests and transnational labor migration. As a portrayal of how globalization intersects a number of complex issues, *Syriana* presents a dazzling array of social and political issues with pronounced nuance. In particular, the class differences of the various factions of the Muslim world are dramatized in a realist spectrum that includes drug-addled parties in Tehran, Hezbollah arms dealing, the oil politics of the Arab Gulf, and finally the harsh realities of transnational workers. This last category serves the purpose of explaining terrorism on the ground, that is, the recruiting methods and tactics to motivate youth toward violence. Unfortunately, the narrative of the film rehashes the hackneyed explanatory framework of class warfare and ultimately provides a less nuanced account of what could have been an illuminating foray into the motivations and torments of transnational labor migration.

Historically, labor migrants began going to the Middle East from various parts of South Asia in the first half of the twentieth century and en masse since the early 1970s.[25] Labor migrants reflect the needed foreign workforce in the Arab Gulf to occupy the middle and lower tier of the service economy including the oil fields, massive construction projects, driving, janitorial work, and the professional fields including engineering, health, accounting, and information technology. Building entire cities from the ground up, South Asian laborers are an integral aspect of the economy and development of the Arab Gulf. Indeed, much of the depiction of laborers in *Syriana* was shot on location in well-known worker camps outside of Dubai in the United Arab Emirates to add a sense of ethnographic realism to the narrative. One of the subplots in the story builds on the dilemmas of a teenager from Pakistan who is increasingly disaffected from his life as a labor migrant. He faces, along with his father, the humiliation of limited opportunities and degrading work conditions. In a scene following their dismissal from work in the oil fields, the two are beaten for speaking in a queue while waiting to update their immigration papers. Depicting the quotidian brutality of the tight regulation of labor migrants through a highly disciplinary police state, as labor migrants their coreligious affiliation is unclear in the workplace. The father of the Pakistani youth dreams of what he refers to as the snow-capped mountains of Pakistan, an allusion to the recently dubbed Khyber-Pakhtun Khwa province, an area often surmised in U.S. media to offer refuge to Islamic militants such as Al-Qaeda and the Taliban. The dream of economic freedom is tied to ideas of family reunification and the aspiration of one day making enough to buy a home. The seeming impossibility of this dream in the face of the hardships of working in a foreign country lends itself to the Pakistani teenager's desperation and eventual impressionability. Through the tension of teenage angst, the Pakistani youth falls into the hands of militant Islamists seeking susceptible youth for their ulterior motives. This overly simplified resolution in the film too easily derives from an explanation of "susceptible youth and bad influences" without questioning the assumptions that form the basis of this conclusion.

To begin with, the film establishes a narrative logic of dangerous nationalities. Out of the context of the many South Asian labor migrants in the Arab Gulf—Indians, Pakistanis, Bangladeshis, Sri Lankans—it is Pakistanis in the film that emerge as dangerous and susceptible to Islamic militancy. This logic is pervasive in defining these labor migrants as a whole. For

Fig. 9.2. Film still from *Syriana,* Warner Bros., 2005.

example, a cast member is credited as a "Pakistani translator" rather than an Urdu, Hindi, or Hindustani translator, in a scene in which the official wears the head garb and beard of an Indian Sikh. Later, viewers are made aware of the dangers of Pakistani youth who are led by militant Arabs in madrassas who preach anticapitalist, anti-Western messages in favor of an Islamic utopia. Following a long list of visual cues and popular culture references throughout this film, Pakistan becomes a central part of the Muslim world responsible for the dirty work of Islamic militancy. In a further irony, this parallels their role as a laboring class that does the muscle work for the ideological base of the Arab employers throughout the Gulf. In this imagined world, Pakistanis are not from the Middle East, but as guest workers they become part of an indistinguishable Middle East ruled by their Muslim coreligionist Arabs.

Syriana is certainly to be hailed for its attempt to present a complex Muslim world divided by religious sect, ethnicity, nationality, and economic standing. Yet, there is little to differentiate the film's characters aside from classifying them through the dyads of Muslim/Arab/Pakistani versus American, wealthy versus destitute, and corrupt versus militant. From the perspective of U.S. foreign policy, geostrategic security translates into a map of political and economic interests.

> India is now our ally, Russia is now our ally, even China will be an ally. Everybody between Morocco and Pakistan is the problem. Failed

states and failed economies, but Iran is a natural, cultural, ally of the US. Persians do not want to roll back the clock to the 8th century. I see students marching in the streets, I hear Khatami making the right sounds. And what I'd like to know is, if we keep embargoing them on energy, then someday soon, are we going to have a nice secular, pro-Western, pro-business government? (CIA Assistant, *Syriana*, 2005)[26]

As a cultural mapping of the Muslim Middle East, North Africa, West Asia, and South Asia are the boundaries of a world noncompliant to the interests of twenty-first-century U.S. empire. In what is often described in film reviews as a confusing narrative and a barrage of characters,[27] the figure of the Muslim ends up uniformly racialized as a problem. The Muslim social and cultural world is thus understood through the racialized tropes of Islam and oil glossed in terms of the geostrategic terms of energy, governance, and economy. In this framework the problem of Muslim assimilation translates arms, drugs, terror, and labor migrants into the same commodity as forms of illegality and criminality. As markets and economies that do not cooperate with the neoliberal marketplace crafted in the U.S. empire, the countries in these diverse regions are made into problems requiring the diplomatic strategy of economic sanctions and embargoes, and justifying the war strategy of violent military force.

In this logic the potentiality to do harm through terrorism is considered a social and cultural attribute. In the emergent Muslim racial formation, this potential is found in the bodies of those read as Muslim and then essentialized as potential terrorists. This is based on phenotype, dress, and bodily comportment, and additionally religious belief and practice. As a biological metaphor of naturalization, cultural and social traits of religious comportment and belief are potentially violent, militant, and ultimately, transmittable. That is, in this blunt cultural racism, terror and its ideology are understood as socially and culturally learned and simultaneously internalized within the body. Going against a logic that regards essentialism as opposing the idea of learned behavior, the racialization of Muslims incorporates both. In the context of the Muslim world, to argue against the worldview of the U.S. empire felt through the alienation of capitalism immediately signifies an anti-American attitude that naturalizes terrorist violence to critical Islamic discourses. Indeed, in the coda of *Syriana* the metaphor is quite literal in the use of the body as a weapon or instrument of terror when the Pakistani youth drives a boat loaded with a missile on a suicide mission into a U.S. naval ship. Alongside the missile, their bodies act as forces of rage and violence against a system that has marginalized them. Yet, such an analysis is far from apparent, and although the act itself is supposed to speak for itself, it remains quixotic and inexplicable. In this sense terror and violence are coded as part of a spectrum of general Muslim disenchantment that requires vigilance. It is with this in mind that the established rubric of the domestic War on Terror mandates that migrants from the Muslim world become the primary targets of controlling terror. Specifically, South Asian workers in the Arab Gulf are imagined as the same migrants that go to Europe and North America, and as part of an endlessly expanding threat, problem, and potential of terrorism.

Consolidating the Racialized Muslim

In the immediate aftermath of 9/11, as everyday racial violence through an assortment of hate crimes against Muslims, Arabs, and South Asians increased dramatically, working-class immigrants became the central targets of the U.S. security state that used systems of detention and deportation to control immigration.[28] As a lingering threat of the figure of the racialized Muslim, transnational workers are the hardest to imagine and codify in processes of globalization. This is partly an act of obfuscating working-class lives, but also a basic misunderstanding of how such transnational laborers are incorporated into the system of globalization. Labor migration throughout the twentieth century became part of a global racial system that depended on the dictates of the global economy and newly configured forms of social stratification. Working-class migrations across the globe are racialized by imperial economies that extract surplus value as new forms of sociality and subjectivity are constructed. Racializing the figure of the Muslim and placing Pakistan into a geographic logic of the Middle East serves the purpose of creating a visible population as a racialized threat.

The use of ethnographic cinema as imperial spectacle for the aims of U.S. foreign policy derives from a history of geopolitical strategies of containment and economic control.[29] The consolidation of a Muslim racial formation in post-9/11 ethnographic cinema demonstrates how Arabs and South Asians are combined into the racial figure of the Muslim. As emblematic problems in the War on Terror, Palestine and Pakistan are used to reconfigure the geography of the Middle East and the Muslim world to construct targets, enemies, and racial figures. This racial formation mobilizes a racial logic based on essentializing such phenotypic attributes as skin color—olive, brown, and dark-skinned—with notions of religious comportment, dress, and cultural practice. In the Age of Terror, the examples of visual culture examined in this essay point to the fear of multiculturalism as a ploy to cast a wide range of terror threats that are racialized through notions of cultural practice in the narrative logic of the *Sleeper Cell* series, while the racial figure of the Muslim is cast as homogeneous through a vast array of geopolitical realities in the Islamic world that ultimately offers class conflict as an explanation of terrorist violence in *Syriana*. Such narrative anxieties speak to the ambiguity of the racialized Muslim figure in its multiracial diversity, and the implied analysis of post-9/11 terror that fails to account for such complexity. Instead the portrayal of histories of conflict with the American empire emerging out of the confluence of oil politics, Islamic ideology, and transnational labor migration, all further naturalize the connection of terrorism and Muslims through a covert logic of cultural racism.

Although I argue that there are particular devices and strategies for manufacturing the racialized figure of the Muslim through imperial spectacles such as dissimulation, passing, multiracialism, and class warfare, these ideas draw on historical processes of subjugation at work in the U.S. racial formation. The process of consolidating an idea of the racialized Muslim involves the conflation of multiple populations in relation to histories of racialized oppression in the United States. For this reason, this includes the imagining of a broad geography from North Africa to South Asia that makes Palestine, Iraq, Afghanistan, and Pakistan part of the central conflicts in the global War on Terror. Pakistan thus becomes part of the Middle East through imagined geographies of conflict and through the construction of the figure of the Muslim in the global racial system. Thus to conflate multiple populations such as Arabs and South Asians into the racialized Muslim produces a visible target of state regulation and policing for consuming publics.

NOTES

This essay is an abridged and modified version of Chapter 3 "Imperial Targets" in *Terrifying Muslims: Race and Labor in the South Asian Diaspora* (Duke, 2011).

1. Throughout this text I refer to *transnational migration* as a semipermanent workforce that travels to numerous locations and engages in multiple patterns of migration (e.g., chain, step, seasonal, radial/circular), whereas *international migration* is often a term used to describe one-way migrations. My emphasis of the transnational aspect of this experience points to the often liminal state that labor migrants exist in, in relation to nation, race, and legality, to name a few of the central concepts that shape their subjectivity.

2. Vijay Prishad, *The Karma of Brown Folk* (2000); Biju Mathew, *Taxi! Cabs and Capitalism in New York City* (2005), 119.

3. For more on the rivalry between British and Russian colonial powers and the formation of New Great Game in Central Asia between multinational interests and the American imperial war in Afghanistan, see Ahmed Rashid, *Taliban: Militant Islam, Oil, and Fundamentalism in Central Asia* (2001); *Jihad: The Rise of Militant Islam in Central Asia* (2002); and *Descent into Chaos: The US and the Failure of Nation Building in Pakistan, Afghanistan, and Central Asia* (2008).

4. Historically occupied by the Pashtun ethnic group, since 2008 this cross-border region was dubbed "AfPak" by White House strategist Richard Hobrooke.

5. Numerous postcolonial feminists have thoroughly critiqued the logic of these rescue narratives. See Inderpal Grewal, *Home and Harem: Nation, Gender, Empire, and the Cultures of Travel, Post-Contemporary Interventions* (1996); Chandra Mohanty, "Under Western Eyes: Feminist Scholarship and Colonial Discourses," in *Third World Women and the Politics of Feminism*, ed. C. Mohanty, A. Russo, and L. Torres (1991); Ella Shohat, *Taboo Memories, Diasporic Voices* (2006); and Gayatri Spivak, "Can the Subaltern Speak?" in *Marxism and the Interpretation of Culture*, ed. C. Nelson and L. Grossberg (1988).

6. Sherene Razack, *Casting Out: The Eviction of Muslims from Western Law and Politics* (2008).

7. Junaid Rana, "The Story of Islamophobia," in *Souls: Critical Journal of Black Politics* 9, no. 2 (2007): 148–61.

8. Leith Mullings, "Interrogating Racism: Toward an Antiracist Anthropology," *Annual Review of Anthropology* 34 (2005): 667–93; Howard Winant, *The World Is a Ghetto: Race and Democracy Since World War II* (2001); and Winant, *The New Politics of Race: Globalism, Difference, Justice* (2004).

9. Minoo Moallem, *Between Warrior Brother and Veiled Sister: Islamic Fundamentalism and the Politics of Patriarchy in Iran,* 2005; Shohat, *Taboo Memories*.

10. Steven Salaita, *The Holy Land in Transit: Colonialism and the Quest for Canaan* (2006).

11. In historian William A. William's well-known argument, the strategy of American empire from the Civil War onward was of "annihilation unto unconditional surrender" (1980). As a foreign policy after World War II, this approach transformed the expansive reach of American capitalism through the surrogacy of multinational corporations and the market reform of the international banking system. By creating a global marketplace, American power would dictate the terms of economic reform while maintaining "imperialism without colonies" (Harry Magdoff, *The Age of Imperialism: The Economics of U.S. Foreign Policy,* 2000; Magdoff, *Imperialism without Colonies,* 2003). In such a configuration, the American military and intelligence branches would be used as a force in state-sponsored violence (Lesley Gill, *The School of the Americas: Military Training and Political Violence in the Americas, American Encounters/Global Interactions,* 2004), while maintaining minimal disruption to domestic life and security. Such an empire launched a systematic approach of accumulation by dispossession through imposing an economic framework through violent means of permanent war and the politics of spectacle (David Harvey, *The New Imperialism,* 2003; Retort and Iain Boal, *Afflicted Powers: Capital and Spectacle in a New Age of War,* 2005).

12. Michal Rogin, "'Make My Day!' Spectacle as Amnesia in Imperial Politics (and the Sequel)," in *Cultures of United States Imperialism*, ed. A. Kaplan and D. E. Pease, 1993.

13. Amy Kaplan, *The Anarchy of Empire in the Making of U.S. Culture* (2002).

14. Fatimah Tobing Rony, *The Third Eye: Race, Cinema, and Ethnographic Spectacle* (1996), 9.

15. Ibid., 8.

16. Ella Shohat and Robert Stam, *Unthinking Eurocentrism: Multiculturalism and the Media* (1994).

17. Scholars have pointed to the important connections between anticolonial struggles and the African diaspora to argue that in these linkages African Americans devel-

oped opposition to American foreign policy. For the Nation of Islam this appeared as an anti-American critique of the Cold War (Penny Von Eschen, *Race Against Empire: Black Americans and Anticolonialism, 1937–1957* [1997], 174), and for African American Muslims this anti-imperial resistance fomented transnational exchanges with Arab Muslims through a rejection of American nationalism (Edward E. Curtis, "Islamism and Its African American Muslim Critics: Black Muslims in the Era of the Arab Cold War," *American Quarterly* 59, no. 3 [2007]: 683–710). Contemporary American Islam is also fraught with clashes and conflicts between and within immigrant Islam represented demographically by South Asian and Arab Americans and African American Islam that challenge the possibility of a unified Muslim American *umma*, or community of believers (Sherman Jackson, *Islam and the Blackamerican: Looking Toward the Third Resurrection* [2005]).

18. Even the name Darwyn al-Sayyid clearly represents the contrived intentions of the writers of the show to create this character as a cultural intermediary of reformed Islam. *Darwyn*, of course, is a reference to the founder of modern evolutionary thought, and the surname *al-Sayyid* a title for Muslims often given to those who are direct descendants of the prophet.

19. Sarah Gualtieri, *Between Arab and White: Race and Ethnicity in the Early Syrian American Diaspora* (2009).

20. Sunaina Maira, "Belly Dancing: Arab-Face, Orientalist Feminism, and US Empire," *American Quarterly* 60, no. 2 (2008): 317–45.

21. Tim Jon Semmerling, *"Evil" Arabs in American Popular Film: Orientalist Fear* (2006); Jack Shaheen, *Reel Bad Arabs: How Hollywood Vilifies a People* (2001); Shaheen, *Guilty: Hollywood's Verdict on Arabs after 9/11* (2006).

22. Shohat and Stam, *Unthinking Eurocentrism*, 189.

23. Shohat and Stam, *Unthinking Eurocentrism*, 180.

24. It is important to note that Arab American film critic Jack Shaheen consulted on this film. On his view of the film see Jack G. Shaheen, "Arabs and Muslims in Hollywood's 'Munich' and 'Syriana,'" *Washington Report on Middle East Affairs* (March 2006).

25. Robert Vitalis, *America's Kingdom: Mythmaking on the Saudi Oil Frontier* (2006).

26. Stephen Gaghan, *Syriana* (Burbank, CA: Warner Home Video, 2006).

27. For example, see A. O. Scott's review "Clooney and a Maze of Collusion," *New York Times,* November 23, 2005.

28. See Human Rights Watch, *"We are Not the Enemy": Hate Crimes Against Arabs, Muslims, and Those Perceived to be Arab or Muslim after September 11*, Report, 14 (6-G), November 2002.

29. Shohat and Stam, *Unthinking Eurocentrism;* Melani McAlister, *Epic Encounters: Culture, Media, and U.S. Interests in the Middle East since 1945* (University of California Press, 2005); and Douglas Little, *American Orientalism: The United States and the Middle East since 1945* (2002).

Diaspora, Transnation, & Translation

TEN

"A Strip, A Land, A Blaze"
Arab American Hip-Hop and Transnational Politics

Sunaina Maira

> a festival of lights / a strip a land a blaze
> the sea a mirror of fire
> a casting of lead upon children. . . .
> an army feasting on epiphany / driving future into history
> —Suheir Hammad, "Gaza"[1]

There is an emerging generation of Arab American youth that has come of age listening to the sounds of rap and that is now using hip-hop as a medium to address the question of Arab American identity as well as histories of nation, migration, racism, war, and colonialism. If hip-hop was described as "the Black CNN" by Chuck D of Public Enemy, suggesting its role as a tool for sharing news of the social and political realities of urban, disadvantaged youth of color,[2] it seems that hip-hop is becoming the "Arab American CNN" for a new generation of youth. Arab American hip-hop has developed in the context of a transnational youth culture and political movement that spans national borders, linking the United States and the Middle East. This new genre of hip-hop has become an aesthetic idiom through which Arab American youth sonically connect their experiences to Arab youth outside the United States, as well as to minoritized youth in the United States, and express their political concerns, particularly about the Palestine question that is repressed in the U.S. public sphere, as well as about the global War on Terror.

Drawing on interviews with Arab American artists and analysis of lyrics, this essay briefly discusses some of the main themes in Arab American hip-hop. It demonstrates that Arab American hip-hop forges transnational linkages among Arab communities and offers a critique of U.S. policies in the Middle East, particularly in Palestine and Iraq. This music challenges Orientalist representations of Arabs and Muslims in the United States, in the context of the intensified Islamophobia and Arabophobia since 9/11, and also reflects the racial politics of an Arab American youth subculture that identifies with youth of color and disidentifies with whiteness. Hip-hop serves as a site where these ethnic, racial, and political identities are constructed, imagined, and performed, and where Arab American artists connect the concerns of Arab Americans in the post-9/11 moment to U.S. foreign policy and interventions overseas.

Emerging in the South Bronx of the late 1970s, hip-hop was initially a youth subculture that grew out of and responded to urban restructuring, deindustrialization, poverty, and racism. Marginalized African American and Puerto Rican youth produced a new cultural form, weaving reflections on their current condition with references to histories of exclusion and migration and creating a counterdominant narrative.[3] The idiom of hip-hop expressed their alienation and political abandonment in the postindustrial moment, reimagining the past, present, and possible future. Hip-hop, which consists of rap (by poets known as MCs), graffiti, deejaying, and break dancing, is a "hybrid cultural form" that mixes Afro-Caribbean and African American musical, oral, visual, and dance practices with contemporary technologies and urban cultures.[4] The "heavy reliance on lyricism" makes hip-hop a genre that can be powerfully used for social and political commentary by layering poetry over beats.[5] Arab and Arab American rap, too, can be described as a poetics of displacement and protest. While some Arab American rappers focus on themes such as romance, friendship, and the hyperconsumption of "bling bling," there has been a burgeoning of Arab American hip-hop infused with a searing political critique of racial exclusion, warfare, military occupation, and the ravages of global capitalism.[6]

This essay will focus specifically on political rap by Arab American artists, and largely on Palestinian American youth whose relationship to the United States is heavily mediated by ongoing U.S. support for Israel and who are using hip-hop to challenge the silencing of Palestinian histories. At the same time, it is important to note that Arab American hip-hop is rapidly evolving, and Arab American youth are a diverse population.[7] Arab American hip-hop is transnational, not just in its social and political linkages to Arab youth and Arab homeland politics but aesthetically and culturally as well, as a hybrid genre that samples and recreates Arab musical and poetic traditions.[8] Will Youmans, a Palestinian American activist, writer, and hip-hop artist ("Iron Sheik"), points out that there are forms of improvised and folk poetry in Arabic, such as zajal, mawwal (mawwaliya), and saj', that could be likened to spoken word, not to mention the percussiveness and lyricism of Arabic music. He also argues that the major impetus for Arab American hip-hop is the mainstreaming and globalization of rap.[9] The question of cultural influences is not an either/or one; clearly, Arab American MCs are responding to the global popularity of hip-hop as well as to the Arabic music and poetry they have grown up with and are incorporating them into a new cultural form.

As hip-hop has crossed ethnic and class boundaries, it has become a multiethnic and globalized art form, but it has also become increasingly mainstream in the United States. Many fans of political or so-called conscious rap lament that the oppositional thrust of hip-hop has waned as it has become intensely commercialized; some argue that this commodification of youth culture is part of the "politics of containment" directed at youth of color in the post–civil rights era.[10] It is apparent that while hip-hop culture may in some instances be critical or implicitly subversive of consumerism, it is always engaged with the realm of commerce and is not outside of global capitalism—like all other forms of popular culture that are marketed, distributed, and consumed.[11] Arab American hip-hop is still a largely underground music that has not yet entered the mainstream music industry and is distributed via the Internet and Arab American stores. Yet young Arab American rappers who are part of the hip-hop underground are receiving greater recognition by the larger hip-hop community, such as Iron Sheik (from Oakland, California; later based in Ann Arbor, Michigan); Excentrik (Oakland); the Philistines and NOMADS (Los Angeles); and the Brooklyn-based Hammer Brothers, who wrote a "Free Palestine" anthem. There are numerous other Arab American MCs around the United States who do political rap, such as Poli Heat (San Francisco), Patriarch (Hayward, California), MC Shaheed (New Orleans), Gaza Strip (New York), Hasan Salaam and ASH ONE (New Jersey), and Arabic Assassin (Houston), not to mention well-known music producers such as Fredwreck (Los Angeles) and spoken word poets such as Remi Kanazi and Suheir Hammad, star of Def Jam Broadway, from New York.[12] In fact, Iron Sheik, who was inspired to produce and write rap in high school because of politically conscious groups such as Public Enemy and A Tribe Called Quest, suggests that the "message rap" produced by Palestinian and Arab American youth is reinvigorating the progressive potential of hip-hop; he comments, "I feel ambivalent about what hip hop has become in the U.S. and I'm happy to see messages in rap again."[13]

Arab American hip-hop artists are part of a transnational Arab hip-hop movement that includes young artists in the Arab world, such as Palestinian MCs DAM, MWR, Abeer, and Saz in Israel; Tashweesh, Palestinian Street, and Boikutt in the West Bank; PR (Palestine Rapperz) in Gaza; Clotaire K, Aksser, and DJ Lethal Skillz in Lebanon; MBS in Algeria; as well as MCs in the larger Arab diaspora (for example, Euphrates in Canada; I AM and MC Solaar in France; Shadia Mansour in Britain; Isam Bachiri of Outlandish in Denmark; and Palestine a.k.a. Ref-UG in Sweden) who increasingly perform all over Europe and North America.[14] Arab and Arab diasporic rap speaks to transnational connections between these various sites and, in the United States, to cross-ethnic linkages with African American, Asian American, Native American, and Latino(a) experiences. This essay illustrates how Arab American youth, who have grown up identifying with the experiences of racism shared with other youth of color, are increasingly vocal about critiquing their profiling after 9/11 and linking it to older structures of Orientalism and anti-Arab racism.

In 2007, a new Arab American musical project, "The Arab Summit," was formed, releasing an eponymous album that speaks powerfully to the constitution of Arab American political identity at this historical moment. The Arab Summit consists of Excentrik (Tarek Kazaleh of Rogue State); Ragtop, who is part of the Filipino-Palestinian American hip-hop crew, the Philistines; Omar Offendum, a Syrian American member of the NOMADS (who says he is from "Los Shem-geles," a play on the Arabic name for Syria); and Narcycist of Euphrates, an Iraqi Canadian artist from Montreal. Members of Arab Summit have performed at political and community events around the country. For example, at the inauguration of the mural honoring Edward Said at San Francisco State University in 2007, Excentrik and Narcycist performed for an enthusiastic and diverse crowd, including Palestinian and Arab Americans from the campus and local community, while students waved Palestinian flags. For Narcycist a.k.a. Jamal Abdul Narcel, the agenda of the collective is "to speak on the issues that have touched us and affected our lives indirectly or directly. I want to further investigate the study of Arab identity in the West vis-à-vis hip-hop cultural belonging."[15] He suggests that hip-hop is a tool not just for documenting but also for analyzing the conditions of growing up Arab in the diaspora; it has become an archive of historical memories and collective experiences of Arab youth in the Americas.

Archives of Affiliation: "At Odds With Lessons We Learn"

Tell me why all our children gotta die, why our mothers and fathers gotta cry?
Ramallah-wide born in California, seen a potent portion of the pride.
Even if you see the evil with your 3yn, it can only be deflected with your pain.
Always at odds with lessons we learn. It's a beautiful thing we can't explain.
—Excentrik, "Somebody Please"[16]

The music of Arab Summit, like that of other progressive Arab American rappers, offers counternarratives by youth whose identities are shaped by histories of exclusion and violence, in the United States and Middle East, and who recreate the collective memory of exile and migration. For many of these Arab American MCs, the Palestine issue is a salient part of this collective history that is "always at odds" with official narratives in the United States that present the perspective of Israel, the occupying power it supports. Palestinian American youth who are part of this growing Arab American hip-hop movement are the second or third generation of Palestinians living in the United States, many of whom are challenging the dominant Israeli perspective on Palestine and the Middle East that is circulated in American mainstream media and public discourse. As Excentrik suggests, this generation is asserting their Arab and Palestinian pride and national identities, drawing on an untold pain that is also inexplicable beauty, not easily explained or consumed. The websites of Palestinian American MCs from New Jersey to Texas, who have names like Palestine Free 4 Eva and Palestine Till Death, are adorned with red, white, green, and black proclamations of their love for Palestine and web links to Palestine solidarity campaigns. Like Excentrik, who is part of a large community of Palestinians from the Ramallah area living in the San Francisco Bay Area (many of whom are Christian), they identify not just with Palestinian refugees but also with Palestinians currently living under occupation or facing apartheid-style discrimination.

Diasporic communities generally display a politics of nostalgia, a fantasy of the home country and a longing to return that is not always a concrete desire to go back; for Palestinian youth from refugee communities, these dreams and desires are intertwined with an ongoing political struggle to challenge occupation and exclusion in Palestine-Israel. Youth in the Palestinian diaspora use rap to evoke collective memory and nationalist symbols of the "homeland" to connect to politically tangible issues such as refugee rights and the right of return.[17] The cause of Palestine remains a touchstone of identity for young Palestinians across the diaspora and also a unifying axis of mobilization for Arab and Muslim American youth. Iron Sheik, whose family is from Nazareth in Galilee, which became part of Israel after the 1948 war, has used music to address issues of displacement, the right of return, the history of Zionism, Orientalism in the media, and anti-Arab racism. On his first underground album, *Camel Clutch,* Iron Sheik recorded songs such as "Olive Trees" and "194" that he has performed at political events to educate and galvanize audiences and that invoke symbols of Palestinian nationhood (the olive tree) and international laws supporting the rights of Palestinian refugees (UN Resolution 194). The refrain of "Olive Trees" is, "They exiled us and stole our homes / Now all we have is old keys and new poems,"[18] alluding to the dispossession of refugees who still have the keys to their lost homes and also the political aspirations of new generations of Palestinians. Iron Sheik's lyrics reflect not a romanticized vision of homeland, nor an easy invocation of liberal human rights discourse, but the use of hip-hop as a political tool that connects different histories of colonialism and displacement, and speaks musically and aesthetically to hip-hop fans in the United States and globally.

The cultural production of Palestinian immigrant communities in the United States have always been shaped by the politics of their homeland and its relationship with Israel and the United States. Arab immigration from what is today Syria and Lebanon formed the bulk of migration to the United States before World War I. The first Palestinian immigrants came to the United States in the early twentieth century. The second major wave of Arab immigration and the influx of Palestinian refugees was after World War II and the Nakba (catastrophe) in 1948 that led to the exodus of more than 700,000 displaced Palestinians.[19] The Arab-Israeli wars of 1967 and 1973, as well as the U.S. Immigration Act of 1965, led to a third wave of increased Palestinian immigration to the United States. These later Palestinian and Arab immigrants predominantly settled in urban areas and were employed in the industrial sector, particularly the automobile industry centered in Detroit, Michigan, home to the Ford Motor Company.[20] The immigration history of some of the rappers I interviewed can be traced back to this period. Kazaleh's great-grandfather, for example, came to the United States in the early twentieth century and worked in a paper factory in Detroit.[21] His grandfather left Ramallah to join him in Detroit in the 1930s, then went back to Palestine to have children, but returned in 1952 when he lost all his land. Kazaleh is thus fourth-generation Palestinian American; his father worked at two jobs, at the store and at the Ford factory in Detroit. Kazaleh, who remembers growing up with the older generation of Arab immigrants still working in the auto factory, lived in an Arab American neighborhood before moving to the Bay Area. Although the Palestinian immigrant community has grown through chain migration and relatives' sponsorship, it has been marked by an identity that was rendered invisible and by a history that was generally not recognized in the United States.[22] While some Arab Americans may be ignorant of the history of people of color in the United States, it is also true that many Americans, including people of color, do not know the full history of Palestinian and Arab struggles. Moreover, Arab identity is racially ambiguous in the United States, and Arabs and Palestinians have been variously classified as white, Asiatic, Syrian, and "Mohammedan" throughout the twentieth century, being "not quite white" within the black/white racial polarity of the United States.[23] As Iron Sheik, who grew up between Black and White neighborhoods in the Detroit area, notes, "There is a very ambiguous racial positioning for Arab Americans. Hip hop is a way to . . . express solidarity with people of color. A good example is Suheir Hammad, whose book of poems was titled *Born Palestinian, Born Black.*[24] Hammad has noted, "I grew up in New York City, in Brooklyn, and I grew up around Puerto Rican people, Latino people, Black people, African-Americans. In the beginning of *Born Palestinian, Born Black,* there is a section where it discusses the different meanings of the word black in different cultures. . . . What the book tries to do is . . . say that this is something that is about survival, something that is positive."[25] In using a cultural form such as hip-hop that was created by African American and Latino/a youth and helped produce an oppositional youth subculture, some Arab American youth are aligning themselves with other youth of color, culturally and politically. Yet both Excentrik and Iron Sheik are acutely aware of the racial and class tensions that exist between African and Arab Americans in urban areas such as Detroit and also in the Bay Area, commenting on issues of mutual suspicion and racial segregation, and do not romanticize this cross-ethnic affiliation.

In my previous research on second-generation youth drawn to hip-hop,[26] I examined the ways young Indian Americans negotiated the contradictions of being neither "black" nor "white," of being part of an upwardly mobile community while also appropriating the styles and sounds of a subculture associated with youth of color. Yet hip-hop has increasingly crossed ethnic, racial, and class boundaries, and even national borders, leading to increasingly contested debates over its identification with "blackness" concerning what defines "authentic" hip-hop and keeps it "real."[27] As Excentrik observes, "People of different voices find a place in hip hop because there's so much room for voices in hip hop. . . . Hip hop . . . is so accessible, it's trendy, and so people gravitate toward that."[28] It is possible that this (sub)cultural capital is part of rap's allure for some Arab American youth, who have grown up in suburban, middle- or upper-middle-class families and who identify with what has become a hugely popular and vastly profitable American, and also global, subculture. At the same time, working-class Arab American communities, such as those in Dearborn, have also been shaped by the politics of deindustrialization that affected African American and other blue-collar workers in depressed urban areas similar to those where hip-hop was created.[29] Excentrik, who began doing spoken word while he was in high school, commented: "We were ridiculed for being into hip hop in high school. . . . I don't see it as an over-important cultural phenomenon, I grew up in hip hop in the city. . . . I grew up in cities—many Palestinians in the suburbs don't know what gave birth to hip hop."[30] It is this experience of being urban and suburban, white yet not white, immigrant and second- or third-generation, Arab Muslim and Arab Christian, refugees and immigrants, that shapes the politics of Arab American hip-hop.

The post–civil rights discourse of ethnic pluralism and the emphasis on multicultural diversity in the United States in the 1980s and 1990s promoted the popular expression of ethnic identity in music, dance, and the arts. Yet, strikingly, Arab American identity, not just Palestinian American identity, was not promoted or celebrated by this rhetoric of inclusion, even within the confines of a liberal multicultural model. "Arab" identity has historically been difficult to perform in the public sphere in the United States due to repressive domestic policies targeting Arab Americans, which have accompanied U.S. overseas interventions in the Arab world and support for Israel.[31] Some argue that this repression and broader anti-Arab racism led to a general cautiousness within Arab American communities about publicly displaying Arab identity; a reticence that partly dissolved in later generations and with the growth of Arab nationalism in the 1960s that spread to communities in the United States.[32] Newer immigrants from the Arab world helped forge a pan-Arab identity and a heightened political consciousness in the 1960s and 1970s that was increasingly overtly expressed in Arab American communities such as that in Dearborn.[33] The 1967 Arab-Israeli war, and the anti-Arab representations in the U.S. media at the time, galvanized a younger generation of Arab Americans who supported the Palestinian struggle and also formed pan-Arab American political organizations, such as the Arab American University Graduates in 1967 and the American Arab Anti-Discrimination Committee in 1980.[34] In 1973, during the October Arab-Israeli war, two thousand Arab Americans from the Southend, a largely working-class community in Dearborn, staged a demonstration in front of the United Auto Workers (UAW) office to demand that the UAW divest from Israel, and later organized a massive protest at a B'nai Brith event that involved Arab American high school students and auto workers.[35] In fact, Gregory Orfalea describes 1972–81 as a period of "political awakening" for Arab American collective organizing and entry into U.S. electoral politics.[36]

These events are important for situating Arab American youth activism within a larger historical context. Palestine activism spearheaded by Arab nationalists, as several scholars have pointed out, has a long history in the United States that predates the Six-Day War of 1967, but which is rarely acknowledged.[37] Contemporary political hip-hop focused on the Palestine issue seems to be, in part, an expression of the politicization of a new generation of Arab Americans who are countering the message of some of their parents and families to stay away from politics, and to avoid raising controversial issues in public.[38] The Iron Sheik says, "I also want Arab Americans . . . to gain a view that it's cool to be political, it's OK . . . to speak truth to power."[39] Nowhere in the United States is the question of the politics of freedom of expression clearer, arguably, than in the case of the highly controversial Palestine question. The fear of taking a public stance on Palestine is a result of the repression of that question and the possibility of reprisals, including the targeting of Arab and Muslim American youth presumably "radicalized" by U.S. and Israeli atrocities and viewed as anti-Semitic "terrorist sympathizers."

Resistance: "The Lyrics are the Stones"

Despite this repressive political climate in the United States, and the surveillance and criminalization of Arab and Muslim youth activism, some Arab American youth have publicly challenged racist profiling and the larger War on Terror, subverting the Orientalist images of Arabs/Muslims as terrorists and fundamentalists that suffuse mainstream discourse, whether implicitly or explicitly. Excentrik remembers being harassed while growing up and being called "terrorist" and "Saddam,"[40] gesturing to the long history of Islamophobia and Arabophobia in the United States that precedes 9/11 and is entangled with various U.S. interventions in the Middle East. Ragtop, whose MC name is a play on the racist slur of "camel jockey" and "raghead," comments on the critique offered by The Arab Summit in their music: "The inspiration to do what we do definitely came from a mixture of personal and political feelings . . . for me it was the backlash following 9/11, both in the media and [against] our communities, that really drove me to try and make my voice heard."[41]

Ragtop's song "We Need Order," for example, alludes both to the domestic criminalization and deportation of youth of color in the "law and order" regime and the violence and surveillance of the New World Order. It suggests that hip-hop, too, is a form of tracking and recording that potentially subverts the privatized national security state and the war economy and would be a form of countersurveillance:

> Order in the court—order him deported, it's plethoras of his sort up in our borders . . . use they dollars to shoot launch bombs into orbit more troops—Cameras on every front stoop, and their porches. GPS systems in they coupes and Porsches so they movements is tracked don't lose the coordinates. Me?—I'm a MC—I'll never forfeit. Catalogue it on an analog disc—record IT . . .

Ragtop and Narcycist both speak of the profiling and "special security" searches they have experienced while traveling across borders in the United States, Canada, and Israel. At the same time, Offendum is acutely aware that the detention suffered by many Arab and Muslim political prisoners, from

Guantánamo to Israel, is far graver.[42] In fact, the video for P.H.A.T.W.A, a track on Narcycist's album *The Narcycist*, 2009, suggests that the profiling, interrogation, and harassment of Arabs at North American airports is linked to detention and torture in Guantánamo and Abu Ghraib through a globalized security regime. Narcy's T-shirt proclaims, "Same shit, different Saddam."[43]

Playfully challenging gendered and racialized representations of sheiks, terrorists, harems, and camel jockeys, Arab American MCs counter Orientalist stereotypes through their names and album titles. They play with the hysteria about Arab terrorism and reappropriate signifiers of the "exotic" Middle East in the imagery on their album covers, websites, and music videos, as well as in their names. For example, the cover of *The Arab Summit* album is imprinted with the motto "Arabs at it again!" and a slyly mocking seal for the "Department of Arab-man Security." The name of the hip-hop crew NOMADS actually stands for "Notoriously Offensive Male Arabs Doing S——," a tongue-in-cheek riff on images of Arab male terrorists as well as on exotic, wandering tribes. Iron Sheik takes his MC name from that of a 1980s wrestling star who used to wear a red kaffiyeh and represent the "bad guys," countering the Orientalist racialization of Arab and Middle Eastern masculinities.[44] These artists also seem to be aware of the pitfalls of self-Orientalization and the commodification of a culture that is simultaneously desired and maligned as antimodern, antidemocratic, and fundamentally "other" to the West.[45] Excentrik hints at the dangers of liberal Orientalist fascination with Arab music: "If I'm playing my 'oud [an Arab stringed instrument], some old Berkeley lady wants to take my picture, talking about my 'exotic' culture."[46]

Given the massive Orientalist investment in images of Arab and Muslim masculinities and femininities in the United States, an important issue that deserves greater reflection is the gendered and sexual politics of Arab American hip-hop. This is a complex issue given the virtual absence of Arab American women MCs and the historical exclusion of women from deejaying and MCing, in general. Popular culture is a field that changes rapidly, but at least at the time of this research, prominent Arab American women in hip-hop seemed to be DJs (such as DJ Mutamissik in New York and DJ Emancipation in San Francisco) or spoken word poets (most famously, Suheir Hammad, and also younger figures such as Tahani Salah from New York and several emerging poets in the San Francisco Bay Area). There is also a queer Lebanese American hip-hop crew, NaR, in the Bay Area. Interestingly, there are some well-known female Arab rappers outside the United States who are Palestinian, such as Abeer from Lid and Arapeyat from Acca in Israel, as well as Shadia Mansour in Britain. Iron Sheik likens male-dominated

Arab American hip-hop to "early 1990s hip hop" in the United States, which became hypercommercialized and male-dominated.[47] Arab American hip-hop is a relatively new genre within a larger music industry that continues to be shaped by deeper problems of racial, gender, and sexual exclusion. It is also apparent that the image of the "angry Arab" man, however oppositional, is more marketable in American (and global) popular culture than that of a defiant and militant Arab woman MC, not to mention the gendering of hip-hop that is evident for all artists, not just for Arab Americans.[48] At the same time, the poetry performed by young women in hijab who speak unflinchingly about war and occupation using the idioms of urban poetry, such as Salah in "Hate," challenge the dominant images of passive, voiceless, and veiled Muslim and Arab women. These are issues that cannot be fully addressed here but need to be explored in future research.

Hammad and Salah are just two of a growing community of young Arab American artists who connect anti-Arab racism and Islamophobia, particularly in the wake of 9/11, to a longer history of Orientalist representations of Arabs, and to the racism of occupation and apartheid in Palestine and the war in Iraq. Timz (a.k.a. Tommy Hanna), an Iraqi American rapper from San Diego, burst into the media in 2007 with the video for his searing song, "Iraq," a condemnation of the U.S. invasion and Abu Ghraib.[49] The video portrays the daily violence and persecution suffered by Iraqis living under a privatized occupation, denouncing George W. Bush and Condoleeza Rice as well as Halliburton. The Arab Summit has a song, "Tomorrow's Justice," which layers a sample from a famous Bob Marley song about struggling for rights, in the face of deception and deferred hopes, over Fairuz's stirring ode to Jerusalem, which remains under Israeli occupation, in "La Fleur Des Cites (Zahrat El Mada'en)." Ragtop insightfully comments on this linkage of musical archives from various locations: "'Get up, stand up' is of course a reference to the classic Bob Marley line recorded [in 1973] and [which] reinforces the idea that little has changed."[50] The sampling of songs from different historical moments and political struggles allows hip-hop artists to articulate an analysis of historical continuities across time and place. "Tomorrow's Justice" from Arab Summit, 2007, begins by tracing the links between refugees from Palestine ["the P"], Haiti, and post-Katrina New Orleans and between poverty in Los Angeles and the Philippines, suggesting that there will always be injustice as long as the ravages of imperialism and global capitalism persist.

> Ain't no justice ain't no peace, ain't no place safe left to be. We got refugees from Haiti to the P. to those fleeing toes freezing wet from New Orleans, we got people waiting for their piece of the cake and

> it's a long line of empty plates—From L.A. to the Bay to Wastes of Manila, where your waste is their food, shit that you'd throw away gets consumed with a little bit of regret. . . .

While the politics of cross-racial solidarity espoused by Arab Summit, Iron Sheik, and other young hip-hop artists has inspired audiences, they have also argued for the need for Palestinian and Arab American youth to make stronger alliances with other communities rather than indulge in a discourse of exceptionalism. Iron Sheik, for example, has explicitly commented, "The Palestinian experience is not unique in the twentieth century. Displacement and dispossession have happened throughout world history."[51] His songs make links to the genocide against Native Americans ("As a Palestinian / feel more like an Indian / driven into reservations / living under occupation / as a shattered nation / a Western creation"), a persistent theme in Palestinian and diasporic hip-hop that articulates a politics of indigeneity and critique of settler colonialism in the United States and also in Israel.[52] In "Tomorrow's Justice," Excentrik invokes the history of slavery and migration and the violent annihilation of indigenous peoples by settlers and missionaries in the New World, suggesting a new term ("Palest-indians") to challenge the notion of lands empty of people that can be "civilized" by colonial settlement.

> . . . whether you an immigrant or children of slaves you can see it in the difference / of the living in conditions like missions tortured indians / force 'em to Christians we call 'em Palest-indians / we ain't missing

These artists have made connections between colonialism, repression, segregation, and militarism in the United States as well as in the Middle East and Israel, offering a musical critique of global structures of imperialism, racism, and war. Given the censorship of the Palestinian struggle in the United States, as well as in Canada, underground Arab American hip-hop performs the work of helping to shatter silence around this taboo issue.

The growing Arab / Arab American hip-hop movement has also allowed youth in the diaspora to communicate with one another, sharing their stories and views across national borders. For example, DJ Lethal Skillz from Beirut has collaborated with Omar Offendum of the NOMADS, Excentrik has performed with MWR, and DAM has a song ("Mes Endroits / My Hood") with a Moroccan French rapper in which they link "the ghettos of Palestine to the ghettos of France." DAM has also performed with the Philistines in Los Angeles; Ragtop, who is part of the Philistines, speaks of how "cats like our boys the Palestinian [MCs] DAM" are engaged in a similar project of creating an "honest expression of their lives."[53] DAM did their premier concert in the United States in 2005, at a New York benefit for the album "Free the P," released to support a documentary film about Palestinian hip-hop, "Slingshot Hip Hop: The Palestinian Lyrical Front," directed by Jackie Salloum. DAM shared the stage with Latino and African American hip-hop artists, as well as with Invincible, an Israeli American woman from Detroit whose song on the album, "No Compromises," addresses issues of occupation, resistance, and the apartheid wall, and also police brutality and racism in Detroit.

Reportedly the first Palestinian hip-hop group, DAM (or Da Arabian MCs; *dam* also means "to persist" in Arabic), became globally famous with their first single and music video, the searing song "Meen Erhabi (Who's the Terrorist?)" released in 2001, and they have become immensely popular among Palestinian and Arab American youth, touring across college campuses in the United States. DAM's music is an incisive commentary on the contradictions of being Palestinian citizens of Israel, the so-called '48 Palestinians who represent 19 percent (1.2 million) of the Israeli population.[54] In "Meen Erhabi," they astutely critique the notion that Israel is a democracy with equal rights for all its citizens, by pointing out that there is no neutral arbiter of justice in a state where discrimination is built into citizenship and the law.[55] The song turns on its head Orientalist representations of Palestinian terrorists by highlighting the specter of state terror, illustrated by video images of bulldozed homes and brutality by Israeli soldiers: "Who's a terrorist? / Me, a terrorist? / How am I a terrorist / When you've taken my land? / You're the terrorist! / You've taken everything I own while I'm living in my homeland / You want me to go to the law? / You're the witness, the lawyer, and the judge."

The songs of DAM, MWR, and Saz are full of outrage at police brutality, inner-city poverty, and the failure of the Israeli state to protect the rights of its minority citizens, resonating with political rap in the United States. DAM challenges U.S. support and funding for Israel and settler colonial policies that displace indigenous peoples who remain imprisoned by treaties and agreements, similar to Native Americans: "We've been like this more than 50 years / Living as prisoners behind the bars of paragraphs / Of agreements that change nothing . . . The U.S. has made it their 51st state / Cleaning the Middle East of its Indians / Hitting us then blaming us."[56] They expose the hypocrisy and racism of "national security" and "anti-terrorist" policies in both Israel and the United States as a cover for subjugation and hegemony, challenging images of the "Arab terrorist" from Palestine to Iraq and calling for a lyrical resistance among youth. In "Kalimat" (Words), DAM raps, "Lyrics are like a witness / They witnessed the past and forecast the future" and in

"It's DAM," they proclaim, "The pen is my sledge hammer, the pages are my ground." DAM and other MCs situate their music in a tradition of poetry resisting colonialism and occupation like "the stones" of the Intifada and perform at political and community events for Arab as well as non-Arab audiences around the world, including for boycott and divestment campaigns.

Tensions: Between a Rock and a Hard Place

There are some potential, and productive, areas of tension experienced and debated by Arab American rap artists and their fans. Some artists discussed a potential conflict between their artistic development and political motivations. Iron Sheik sees himself as an "activist first, then an MC" and says, "I got back into producing hip hop as an alternative way to communicate the messages and ideas I work with." For him, there is no conflict for he comments, "If it weren't for the politics, I wouldn't be doing it."[57] Iron Sheik increasingly shifted to hosting shows and writing articles, rather than producing hip-hop, and has a political blog, Kabobfest.[58] He views this is as the most effective medium for his political activism given the profusion of Palestinian/Arab rap around the United States. Although there is no inherent contradiction between "art" and "politics," there is a tension that has long been experienced by "committed" artists; as Palestinian poet and writer Mourid Barghouti commented, "Poetry is not a civil servant, it's not a soldier."[59] Excentrik exclaims, "We're not just Arab hip hop, I'm not f——ing McDonald's, I'm not going to give you the same burger every time. It's art!" But he also acknowledges that "politics" suffuses his art and identity: "I don't see anything that isn't 'political' in regards to being Palestinian and an artist."[60]

Excentrik, who is interested in producing experimental music and electrifying the 'oud, seems to be concerned with the burden of representation that many minority artists feel. Since September 11, 2001, there has been increased pressure on Arab and Muslim American artists to speak on behalf of an identity category. In the words of Excentrik, "After 9/11, I was no longer just a hip hop artist, I was an Arab hip hop artist. Now I'm in a box, I'm in a metal cage. The media totally puts us in that box."[61] Iron Sheik, meanwhile, observes that there is a difference between being an "Arab American hip hop artist," who speaks to Arab American identity and politics, and an "Arab American *in* hip hop" who does not specifically address Arab American issues; while he thinks there is room for both positions, other artists feel it is not always a choice.[62] This dilemma, however, is situated in the larger context of the racism and backlash that Arab American hip-hop artists have experienced, especially those who do progressive rap. For example, Iron

Sheik and Excentrik are just two of many artists in the United States who have had their shows cancelled due to Zionist pressure. Excentrik recalls that he was almost attacked by a white man with a crowbar at a Detroit club after 9/11. The African Americans in the audience threw the assailant out, and told Excentrik, "You're the new niggaz, welcome to our world! We've dealt with this for years."[63] Narcycist, in P.H.A.T.W.A., observes wryly before being thrown against the wall by security personnel at the airport, "Iraq is the new Black." This "blackening," or at least resonance with the exclusion and opposition of African Americans, underlies the disidentification with whiteness and the identification with other racial minorities for some Arab American youth that drives their turn to hip-hop.[64]

Related to the issue of categorizing and marketing Arab American hip-hop is the thorny question of commodification, not just of Arab American identity but also of political activism. The proliferation of hookah bars and resurgence of belly dancing classes is often intertwined with Orientalist images of Arab and Middle Eastern cultures,[65] but there is also a consumption of progressive symbols of solidarity. For example, for some American college students and activists, the kaffiyeh denotes a visual symbol of solidarity with Arabs, especially in relation to Palestine or Iraq, but for many in the mid-2000s, it was simply a trendy fashion item available in different colors.[66] There is a range of products that one can purchase to express or embody solidarity with Palestine, from T-shirts and pendants to wristbands in red, green, and black (the colors of the Palestinian flag). However, cultural resistance, or resistance through symbols, cannot be substitutes for political resistance and education. Arab American hip-hop is a site where oppositional identities are being produced and performed, but the question of commodification of culture, and also solidarity, is ever present. Arab American rappers challenge hip-hop's conflation with American consumerist "lifestyles" and perform at antiwar and pro-Palestine rallies, on college campuses, and at community festivals, in spaces that are Arab American as well as multi-ethnic. For the artists discussed here who are outside mainstream popular culture, this production of political identities is linked to movements against war and occupation and in relation to music produced outside the borders of the United States.

Arab American hip-hop has become a popular cultural site of political pedagogy and alliance-building for youth that bridges Arab American and other communities. It is also an aesthetic form that resonates with the experiences of different groups of youth, in the United States and globally, who share an oppositional critique of colonialism and racism.[67] Political alliances between Arab Americans and other groups exist to varying degrees and are often nascent or tenuous, but Arab American hip-hop artists are able to translate their political concerns to youth from other communities whose understanding of such issues as the Palestinian struggle and the war in Iraq may be limited to the dominant discourse. In doing so, this musical critique resists the pervasive U.S. narrative of civilizing and progress and the discourse of exporting "freedom" and "democracy" to the Middle East and elsewhere. Arab American hip-hop enacts a diasporic identity that excavates cultural histories from sonic archives, reimagining the geographies of Arab America within national and transnational contexts through sounds of affiliation and resistance.

NOTES

My thanks to the artists who generously shared their time and insights with me and to the editors for their support, encouragement, and interest in my work. This is a revised and updated version of an essay that appeared in the *New Centennial Review* 8, no. 2.

1. Suheir Hammad, excerpt from "Gaza" written after Israel's war on the Gaza Strip in winter 2008–9, "Operation Cast Lead," which killed at least 400 children. http://shailja.com/news/newsletterblog/2009/01/gaza-poem-by-suheir-hammad.html (accessed December 3, 2009).

2. Tricia Rose, *Black Noise: Rap Music and Black Culture in Contemporary America* (1994); Murray Forman *The 'Hood Comes First: Race, Space, and Place in Rap and Hip-Hop* (2002).

3. Jeff Chang, *Can't Stop, Won't Stop: A History of the Hip-Hop Generation* (2005); Rose, *Black Noise*.

4. Rose, *Black Noise*, 82.

5. Will Youmans, "Arab American Hip-Hop," in *Etching Our Own Image: Voices from within the Arab American Art Movement*, ed. Anan Ameri and Holly Arida (Newcastle, UK: Cambridge Scholars Publishing, 2007), 42.

6. There is also a growing genre of Muslim American hip-hop and African American hip-hop artists who resonate with Arab issues via Islam; for example, Mos Def, Eric B., and Rakim ("Know the Ledge"), as well as Black rappers who are Five Percenters—a splinter group of the Nation Of Islam—such as Wu Tang Clan, Busta Rhymes, and Poor Righteous Teachers (see Hisham Aidi, "Jihadis in the Hood: Race, Urban Islam and the War on Terror," *Middle East Report* 224 (2007); Samy H. Alim, "A New Research Agenda: Exploring the Transglobal Hip Hop Umma," in *Muslim Networks from Hajj to Hip Hop*, ed. Miriam Cooke and Bruce B. Lawrence (Chapel Hill: University of North Carolina Press 2005), 264–74; Michael Muhammad Knight, *Blue-Eyed Devil: A Road Odyssey through Islamic America* (2006).

7. It is worth noting that there are hip-hop and spoken word artists who are not Arab / Palestinian American and who increasingly address the issue of Palestine; for example, Talib Kweli, Method Man ("PLO Style"), Immortal Technique, Lupe Fiasco, and spoken word poet Mark Gonzalez.

8. For example, Joseph Massad situates Palestinian political rap in a longer tradition of revolutionary, underground Arabic music that supported Palestinian liberation since the 1950s and mixed nationalist poetry with hybrid Arab/Western musical

instrumentation. "Liberating Songs: Palestine Put to Music," in *Palestine, Israel, and the Politics of Popular Culture,* ed. Rebecca Stein and Ted Swedenburg (Durham: Duke University Press, 2005), 175–201.

9. Youmans, "Arab American Hip Hop," 46–47.

10. Chang, *Can't Stop, Won't Stop* (2005).

11. George Lipsitz, "We Know What Time It Is: Race, Class, and Youth Culture in the Nineties," in *Microphone Fiends: Youth Music, Youth Culture* (New York: Routledge, 1994), 17–28; Robin Kelley, *Yo' Mama's Disfunktional! Fighting the Culture Wars in Urban America* (1997).

12. Alim, "A New Research Agenda: Exploring the Transglobal Hip Hop Umma" (2005); Davey D, "Fear of an Arab Planet: Hip Hop is Everywhere," *The Hip Hop Cosign: Breakdown FM* (November 2007); Youmans, "Arab American Hip Hop."

13. Will Youmans (aka The Iron Sheik) in discussion with the author, 2008.

14. See Joan Gross, David McMurray, and Ted Swedenburg, "Arab Noise and Ramadan Nights: Rap, Rai, and Franco-Maghrebi Identities," in *Displacement, Diaspora, and Geographies of Identity,* ed. Smadar Lavie and Ted Swedenbur (Durham: Duke University Press, 1996), 119–55.

15. Stefan Christoff, "Arab Hip-hop Forces Unite for Justice," interview with Arab Summit. *The Electronic Intifada,* October 1, 2007.

16. *The Arab Summit* (2007).

17. Juliane Hammer, *Palestinians Born in Exile: Diaspora and the Search for Homeland* (Austin: University of Texas Press, 2005), 83.

18. Iron Sheik, *Camel Clutch* (2003).

19. Sameer Abraham, "Detroit's Arab-American Community: A Survey of Diversity and Commonality," in *Arabs in the New World: Studies on Arab American Communities,* ed. Sameer Abraham and Nabeel Abraham (Detroit: Wayne State University Center for Urban Studies, 1983), 84–108.

20. Ibid.

21. Kazaleh (rapper) in discussion with author, 2007.

22. Edward Said, *The Question of Palestine* (1979); "America's Last Taboo," *New Left Review* 6 (November–December 2000): 45–53.

23. Helen Samhan, "Not Quite White: Race and the Arab-American Experience," in *Arabs in America: Building a New Future,* ed. Michael W. Suleiman (Philadelphia: Temple University Press, 1999), 209–26.

24. Suheir Hammad in discussion with author, 2008; idem, *Born Palestinian, Born Black* (1996).

25. "Drops of Suheir Hammad: A Talk with a Palestinian Poet Born Black," interview with Nathalie Handal, *Al Jadid* 3, no. 20 (Summer 1997). http://leb.net/~aljadid/interviews/DropsofSuheirHammad.html (accessed December 1, 2009).

26. Sunaina Maira, *Desis in the House: Indian American Youth Culture in New York City* (Philadelphia: Temple University Press, 2002).

27. See, for example, Oliver Wang, "Rapping and Repping Asian: Race, Authenticity, and the Asian American MC," in *Alien Encounters: Popular Culture in Asian America,* ed. Mimi Thi Nguyen and Thuy Linh Nguyen Tu (Durham: Duke Press, 2007), 35–68.

28. Excentrik in discussion with author, 2007.

29. Sameer Abraham, Nabeel Abraham, and Barbara Aswad, "The Southend: An Arab Muslim Working-Class Community," in *Arabs in the New World: Studies on Arab*

American Communities, ed. Sameer Abraham and Nabeel Abraham (Detroit: Wayne State University Center for Urban Studies, 1983), 164–81.

30. Excentrik in discussion with author, 2007.

31. Nabeel Abraham, "Anti-Arab Racism and Violence in the United States," in *The Development of Arab-American Identity,* ed. Ernest McCarus (Ann Arbor: University of Michigan Press, 1994), 155–214; David Cole and James Dempsey, *Terrorism and the Constitution: Sacrificing Civil Liberties in the Name of National Security* (2002); Steven Salaita, *Anti-Arab Racism in the USA: Where It Comes From and What It Means for Politics Today* (2006).

32. Abraham, "Detroit's Arab-American Community: A Survey of Diversity and Commonality" (1983); Gregory Orfalea, *The Arab Americans: A History* (2006).

33. Abraham, Abraham, and Aswad, "The Southend: An Arab Muslim Working-Class Community," 177–78.

34. Abraham, "Detroit's Arab-American Community: A Survey of Diversity and Commonality" (1983); Gregory Orfalea, *The Arab Americans: A History* (Northampton: Olive Branch Press, 2006).

35. Abraham, Abraham, and Aswad, "The Southend: An Arab Muslim Working-Class Community," 178–79.

36. Orfaela, *The Arab Americans: A History,* 216.

37. See Lawrence Davidson, "Debating Palestine: Arab-American Challenges to Zionism, 1917–1923," *Arabs in America: Building a New Future,* Michael Suleiman, ed. (Philadelphia: Temple University Press, 1999), 227–40.

38. Orfalea, *The Arab Americans: A History.*

39. Laila Weir, "The Iron Sheik: Rapper Will Youmans taps into the American minority experience to address the Palestinian-Israel conflict," *San Francisco Chronicle,* August 22, 2004.

40. Excentrik in discussion with author, 2007.

41. Quoted in Christoff, "Arab Hip-hop Forces Unite for Justice" (2007).

42. Ibid.

43. The Narcysist, http://www.myspace.com/euphrates (accessed June 15, 2009).

44. Weir (2004).

45. Edward Said, *Orientalism,* 1978.

46. Quoted in Christoff, "Arab Hip-hop Forces Unite for Justice" (2007).

47. Chang, *Can't Stop, Won't Stop,* 445–46.

48. See Nancy Guevara, "Women Writin' Rappin' Breakin,'" in *Droppin' Science: Critical Essays on Rap Music and Hip Hop Culture,* ed. William E. Perkins (Philadelphia: Temple University Press, 1996), 49–62; Rose, *Black Noise.*

49. TIMZ "Iraq" Music Video, 2007. http://www.youtube.com/watch?v=DRiy4yfh-IM (accessed June 15, 2009).

50. Quoted in Christoff, "Arab Hip-hop Forces Unite for Justice" (2007).

51. Iron Sheik in discussion with author, 2008.

52. Weir (2004).

53. Quoted in Christoff, "Arab Hip-hop Forces Unite for Justice" (2007).

54. Dan Rabinowitz and Khawla Abu-Baker, *Coffins on Our Shoulders: The Experience of the Palestinian Citizens of Israel,* 2005.

55. Nimer Sultany, *Citizens Without Citizenship: Israel and the Palestinian Minority 2000–2002* (Haifa, Israel: Mada—Arab Center for Applied Social Research, 2003); see

articles in *Adalahs' Review—The Journal of the Legal Center for Arab Minority Rights in Israel*, 3 (2002).

56. "Mali Huriye / I Don't Have Freedom," *The Arab Summit*.
57. Iron Sheik in discussion with author, 2008.
58. See Youmans, "Arab American Hip-Hop."
59. Quoted in Ahdaf Soueif, "Art of Resistance," *The Guardian*, 21 October 2006.
60. Quoted in Christoff, "Arab Hip-Hop Forces Unite for Justice" (2007).
61. Quoted in Christoff "Arab Hip-hop Forces Unite for Justice" (2007).
62. Iron Sheik in discussion with author, 2008.
63. Excentrik in discussion with author, 2007.
64. See Moustafa Bayoumi, "How Does It Feel to Be a Problem?" *Amerasia Journal* 27, no. 3–28, no. 1 (2001–2): 69–77; Nadine Naber, "Ambiguous Insiders: An Investigation of Arab American Invisibility," *Ethnic and Racial Studies* 23, no. 1 (2000): 37–61; Therese Saliba, "Military Presences and Absences," in *Food for Our Grandmothers: Writings by Arab-American and Arab-Canadian Feminists*, ed. Joanna Kadi (Boston: South End Press, 1999), 125–32.
65. Maira (2008).
66. See "Modern Chronology of the Keffiyeh Craze," by QuiQui, and the satirical video, "Keffiyeh Infiltrates Our Nation's Youth" at the Kabobfest blog. http://www.kabobfest.com/2007/07/modern-chronology-of-keffiyah-kraze.html (accessed December 3, 2009).
67. For example, M.I.A., a British Sri Lankan hip-hop artist raps in "Sunshowers": "Like PLO, I don't surrender" (Ben Sisario, "An Itinerant Refugee in a Hip-Hop World," *New York Times*, August 19, 2007).

ELEVEN

Muslim Digital Diasporas and the Gay Pornographic Cyber Imaginary

Karim Tartoussieh

In recent years, Arab American youth have been capitalizing on the potential and reach of digital technology to help create a virtual public sphere for participation, networking, and activism. The rampant developments in cyber technologies have enabled the rise of digital diasporic communities in the United States where Arab migrants and Arab Americans increasingly find forums to reconnect with their countries of origin. Indeed, the Internet has helped to create new avenues for participation in the political, social, cultural, and religious issues that are pertinent to the Arab and Muslim Diaspora in the United States. This essay argues that currently, there is an ascending moment in which new media culture and practice is dovetailing with a neoliberal mutation of post-Islamism—one that is evident since the 1990s and is characterized by its embrace of media technology as a tool for fashioning an Islamic citizen/consumer. This new media moment provides the requisite technological scaffolding for the emergence and accretion of digital diasporic communities that may be organized along different affiliative axes, for example, religious (Muslim/Christian/secular, Sunni/Shia') and/or sexual (queer/ heterosexual). These emerging digital communities are reimagining and redefining notions of citizenship, both sexual and religious in the United States. Taking the United States as a real national space, I demonstrate how these virtual digital sites, which are transnational in nature, that is, not confined to the actual borders of a nation-state, can have immense impact on societies and cultures within the confines of an actual territorial space.

This essay doesn't purport to offer an exhaustive survey of the different digital Arab communities in cyber space. The focus here will be on two sites of digital diasporic expression: first, digital Muslim networking through Islamic portals that service the Arab American community, and second, cyber representations of male Arab queerness in gay pornography websites. By juxtaposing these two digital sites that offer two different snapshots of the cyber imaginary, I investigate the ways in which Arab Americans are socially, politically, and sexually inscribed in the United States especially after the attacks of September 11. Undoubtedly, the rise of Islamophobia coupled with a lack of knowledge about Islam has resulted in a backlash against the Arab American community, subjecting it to a deluge of racial profiling and misrepresentations in the media. Furthermore, such a highly anxious climate resulted in conflating "Muslim" and "terrorist" in the popular imaginary. Such an assemblage has negatively affected the Arab American community who felt their affiliation with the Middle East or profession of the Islamic faith automatically put them under suspicion.

It is within the post–September 11 context that my essay analyzes these two digital sites (Islamic networking portals and gay pornographic websites). I make the following arguments: first, I contend that the sense of alienation felt and experienced by Arab Americans post–September 11 has necessitated the creation of safe spaces for the community to mobilize, share experiences, and assert their citizenship rights. Islamic digital networks helped create a virtual public sphere for the community. Second, I contend that pornographic digital sites have capitalized on the clustering of "Muslim" and "terrorist," and this gave rise to a whole new genre of sexual fantasy and fetish. Third, looking at both the Islamic portals and the pornographic gay websites in relation to each other demonstrates how the Muslim Arab body becomes a signifier of danger and violence, in both a real and pruriently-inspired sense. Hence, my investigation will map out the ways through which their representation has been discursively shaped and influenced by the proliferation of transnational digital technologies in light of current discourses on Islamic fundamentalism and terrorism. Furthermore, networked texts such as blogs, Twitter feeds, YouTube videos, Facebook pages, SMS, and cell phone films are pushing the boundaries of cultural production, dissemination, and consumption; they are giving rise to new transnational media regimes that are global in reach and broadening the discussion around globalization and the directionality of media flows.

Much of the debate around globalization centers on the unidirectional flow of globalization that is structured around what Inderpal Grewal and Caren Kaplan call "the problematic notion of a homogenizing West." A key idea within this formulation is the unidirectionality of cultural flow from the center (the West) to the periphery (the rest), which makes such approaches not only ethno- and eurocentric but also inaccurate.[1] In this formulation the notion of cultural homogenization is equated with Americanization. Furthermore, this formulation assumes a binarist separation between center/periphery and local/global, denying spatial and temporal relationality. Ella Shohat and Robert Stam have argued that "it is simplistic to imagine an active First World unilaterally forcing its products on a passive Third World . . . [also] there are powerful reverse currents as a number of Third World countries (Mexico, Brazil, India, and Egypt) dominate their own markets and even become cultural exporters."[2] This essay builds on Shohat and Stam's formulation by exploring how Islamic portals like Islam online and the prolific digital religious preaching products of the influential Egyptian preacher Amr Khaled have had an enormous impact on Muslim diasporic communities in the United States and Europe. It also examines the Eurocentric ways in which queer Arab men are consumed in gay porn sites during the War on Terror.

The past decade has been characterized by a media revolution in the Arab World. This has been facilitated by two events: the spread of cyber technologies and the proliferation of transnational satellite channels with twenty-four-hour programming. These developments had an immense impact on Arab societies both at home and in the diaspora. One of the most salient projects to have tapped into the potential of these transnational media technologies is an Islamic revivalist movement, or what Asef Bayat calls "Post Islamism"[3]—a movement that has effectively used transnational media technologies, particularly the Internet, to help in forming an Islamic (trans) nation connecting Muslim diasporas with an imagined Islamic nation. These Islamic communication tools have facilitated the production of communities who are not confined to the political borders of the Middle East but extend beyond the spatial and temporal confines of Muslim nation-states, giving these communities a transnational character. This process echoes Jasbir Puar and Amit Rai's formulation of the nation (in this case an Islamic nation) reterritorializing itself in the diaspora.[4]

These media products (discussed below) have triggered a transnational imaginary resulting in what Arjun Appadurai calls a "model of disjunctive flows," whereby the flow of people (through migratory practices), cultural products (through electronic mass media), capital, and technologies creates a theory of rupture in intersocietal relationships that has an impact on "the work of imagination, which is a constitutive feature of modern subjectivity."[5] Key to Appadurai's formulation is how both electronic mediation and mass migration mark our present world and unleash the work of the imagination. Thus, "the work of the imagination as social practice," viewed through this lens, is not simply purely emancipatory or hegemonically disciplined but "a space of contestation in which individuals and groups seek to annex the global into their own practices of the modern."[6] My work here dialogues with

Minoo Moallem's work on Iran, which contends that to understand Islamic nationalism and fundamentalism, not only do various forms of nation-state governmentality need to be explored but also "postmodern circuits of goods, technologies, and ideas . . . consumer culture, and transnational media in both national and diasporic spaces."[7] Finally, I examine these cases to help in understanding the linkages between transnational digital production, citizenship, and identity formation. A common thread that runs throughout these cases is the fact that they are situated at the intersection of religion, media, and power. Here a caveat is in order: not all Arabs are Muslims, and for the purposes of this essay, I focus on the Muslim population of the Arab American community.

Halal Dating, Cyber Preaching and Online Islam

The last decade has witnessed a plethora of scholarly work that explores the relationship between religion, technology, and society.[8] In fact, research has shown that religion has capitalized on the power and potential of the Internet to establish a solid presence online.[9] Islam is no exception. Islamic portals and networking tools have proliferated in the past decades offering an array of resources and online services to Internet surfers and subscribers. Gary R. Bunt contends that these portals act as central information resources on Islam.

> In order to enhance their position in the cyber-marketplace, those with appropriate financial and technical resources can apply wide-ranging communication management strategies and utilize specific forms of religious symbolism and language. Loyalty is encouraged through schemes such as membership benefits and through the provision of facilities including chat rooms, Islamic software (such as prayer timetables and Islamic screen savers), Qur'an resources, and free e-mail accounts and Web space.[10]

Three popular Islamic social networking portals in the United States are Islamic matrimonial sites: www.muslimsingle.com, www.Qiran.com (the word *qiran* in Arabic translates to matrimony or marriage), and iKhitba.com (*khitba* is the Arabic word for engagement). The *iKhitba* portal is based in the United States and specializes in providing its services to the Arab American community. In the introduction section of the *iKhitba* website the intention of the site is made clear in its targeting of the Arab American community in particular.

> *iKhitba.com* is dedicated for Arab Americans interested in getting married and searching for their life partner. You can do your own search and contact members registered at *iKhitba.com* until you find your life partner. *iKhitba.com* makes finding your life partner easier and achievable. The intention of iKhitba.com is to provide these services in a manner that reflects a genuine respect for the people that are using the site as well as with a sincere and sustainable concern for the Arab American culture and society.[11]

While the Single Muslim portal is based in the United Kingdom and the *Qiran* portal is based in Canada, both websites allow the user to choose their geographical location in order to customize the search result according to the location of the user. Both websites are available to users in the United States and, according to the information listed on their respective sites, are highly popular in the United States attracting heavy user traffic. The singlemuslim.com website includes the following description of its mandate and services.

> *SingleMuslim.com* provides the best possible help for our brothers and sisters to find their ideal Muslim marriage partner and complete their faith within a happy and successful Islamic marriage. We do this using modern technology, coupled with Islamic principles, so you can be confident that our service is the *halal* choice.[12]

In fact, the three websites emphasize the *halal* nature of their services. Such a designation entails the following: proper intention (the intention of finding a proper pious marriage partner), parental involvement, and modesty and faith. When there is a potential for a possible match, the subscriber can request a parentally sanctioned video interview. In fact, the *ikhitba* website states explicitly in its eligibility for registration section that "married Ladies may not become registered users. By registering to iKhitba.com site, you have to represent and warrant that you are not married."[13] If a match is made and results in marriage, the websites offer tickets to the Muslim Holy Land for an *Umrah* as wedding gifts.[14] The websites encourage subscribers who have found their marital match through the service to share their success stories online to provide encouragement to "fellow Muslim brothers and sisters." Another feature that ensures the *halal* designation of these websites is their position vis-à-vis same-sex dating. The three websites prohibit gay users from using their services, and the menu-driven identity that the registered user must construct in order to use the service is heterosexually biased by not allowing a male to search for another male or a female to search for another female. The frequently asked questions section of the *iKhtiba* site explicitly addresses this issue.

> Is there a way to contact same sex member?
> You can't send messages or show interest to same sex members. *iKhitba.com* is meant to be for marriage only.[15]

It is salient to note the logic inherent in the above question and answer. The website defends its heterosexist bias not out of discrimination against same-sex people but because the site is strictly for marriage purposes. And since gay marriage is not federally sanctioned in the United States, therefore the main function of the website will not be met, and this justifies exclusionary measures against members of the queer Arab American community.

The case of online *halal* dating indefatigably brings out the following conclusions: first, the creation of a virtual marriage marketplace has an empowering effect on the members of the Arab American community, due to the precarious position that Arab Americans found themselves in after the attacks of September 11. Many were the target of attacks and slander. The vitriol the community encountered has exacerbated a feeling of atomization and alienation. Many of the testimonies by users of such websites highlight how these sites provide a safe space for them to interact and build community while feeling protected by the digital space that these sites provide. One has to consider the plethora of documented attacks on Arab Americans in the wake of September 11, 2001, where mosques and community centers have been the targets of acts of vandalism and sabotage. Surely, the current hostile backlash resulting from what has come to be known as the "Ground Zero Mosque" is a case in point. Islamic community centers and mosques provide meeting places for members of the Arab American community where they can interact, socialize, and mobilize. Having become dangerous zones for congregation, these traditional spaces have been to a large extent replaced by safe digital spaces. Second, despite the significance of such sites in fostering digital diasporic communities that aided in cementing alliances, these sites have been exclusionary of a segment of the Arab American community, namely, queer Arab Americans who are deprived of participation in such virtual communities.

Islamic preachers in the Middle East have been active in using electronic mediation to reach Muslims in the diaspora. One of the best examples of such a trend is the Egyptian preacher Amr Khaled, who has become a transnational phenomenon. In April 2006, the *New York Times* magazine published an investigative piece by Samantha M. Shapiro on Amr Khaled, featuring on the cover a full-length photo of a visibly pious Amr Khaled. The caption reads: "Amr Khaled is the World's most famous and influential Muslim televangelist. So what's his message, exactly?" The piece functions as an introduction of Mr. Khaled to an American audience. Amr Khaled's popularity in the Arab world, his brand of preaching—preaching that is an amalgam of traditional Islamic hermeneutics coupled with self-help and management skills—is close to evangelical Christianity in America. More important, in contradistinction to the preachers of radical Islam, Khaled's message stresses the reconcilability of modern life with Islam and eschews politics by underscoring personal values and norms necessary for modern ethical living. All these characteristics have made Khaled a favorable candidate for Europeans and the Americans in their war against radical Islamism—a point that Shapiro intelligently highlights in her article.

> In the wake of Sept. 11 attacks, the Madrid train bombings, the London tube bombings and the cartoon riots, many European governments and philanthropic groups have been looking for a point of communication with Muslims, and a few are beginning to come to the conclusion that they have found it in Amr Khaled.[16]

In addition, Shapiro quotes a State Department official who echoes Shapiro's hope for establishing a meeting with Khaled when the preacher visits the United States since the official thinks that Khaled's message is in sync with the message that the United States wants to communicate to the Muslim world, which is that the United States' problem is not with Islam per se but with terrorism. Indeed media technology has connected Amr Khaled to a wide constituency of Muslims in the diaspora in Europe and the United States. The *New York Times* article states that "Khaled's Web site, where followers can chat with one another and download sermons, received 26 million hits last year, more than Oprah's; it is the third most popular Arabic website in the world, behind Al Jazeera."[17]

A salient part of the power of Khaled's message lies in its mode of transmission. Relying on the Saudi-financed Religious Satellite channel, Iqra, and his astoundingly popular website (www.amrkhaled.net), the preacher has enjoyed an amazing geographical reach that has transcended the borders of the nation-state. In fact, his use of transnational media technologies such as the Internet and satellite television has enabled him to escape the censorship and silencing of the Egyptian state. Due to the extreme popularity of the preacher, specifically with the upwardly mobile and youth segments of Egyptian society, and his ability to galvanize these segments into action, the Egyptian state felt threatened by the reach and strength of his preaching power and deemed him persona non grata. To my mind this hostile attitude toward Khaled derives from the realization that the state's official religious institutions cannot offer much competition. Both the content and packaging[18] of this private-sector preacher make him much more appealing than his public, state-sanctioned competition. Speaking in simple colloquial Egyptian and dressed fashionably in suits and jeans, Khaled sugarcoats his religious message with modern parables that speak to the dreams and desires of young people such as his "fun in the sun" series where he explains how one can enjoy the beach in summer in an Islam-sanctioned manner. By contrast, the preachers of the state, adhering to classical Arabic and dressed in traditional garb, are seen as fossilized and antiquated in terms of their appearance and message by comparison to Khaled's.

In 2007, Amr Khaled was placed in the "Heroes and Pioneers" category of *Time* magazine's list of the 100 most influential people of the world. Khaled made his first trip to the United States in order to accept the award. On May 12, 2009, Khaled was invited by the Maryland and Virginia chapter of the Council on American-Islamic Relations (CAIR-MD/VA) and the Islamic Society of North America (ISNA) to give a lecture on Muslims in the United States. His message was simple: Muslim Americans have a religious obligation to better their lives and their communities. Using parables from *The Quran* and *Hadith* (sayings of the Prophet Muhammad), he outlined five messages to Muslims in America.

> 1. Balance between materialism and the spirit; 2. Be good emissaries for Islam; 3. Don't be embarrassed of your faith or your background, don't hide or be ashamed of your *hijab,* your identity, your faith. Always be proud of your faith, your background. Be proud of your service to your society; 4. Have hope and raise your kids to have hope that the country they live in will improve and Islam will be fine; and 5. Renew your lives, promise God a new beginning and repent to God.[19]

As illustrated above, the phenomenon of Amr Khaled and his influence extends beyond Muslim populations in the Middle East to include Muslim diasporic communities. Such development draws our attention to the multidirectionality of cultural flows, characteristic of our current globalized terrain. But beyond the point of multidirectionality of digital media flows, the enthusiastic reception of Khaled's outreach efforts to the Muslim communities in the United States after September 11 and his popular reception are due both to the form and content of his digital preaching. In terms of form, his modern personal sartorial style coupled with his use of simple colloquial Arabic and Internet linguistic codes make him easily accessible to Arab Americans, who can relate to his modern appearance and are not intimidated by simple everyday Arabic. In terms of content, his message to diasporic communities of integration within their adopted societies while remaining proud of their heritage appeals especially to young Arab Americans. And it is precisely this aspect of his preaching that endears him to the West by deeming him an "enlightened" Muslim scholar who can build friendly bridges of communication between Western governments with their Muslim constituencies, and thus he is a frequent guest speaker in Europe and the United States.

The third example of diasporic community building in cyber space is the interactive forum Islam Online. According to the gatekeepers of the website, the mission of the multilingual site is "To create a unique, global Islamic site on the Internet that provides services to Muslim community and non-Muslims in several languages. To become a reference for everything that deals with Islam, its sciences, civilization and nation. To have credibility in content, distinction in design, and a sharp and balanced vision of humanity and current events."[20] Islam Online provides a cogent example of cyber technology that reterritorializes a virtual Islamic nation in the diaspora. This goal becomes evident in the introductory work of Dr. Yusuf Qaradawi, one of the main scholars and founders of the service.

> It is our [Muslims'] duty to carry this religion to all people around the world until they understand it, become interested in it, look for it, and enter it in surges as God would like. This is the duty of the Islamic nation. It is a collective obligation for this nation to propagate the message of this religion to the corners of the globe, and it is an individual obligation for the scholars of this religion to propagate Islam in all languages and tongues.[21]

Because of its interactive nature, Islam Online has proven to be a very popular destination for questions around Islam. The content of the site underscores the compatibility of Islam with modernity. One of the more popular services that the site provides is an interactive ask-a-scholar service and online *Fatwa* section (nonbinding Islamic opinions). Randomly surveying these sections reveals that the service is very popular among Muslim diasporic communities. Arab American Muslims are frequent users of the service. A sample of the questions posed to the online scholars from Muslims in the United States provides a sense of some of the issues with which this community is concerned. More important, most of the answers provided stress the need for integration and positive engagement within the wider American society without compromising Islamic values. Here are some examples of these inquiries and abridged responses.

QUESTION:
Dear Scholar, As-salamu `alaykum. I find it so difficult to strike a balance between my religious ordinances and the idea of enjoying summer, particularly at beaches. My family asks me for a summer vacation, but I don't know how to organize a summer vacation that is sin-free and enjoyable. Thanks.

ANSWER:
In summer time, all members of the family should try their best to help one another lead a sin-free and enjoyable life. This can be achieved by staying away from all sources of temptations that affect one's behavior negatively. In addition, one must strike a balance between one's religious duties and enjoying summer in order to remain attached to one's religion and safe from decline.

QUESTION:
Is it allowed for Muslims living in the West or in non-Muslim countries not to file their taxes or to conceal their full income or business profits?

ANSWER:
It is the duty of Muslims, especially those living in Western countries to reflect the true image of Islam and commit themselves to the proper Islamic manners both in theory and practice. Indeed, concealing one's income to evade paying taxes is a prohibited act for a Muslim. It is a kind of lying, which is totally prohibited in Islam.

QUESTION:
As a Muslim minority, can we join non-Muslim political parties and take part in elections?

ANSWER:
Muslims are encouraged to join non-Muslim political parties and take part in elections. This is part of the Islamic duty to command that which is good and forbid that which is evil. Moreover, Muslims should elect candidates who uphold the values or principles they cherish dearly; so if they find a candidate who is upholding all of the values or principles that they cherish, they should support him.

This sample of ask-a-scholar questions and answers gives a sense of the issues and challenges diasporic communities face while living in their adopted societies. Questions regarding taxation and political participation highlight the sense of precariousness that these communities feel vis-à-vis naturalized home states and an uncertainty toward assimilation. The tragic events of September 11 buoyed the urgency of questions of citizenship and participation. These excerpts illustrate how through interactive services such as those Islam Online provides, Arab American digital media participants are able to voice their questions regarding integration in their new societies and preserving a sense of identity—one that is derived from their religious background. In fact the three examples, which I explored in this section on digital diasporic community building, underscore the importance of the Internet and new media technologies in providing a safe virtual terrain where Muslims in the diaspora can tread without fear of persecution or stigmatization. Furthermore, participation in these digital landscapes represents mutations of the notion of citizenship. Indeed, the participants in these new media forms are digital citizens in their own right. Their digital citizenship allows them flexibility to construct their identities in a multivalent manner: They are Americans but are also Muslims; they can assimilate but without compromising their religiosity. While historically many diasporic communities in the United States have been able to define themselves through a pastiche of old and new influences (think about Italian Americans or Irish Americans), the social and political climates post–September 11 have made it very difficult for Arab Americans to do the same, and here the Internet and digital technology have forged a way to facilitate identity construction in a time of rampant Islamophobia.

"Fuck me, Osama!" or The Orgasmic Specter of the Homoterrorist

So far I have outlined how Muslim Americans have digitally mobilized around issues of interest to their community. Examples of such digital mobilization include social networking / Islamic marriage portals, cyber preaching, and interactive Islamic websites. I have argued that in light of rampant Islamophobic attitudes in the United States post-9/11, these digital diasporic communities have been able to harness the potential of new media technology to create virtual public spheres for the exchange of ideas, thoughts, and concerns. However, unfortunately, membership in these digital diasporic communities has not been inclusive to all Arab Americans. Queer Arab Americans are denied membership to the dating websites I have analyzed. The position of the cyber preachers who run Islam Online and other sites regarding homosexuality is unanimous: it is an unnatural act—one that is destructive to the social fabric of society—and hence, cannot be tolerated. Despite the emergence of some attempts to create digital platforms that tackle queer Arab issues, these attempts remain on the fringe of cyber mainstream. Here I explore how queer Arab Americans are signified in the pornographic digital imaginary particularly after September 11.

Nowhere and at no other time has the collapse of the category "Terrorist" and "Arab" been as palpably discernible as in the United States post–September 11 and the ensuing War on Terror. In fact, Jasbir Puar contends that at this historical juncture, the invocation of the terrorist as queer, nonnational, and acutely racialized becomes ubiquitous.[22] This conflation between terrorist, Arab, and queer has had a dehumanizing effect on the Queer Arab American community. It is pertinent to add here that such representations are not entirely the fabrication of a heteronormative Islamophobic power bloc. This stigmatization of the male Arab is highly palpable within the American queer community too. Consequently, the analysis of how gay Arab Americans are represented in pornographic websites exhibits a collusion between two types of normative power vectors that Arab Americans, both straight and gay, have to contend with: heteronormativity and what Lisa Duggan calls a new emerging homonormativity in the United States post–September 11. According to Duggan, homonormativity is "a new neo-liberal sexual politics that hinges upon the possibility of a demobilized gay constituency and a privatized, depoliticized gay culture anchored in domesticity and consumption."[23] Within this power constellation of hetero- and homonormativity, the Arab American body is a "dangerous" body; the only difference is that for the homonormative imaginary this "dangerous" body is desirous and is sanctioned within the realm of sexual fantasy.

Take, for example, this question that was posed to the sex expert Jamie Bufalino who writes a section called "Get Naked" answering questions on sex in *Time Out New York* magazine.

QUESTION:

I'm a gay male Muslim, and my boyfriend is Jewish. A few months ago, my boyfriend suggested I grow a beard, but I am blond, so my beard was very light, and he suggested I dye it brown. A few days ago, as I was fucking him, he said, "Fuck me, you fucking Muslim terrorist," and stuff along these lines. I stopped; he apologized and said he didn't mean it. I am sure he called me a Muslim terrorist and asked me to dye my beard because the idea of him being fucked by a Muslim fanatic turns him on. I have to admit, it turns me on too. However, my dilemma is that I grew up in cosmopolitan Beirut, speaking French along with Arabic, and like the current Lebanese-American Miss USA, I attended Catholic school there. My mom was a single mother who worked and went to the beach in a bikini, and that—along with my blond hair—makes me not fit the stereotype that my boyfriend fantasizes about. I know he doesn't think all Muslims are terrorists, and certainly not me, but I am caught between the fear of fulfilling his fantasy and thus propagating the Muslim stereotype and the fear of failing to fulfill his fantasy.

ANSWER:

At first I thought this letter was a complete goof, but by the end I actually started taking it seriously (nothing shuts down my bullshit meter quite like a Muslim mom in a bikini). Here's the deal: if you truly believe that your boyfriend doesn't harbor extreme prejudice against everyone of the Muslim faith, then I say the bedroom action can get as freaky as you both want to get. If you start questioning the social implications of all of your sexual activities, you'll just end up with a headache and a limp dick. Think about it: Would you say, "Hmm, I wonder if sucking this cock plays too much into the gay stereotype?" or "Does being this aggressive in bed make me too much of a male cartoon?" I think asking someone to dye his beard for role-playing purposes is a bit much (that's what imaginations are for, people), but if you're okay with it, who am I to judge.[24]

The question and answer, notwithstanding Bufalino's problematic response, highlights the bind that the French-speaking, Catholic-educated (read: secular) young gay questioner finds himself in. On the one level, he is uneasy about fulfilling his partner's sexual demands lest he be implicated in propagating the stereotype of the "angry male Arab," and on the other hand, he feels scared of alienating his boyfriend by denying him his fantasy. Furthermore, his resorting to *Time Out New York* for advice is understandable given the difficulty of posing such question to a cyber preacher or submitting his query to the Islam Online ask-a-scholar section, for example.

One might say that this is an isolated case that shouldn't be generalized. However, I believe the case (the homoterrorist fantasy) is ubiquitous enough that it has provided creative fodder for an off Broadway play shown in New York in 2007. *All that I will ever be* is a play by Alan Ball (who wrote the screenplay for *American Beauty*) that was performed at the New York theater workshop. The play tells the story of Omar, an Arab American bisexual salesperson and hustler living in the United States post–September 11. We are first introduced to Omar as he is servicing one of his white American clients, who shouts at Omar, "That's it, fuck me, Osama! Sandnigger!" In a review of the play in the *New Yorker*, the critic John Lahr reflects on Omar's predicament by stating, "Omar finds himself variously ignored, abandoned, and paid to leave. His particularly robust sexual expertise is a testament to his desire to find a place for himself in the alien American landscape, to root himself somehow in the imagination of another person."[25]

A preliminary survey on the Internet reveals a plethora of websites dedicated to exhibiting Arab male bodies pornographically. The intended consumers of these websites seem to be white middle-class American and European gay men. The racism inherent in these hypersexual spaces of representation reveals itself on several levels. The names of the websites are indicative of the preconceived attitudes and stereotypes that these websites convey and solidify: *Arab Studs, Arab Cock, Arab Meat, Arabian Sex, Arab Ass Fuckers, Hung Egyptian Men, Arabian Heat,* and *Baghdad Boy.* Surely, one has to wonder what exactly "Arabian sex" is and how it differs from, say, "American sex." In fact the pornographic industry subjects blacks and Asians to similar racist attitudes. Richard Fung cautions us that "it is important to recognize the different strategies used for fitting an Asian actor [or, for that matter, an Arab or a black] into the traditionally white world of gay porn and how the terms of entry are determined by the perceived demands of an intended audience."[26]

The content of these websites reveals the intransigence of a Eurocentric homoerotic Orientalist desire vis-à-vis the representation of Arab men. The same colonialist racial hierarchies that were discussed earlier permeate pornographic cyber space. Thus we find the same racist tendency to feminize the Asian and hypermasculinize the black and Arab. As Fanon tells us, how the Negro is eclipsed is that he is turned into a penis,[27] and the Arab in these websites is also turned into a penis (*Arabian Meat, Arab Cock*). Furthermore, the content of these websites reveals the persistence of the Orientalist trope through which Arab Men are perceived as the dangerous, unrestrained, violent "Other" of Europe's "civilized" masculinity. To elucidate this point, consider these quotes taken out of these websites: "Brutal Arab tops in hard hot action . . . They fuck with force and fuck to hurt,"[28] "Arab Studs with attitude will fuck your ass deep and hard with their cut huge Arab cock," and "Active circumcised horse-hung Arab studs fuck hard in violated Assholes. When they shove their cocks up a hole all they fucking care about is their own penis pleasure."[29]

The above quotes reveal what Shohat and Stam call the "animalization trope," whereby "colonial/racist discourse renders the colonized as wild beasts in their unrestrained libidinousness."[30] On one level, it is a source of fascination and obsession (particularly pertaining to penis size), but on another level, the Arab body is aggressive, belligerent, violent, and unrestrained. However, the fact that these Arab male bodies inhabit the virtual realm of cyber space allows the intended audience to marvel and indulge in this ambivalent fascination from the safe power position of cyber hyperreality. In a sense the Arab body is contained and restrained in cyber space; its power to violate and hurt is allowed to manifest itself to the Arab fetishistic gaze specifically because of its powerlessness due to its containment within the virtual borders of cyber space. Hence, the cultural is reduced to the biological, and the colonized associated with the instinctual, as opposed to the learned and cultural.[31] This penchant for animalization is conspicuously evident in these Arab gay pornography websites; the epithet "horse-hung" that describes the Arab bodies represented in these websites is one example of this animalization.

The association of the Arab with barbarism, violence, aggression, and beastlike behavior is undeniable in these websites and enforces this colonialist animalization trope. The use of words like *force, brutal, hurt, violated, hard* attest to that image of the Arab as aggressor and violator. Faithful to the Orientalist homoerotic narrative, these quotes also show the ambivalent attitude that the intended audience (white gay European and American men) has vis-à-vis the Arab male body. While some would say (as the sex columnist Jamie Bufalino has in the example I provided above) that these pornographic depictions of the Arab male lie within the realm of fantasy and make-believe, and have no bearing on how the consumers of these pornographic sites really view Arabs and Arab Americans, I believe that such representations are damaging not only to queer Arabs but also to heterosexual Arab Americans. In fact, one cannot dissociate the prurient pornographic imagination from a wider sociopolitical context that is belligerent to Muslims in America. Here the realms of fantasy and politics are harmoniously coupled.

A decade after the attacks of September 11, the current vitriolic debate about the construction of an Islamic community center near Ground Zero, the rise of the birther movement, and the erroneous belief held by some Americans that President Obama is a "closeted Muslim" highlights the rise of Islamophobia in the United States—a sentiment that puts in peril millions of Muslim Americans. The Internet allows Muslims in the United States to cope with their sense of alienation by providing platforms through which they can connect with other Muslims both in the diaspora and the homeland. The examples illustrate how Muslims are using such platforms to find a suitable marriage partner, know more about their faith, and ask questions about issues that concern them. The multidirectionality of new media flows reveals itself in the ways in which cyber preachers like Amr Khaled through Islamic websites are reaching out to Muslim populations in the diaspora and are reterritorializing these diasporic communities by creating an imagined virtual Islamic community. Furthermore, these digital platforms help the community deal with the stigma and stereotype attached. On the other hand, my survey of gay pornographic websites reveals that this stigma and stereotype gains traction; nothing attests to that more than the rise of the homoterrorist fantasy. In both instances the Muslim Arab body is inscribed as "dangerous," and whether that "danger" is real or pruriently imagined is beside the point.

NOTES

1. Inderpal Grewal and Caren Kaplan, "Introduction," in *Scattered Hegemonies: Postmodernity and Transnational Feminist Practices,* ed. Inderpal Grewal and Caren Kaplan (Minneapolis: University of Minnesota Press, 1994), 12.
2. Ella Shohat and Robert Stam, *Unthinking Eurocentrism: Multiculturalism and the Media* (New York: Routledge, 1994), 31.
3. See Asef Bayat, *Making Islam Democratic: Social Movements and the Post-Islamic Turn* (California: Stanford University Press, 2007).
4. Jasbir K. Puar and Amit S. Rai, "The Remaking of a Model Minority: Perverse Projectiles under the Specter of (Counter) Terrorism," in *Social Text* 80, vol. 22, no. 3 (Fall 2004).
5. Arjun Appadurai, *Modernity at Large: Cultural Dimensions of Globalization* (Minneapolis: University of Minnesota Press, 1996), 3–4.
6. Ibid.
7. Minoo Moallem, *Between Warrior Brother and Veiled Sister: Islamic Fundamentalism and the Politics of Patriarchy in Iran* (Berkeley: University of California Press, 2005), 22.
8. See Castells, *The Internet Galaxy: Reflections on the Internet, Business, and Society* (2001); Slevin, *The Internet and Society* (2000); Wellman and Haythornthwaite, *The Internet in Everyday Life* (2000); Rheingold, *The Virtual Community: Homesteading on the Electronic Frontier* (1993).
9. Consult Lorne L. Dawson and Douglas E. Cowen (eds.), *Religion Online: Finding Faith on the Internet* (New York: Routledge, 2004).
10. Gary R. Bunt, "'Rip. Burn. Pray.' Islamic Expression Online," in *Religion Online: Finding Faith on the Internet,* ed. Consult Lorne L. Dawson and Douglas E. Cowen (New York: Routledge, 2004).
11. www.iKhtiba.com/DefaultEn.aspx.
12. www.singlemuslim.com/ about_us.php.
13. www.iKhtiba.com/DefaultEn.aspx.
14. *Umrah* is a pilgrimage to Mecca, Saudi Arabia, performed by Muslims, that can be undertaken at any time of the year. In Arabic *Umrah* means "to visit a populated place."
15. www.iKhtiba.com/DefaultEn.aspx.
16. Samantha M. Shapiro, "Ministering to the Upwardly Mobile Muslim," in *New York Times Magazine,* 30, April 2006.
17. Ibid.
18. Khaled told Shapiro in the *New York Times* article that he has a weakness for Hugo Boss suits.
19. A transcript of the lecture is found on *Jaihoon.com: Old World, New Ideas.* http://www.jaihoon.com/347.htm.
20. See http://www.islamonline.net/English/AboutUs.shtml.
21. See http://www.islamonline.net/English/Qaradawi/index.shtml.
22. Jasbir K. Puar, "Mapping US Homonormativities," in *Gender, Place and Culture* 13, no. 1 (New York: Taylor and Francis, February 2006), 67–68.
23. Lisa Duggan, "The New Homonormativity: The Sexual Politics of Neoliberalism," in *Materializing Democracy: Toward a Revitalized Cultural Politics,* Russ Castronovo and Dana D. Nelson, eds. (Durham: Duke University Press, 2002), 175–94.
24. *Time Out New York,* June 2009, 24–30.

25. http://www.newyorker.com/arts/critics/theatre/2007/02/19/070219crth_theatre_lahr.

26. Richard Fung, "Looking for My Penis: The Eroticized Asian in Gay Video Porn," in *How Do I Look? Queer Film and Video,* ed. Bad Object-Choice (Seattle: Bay Press, 1991), 150.

27. Frantz Fanon, *Black Skin White Masks* (London: Paladin, 1970), 120.

28. www.arabgayandbisexportal.com (May 2007).

29. www.Arabstuds.com (accessed May 2007).

30. Ella Shohat and Robert Stam, *Unthinking Eurocentrism: Multiculturalism and the Media* (New York: Routledge, 1994), 137.

31. Ibid.

TWELVE

Drawing the Line
*A Rhetorical Analysis of the
Mohammed Cartoons Controversy as It
Unfolded in Denmark and the United States*

Helle Rytkønen

Images of angry Muslims in Africa and the Middle East torching Scandinavian embassies, stomping on Danish flags, and chanting death threats against Danish cartoonists and politicians circulated the world in the first months of 2006. The immediate cause of the anger was twelve cartoons of the Prophet Mohammed published in *Jyllandsposten,* a major Danish newspaper. Any portrait of the Prophet is a violation of the Judeo-Muslim prohibition on depicting a holy figure; cartoons of Islam's most sacred prophet as a terrorist infuriated many. An estimated hundred people died and eight hundred were injured in the demonstrations that followed. Muslim countries boycotted Danish products, and several Muslim ambassadors were withdrawn from Denmark. Denmark was, in the words of its prime minister, facing its worst foreign policy crisis since World War II.[1]

Amidst the turmoil, many European politicians called for "rational calmness" from Muslim leaders and urged "the West" to stand united in what was very early on framed by the governing European[2] discourse as a fight for Western values like freedom of speech against the threat of "a reactionary, Medieval Muslim culture." The cartoons were soon reprinted in several European newspapers[3] in support of the "Danish cause," and "Buy Danish" campaigns popped up around the world. However, the U.S. reaction to the cartoons was starkly different. While the U.S. news media followed the controversy closely and circulated images of Muslims protesting violently in the Middle East, only a handful of papers reprinted the cartoons.[4] And while the Danish government eagerly awaited U.S. support for its "cause," American politicians were at best lukewarm in their responses. President George Bush cautioned that "with freedom comes the responsibility to be thoughtful to others,"[5] and former president Bill Clinton condemned the publication of the cartoons as "shameful."[6]

This article tries to make sense of why the responses to the publication of the Mohammed cartoons were so different in the United States and Europe (with special focus on Denmark). The analysis is based on a discourse analysis of original documents (political statements, speeches, letters, the cartoons) and dominant Danish and U.S. media representations of the case during and after the publication. I situate these representations in relation to ongoing political debates about Muslims in the West and pay particular attention to how Islam was mobilized and "packaged" in the imagining of Danish and U.S. identities.[7]

I argue that the cartoons and the Danish prime minister's subsequent framing of the debate as an issue of freedom of speech under attack from Muslims are acts of "foreign-making,"[8] and symptomatic of how Islam is continuously imagined as incompatible with "Western values" and Danish identity. Furthermore, despite a Danish rhetoric of inclusion and freedom of speech for all, the concerns of Danish Muslims who demonstrated peacefully against the publication of the cartoons were marginalized and silenced.

The very different U.S. reaction to printing the cartoons, I argue, was not a given. While the Muslim population in the United States is better integrated than the Muslim population in most countries in Europe, and while America prides itself on being a multicultural society, the United States also has a history of employing Muslims' (real or imagined) differences in the dominant narrative of its identity.[9] After 9/11, these differences have often been framed in a security discourse or "securitized"[10] and constructed as foreign to America and a "Western way of life."[11] However, more complex, nuanced, and favorable images of Muslims have also been part of the post 9/11 climate and, notably, the cartoon crisis came at a time when the Bush administration was desperate to win public support for its unpopular War on Terror. Emphasizing empathy for Muslim sentiments helped the government consolidate the idea of the United States as religiously tolerant despite leading wars in Muslim countries.

The U.S. response therefore reflects the overlapping, competing, and conflicting representations of Muslims that continue to frame debates about American identity.

An Invitation into a Culture of "Insult, Mockery and Ridicule"

"We are in the midst of a 'culture and value battle,'" argued Denmark's Conservative minister of culture, Brian Mikkelsen, less than a week before the

Mohammed caricatures were first published in 2005.[12] The minister argued that the battle was against a "Medieval Muslim culture" that would never be as "valid" as the Danish culture.[13] The threat, he continued, comes from immigrants from Muslim countries who "refuse to acknowledge Danish culture and European norms" with their "medieval norms and undemocratic ways of thinking."[14] The minister expressed concern that a Danish stand-up comedian, Frank Hvam, commented in a television interview that he was afraid to publicly "piss on the Koran" out of fear of angering fundamentalist Muslims. A Danish children's book author, Kåre Bluitgen, had furthermore complained in an interview that he couldn't find an illustrator for his otherwise uncontroversial book about the Prophet Mohammed. According to Bluitgen, two illustrators had declined the job with reference to Dutch filmmaker Theo van Gogh, murdered after having made a film critical of Islam.

Discussions about Muslim immigrants and their perceived lack of compatibility with Western norms have dominated Danish local and national elections in the past ten years, even though Denmark's Bureau of Statistics estimates that only 3.8 percent of the Danish population is Muslim.[15] Mikkelsen's declaration of a culture war also came amidst broader European discussions of whether Muslim women have the right to wear a head scarf in public, and of citizenship tests to screen immigrants, especially Muslims, for their adherence to "Western values"[16] such as gender equality and sexual tolerance.[17]

Jyllandsposten, a major Danish newspaper, was provoked by the minister's speech and the statement from the comedian and decided to challenge what it called "self censorship" in Denmark caused by a fear, "real or not," of violent Muslim reactions. There has been "an intimidation of the public space," argued Flemming Rose, the cultural editor of *Jyllandsposten*, as an explanation for why the paper had asked forty Danish cartoonists to draw the face of the Prophet Mohammed "as they imagined him."[18] Twelve artists submitted caricatures, and their work was published on the front cover on September 30, 2005. In a quote accompanying the caricatures, Flemming Rose explained why the newspaper published them.

> The modern, secular society is rejected by some Muslims. They demand a particular [sær-stilling] position when they insist on special [sær-lig] considerations for their religious feelings. This is incompatible with a secular democracy and freedom of speech where you have to be prepared to tolerate insult, mockery and ridicule.[19]

Aside from ignoring how deeply embedded in Protestant traditions and culture the Danish "secular" society is, Rose narrowly frames the delicate negotiations between freedom of speech and respect for minorities in terms of having a sense of humor or not.[20] The importance of humor and Muslims' perceived lack of it was later to be emphasized again and again by other cartoonists, media pundits, and the Danish prime minister in his 2006 New Year's speech to the nation. The ability to "laugh at oneself" or to tolerate "insult, mockery and ridicule" became a litmus test for adherence to Western values and should, Rose insisted, be seen as an "invitation" into Danish community, not an act of disrespect or exclusion. In a later defense of the publication of the cartoons, he emphasized this point, again sidestepping the issue of rights versus responsibilities.

> The cartoonists treated Islam the same way they treat Christianity, Buddhism, Hinduism and other religions. And by treating Muslims in Denmark as equals they made a point: We are integrating you into the Danish tradition of satire because you are part of our society, not strangers.[21]

By far the most infamous of the twelve caricatures, "Mohammed's Face," is a sketch of the Prophet Mohammed as an angry-looking man wearing a bomb-shaped turban with a lit fuse, clearly about to blow himself up. The bomb/turban has an emblem on it with the Muslim creed "There is only one God, Allah, and Mohammed is his Prophet." Cartoonist Kurt Westergaard later explained that his cartoon depicts a terrorist "who looks like he was coming down from the mountains in Afghanistan."[22] It was, he explained, meant to show that "terrorists get their spiritual ammunition from Islam" and was not meant to critique the entire religion.[23] Five years after the original publication Westergaard was asked by *National Public Radio* if his cartoon depicted the Prophet Mohammed, and he replied that "[he] [didn't] know anymore."[24] Regardless, the caricature appeared under the heading "Mohammed's Face," and it incongruously links seventh-century Mohammed, the most prominent symbol of Islam, with recent acts of violence, thereby recycling the trope of Muslims as foreign and a threat to the West. Interestingly, and maybe telling of the lack of knowledge of minorities, it also fell prey to the stereotypical error that Arab Muslims wear turbans (in actuality associated with Sikhs).

Of the twelve cartoons, seven invoke the trope of male Muslim fanaticism and violence and/or oppression of women: in Rasmus Høyer's caricature, the Prophet is again an angry, heavily armed man. Behind him are two women in black burkas with only their alarmed eyes showing. The Prophet, with a black bar covering his eyes, has a sword in one hand and holds out the other as if to keep the women back. This cartoon again links male Muslim bodies with violence and shows Muslim women literally immobilized by the restrictive veil of Islam (symbolized by the burkas). Understood in its "intertextuality,"[25] the caricature inevitably invokes recent years' ferocious debates in Europe over head scarves, forced marriages, genital mutilation, and other examples of what are seen as Muslim practices of female oppression. Some of the same themes are present in the cartoon by Jens Hansen, where the Prophet Mohammed has taken Saint Peter's place at the Gate of Heaven. Mohammed greets a line of Muslim suicide bombers and tells them, "Stop, stop. We've run out of virgins!" The line of tattered men, their clothes in shreds, smoke rising from their bodies, look at the cartoon Mohammed with dismay. By depicting the Muslim terrorists as exposed, literally with their pants down, the caricature questions whether there are any real political, social, economic, or religious motives behind Muslim violence. It lends itself, in a fashion meant to be humorous, to the idea that the true motive behind terrorism is lust for something as profane (and Western?) as sex with virgins. While this is "just" a cartoon, it reflects the way terrorism, itself a politicized term, is taken out of any historical and geopolitical context and explained by sexual motives and frustrations in Western media.[26] It suggests that the roots of terrorism are an "internal" problem for Muslims and ignores that the West might be implicated in world politics in such a way that terrorist acts could be a (poor or understandable, depending on viewpoint) response to it. The cartoon also reconfirms a gendered notion of Islam, as the Muslim woman is invoked in her very absence (there are no more virgins) and represented without any agency of her own, a prize fully at the disposal of Muslim men.

However, while most of the artists made no effort to distinguish Muslim "terrorists" from the founder of the religion, nor to shake themselves loose from the lockstep of female oppression and terrorism, Lars Refn's cartoon is an example of how political cartoons can challenge stereotypes and create greater dialogue about Muslims in the West. In his drawing, which has received almost no attention in the subsequent coverage of the cartoons, Mohammed is not a prophet but an ordinary-looking seventh-grade student standing in a classroom in Valby school, in a suburb of Copenhagen.[27] Mohammed wears a T-shirt with the local soccer team's logo, *Frem* (Forward), but his T-shirt cleverly says *Frem-tiden* (the future, or, literally, forward time). This Mohammed is not "Orientalized" or exoticized in any way, and he is not angry or threatening. Instead, he sticks out his tongue like any sly schoolboy who's done something naughty, and points grinningly to his writing on the blackboard. The writing in Arabic, which *Jyllandsposten* said they did not understand at the time of publication, translates to "*Jyllandsposten*'s editors are a bunch of provocateurs."

Refn's Mohammed demonstrates that he is very familiar with "Western" style satire and "skepticism of authorities," the very rhetorical strategies President Bush and Danish prime minister Fogh Rasmussen would later say constitute Western democracy. In contrast to the other cartoons in *Jyllandsposten*'s series, this Mohammed is not using his agency to oppress Muslim women or incite terrorism. He is neither a victim nor a convert. The drawing thereby defies the binary opposition between the West and Islam, which Kurt Westergaard's drawing and *Jyllandsposten*'s campaign invoked. Seventh-grader Mohammed is *not* representing a "medieval" foreign culture; he is a part of "us" and is already here in our classrooms, in the heart of the West, wearing the team colors. And he is playing for the future. The cartoon thereby deterritorializes culture and exposes the limits of the public discourse, which sees Muslims as "little islands of foreignness" in Western space.[28] Refn's cartoon creates a mocking bond between author and audience instead of merely pointing an accusatory finger at an already marginalized minority. It suggests that the debate could be framed in ways other than as a fight over fundamental Western values.

However, just as cartoons like Refn's have the potential to be subversive, laughing at someone is also among the "strongest markers of social exclusion" (Kuipers), and caricatures that portray Mohammed as a terrorist "police" the social, geographical, and moral boundaries of Danish identity. They do so by casting Muslims as a horizon of abnormality against which a decent, rational Danish identity is constructed. More significant, the ridicule is part of broader political and cultural discourses, which legitimize stricter immigration laws in Denmark specifically,[29] and broader Western or neo-European "civilizing" projects, of which the War on Terror is the most recent example.[30]

The Enemy Within

The act of representing the Prophet Mohammed is itself a violation of the Judeo-Muslim prohibition against embodying an infinite God in finite materials.[31] In the minds of many (Muslim or not), the insult was aggravated by the nature of the caricatures and the sense that they were only adding fuel to an already rather heated immigration debate.[32] In the days following the publication, *Jyllandsposten* received about 100 letters to the editor, 17,000 signatures were collected, and 3,500 Muslims demonstrated peacefully against the cartoons under banners of "NO to racism and fanaticism, YES to peace and coexistence." The demonstrators demanded an apology from *Jyllandsposten* and from the Danish government, and organizer Adel Hassan strongly condemned threats against the cartoonists and warned that

Fig. 12.1. Seventh grader Mohammed by Lars Refn, originally published in *Jyllandsposten,* September 30, 2005.

"the violent road leads nowhere."[33] *Jyllandsposten,* a conservative paper with generally strong immigrant-critical perspectives, refused to apologize, and the Danish government was silent on the issue. On October 12, 2005, at the initiative of Muslim organizations in Denmark, eleven Muslim ambassadors[34] wrote a letter addressed to both the Danish prime minister and the Danish foreign minister. The wording of the letter subsequently became the center of heated debate, and the interpretation of it shaped what was to follow. In the letter, the ambassadors asked for a meeting with the Danish prime minister and expressed concern with the "on-going smearing [*sic*] campaign" against Islam and Muslims. The letter specifically referred to four recent examples of the "Islamophobic" tone of the Danish debate of which *Jyllandsposten*'s cartoons was just the most recent. The letter appealed to "the spirit of Danish values" such as "tolerance" and "civil society" and specifically stated that the Muslim ambassadors were in agreement with the Danish prime minister that just as terrorists should not be allowed to abuse Islam for their crimes, the Danish press should also not be allowed to abuse Islam in the name of "democracy, freedom of expression and human rights, the values that we all share."[35] What would later become the most important part of the letter appeared at the end where the Muslim ambassadors asked the Danish prime minister to "take all those responsible to task under law of the land."[36]

Nine days later, the ambassadors received a reply from the Danish prime minister, Anders Fogh Rasmussen, ignoring their request for a meeting, and reiterating that "freedom of expression is the very foundation of the Danish democracy."[37] Rasmussen went on to say that the Danish government has "no means of influencing the press." And while the ambassadors had stressed in their letter that they shared the values of democracy and freedom of expression, Rasmussen chose to interpret "under the law of the land" as a demand for government intervention in the free press and a request to curtail free speech. As critics of Rasmussen's handling of the case later suggested, the ambassadors' concerns might have been assuaged had the prime minister simply spoken with his minister of culture about the "culture war," or had Rasmussen publicly recognized, as he would much later, the hurtful effect of the cartoons and hostile tone of the Danish public discourse.

Instead, Rasmussen told the ambassadors that "Danish legislation prohibits acts or expressions of a blasphemous or discriminatory nature" and that "the offended party" can take their case to court.[38] By indicating that the Danish courts were the place to determine whether Muslims in Denmark had been victims of blasphemous or discriminatory "acts or expressions," Rasmussen reduced the debate to a legal issue of free press and brought the complex issue of respect for religious minorities from the nuanced and contested terrain of politics and culture to the supposedly value-neutral judicial domain.[39] The debate about how to coexist respectfully in a multicultural society was thereby condensed into whether *Jyllandsposten* had a legal right to publish the cartoons or if they violated the law against blasphemy (not surprisingly, the courts later found that the newspaper was in its *legal* right to publish the cartoons, stating that the court is not the place to determine whether it was a wise or morally right thing to do). The prime minister thereby framed the debate in an all-too-familiar Western discourse about Muslims in the West and cast the Danish nation as a protector and securer of both fundamental human rights like freedom of speech *and* a society tolerant of different religions (emphasizing that the courts were there to rule against any intolerance). Hence, Rasmussen participated in the silencing or marginalization of the more nuanced and complex concerns brought forth by the Danish Muslims' peaceful demonstrations and by the Muslim ambassadors' letter. He isolated the debate from any global or local context and considered only its legal ramifications. Rasmussen's narrow definition of freedom of speech also allowed for little consideration of responsibilities ("there is no 'but'" as Rasmussen kept insisting). Interestingly, the American response to the issue would be very different.

The letter from the prime minister became hotly debated in Denmark. In an unusual and harshly worded public letter, twenty-two former Danish ambassadors criticized Rasmussen for not meeting with the Muslim representatives.[40] The criticism resonated with the views of some politicians and cultural icons that called *Jyllandsposten* "populistic" and Rasmussen "insensitive."[41] However, these critical voices were in the minority; by far the majority of the Danes supported Rasmussen's handling of the case. And in his New Year's speech to the nation, Rasmussen again referred to the cartoons and harped on the importance of freedom of speech for Danish democracy: "We in Denmark have a healthy tradition for critically scrutinizing all authorities, whether political or religious. . . . [It] is this inclination to critically debate everything which has created the progress in our society. . . . That is why freedom of speech is so crucial."[42]

Two months after the publication, five imams from Denmark went to Egypt, Syria and Lebanon to meet with leaders of the Arab League and advisers to Arab governments. The imams voiced their concern with the Danish representations of Muslims in politics and in the media.[43] These meetings would later influence how Muslims were seen within the Danish nation. Polls show that an overwhelming majority of the Danish population believed that the imams had manipulated the Arab world into turning on Denmark.[44] Subsequently, the imams were compared to "enemy sympathizers within our own ranks,"[45] an idea borrowed from World War II. Politicians from the immigrant-critical Danish People's Party also suggested revoking the imams' citizenship or legal residency visas. The Danish debate framed the Muslim imams' journey within a narrative in which Danish national culture was the organizing grammar (i.e., enemy within; anti-Danish behavior). Within this narrative, the imams' allegiance with Muslim communities in the Middle East trumped their Danish-ness. By bringing into question the Muslims' allegiance to Denmark and Western values, the imams' (and by extension Islam's) assumed foreignness was once again confirmed.[46]

Whether spurred on by the imams from Denmark or not, criticism from Middle Eastern governments and religious organizations increased in the first months of 2006. Tens of thousands of demonstrators filled the streets of Pakistan, Kenya, Somalia, Egypt, Jordan, Iran, Turkey, Pakistan, India, Bangladesh, Sri Lanka, the Philippines, Malaysia, Nigeria, and Venezuela.[47] The demonstrations expanded to include criticism of U.S. involvement in the Middle East, Israeli occupation of Palestinian territories, and Denmark's alliance with the United States in the war in Iraq. In response, several European newspapers reprinted the cartoons in solidarity with the Danish cartoonists and editors, and many European politicians from all points on the political spectrum spoke out in support of what was now portrayed exclusively as a battle for or against freedom of speech.[48] This interpretation relied on a conflation of all Muslims and allowed violent demonstrators in Africa and the Middle East to be seen as representatives of Islam. It disregarded that the Muslims in Denmark had already demonstrated their adherence to democratic values when they peacefully expressed their objection to the cartoons, and it ignored that the Muslim ambassadors, in their letter to the Danish prime minister, had confirmed that freedom of speech and human rights are values that "we all share." It further participated in the marginalization of the Danish Muslims' initial concerns about the "Islamophobic" nature of the debate in Denmark (of which the publication of the Mohammed cartoons was just the latest example), and normalized "the West" as a homogeneous, stable identity with a monopoly on values like freedom of speech and human rights. Whatever concerns the Danish Muslims might have wished to discuss with official Denmark was silenced when the debate was framed only in terms of fundamental Western values under attack from Islam.

U.S. Coverage of the Demonstrations

The demonstrations across the Middle East and Africa were "breaking news" in the U.S. news media in early February 2006, whereas the cartoons themselves were hardly seen. Most of the news coverage focused on the protests and emphasized the "extraordinary" and violent aspect of the "wall climbing, gate busting, flag burning" Muslim protesters—incited by "cartoons printed in *one* Danish newspaper and reprinted in a few others" as CBSNEWS formulated it.[49] Political commentators, Internet sites, and political cartoons ridiculed Muslims for failing to distance themselves from 9/11, only to be infuriated "beyond reason" by a series of cartoons. The *Washington Post* followed every "new round of flag-burning demonstrations" and cited Muslims like Mohammed Hussein for calling on his worshippers to "express [their] anger" during a sermon at the al-Aqsa mosque in Jerusalem, the third-holiest site in Islam.[50] On the web and on television, *CNN* reported that "protesters burn[ed] consulate over cartoons," and "tens of thousands of Muslims launched fresh worldwide protests" because of the images.

The stories were accompanied by images of angry, yelling, often armed Muslim protesters burning down Scandinavian embassies, Danish flags, and effigies of the Danish prime minister: dramatic illustrations of "Muslim rage." The images conveyed a sense of chaos and of protesters literally trying to knock down the walls to the West, symbolized by the Western embassies, flags, and businesses. The "busting of gates" was also narrated as a threat to "Western values" such as property rights and free speech. In contrast, the cause of the anger was attributed to the cartoons and thus to a Muslim culture unable to "take a joke," and thereby understand Western values.[51] Hence, the U.S. media participated in the global circulation of representations of Muslims as fanatics and a threat to the West—incited by something as seemingly insignificant as a cartoon. These representations are all too familiar, as Said reminds us. Reductive representations of the fanatical "Oriental man" have dominated U.S. encounters with the Middle East since colonial times and have been evoked more ferociously since 9/11.[52] They mark Muslim bodies as dangerous and possibly undeserving of citizenship rights. Debates over cultural or ethnic differences are often framed in a "security discourse"[53] where the very foundation of the West is under threat from Muslim life. The PATRIOT Act is an example of this, and polls and surveys in the United States show that since 9/11 an increasing number of Americans are in favor of discriminating against American Muslims' rights to organize social and religious programs.[54] This discourse of "regrettable but necessary" exceptions to Muslims' rights reconfirms a "moral geography"[55] in which loyalties and rights are believed to run parallel with the boundaries of nation-states (or "the West"). One of the problems of conceptualizing Muslims and the West in such binary terms, Stolcke reminds us, is that it completely marginalizes the "root causes" of immigration and the political privileging of geopolitical identity categories like immigrant and citizen.[56]

I do not want to reduce a very complex issue—that of flows of people across political and territorial boundaries—into a problem which is simply caused by Western colonialism, imperialism, need for cheap labor, trade negotiations, or barriers, for which the West in some shape or form should accept guilt. I do, however, find it thought-provoking that the "problem" of Muslims in relation to the West is frequently framed as a problem with "their outdated" culture. Both the broader and the more local contexts are all too often ignored, and the Muslims in Denmark who protested peacefully against what they saw as a disturbingly Islamophobic tone in the public debate were consistently ignored by both Danish and American media.

"Not Censorship, Editing"

However, the reaction in the United States to the printing of the cartoons was strikingly different from the European. While the U.S. media covered the demonstrations on a daily basis, thereby feeding into a narrative of Islam as a violent religion, only a handful of primarily minor U.S. newspapers reprinted the actual cartoons. U.S. politicians also either outright condemned the publication of the cartoons or argued that while they supported freedom of speech and condemned violent actions, they also understood Muslim frustrations. This, I argue, reflects the overlapping and conflicting ways in which Muslims are mobilized in the United States and speaks to the particular geopolitical circumstances at the time.

Major news organizations like CNN, the *New York Times*, the *Washington Post*, the *Los Angeles Times*, the *Wall Street Journal*, and the *Chicago Tribune* did not print the controversial cartoons. "We didn't want to publish anything that can be perceived as inflammatory to our readers' culture when it didn't add anything to the story," said Robert Christie, a spokesman for Dow Jones & Company, which owns the *Wall Street Journal*.[57] Many shared his sentiment: "This is a clear example of something people will be offended by so we don't see the point in doing it [publishing the cartoons]," as Keith Richburg, foreign policy editor at the *Washington Post*, expressed it.[58] The *New York Times* showed a picture of *Jyllandsposten*'s cover page but blurred the images, and TV stations like CNN and CBS News explained to their viewers that they decided not to show the cartoons out of concern for the audiences. Some critics in the United States saw this as a concession to "radical Islamists" and a victory for their "war of intimidation"[59] against Western media, but the majority of the U.S. media disagreed. Garry Trudeau, the political cartoonist responsible for the Doonesbury cartoons, argued that editors not only have a right to delete material they feel is inappropriate for their readership, but a responsibility: "That's not censorship. It's editing."[60]

American politicians were also not nearly as outspoken in Denmark's defense as Danish politicians had anticipated. Secretary of State Condoleeza Rice met with Danish minister of foreign policy Per Stig Møller to be briefed about the controversy in late January 2006, and U.S. president George Bush didn't comment on the controversy until the demonstrations were at their fiercest. In his statement, Bush condemned the violent reactions to the cartoons and called on its ally Saudi Arabia to use its influence to calm Muslims,[61] but he also said that he understood why the cartoons could be seen as offensive: "We also recognize that with . . . freedom comes the responsibility to be thoughtful about others."[62] Former U.S. president Bill Clinton called the caricatures "shameful,"[63] and U.S. State Department spokesperson Steve McCormack told a group of reporters that while the United States defended the right of individuals to express their opinion, "anti-Muslim images are as unacceptable as anti-Semitic images, as anti-

Christian images or any other religious belief."[64] This was echoed by the *Boston Globe,* which argued in an editorial that depictions of the Prophet Mohammed as a terrorist were just as hurtful as "Nazi caricatures of Jews or Ku Klux caricatures of blacks." The *Boston Globe* argued that "newspapers ought to refrain from publishing offensive caricatures of Mohammed in the name of "the ultimate Enlightenment value: tolerance."[65] State Department spokesperson Kurtis Cooper sided even more strongly with Muslim protesters: "These cartoons are indeed offensive to the belief of Muslims. . . . We all fully recognize and respect freedom of the press and expression but it must be coupled with press responsibility. Inciting religious or ethnic hatreds in this manner is not acceptable."[66] State Department spokesperson Justin Higgins added, "We call for tolerance and respect for all communities and for their religious beliefs and practices." These statements framed the debate less as a clash between Muslims insisting on their religious particularities and the West trying to secure free expression, and refrained from reducing the debate to mere legalities. Instead, they invoked the common sensitivity of all cultures, peoples, and religions, or what Kuipers calls "normative communities of humor."[67] Rather than insisting, as Flemming Rose, the cultural editor of *Jyllandsposten* did, that the cartoons were a sign that Islam is equal to "Christianity, Buddhism, Hinduism and other religions" (i.e., they too must tolerate "ridicule and mockery"), U.S. politicians and media representatives situated the cartoons within the "shameful" Western history of anti-Semitism and slavery. They thereby invoked and acknowledged the sensitive nature of the relation between minority and majority cultures.

The response was somewhat surprising since, as I argue above, the United States certainly has a long history of casting Muslims as foreign to the nation. Furthermore, the United States has positioned itself as the world's defender of human rights and democratic values, like freedom of speech. Denmark is a U.S. ally in the war in Iraq and Afghanistan, and the Danish government clearly expected the U.S. government to provide much stronger support.[68] However, the Bush government walked on eggshells because of its highly unpopular War on Terror, and the scandal in Abu Ghraib prison was still fresh in the world's and American citizens' collective memory. Bush had repeatedly argued that he was *not* engaged in a war against Muslims and Islam, and his outspoken empathy with Muslim sentiments over the cartoons helped him confirm that the United States respects religious minorities despite the wars in Iraq and Afghanistan.[69]

Furthermore, while representations of Arabs and Muslims as "terrorist" and "fundamentalist" have replaced that of the "rich oil sheik," circulating frequently in the United States since 9/11, more complex, nuanced, and favorable images have also been part of the post-9/11 climate.[70] In general, news reports about Muslims in America increased dramatically after 9/11, Nacos and Torres-Reyna's study shows, and Muslims went from being "almost invisible" to "hyper-visible."[71] This is less true in Denmark where news or political stories about Muslims predominantly emphasize their (real or imagined) differences in clothing, eating habits, family structure, and so forth. In contrast, many of the stories in the U.S. media were less "essentialized caricatures" of Muslims and gave voice to patriotic, educated, well-integrated, and financially successful American Muslims in pursuit of the American dream.[72] The more favorable media representations might very well reflect the different history of Muslims in America as compared to Muslims in Europe. While it is difficult to get exact numbers, as census data does not track religion, fewer Muslims in America than in Europe are of immigrant backgrounds (an estimated 30 percent are African American Muslims), and contrary to many Muslim Europeans' social isolation in suburban ghettos (le banlieue de l'Islam in France and Gellerup in Denmark, for example), American Muslims are geographically dispersed and only one city, Dearborn, Michigan, is estimated to reach a 30 percent Muslim population. American Muslims are also primarily middle-class and solidly integrated with their non-Muslim neighbors,[73] and Muslims in America tend to have higher educational levels and higher incomes than average Americans.[74]

Muslim leaders in the United States were also quick to voice their opposition to the violent demonstrations. National Communication's director Ibrahim Cooper from the Council on American-Islamic Relations (CAIR) regretted the stereotyping "on both sides" and called on all Muslims to consider the controversy a "teaching moment," to show forgiveness, and exemplify the Prophet's teaching through "dignified behavior in the face of provocation and abuse."[75] The Muslim Public Affairs Council (MPAC) commended Bush's position on the cartoons controversy and applauded American Muslims for responding to the incident with "calm and reason."[76] The Canadian Arab Federation (CAF) condemned the "hateful depiction of Islam" in the Danish cartoons, which did "nothing to bridge the widening gap between Muslims and Western nations." But CAF also reminded its members that it opposed violence and called on "all parties to establish an open dialogue."[77]

Danish Muslim organizations expressed similar nuanced views but, as I argued above, their voices were not heard in the debate, or their concerns were reduced to legalities.

The most current U.S. debate over whether or not to print the caricatures took place in the fall of 2009 when Yale University Press decided *not* to print them in a book titled *The Cartoons that Shook the World*. Yale University vice president and secretary Linda Lorimer argued that Yale's decision was made after consultation with "counter-terrorism experts," senior academics, and diplomats who expressed that there were "serious concerns of violence" if the cartoons were published.[78] It is not, Yale University Press argued, a stifling of the right to free speech, as the cartoons are readily available on the Internet.[79] However, the president of the American Association of University Professors, Cary Nelson, "deplored" Yale's decision,[80] and the *New York Post* called Yale's stance "cowardly" and "shameful."[81] Alumni also wrote an open letter asking Yale to reconsider the decision.[82]

The debate about Yale's decision is interesting not least because it is less about respect for religious sensitivities than it is about the fear of invoking "Muslim anger." This is a reminder that U.S. concern for Muslim sentiments thrives side by side with a discourse in which events like 9/11 are explained by Muslims' hate and envy of Western values. "They [Muslims] hate our freedoms," President Bush said to the American people in 2001.[83] While America now has a new president, discussions like Yale's about "Muslim anger" are symptomatic for the constantly shifting, overlapping, and sometimes conflicting ways in which Muslims are mobilized as potential threats to American and Western identities (the 2010 debate about the plans of Florida's Rev. Terry Jones to publicly burn copies of the Quran on the anniversary of 9/11 is another case in point).

To Print or Not to Print

The debate continues. Seventeen European newspapers republished the cartoons in 2008 after Danish police arrested three men accused of plotting the murder of cartoonist Kurt Westergaard.[84] Meanwhile, calling his caricature a "test" of Muslim immigrants' willingness to respect democratic values including free speech, Westergaard has defiantly announced that he will auction off signed copies of his drawing.[85] And five years to the day of the initial publication of the cartoons, Flemming Rose, cultural editor of *Jyllandsposten,* published the cartoons again in his book *Tavshedens Tyrani* (The Tyranny of Silence).[86]

The caricatures as well as political and media representations of the demonstrations and the subsequent discussions about later reprints, reflect dominant discourses in Denmark that continue to mobilize Muslims in the imagining of Danish and Western identities. A 2009 Danish political proposal to make it illegal to wear burkas dominated public debates for months, even though critics pointed out that the debate once again vilified Muslim men (suspecting them of forcing their daughters and wives to veil themselves) and victimized Muslim women as having no say in the matter.

As Danish journalists scrambled, mostly in vain, to find burka-clad women to interview, critics mused that there might only be four such women in all of Denmark.[87] This debate was soon followed by the governing party's proposal to better integrate non-Western immigrants by "rewarding" immigrant women 15,000 Danish kroner ($2,500) if they completed a course in Danish language and democracy.[88] Such proposals, I argue, continue to ignore the possibility that "poor integration" might also be the result of Danish exclusionary policies and discourses, and instead identify non-Western cultures as the cause of the "problem." Similarly in the debates about the cartoons, values such as freedom of speech are monopolized as "Western" despite many Muslims' insistence that in the dominant Danish discourse, these are values "we all share." Danish and Western identities are therefore continuously imagined as static and homogenized. They are not understood as contested, contrasting, and conflicting sites for negotiation of what it means for different cultures, religions, and ethnicities to live together.[89] The debate is framed in such a way that Muslim Danes' concerns are often silenced despite an official rhetoric of inclusion.

In contrast, the cartoons have still only been printed in very few U.S. media outlets, and, with a few exceptions, U.S. politicians and media representatives abstained from framing the debate about the cartoons as an issue of fundamental Western values under attack from hostile Muslims. Part of the explanation for this difference in the response to the publication of the cartoons, I argue, can most likely be found in the different history between majority and minority identities in the United States, and in the fact that American Muslims are better integrated and have a more powerful voice in the public debate. It was also in the strategic interest of the Bush government to make it clear to the United States and the international community that its highly unpopular war in Muslim countries was not a war against Islam. And it is imperative to remember that this nuanced and complex understanding of freedom of speech and respect for religious minorities exists side by side with more antagonistic discourses in which Islam is seen as a violent religion and Muslims are cast as a threat to American identity. As Campbell reminds us, these acts of "foreign-making" are intimately related to identity construction, and agonistic difference can quickly turn into antagonistic sentiments under the right (or wrong) circumstances such as a nation under pressure or during war.

While it may seem surprising that twelve caricatures printed in one of the smallest countries on earth can "shake the world" as Klausen argues,[90] this paper therefore argues that the continued debates about them reflect the different and ongoing negotiations in Denmark and the U.S. of where to draw the line around who "we" are and what "we" stand for.

NOTES

1. "70,000 Gather for Violent Pakistan Cartoon Protest," *Times Online,* February 15, 2006.

2. There was great variance among the European countries (almost no British media published the cartoons, for example), and there was not always an overlap between media and political responses in each country. What is important here is that the dominant European response was markedly different from the American.

3. The cartoons were published in newspapers in Norway, Italy, Spain, Germany, Switzerland, Holland, Egypt, Morocco, Bosnia-Herzegovina, and Romania in 2005 and early 2006. Later, they were reprinted in several other papers.

4. Fox TV, *Philadelphia Inquirer, Austin American-Statesman,* and the *New York Sun* published all or parts of the cartoons. *Harper Magazine* featured an article by *New Yorker* cartoonist Art Spiegelman in which all twelve cartoons were evaluated.

5. "Bush Urges World Leaders to Halt Violence Over Cartoons," *New York Times,* February 8, 2006.

6. *Ritzau,* January 30, 2006.

7. See Evelyn Alsultany, *Arabs and Muslims in the Media: Race and Representation After 9/11* (New York University, 2012); "The Changing Profile of Race in the United States: Media Representations and Racialization of Arab- and Muslim-Americans post-9/11," 2005; Ella Shohat and Robert Stam, *Unthinking Eurocentrism: Multiculturalism and the Media,* 1994, Routledge, London and New York; and Benedict Anderson, *Imagined Communities: Reflections on the Origin and Spread of Nationalism,* 1983, Verso, London and New York.

8. See Richard Ashley, "The Geopolitics of Geopolitical Space: Toward a Critical Social Theory of International Politics," *alternatives* 12, no. 4 (1987); Michael J. Shapiro "Moral Geographies and the Ethics of Post-Sovereignty," *Public Culture,* vol. 6 (1994): 479–502; William E. Connolly, *Identity/Difference: Democratic Negotiations of Political Paradox,* 1991, Cornell University Press; and David Campbell, *Writing Security—United States Foreign Policy and the Politics of Identity,* 1992, University of Minnesota Press.

9. See Alsultany; Melani McAlister, *Epic Encounters: Culture, Media, & US Interests in the Middle East since 1945,* 2005, xviii, University of California Press; and Amaney Jamal and Nadine Naber in *Race and Arab Americans Before and After 9/11,* 2008, Syracuse University Press.

10. Ole Wæver "Securitization and Desecuritization," in Ronnie D. Lipschutz, ed., *On Security* (1995): 46–86, Columbia University Press, New York.

11. See Alsultany; Jamal and Naber.

12. Minister of culture Brian Mikkelsen in his speech to the Conservative Party's annual congress, "Minister kalder til ny kulturkamp" (Minister declares new culture war) in *Berlingske Tidende,* September 26, 2005.

13. "Minister kalder til ny kulturkamp" (Minister declares new culture war) in *Berlingske Tidende,* September 26, 2005.

14. "Kulturkampen bliver lang og sej" (The culture war will be long and tough) in *Information,* July 26, 2007.

15. *Tørre tal om troen. Religionsdemografi i det 21. århundrede* (Dry numbers on faith: Religion demography in the 21st century) from the Danish Bureau of Statistics website http://www.dst.dk/OmDS/Bib/spoerg/oss/religion.aspx.

16. The West is referred to both in a concrete sense, as a specific geographically

defined identity (U.S., Europe, etc.), and on a more abstract level, as a discourse, a set of values, and a mode of thinking and "packaging" issues that makes some identities, cultures, and problems seem natural and normal and others not. The latter way refers to the West as a floating signifier or a referent only loosely connected to a territorial space.

17. The German regional states Baden-Wurttemberg and Hesse first proposed what opponents have called "Muslim tests," but Holland, Britain, and Denmark were also considering similar tests.

18. "Muhammeds ansigt" (Mohammed's face), in *Jyllandsposten,* September 30, 2005.

19. *Sær* in Danish means odd or out of sorts. "Muhammeds ansigt" (Mohammed's face) in *Jyllandsposten,* September 30, 2005.

20. This is not an unusual accusation. Humor scholars John Morreal and Malcolm Kushner have made similar arguments. See Paul Lewis, "The Muhammed Cartoons and Humor Research: A Collection of Essays," in *Humor—International Journal of Humor Research* 21 (2008): 1.

21. *Washington Post,* February 19, 2006.

22. "Danish Cartoonist in Hiding after Attack" *National Public Radio,* January 10, 2010.

23. Art Spiegelman, "Drawing Blood: Outrageous Cartoons and the Art of Outrage," in *Harper's Magazine,* June 2006.

24. "Danish Cartoonist in Hiding After Attack."

25. See Julia Kristeva, *Desire in Language: A Semiotic Approach to Literature and Art,* 1980, Columbia University Press, New York.

26. See Alsultany.

27. The role of education has been crucial in recent Danish integration policies. In 2000, the Danish immigration law changed the age limit for the right to family reunification from eighteen to twenty-four years, giving, as the minister of interior explained it, the young immigrant woman additional "breathing room" to finish an education and to become mature enough to withstand her Muslim parents' "oppressive authorities" (Minister of Interior Karen Jespersen, *Ekstra Bladet,* April 4, 2000, and Prime Minister Poul Nyrup Rasmussen, New Year's Speech, January 1, 2001). Guarding the Muslim woman's body thereby became a way of also guarding the Danish borders against foreign (Muslim) penetration too (Helle Rytkønen, *Europe and Its "Almost-European" Other: A Textual Analysis of Legal and Cultural Practices of Othering in Contemporary Europe,* 2002, Ph.D. dissertation, Stanford University).

28. See Ashley and Shapiro.

29. See Rytkønen.

30. See Alsultany.

31. Shohat and Stam, *Unthinking Eurocentrism,* 27.

32. Five days after *Jyllandsposten* published the cartoons, the Arab TV station *Al Jazeera* put a story on their website about Danish Muslims' objection to the cartoons.

33. Larsen and Seidenfaden, *Karikatur krisen. En undersøgelse af baggrund og ansvar* (The caricature crisis: An investigation of background and responsibility), 2006, 59, Gyldendal, Copenhagen, Denmark.

34. The letter was written on behalf of ambassadors from Turkey, Saudi Arabia, Iran, Pakistan, Egypt, Indonesia, Algeria, Bosnia-Herzegovina, Libya, the Moroccan chargé d'affaires, and the leader of the Palestinian delegation.

35. Letter to prime minister Anders Fogh Rasmussen, reprinted in Larsen and Seidenfaden p. 324.

36. Letter to the eleven Muslim ambassadors from Danish prime minister Anders Fogh Rasmussen, October 21, 2005, reprinted in Larsen and Seidenfaden, 329.

37. Letter to the eleven Muslim ambassadors from Danish prime minister Anders Fogh Rasmussen, October 21, 2005, reprinted in Larsen and Seidenfaden, 329.

38. On October 26, 2006, a Danish city court ruled that *Jyllandsposten*'s editors were not guilty of inflammatory statements when they published the Mohammed caricatures.

39. While critical legal scholars have emphasized the historical, political, and socio-economic power relations at work in the making and upholding of laws, the legal domain still has an air of neutrality about it (Giorgio Agamben, *Homo Sacer: Sovereign Power and Bare Life,* 1998, Stanford University Press, Stanford, California).

40. "Danish ambassadors criticize Anders Fogh Rasmussen," *Politiken* December 12, 2005.

41. Later, Rasmussen distinguished between his political and personal identity and acknowledged that as a religious man he would personally never have published cartoons that ridiculed any religious figure. *TV2 News,* January 30, 2006, at 7 p.m.

42. Prime Minister Anders Fogh Rasmussen's New Year Speech to the nation, January 1, 2006, http://da.wikisource.org/wiki/Statsministerens_nytårstale_2006.

43. See Larsen and Seidenfaden.

44. The cartoons were not on the official agenda but the "imams' folder" circulated in the corridors and international commentators later argued that the OIC conference brought the controversy to the government level in countries like Iran and Syria. "At Mecca Meeting Cartoon Outrage Crystallized," *New York Times,* February 9, 2006.

45. Pia Kjærsgård in *Ugebrev* January 9, 2006.

46. Fiona Adamson, *Civil Society, Immigrant Mobilization and the Limits of Liberalism: The Challenge of Janus-Faced Civil Society,* 2006, conference paper.

47. Klausen argues that the cartoons played into the hands of Middle Eastern extremists who were already involved in violence. The response to the cartoons, she argues, was therefore more about politics than a clash of cultures (Jytte Klausen, *The Cartoons that Shook the World,* 2009).

48. See Larsen and Seidenfaden.

49. "Iran, Syria Stoking Protests?" *CBSNEWS,* February 8, 2006.

50. "Irate Muslims Stage New Protests," *Washington Post,* February 4, 2006.

51. "Top Saudi Official Urges Restraint over Cartoon Protests," *CNN Wire,* February 6, 2009.

52. See McAlister; Jamal and Naber.

53. See Waever.

54. Brigitte Nacos and Oscar Torres-Reyna, *Fueling Our Fears: Stereotyping, Media Coverage, and Public Opinion of Muslim Americans,* 63–64, 2007, Rowman & Littlefield.

55. See Shapiro.

56. See Agamben; Stockle Verena, "Talking Culture: New Boundaries, New Rhetorics of Exclusion in Europe," in *Current Anthropology* 1, no. 2 (1995).

57. "US Says It Also Finds Cartoons of Mohammed Offensive," *New York Times,* February 4, 2006.

58. "Amerikanske aviser hopper ikke på tegninger" (American newspapers don't buy the idea of publishing cartoons) in *Politiken,* February 3, 2006.

59. Conservative William J. Bennett and liberal Alan M. Dershowitz in "A Failure of the Press," *Washington Post,* February 23, 2006.

60. "When Cartoons Are the News. Artists Confront Issue of How to Address Protests Sparked by Mohammed's Image," *San Francisco Chronicle,* February 7, 2006.

61. Many influential Muslim leaders like Iran's foreign minister Manouchehr Mottaki and Malaysia's prime minister Abdullah Ahmad Badawi cautioned against responding violently to the publication of the cartoons while at the same time reminding Western media to not demonize Muslims (*BBC News,* February 10, 2006, and *BT,* February 20, 2006).

62. Scott Benjamin, "Bush Cautions Press, Urges Peace," CBSNews, February 8, 2006. http://www.cbsnews.com/stories/2006/02/08/world/main1294287.shtml

63. *Politiken,* February 4, 2006.

64. "A Clash of Rights and Responsibilities," *BBC News Website,* February 6, 2006.

65. "Forms of Intolerance," *Boston Globe,* February 4, 2006.

66. "How Cartoons Fanned Flame of Muslim Rage," *guardian.co.uk,* February 5, 2006.

67. Giseline Kuipers, *Good Humor, Bad Taste,* 2006. De Gruyter Mouton.

68. See Larsen and Seidenfaden.

69. To some extent, this is probably true. Public displays of non-Christian religious practices are less controversial in the United States than in Denmark, has no separation between state and religion and which imagines itself as more homogeneous and with a common Protestant culture. American Muslims confirmed this difference at a meeting in Denmark in 2006. Contrary to the experience of Muslims in Europe, they didn't find it hard to practice their religion in the U.S. They did, however, feel discriminated against because of their ethnicity. This obviously does not mean that religion doesn't inform U.S. politics as current concerns over gay marriage is a sad testimony of.

70. See Alsultany; McAlister; Jamal and Naber, 37; Nacos, 18.

71. See Alsultany; Jamal and Naber.

72. Nacos, 118.

73. Spencer Ackerman, "Religious Protection: Why American Muslims Haven't Turned to Terrorism," *New Republic,* December 12, 2005. http://www.tnr.com/article/politics/religious-protection.

74. Daniel Pipes, Muslim Immigrants in the United States, Middle East Forum, August 14, 2002. http://www.danielpipes.org/453/muslim-immigrants-in-the-united-states.

75. "What Would Muhammad Do? Muslim Response to Cartoon Controversy" *about.com:islam* February 4, 2006.

76. MPAC Commends Bush Administration for Condemning Danish Cartoons, February 4, 2006. http://www.mpac.org/issues/islamophobia/mpac-commends-bush-administration-for-condeming-danishcartoons.php.

77. "CAF Condemns Hateful Depictions of Islam," February 3, 2006.

78. "Yale Press Panned for Nixing Cartoons of Muhammad," *Yale University Press,* August 16, 2009, and "Statement by John Donatich," *Yale University Press,* September 9, 2009.

79. "Yale Press Bans Images of Muhammad in New Book," *New York Times,* August 12, 2009.

80. "Yale Press Panned for Nixing Cartoons of Muhammad," *Yale University Press,* August 16, 2009.

81. "Censorship at Yale," *New York Post,* August 16, 2009.

82. "Alums Submit Letter Criticizing Yale Press," *Yale Daily News,* September 8, 2009.

83. "Address to a Joint Session of Congress and the American People," September 20, 2001, http://www.washingtonpost.com/wp-srv/nation/specials/attacked/transcripts/bushaddress_092001.html.

84. However, no newspapers reprinted the cartoons after a suspected murder attempt on Kurt Westergaard on January 1, 2010, by a Somali man who has been linked to the radical al-Shabab militia ("Somali Charged over Attack on Danish Cartoonist," *BBC News,* January 2, 2010).

85. Westergaard, quoted in "Jonathan Kay on Kurt Westergaard, Free Speech, and Leftist Refuseniks," *Canadian National Post,* October 5, 2009. Westergaard is quoted as saying, "We gave them everything—money, apartments, their own schools . . . In return, we asked one thing—respect for democratic values, including free speech."

86. Tavshedens Tyrani, Flemming Rose, Jyllandspostens Forlag, Denmark.

87. Similar debates take place in France where the French president's party, the UMP proposed a law that would fine women for wearing the burka in France even though French intelligence service estimates that fewer than 400 women in all of France wear the full veil. Men who force their wives or daughters to wear the burka would get an even higher fine. In "France to Ban Full Face Veil, Says Ruling Party Chief," *radiofranceInternationale,* December 16, 2009.

88. "Kontant Bonus for at lære Dansk" (Cash bonus for learning Danish), *Jyllandsposten,* December 25, 2009.

89. Sherene Razack, *Casting Out,* 2008. University of Toronto.

90. Jytte Klausen, *The Cartoons That Shook the World,* 2009, Yale University Press, New Haven & London.

THIRTEEN

Turcophobia or *Turcophilia*
Politics of Representing Arabs in Latin America

Heba El Attar

Upon gaining their independence from Spain, Latin American countries began the process of constructing their new national identities. Throughout the nineteenth and early twentieth centuries, Latin American intellectuals and writers started invoking an image of the Orient in general, and the Arab Other in particular, to assert a civilized self in the face of an inferior and barbaric Other. An Orientalist discourse ensued and later increased with the influx of Middle Eastern immigrants flowing from the Ottoman Empire. *Turcophobia*—anti-Arab prejudice institutionalized by that discourse—arose as a fierce challenge to the assimilation and integration of Arab immigrants. Desperate, some first- and second-generation Arab authors were forced to practice auto-orientalism, either silencing their heritage or reproducing stereotypical images of the Orient as a means to insert themselves in the nationalist discourse of Latin American countries.[1] Nevertheless, in the second half of the twentieth century, particularly since the 1980s, Latin America started recognizing the heterogeneity of its societies and tolerating the diversity created by all of its immigrants. Unlike the *civilización-barbarie* dichotomy long supported by Latin American intellectuals of the late nineteenth and early twentieth centuries, renowned Mexican novelist Carlos Fuentes today underscores how the Latin American imaginary acknowledged the peculiarity of its hybrid identity of which the Middle Eastern Semitic (both Arab and Jewish) formed an integral part that could be traced back to medieval Spain.[2] Also, unlike the vilified portrayal of the Arab Other in the press of the nineteenth and twentieth centuries, Latin American media today, especially its public television and film, is changing its depiction of that

Other. In the last decade alone, two Latin American soap operas widely watched locally and/or internationally, *O Clone* (Brazil, 2001) and *Los Pincheira* (Chile, 2004), set their main plotlines around a romance and intrigue between a Latin American man and an Arab immigrant woman. Though stereotypical in some aspects regarding the Arab Other, the stories nonetheless drew attention to the culture of that Other, and also to the visibility of Arabs in Latin America today. Meanwhile, in what appears to be an attempt to find the "us" in the "them," the movie *Callejón de los Milagros* (Mexico, 1995) adopted and adapted the Egyptian novel *Midaq Alley* by Naguib Mahfuz to current Mexican social, economic, and political realities.

Hence, several questions seem inevitable. For instance, how has *Turcophobia* regarding the Arab Other shifted toward *Turcophilia*? And subsequently, how intensely is Orientalism practiced by Latin American intellectuals today? Are Latin American cultural productions creating commonalities between Latin American culture and that of the Other? Moreover, have these possible shifts in Latin American perceptions and depictions of the Arab Other had an impact on Arab immigrants' counterrepresentations? I begin this essay by examining representations of the Arab Other in Latin American fiction of the second half of the twentieth century, particularly in two novels from Colombia and Honduras. I then examine counterrepresentations by Arab immigrants during the same period by looking at two examples from their poetry and press in Chile.

Deconstructing Turcophobia

In the 1980s, Gabriel García Márquez, Colombian author and winner of the Nobel Prize in Literature, wrote *Chronicle of a Death Foretold*.[3] The main character of the novel is Santiago Nasar, the wealthy young son of an Arab immigrant, most probably of Palestinian origin,[4] involved in the cattle business. In the same decade, Honduran author Jorge Luis Oviedo wrote *La Turca* (The Turkish Woman),[5] whose protagonist is known only as the Turca, an Arab immigrant lady from Palestine, who begins as a peddler and manages to amass great wealth. The two novels share many characteristics: both protagonists are killed at the end, and both novels are woven with two main threads. The first shared thread is a realm of constant rumors generated by the townspeople, in which both characters are perceived as immoral, mundane yet exotic, and insensitive to the poor population around them. The second thread is the sociopolitical reality of the Arab collectivities in Colombia and Honduras, which constitute the ethnic background of Santiago and the Turca, respectively. Thus, although the reader may initially find the depiction of the two characters and their deaths to be quite typically Orientalist, the nuances of the two threads challenge such reading and lead one to discover the author's awareness of a cognitive dissonance behind the prejudicial rumors about Santiago and the Turca and acknowledge the absurdity of their deaths at the end.

In *Chronicle of a Death Foretold*, Santiago Nasar is thought to be guilty of deflowering a girl whose brothers then kill him without further investigation. However, the text provides no authentic facts against Santiago Nasar, only rumors generated by almost all the people in that Colombian town who viewed Santiago through their prejudiced lens and encouraged the brothers to blindly avenge their sister's honor. Such prejudice becomes even more apparent when, in parallel, García Márquez depicts the town's reaction to a non-Arab young man arriving from another town to marry the deflowered victim. Despite the many similarities between both men in wealth, attractiveness, power, and religious commitment, the people of the town were predisposed to think highly of the non-Arab newcomer while thinking the worst about the Arab son of their own town, Santiago. In the view of the townspeople, Santiago was thinking that his money would make him invincible just "like all Turks."[6] Their prejudice becomes more explicit when in the wake of Santiago's death the narrator, a journalist who comes to investigate and write about the story, interviews each of the subjects in that town and in the comparison of their testimonials makes clear that no real facts are being presented. The reader is left questioning whether all the people in the town were not simply eager to get rid of the "turco" for the cognitive dissonance he generated in them. Santiago was supposed to be the inferior and exotic Other. Instead he was a wealthy, powerful, and attractive young man who was successful in both business and love. He was also white and Christian.[7] Eager to regain their cognitive consonance, the people in the town implicitly urged the elimination of the cause of that dissonance—Santiago.

Now, if any attention was ever paid to Santiago's Arab identity, it would have been to unlock it within a contemporary sequel to the Christian-Moorish conflict. His conveyed Arabness, however, denotes a Latin American perception, representation, and even to some extent validation of the Arab Other's mobility in Colombia's recent political and economic history. Like many Arabs in the Colombian Caribbean, the Nasar family was involved in the cattle business, which contributed to their rapidly gathered wealth and their rising social status. Certainly, this social ascendance later enabled their political visibility. Subsequently, Gabriel García Márquez depicts the Nasars as constantly living in apprehension, sleeping with guns under their pillows. The Nasars' possession of weapons is an aspect that has intrigued some scholars. In a small humble town of defeated people, amassing a huge arsenal was uncommon, as there was nothing that would require such a collection of weapons unless intended for hunting. Nevertheless, in the Colombia of the 1940s, when the main plot of *Chronicle of a Death Foretold* takes place, the Nasars would have been quite justified in their apprehension. During that period, Colombia witnessed horrendous waves of violence, a situation that was aggravated by the political rivalry between the Conservative and Liberal parties. More important, the Liberal parties were known for adopting progressive political measures toward foreign migrations and exports, and extended their hegemony across the Colombian Caribbean.[8] It is in that particular region that the plot of *Chronicle of a Death Foretold* developed. And not only were Arab immigrants established in that region, but they were potentially affiliated with the Liberal Party[9] whose leadership was at some point headed by the Arab Colombian politician Gabriel Turbay.[10] Shown against this backdrop, the dimension of cognitive dissonance generated by Santiago's figure in that fictional Colombian town depicted in García Márquez's novel becomes clear, as does the urgency to eliminate him and thus restore the cognitive consonance.

The death of the Turca in Jorge Luis Oviedo's novel was as unwarranted as that of Santiago in García Márquez's. And her elimination from the scene was as urgently sought, as the cognitive dissonance she had created was even more aggressive than that generated by Santiago. Sharply caricaturized, the depiction of the Turca in the novel initially seems to follow the odalisque style, as everyone in that Honduran town viewed her at first as an exotic female Other, subjected, passive, lusty, and penetrable. To their consternation, however, the Turca, a white Arab female immigrant, turned out to be a woman who did not await Western penetration but rather initiated the penetration of a Western space physically, economically, politically, and culturally. An independent female immigrant, she begins as a peddler and crosses through numerous Honduran towns selling her merchandise. The number of towns she visits, as the novelist remarks ironically, exceeds those visited by any Honduran politician. Soon she is able to save a huge sum of money, build a hotel and a local pub, and in doing so provide jobs and a recreational space for the locals. And yet the rumors continue to fly that maintain that she is insensitive to the townspeople. Meanwhile, her image as a lusty Oriental woman does not seem to subtract from her agency, for throughout the novel she makes enormous efforts to find a man capable of satisfying her desires. When she finally does, she invites all the people in the town, representatives of the Honduran authorities, and officials of the U.S. bases in Honduras to her wedding. And to everyone's surprise, instead of ordering the orchestra to play European waltzes, the Turca orders the musicians to play Latin American classics, thus both validating local culture and positioning herself as one of them. Or as the narrator puts it, "La Turca nos dio una lección, una muestra muy evidente de patriotismo e identidad latinoamericana"[11] (The Turca gave us a lesson, an evident performance of patriotism and Latin American identity). In the face of such a disturbance to their cognitive consonance, the other townswomen along with the priest and the local business owners start to increase their production of prejudicial rumors against the Turca, until only her death is able to put an end to such painful dissonance.

In the novel the *Turca* arrives in the 1970s, but waves of Arab migration, mainly Orthodox Christian Palestinians, have been arriving in Honduras since 1860.[12] And as was the case with the rest of Middle Eastern immigrants to Latin America, the Palestinian-Hondurans' mobility improved their economic and social status and won them political visibility. In such mobility, Palestinian-Honduran women played a substantial role,[13] which leads us to think that the main character in *La Turca* has been intentionally gendered by the author, especially as the novel surpasses the odalisque clichés in its depiction of the Arab female Other.

In fact the depictions of Santiago and the Turca in *Chronicle of a Death Foretold* and *La Turca*, respectively, are not quite *turcophilic*, but neither can they be considered *turcophobic*. But unlike earlier Orientalist practices in Latin American fiction that simplistically perceived and represented the Arab Other, Gabriel García Márquez and Jorge Luis Oviedo carefully expose subtexts that reveal the true factors and motivations behind the negative perception regarding the Arab characters. Such exposure is diligently carried out by both novelists through the different commonalities traced by the authors between Arab and Latin American individuals in the two towns, who would have acknowledged those similarities had only Santiago and the Turca not been Arab. It can then be argued that in *Chronicle of a Death Foretold* and *La Turca*, the two novelists are questioning the portrayer/"us" instead of the portrayed/"them," hence deconstructing the anti-Arab prejudice—*Turcophobia*. Subsequently, it can be contended that such deconstruction constitutes a shift from the Eurocentric Orientalism practiced by Latin American authors and intellectuals during the nineteenth and twentieth centuries.

Arab-Latin Americans

As I mentioned previously, the Orientalist representation of the Arab Other has earlier induced the practice of auto-orientalism in the writings of Arab immigrants published in Latin America before the 1950s. If there has been a possible shift in the Latin American representation of that Other during the second half of the twentieth century, as seen in the novels of García Márquez and Luis Oviedo, then it is likely that there was a similar change in counterrepresentation. For this purpose, I look at examples of poetry by the Palestinian-Chilean poet Mahfud Massís (1916–90), specifically his late poems written in the 1970s and 1980s after his self-exile to Caracas in the wake of the Pinochet coup d'état. I also explore the community magazine *Al-Damir* published in Chile since 2000.

Rather than silencing his heritage or reproducing stereotypical images of the Orient, Massís was determined to validate his hyphenated identity. He says of himself both "Soy el árabe oscuro y semental aullando de presagios como el macho cabrio" (I am the dark Arab, purebred, howling like a billy goat), and "Yo, Americano del Sur, entristecido y salvaje" (I, the South American, sad and savage).[14] Also, rather than relying exclusively on Western imagery and culture in his poetry written entirely in Spanish, Massís inserted in his poems fundamental themes of the *Mahjar* literary schools in the Americas (e.g., exile, Arab nationalism). Like the Turca playing Latin American music at her wedding, Massís identifies himself with Latin America in a way that is both emotional and patriotic. By cultivating one of the most particular genres, poetry, in the host nation's official language, Spanish, Massís performed a high degree of assimilation and integration into Chilean national culture. And by bringing in aspects of one of the most important literary movements in Modern Arabic literature, the *Mahjar,* Massís was bridging his national and ethnic cultures, hence forging an intercultural dialogue between Arab and Latin American literatures and cultures.

In his collection *Ojo de tormenta,* Massís traces similarities between his ethnic culture and his national Chilean one. The collection starts with elegies dedicated to icons of Latin American independence and nationalism such as Bolívar and Guevara. Particularly in poems like "Monumento de sangre al guerrillero" (Monument of Blood for the Fighter), or "Oración a Simón Bolívar en la noche negra de América" (A Prayer for Simon Bolivar in the Dark Latin American Night), Massís asserts his Latin American national identity, lamenting the gradual loss of the values institutionalized by Bolívar, hence his call to the leader: "!Despierta / Capitán, despierta / América te llora como una gran viuda apasionada" (Wake up, Captain, wake up! / America is crying for you like a passionate widow).[15] In the following poems of that same collection, however, Massís meaningfully crosses the border back to the Middle East, toward other lands that share similar anti-imperialist struggles and nationalist discourses. Once there, the poet stops at three significant foci: Iraq, Libya, and Palestine, in "Viaje a Iraq en días de Guerra" (A Trip to Iraq in Times of War), "Para Libia una orquídea roja" (A Red Orchid for Libya), and "Guerrilleros de Palestina" (Palestinian Fighters), respectively. In the first two poems, he endorses Arab nationalism and anticolonialism by describing and praising the Iraqi struggle against the British mandate as well as that of the Libyans against the Italian army. Then, right in the third poem, in "Guerrilleros de Palestina," the poet decides to cross the borders back to Latin America vowing in name of the Palestinian fighters: " . . . en vuestro nombre alzo mi voz en Latinoamérica como quien levanta una espada" (. . . in your name I raise my voice in Latin America as if holding a sword),[16] hence explicitly committing himself to bringing the Arab perspective regarding nationalism, resistance, and anti-imperialism to South America.

In fact, Massís's poems published in the 1960s and onward bear a more explicit nationalist tone in comparison with his earlier poetry. This is especially true in the case of "Ojo de tormenta," written between 1960 and 1989, that focuses on both Arab and Latin American nationalism. This growing tendency in Massís's poetry toward incorporating themes of Arab nationalism and anti-imperialism fits in with Cecilia Baeza's contentions[17] regarding the Palestinian communities, particularly in Chile. According to Baeza, despite those immigrants' initial tendency to assert their cultural heritage, over time their relation to their homeland realities became that of a distant follower of events rather than an agent contributor. However, as she observes, that situation has changed since the 1970s, when Arafat started mobilizing the Palestinian diasporas, particularly those in Latin America. Motivated by this new partnership, says Baeza, the Palestinian immigrants in Latin America convoked a conference in São Paolo, in which the Palestinian-Chilean delegation alone formed 20 percent of the attendees. This mobilization, says Amal Jamal, resulted in interconnecting the Palestinian communities in Latin America and binding them to the Palestinian center represented in the PLO. It can then be suggested that Massís's advocacy for the Arab political causes grew stronger with the growing agency of the PLO in Latin America, however his counterrepresentation and assertion of his ethnic heritage can certainly be attributed to the gradual shift in the Latin American stance regarding the Arab Other, especially since the second half of the twentieth century.

The impact of such a shift is not only sensed in the literary writings by Arab immigrants but also in their press. This is evident in *Al-Damir,* a magazine that embodies this new phase in Arab-Chilean communal agency and self-advocacy. Funded by Foundation Bethlehem-Chile 2000, *Al-Damir* is published monthly both in print and online, and though bearing an Arabic name is published in Spanish. *Al-Damir* in Arabic means "conscience," which suggests that the Palestinian-Chileans' utmost goal is to persuade the wider Chilean public that Palestinians are Chilean too, a task endorsed by the degree of professionalism that the newspaper achieves through the type and quality of its coverage. *Al-Damir* does not merely appear as the latest in a series of newspapers and magazines that have traditionally marked the Arab immigrants' cultural contribution in Latin America. It has broader dimensions that are better understood if the magazine is placed within the wider context of the Palestinian press, whether within the Palestinian territories or in the diaspora.

Placing *Al-Damir* within the context of the Palestinian press in the West Bank and Gaza Strip underlines the counterrepresentation of Palestinian Arab immigrants in Latin America today. Media has been influential in Palestinian national politics and strategy, especially after 1967 when the PLO introduced its media outlets in the occupied territories. And later, after the establishment of the Palestinian Authority (PA), important modifications occurred in the Palestinian media in the West Bank and Gaza Strip, embodying a "passage, from the stage of revolution and mobilization toward the stage of administrative centralization, internal pacification, and state-building."[18] Such a shift certainly influenced the Palestinian diaspora's performance in the media as well. For instance, *Al-Damir* indicates an orientation among the Palestinian diasporic communities in Chile toward organized work in favor of the Palestinian territories, this time independent from the political Palestinian center.[19] This translates into more assertiveness on their part regarding their ethnic and cultural heritage, though within the hegemonic context of the host nation.

In addition, placing *Al-Damir* within the broader context of diasporic Palestinian journalism gives insight into the degree of professionalism sought by the Palestinian-Chilean community. In fact, Palestinian journalism in Arab and European countries, observes Samih Shabib (2001),[20] had been highly politicized and influenced by partisanship between 1965 and 1970, before becoming more liberal between 1970 and 1982. However, it was only between 1984 and 1991, he adds, that professionalism was gradually institutionalized in Palestinian diasporic journalism, reflected in the transcendence of revolutionary discourses and the inclination toward persuasiveness and thorough documentation. Such professionalism is key to understanding the level of assertiveness achieved by this group in mastering textual techniques necessary to better voice its hyphenated identity. In this sense, if placed within the context of diasporic Palestinian journalism evoked by Shabib, *Al-Damir* could be considered as incarnating, in the case of Latin America, similar determination for achieving professionalism both in content and format.

Al-Damir developed sections devoted to a wide array of issues (communal profiles and events, correspondence from Palestine, women, culture, fashion, etc.). In addition, the magazine varies its textual formats, alternating between columns or articles of opinion, reports, and interviews, which are always preceded by an editorial. In general, reports or interviews are not limited to traditionally influential figures (Palestinian or Palestinian-Chilean politicians, bankers, investors, etc.) but also include teenagers, young students, and/or professionals from the community. And in general, *Al-Damir*'s overall discourse does not seem to echo that of any Palestinian political party and avoids escalatory intonations especially regarding the Palestinian-Israeli conflict, which is often approached through textual and graphical documentation.[21] By generally avoiding essentialist perspectives and adopting subtle language in the representation of critical political questions, *Al-Damir* seems to be creating a persuasive discourse and reflects the community determination to maintain an intercultural dialogue in Chile.

To reinforce that intercultural dialogue, central to *Al-Damir*'s cultural strategy is the representation of the community's hyphenated identity. In this respect, one of the first things to be aware of is the magazine's transcendence of Andalusian history. In the early Arab press in Latin America, revisiting the glory of *Al-Andalus* formed a crucial part of the Arab immigrant discourse whether in journalism or literature. It is a historic background that the first Arab immigrants, especially Syrians and Lebanese, were eager to validate and project in order to bridge cultural gaps with the local Latin Americans. In contrast, *Al-Damir* does not rely on the Andalusian rhetoric,[22] hence mirroring the inclination of Palestinian-Chileans to prioritize contemporary intercultural dynamics. Therefore, *Al-Damir* is considerably devoted to representing Palestinian-Chilean acculturation and their commitment and loyalty to Chile. This is depicted in reporting about the community protection of and contribution to local Chilean culture, its investment in the Chilean economy,[23] and its representation of Chile in national or international forums and venues.[24] More important, *Al-Damir* acclaims Palestinian-Chileans support to Chile's economic and political visibility in the Middle East. The magazine especially insists on the community's role in upholding Chile's candidacy and actual admission as a permanent observer in the Arab League. Moreover, *Al-Damir* voices Palestinian-Chileans' determination to engage Chile in one of the toughest Middle Eastern issues, the Peace Process, and in vindicating Chile's commitment to fulfilling this role. One salient example is when *Al-Damir* suggestively pictured then Chilean president Ricardo Lagos wearing the Palestinian *hattah* (national scarf), during the ceremony of the fourth anniversary of Foundation Bethlehem-Chile 2000.[25]

Certainly, the *hattah* is an omnipresent symbol of Palestinianness in Chile and often appears in the magazine's graphics. Apart from the nationalist basis of Palestinianness, *Al-Damir* projects the community identity as equally conceptualized on the bases of religion, region, and ethnicity. For instance, the magazine traces the religious heritage of Palestinian-Chileans primarily to the city of Bethlehem, which is covered in numerous reports and advertisements about the city or religious tourism. Obviously, reviving the image of Christ's birth city allows Palestinian-Chileans to identify with mainstream religious culture in Chile and confers holiness on the community in a way that enhances the credibility and digestibility of its discourse.

In any case, it is noteworthy that even while asserting the community's Palestinianness or Chileanness, it does not by any means undermine the assertion of its Arabness, clearly symbolized in the name of the publication itself: *Al-Damir*. In addition, through a series of reports and advertisements about language-learning programs and centers in Chile, *Al-Damir* echoes the communal effort to support the teaching and learning of Arabic language and culture, an effort that had been channeled earlier through the Institute of Arab and Islamic Studies at the University of Chile. It could then be inferred that apart from illustrating the Palestinian-Chilean community efforts in favor of Palestine, *Al-Damir* underscores the current Arab and/or Palestinian-Chilean strategies for counterrepresentation of their hyphenated identity.

Beyond Turcophobia/Turcophilia

By deconstructing the institutionalized *Turcophobia* in Latin America in their novels, Gabriel García Márquez and Jorge Luis Oviedo moved beyond the classic Orientalism inherited from Europe and practiced by Latin American intellectuals at the turn of the twentieth century. Thus, there is a certain inclination toward *Turcophilia*. Such a shift denotes a Latin American disposition to move away from stereotypical generalizations to a more complex understanding of Arab identity. It also indicates its disposition to find some commonalities with that Other, hence engaging in an intercultural dialogue. There are several signs in the two novels that support such argument. For instance, both authors not only stress the Arabness of their respective main characters but more particularly their Palestinianness. In doing so, Gabriel García Márquez and Jorge Luis Oviedo are in fact shifting away from the prejudicial generalization of the "turco" by underscoring the subethnicity of that Arab Other. More important, they are more clearly capturing and depicting fundamental aspects of the reality lived by the Arab collectivities in

Latin America in general. First, the Palestinianness of their main characters matches the crucial changes in the ethnic makeup of Arab migrations to the continent, which has become more integrated with Palestinian subjects over the past several decades compared to the earlier flows of Syro-Lebanese. Second, the prejudice generated around Santiago and the Turca reflects the fears that Latin Americans had regarding the Arab immigrants—their strong connectedness both to the wide public and to the immigrant masses,[26] and their ascending control over commerce and industry. In addition, by emphasizing the whiteness and Christian affiliation of their respective main characters, the two novelists were breaking further away from the stereotypical identification of all Middle Eastern Arabs as being dark or necessarily Muslims. It could then be argued that not only is there a shift in Latin American conceptualizations of its Arab heritage as indicated by Carlos Fuentes, but also a shift in its perception of the Arab Other. Such a shift definitely explains the flexible margin allowed to Arab immigrants to assert their hyphenated identity and attempt to strengthen intercultural bonds within Latin American society as demonstrated in the examples of counterrepresentation in Mahfud Massís's poetry and *Al-Damir* magazine.

Although it is still difficult to contend that *Turcophobia* has been definitively replaced by *Turcophilia,* the examples of representations and counter-representations highlighted in this essay certainly make clear that institutionalized *Turcophobia* is being challenged.

NOTES

1. Civantos, Christina. *Between Argentines and Arabs: Argentine Orientalism, Arab Immigrants, and the Writing of Identity.* Albany: State University of New York, 2006.
2. Fuentes, Carlos. *El espejo enterrado.* Mexico, D. F.: Taurus, 2004.
3. García Márquez, Gabriel. *Chronicle of a Death Foretold.* Translated by Gregory Rabassa. New York: Knopf, 2002.
4. There are several signs in the text that support Santiago's Palestinian origin, such as his family name—the Nasars. Besides being one of the most common among Palestinian families in Latin America, this name evokes the city of Nazareth. Such evocation has in fact encouraged some scholars to trace similarities between the victimized figure of Santiago and that of Christ. See, for instance, Leonilda Ambrozio, "Morte/Nao Morte; O Mito de Cristo Em *Cronica de Uma Morte Anunciada," Revista Letras* 35 (1986): 17–36.
5. Oviedo, Jorge Luis. *La Turca.* Tequcigalpa. Editores Unidos, 1998.
6. García Márquez, op. cit.
7. Throughout the novel, the author seems to stress these two facts about his protagonist (his Christianity and whiteness) to subvert the stereotypical notion of Arabs being necessarily Muslim or dark skinned.
8. Safford, Frank, and Mario Palacios. *Colombia, Fragmented Land, Divided Society.* New York: Oxford, 2002.

9. Second and third generations of Arab immigrants held important positions in municipalities across Colombian cities such as Cordoba or Cartagena. Among thirteen mayors of Arab descent who rose to power in Lorica between 1963 and 1992, eleven were liberals. And all six mayors of Arab descent who took over the power in Cordoba between 1962 and 1994 were liberals. See Viloria de la Hoz, *Presencia Árabe en el Caribe Colombiano. Lorica, un estudio de caso,* http://www.banrep.gov.co/documentos/publicaiones/pdf/lorica_arabes.pdf.

10. Roberto Martín-Guzman, "El aporte económico y cultural de la inmigración árabe en Centro America en los siglos XIX y XX," in Raymundo Kabchi, ed. *El Mundo Árabe y América Latina,* 1991, 155–98.

11. Jorge Luis Oviedo op. cit.

12. Euraque, Dario. "The Arab-Jewish Economic Presence in San Pedro Sula, the Industrial Capital of Honduras: Formative Years, 1880s–1930." In *Arab and Jewish Immigrants in Latin America. Images and Realities,* 94–124. Edited by Ignacio Klich and Jeffery Lesser. London: Frank Cass, 1998.

13. Marin, op. cit.

14. Massís, Mahfed. *Antología. Poemas 1942–1988.* Caracas: Editorial Dialit, 1990.

15. Ibid., 193.

16. Ibid., 199.

17. Baeza, Cecila. "Les pales Tiniens du Chili: De la Conscience disporique à la mobiliation transnationale." *Revue détudes palestiniennes,* no. 95 (printemps 2005), 51–87.

18. Jamal, Amal. *Media Politics and Democracy in Palestine. Political Culture, Pluralism, and the Palestinian Authority.* Portland, Oregon: Sussex Academic Press, 2005.

19. To better understand the value of *Al-Damir,* it is crucial to note that with the territorialization of the Palestinian center after Oslo, the Palestinian diaspora in Latin America fell gradually into marginalization. And it was not until the Second *Intifidah* that Palestino-Latin Americans, especially in Chile, were remobilized. See Cecilia Baeza.

20. Shabib, Sameh. *Palestinian Press in the Diaspora between 1965–1970.* Ramallah, Palestine: The Palestinian Institute for the Study of Democracy, 2001.

21. "Entender lo inentendible," *Al Damir,* Sept. 2006, 20–35. http://www.palestinos.com/AlDamir/AlDamir_n54-Sep06.pdf.

22. *Al-Damir,* however, might occasionally refer to the survival of Andalusian legacy by reporting, for instance, on the predominant Moorish architecture in contemporary Arab-Chileans' residences.

23. Daniela Salvador Elias, "Del negocio textil al éxito de los hipermercados," *Al-Damir,* May 2005, 22–24, http://www.palestinos.com/AlDamir/AlDamir_n44-May05.pdf.

24. Fernando Manzur Chomalí, "El deporte, parte de mi vida," *Al-Damir,* April 2005, 5–11, http://www.palestinos.com/AlDamir/AlDamir_n43-Abr05.pdf.

25. Gwendelen Saffie, "Cuatro años apoyando al pueblo palestino," *Al-Damir,* Sept. 2005, 4, http://www.palestinos.com/AlDamir/AlDamir_n47-Sep05.pdf.

26. Civantos.

FOURTEEN

User-Friendly Islams
Translating Rumi in France and the United States

Ziad Elmarsafy

In the 1960s and 1970s, numerous Anglophone poets and readers discovered Rumi, the thirteenth-century mystic, thinker, and poet who was born in Vakhsh (contemporary Tajikistan), lived most of his life and died in Konya (contemporary Turkey), and wrote in Persian.[1] The affinities between several strands of the New Age movement and the openness of Rumi's message paved the way for its widespread acceptance. By 1997, several American newspapers declared Rumi the best-selling poet in the United States, thanks in no small part to the adaptations of Coleman Barks.[2] This trend was accompanied by the ever-increasing worldwide popularity of the "whirling dervishes," the most visible aspect of the Mawlawi order founded by Rumi.

Over the same period, however, there developed what is looking increasingly like a long-term global conflict between Muslims and non-Muslims. It is thus well worth examining the tensions between the enthusiastic support for the PATRIOT Act, the war in Afghanistan, and (to a lesser extent) the war in Iraq, on the one hand, and the enthusiastic consumption of Rumi, on the other.

In order to better situate this tension in the United States, it would be helpful to compare it with the way in which Islam is seen in another Western country, one which has frequently opposed American foreign policy—namely, France. In what follows I will carry out this comparison as a function of the more widely distributed translations of Rumi. I will argue that the success of the Rumi phenomenon in the United States depends to a large extent on de-Islamicizing his identity, so that he comes across as a symbol of amorphous syncretism. In France, by contrast, Rumi's Muslim identity is foregrounded: here he is presented as a Muslim poet and mystic who bears a message of love. To a certain extent, the image of Rumi propagated by his French translators helps to uncouple the all too frequent association between Islam and terror.

Covering-Up Islam in the English Translation of Rumi

Rumi's popularity in the West is not new, though the remarkable marketing apparatus and commercial spin-off industry surrounding his work certainly are. Before Barks, most English-language readers would probably have read Rumi in the versions of Edward Henry Whinfield (1836–1922), whose abridgment of the *Mathnawī* was first published in London in 1887 and was still being reprinted in New York as a Dutton paperback in the 1970s, as well as the more scholarly translations of Reynold Allen Nicholson (1868–1945), who held the Sir Thomas Adams Chair in Arabic at Cambridge (1922–36), and those of his student and successor to the Thomas Adams Chair, Arthur John Arberry (1905–69). The status of Nicholson's monumental edition, translation, and commentary on the *Mathnawī* is such that Franklin Lewis calls him, along with Badi` al-Zamān Foruzānfar, the greatest Rumi specialist of the twentieth century.[3] Apart from Barks, a number of American poets have also adapted or translated Rumi, usually in collaboration with specialists or speakers of Persian: the list includes Robert Duncan, W. S. Merwin and Robert Bly.[4] More recently, several scholars, including William Chittick, Franklin Lewis, and Annemarie Schimmel, have produced their own translations of various parts of Rumi's oeuvre, usually in the context of research projects or biographies. Still, no set of translations has matched the impressive appeal and sales figures of those produced by Coleman Barks.

One noteworthy attempt at bringing Rumi to a wider reading public was the volume entitled *Rumi, Poet and Mystic,* published in London in 1950 as the first volume in George and Allen Unwin's "Ethical and Religious Classics of the East and West" series. This volume contains a selection of Rumi's shorter poems translated by R. A. Nicholson and edited by his student, A. J. Arberry. The General Introduction explains its purpose as follows.

> As a result of the two Wars that have devastated the world men and women everywhere feel a twofold need. We need a deeper understanding and appreciation of other peoples and their civilizations, especially their moral and spiritual achievements. And we need a new vision of the Universe, a clearer insight into the fundamentals of ethics and religion. . . .

It is the object of this series, which originated among a group of Oxford men and their friends, to place the chief ethical and religious masterpieces of the world, both Christian and non-Christian, within easy reach of the intelligent reader who is not an expert—the undergraduate, the ex-Service man who is interested in the East, the Adult student, the intelligent public generally.[5]

Rumi has become a means of bringing a message of peace and tolerance to a war-ravaged world. The register is unabashedly religious, the purview openly colonial (the ex-serviceman has presumably returned from Asia or Africa), while the tone lies somewhere between didactic and pastoral. It is not particularly clear that the intelligent postwar public actually sought the guidance of the "group of Oxford men and their friends," but the publisher clearly thought such guidance desirable.

The gap separating Nicholson from the protagonists of the fin de siècle Rumi craze is chronologically narrow but ideologically profound. By the late 1960s Robert Bly had established his credentials as a politically committed antiwar poet through his work with American Writers Against the Vietnam War, which he cofounded. At the same time he had made his mark as an active translator, adapting the likes of Lorca, Neruda, Machado, and Rilke. By the early 1970s he had started reading Kabīr and Rumi. In a meeting with Coleman Barks in 1976, he encouraged the latter to rework Arberry's and Nicholson's versions of Rumi. The results, however, are as far from Nicholson as the late 1960s were from Victorian England. To quote David Barber, "This is not your grandfather's Rumi."[6] Indeed, Barks's translations provide the most vivid illustration since Ezra Pound of George Steiner's argument that the quality of a given translation—the "elucidative strangeness" that we recognize and make our own—varies in direct proportion to the distance between the source and target languages.[7] The sound of Barks's Rumi is Whitmanesque, the outlook isolationist.[8] Barks himself presents the ethical and linguistic issues at stake in his introduction to the new edition of his best seller, *The Essential Rumi*. Having ruled out the possibility that "the Middle East warring" will end either in our lifetimes or those of our grandchildren, he adds:

But perhaps hope is overrated. Who needs it. Let us continue on with our battered guidon, which has no recognizable insignia. As Whitman advises us in the 1855 preface to *Leaves of Grass:*

Argue not concerning God . . . re-examine all you have been told at church or school or in any book, dismiss whatever insults your soul . . .

I say that the exclusivity of most of the organized religions *does* insult the soul. We must be open enough to assimilate the insights of indigenous cultures as well as those of the Abrahamic religions, to glory in the clarity of the Rinzai and Bodhidharma as well as that of the dreamtime drawings. Joseph Campbell teaches us this. It feels mean-spirited and academic to dismiss as "syncretic" Rumi's healing universal tolerance. His place among world religions is as a dissolver of boundaries. He is the ocean that acknowledges oneness (the seawater) over the multiplicity of waves (our individual circumstances).[9]

Gone are the conditionals and imperatives of *Rumi, Poet and Mystic*, and with them the well-defined boundaries of a world ruined by war but still familiar with the identities in play. Barks's Rumi is not necessarily an adherent of any organized religion. Furthermore, the social and political impact of Barks's efforts is minimal at best. The routine privileging of passion over reason creates a perspective that turns the word *syncretism*—a not inaccurate description of the uses to which Rumi is put—into an accusation rather than a description. This quietist outlook has more in common with Mahayana Buddhism than Islam, though this, too, is probably an invalid distinction from Barks's perspective. Any possibility of *engagement* or commitment is moot: for Barks, as for Auden, poetry makes nothing happen.

Barks usually stays close to the original.[10] While he does sometimes delete such details as the location of Qur'ānic citation or a *ḥadith*, his notes add numerous helpful explanations for the uninitiated reader. It is, in the last analysis, hard not to be won over by Barks's talent.[11]

If Barks's adaptations of Rumi echo the messages of peace and tolerance that were transmitted by his predecessors, Barks's fellow travelers, especially those of the New Age industry, seem to point the arrow of spirituality in a different direction, placing the Muslim poet and scholar far in the background. Haydn Reiss's 1998 documentary film *Rumi: Poet of the Heart* presents Rumi as a "universal," nondenominational or superdenominational poet, channeled through Coleman Barks.[12] Against a seductive vocal backdrop provided by actress Debra Winger, multiple commentators including Barks himself, fellow poet Robert Bly, mythologist/storyteller Michael Meade, religion specialist Huston Smith, and the ubiquitous Deepak Chopra, all weigh in with their perspective on Rumi. The only cast member with a direct linguistic relationship to Rumi's text and language is the teacher Zohra Eghbal-Mahdjoub, whose name does not appear on the jacket of the DVD. Another name that fails to appear is that of Syrian-born artist and publisher Simone Fattal. Fattal translated Eva de Vitray-Meyerovitch's *Rumi et le soufisme* (1977), long the standard short introduction to Rumi in French.

On screen, however, Fattal is presented as "Publisher, 'Rumi and Sufism,'" the implication being that it is she rather than de Vitray-Meyerovitch who wrote the book. The cast member with what is arguably the most intense institutional involvement with Rumi, namely, Sheikh Jalaluddin Loras, founder and head of the Mevlevi Order of America, does not appear in the credits, nor is his name on the cover. There is, in other words, a relationship of inverse proportion between the visibility of a given name and the proximity of its bearer—linguistic or devotional—to Rumi.

The packaging goes hand in hand with the translation of Rumi into a supranational and supradenominational figure. Rumi's message of peace and tolerance suffers a sea change, courtesy of Deepak Chopra.

> If we look deeply enough, actually, into the heart of science itself, we might discover that what Rumi and what the other great seers and sages and what the wisdom traditions are saying is true: that at the heart of creation, there is only that field of love; that ultimately even our material success comes from the ability to love and have compassion, comes from the capacity to experience joy and ecstasy and share it with others. . . .
>
> We look for all kinds of solutions for our everyday problems; most of the solutions are purely materialistic. . . . If you want to take care of inner cities, pour in the funds over there and it'll solve [the problem]. That's not the crisis of our age, and even if we do see poverty over there, that's the expression of a deeper impoverishment, and that impoverishment is the soul and spirit screaming for nourishment and that nourishment can come from poetry.

Apart from the appalling ignorance of the inner city's lyric forms (rap and hip-hop, inter alia) and the spiritual significance of the black Church inherent in this statement, Chopra's assertion that urban poverty results from spiritual hunger seems to have more to do with *Think and Grow Rich* than with the *Mathnawī*. If only those suffering from economic oppression change their attitude or work on their "capacity to experience joy," the specious argument goes, real wealth will result. The curious logic of these statements takes the viewer away from Islam, which makes alms compulsory, and toward an unreal universe where poetry somehow feeds the hungry, cures the sick, and induces urban regeneration.

The details foregrounded by Reiss's script come close to effacing Rumi's Muslim identity entirely. Consider the life of Rumi as narrated by Debra Winger. "The Sufis," we are surprised to learn, "are an ancient spiritual order." Mysticism may indeed be ancient, but Sufism is bound inextricably with the history of Islam, which is to say that it is no more ancient than the eighth century CE. Nor is it accurate to describe the myriad strands and ways included under the rubric of "Sufism" as a single "order," a term that connotes monasticism and lies outside the ellipse of Sufism with its twin foci of asceticism and ecstasy. Pre-Shams, we are told, "[Rumi's] life seems to have been a fairly normal one for a religious scholar—teaching, meditating, helping the poor." This is no doubt true, but there is much more to the life of a *faqīh* and ascetic than teaching, meditation, and alms. While these are important and commendable activities, the fact that neither prayer nor fasting is mentioned implies, again, a perspective that ignores key aspects of Muslim life. Teaching, meditating, and helping the poor could, in fact, describe the lives of religious figures anywhere. It is precisely this view of Sufism as a multicultural synthesis that emerges in the subsequent commentary by Huston Smith: "They [the Sufis] are the mystics of Islam, and as the mystics of Islam, the Sufis, we can connect with because they're talking about these wonderful sublime truths that have a way of piercing into the human heart wherever it is." Again, this is true, but it leaves the viewer with the impression that interreligious dialogue or "connection" with Islam is only possible if Sufis take part. In fact, the sublime truths in question are frequently expressed through citations from the Qur'ān and *ḥadīth*—orthodox sources to say the least. In the film, Michael Meade follows with this description of Sufism as Unitarian practice.

> The Sufis used to walk, you know, down several roads; visiting with the Christians, visiting with Islam [*sic*], visiting with all the great religions really—I mean, that's part of the nature of this kind of fluid imagination, it crosses boundaries, it penetrates, it slips by. . . . It works in many different ways as if to keep bringing people to some deep human well.

Last but not least, Robert Bly is shown describing the relationship between Rumi and Shams as an illustration of the theories he presents in *Iron John* regarding the mentoring of boys by wild men.

> He [Shams] was an intense, fierce, mountain meditator. . . . One can see here in Shams an older man, who is outside the orthodox spiritual community, who comes in and helps a younger man, who is embedded in that orthodox spiritual community, and then there's a kind of explosion.

Five minutes into *Rumi: Poet of the Heart,* the intelligent viewer knows a fair amount about (a certain version of) Sufism, Rumi, and Shams, but very little about Islam, and still less about Muslim belief and law as a foundation for Sufism. It falls to academic experts like Franklin Lewis to set the record straight.

> Rumi did not come to his philosophy of tolerance and inclusive spirituality by turning away from Islam or organized religion, but through an immersion in it; his spiritual yearning stemmed from a desire to follow the example of the Prophet Muhammad and actualize his potential as a perfect Muslim.[13]

It is unfortunate that this sentence occurs not in *Rumi: Poet of the Heart* but in Lewis's scholarly book on Rumi, thus diminishing the potential impact of his lucid approach on the public.

The excision of orthodox Islam from the portrait of Rumi in Reiss's film can also be seen in a brief passage on the image of wine in Sufi poetry. Now, this is a delicate issue, given the orthodox prohibition against alcohol in Islam, and the frequent reference in Sufi literature to wine as a metaphor for mystic or devotional intoxicated awareness.[14] Barks himself has included in *The Essential Rumi* a short poem, "Why Wine is Forbidden" (a translation of *Mathnawī* 4:2154–58) though here again the reference is to spiritual rather than physical intoxication.[15] About halfway through the film, we see another reference to this liquor (though not necessarily to this snippet from the *Mathnawī*) in a scene showing Zohra Eghbal-Mahdjoub explaining to her Afghan student, Hassina Sharijan, that "it's wine, but . . . it's just all about love." True again, but how is the viewer to discern the multiple levels of significance at work in Rumi's references to wine, especially in view of the prohibition of wine in Islam, from this brief interaction?

One final instance of this tendency is seen in Barks's recitation of "The Sunrise Ruby" halfway through *Rumi: Poet of the Heart*.[16] This poem, as Barks informs us, is a reworking of Nicholson's translation of *Mathnawī* 5:2020–49.[17] On the whole Barks does not stray too far from the content of the original. Nevertheless, it is one of the instances where Barks deletes some references to the Qur'ān and tradition, making its selection for the film seem not exactly innocent. The poem starts with the banter of two heterosexual lovers, she asking him whether he loves her or himself more, he responding that he has dissolved in his love like a ruby held up to the sun, with no resistance to sunlight. This moment of dissolution enables the transition to the moral of the poem, as Barks explains in his introduction to this section: "Being a lover is close to being a worker. When the ruby becomes the sunrise, its transparency changes to a daily discipline."[18]

The fourth stanza of Barks's translation reads:

This is how Hallaj said, *I am God*,
And told the truth![19]

Meanwhile, Nicholson's translation of this verse (2035) reads:

A Pharaoh said "I am God" and was laid low; a Mansūr (Hallaj) said "I am God" and was saved.[20]

Both Nicholson and Barks take the same liberty in translating Al-Ḥallāj's famous cry, "*Ana-l-ḥaqq*," (أنا الحق) cited in the original by Rumi) as "I am God." The difference between them comes in the first hemistich, which is suppressed by Barks. This matters because the autodivinization of a pharaoh in his confrontation with Moses is a recurring topos both in the Qur'ān and the *Mathnawī*.

This occultation of the Qur'anic background continues until the end of Barks's version, where the last two stanzas read:

Submit to a daily practice.
Your loyalty to that
is a ring on the door.
Keep knocking, and the joy inside
will eventually open a window
and look out to see who's there.

In the Nicholson translation, by contrast, the reader is constantly reminded of the details of the Muslim prayer ritual. Nicholson translates verses 2048–2049 as follows:

The Prophet hath said that acts of genuflexion and prostration (in the ritual prayer) [*rukūʿ* and *sujūd*; ركوع و سجود] are (equivalent to) knocking the door-ring of (mystical) attainment on the Divine Portal. [Nicholson's footnote 3: i.e prayer is the means of attaining union with God]

When any one continues to knock that door-ring, felicity peeps out (literally puts forth a head) for his sake.[21]

Nicholson cites two *ḥadīth* as objects of allusion in his commentary on 2048 above, the first of which reads, "Adīmū qarʿa bāb al-malakūt bi-l-rukūʿi wa-l-sujūd" [roughly: "Keep knocking on the door of [God's kingdom] through genuflexion and prostration"].[22] It is precisely the seeker's constant performance of the prayer ritual that metamorphoses him or her into the transparent ruby. Where Nicholson takes pains to make clear the centrality of the prayer ritual to the Sufi, however, Barks substitutes a term redolent of the language used in meditation training: "daily practice." Again, the authorial strategy at work throughout *Rumi: Poet of the Heart* seems to be translating Rumi's poetry into a task that makes physical but not religious or intellectual demands on his readers. Granted, a documentary film aimed at the audience of the PBS network is not a graduate seminar on Persian poetry, and certain elements of the *Mathnawī* are bound to disappear in such a context, but one cannot help suspecting that, if this version of Islam has become palatable to a large public, it is largely at the cost of its creed and law.[23]

Foregrounding Islam in the French Translation

If recent English-language versions of Rumi have a New Age flavor, the French counterpart is filtered through historical events. In addition to the Western view of Islam as the source of the world's ills (especially terror), the French perspective carries with it the long and sad history of France's relationship with its Muslim colonies. Now that France is home to the largest Muslim community in the European Union, books on Islam abound.

Some of the differences in the cultural landscape between France and the United States need to be taken into account at this stage: first, and foremost, the existence of a public sphere that enables dialogue and reflection on matters of import, including Islam and Muslims.[24] Although American equivalents exist, it is difficult to draw parallels between, say, PBS and the state-owned French radio station, France Culture, given the very different role of the state in sponsoring cultural and educational activities. Consider *Cultures d'Islam*, a weekly program on France Culture in which Tunisian-born writer Abdelwahab Meddeb interviews writers of note on various aspects of Islam. Needless to say, the fact that a program that focuses on books about Islam rather than current events has enjoyed such longevity testifies both to a growing Muslim population and a public more literate than its American counterpart. The contours of this public sphere, caught as it is between the academy and the (for lack of a better word) "general public," actually gives intellectuals a certain legitimacy regardless of their academic affiliation, the net result being that the notion of a public intellectual is only loosely centered on university life, and spreads farther and wider than it does in the United States.[25] The sphere is buoyed, moreover, by an extensive network of small- and medium-sized booksellers and publishers, many of them specializing in books on Islam, the Middle East, and North Africa. One happy corollary of all this is a smaller quantity of conformity and jargon in French intellectual life. Another, not unrelated difference is the status of Orientalism in France: it is still more than respectable, as an academic discipline, discursive mode, and aesthetic practice. Although Edward Said is well known, his *Orientalism* has proven far less influential in the hexagon than in the Anglophone world.[26] Admittedly, there is an amnesiac reaction to certain aspects of France's colonial past, as witness the surreal attempts at legislating the teaching of "the positive side of overseas colonization" in 2005–6 and the racist tones frequently voiced in the contemporary debate on "national identity." Similarly, the debate over the *ḥijāb* that shook France in 2003–4 featured precious few links between the colonial origins of many French Muslims and the crisis at hand.[27] (It does bear pointing out, however, that a similarly amnesiac condition is seen in the British debate about the *niqāb* and the assimilation of British Muslims in late 2006, as well as the subsequent British debates about national identity that seem to have inspired the current French government.)

The sheer cultural and political weight of France's colonial past in the Maghreb, the number of Maghrebis living in France, and the tactical decisions made by successive French governments to give this population a stake in France creates a situation in which the face of France is partly Muslim, and France's Islam is to a very large extent Maghrebi.[28] When they are not colored by disastrous current events (wars in the Middle East, suburban riots, and so on), the connotations of the word *Muslim* are frequently associated with the sorts of things that French tourists see when they visit the Maghreb—an exotic fantasy featuring hammams and desert palaces—as well as the culture that the immigrants from the Maghreb brought with them. The economic basis of this culture is not negligible: the fact that the immigrant population was, in the early years, frequently poor and ill-educated entailed frequent recourse to alternative methods of problem solving in the form of religious healers who often claim to be Sufis. The routine Sufi allusions in French rap and raï music aid and abet this tendency, as does the important role played by a number of Sufi orders in interfaith dialogues and synergies in contemporary France.[29] What the French see in their mind's eye when they think about Islam is therefore likely to carry this association regardless of what that person knows about Sufism. Consequently, the average French citizen therefore enjoys greater familiarity with the lived reality of Islam and Sufism than his or her American counterpart.

In stylistic terms, one major difference between France and the United States is the absence of a French Coleman Barks. What we find instead is a large number of academic specialists writing for the general public about

Sufism. Apart from the monumental example of Louis Massignon, whose name has become synonymous with Al-Ḥallāj, it bears pointing out that one of the cofounders of the legendary Éditions du Seuil—one of the most prestigious publishers in France, probably best-known in the Anglophone universe for publishing works by writers and thinkers associated with the journal *Tel Quel,* the vanguard of the French literary theory revolution in the 1960s and 1970s—is Michel Chodkiewicz, a convert to Islam and author of the landmark study of Ibn ʿArabī, *Le Sceau des saints.*

Whereas in the United States there is an effacement of boundaries between faiths and the occultation of Rumi's Muslim identity, in France the opposite takes place: writers represent Rumi as a Muslim first and foremost. As is the case with a number of French writers on Sufism and Islam, the point is to present an image of Islam diametrically opposed to that of the mainstream media: a religion built around love rather than violence. The reasons behind this tactic are not difficult to discern: the Algerian civil war came to France in catastrophic fashion during the 1995 bombing campaign and, together with the rapid rise in fundamentalist movements among France's Muslims, changed the political and religious landscape for Muslim and non-Muslim alike. In reaction, there seems to have been a concerted effort among France's Muslims to reclaim Islam from those who aimed at giving it a more violent persona.[30] These efforts redoubled after the attacks of September 11, 2001, at which point publishers and writers seem to have negotiated a spontaneous contract of cooperation in this regard. The Éditions du Seuil fortified its "Points sagesses" series, and Albin Michel did the same for its "Spiritualités vivantes" collection and added a new one called "L'Islam des Lumières."

For a very long time, French readers of Rumi relied mainly on Eva de Vitray-Meyerovitch's extensive work and expertise. Apart from *Rumi et le soufisme,* she has to her credit a translation of the quasi totality of Rumi's oeuvre. De Vitray-Meyerovitch's translations make clear that Rumi is to be understood as part of an intellectual tradition combining both Islamic and Western philosophy. We are already far from the suppression of reason celebrated in *Rumi: Poet of the Heart.*[31]

Over the past decade, a new generation of translators has picked up the task of translating Rumi into French. The most intriguing figure among them is Christian Jambet, who published a selection from the *Dīwān Shams* under the title *Soleil du Réel: Poèmes d'amour mystique* with the Imprimerie Nationale in 1999. Jambet's political past—he cofounded the Gauche Prolétarienne before becoming a philosopher and Orientalist, working with legendary Iranologist Henry Corbin[32]—seems at first to contradict his current life, producing one study after another of Shiʿi Messianism and gnostic revolt in splendid Parisian isolation. However, the common thread between the two is Jambet's firm and lucid idealism. A self-described Hegelian, Jambet sees his academic activity as an extension of his erstwhile interest in extreme revolutionary movements, all with a view to deconstructing the "Alexandre Adler syllogism: Islam—jihad, jihad—terrorism; therefore Islam—terrorism."[33] In Jambet's words,

> Ben Laden represents the second death of Henry Corbin. He who had such great hope for spiritual Islam would [if he were here today] see that the world has chosen to foreground the Wahhabi executioners, which is to say everything that we thought we had repressed! It's a bit like the story of Marxism, where Pol Pot won out. But I have nothing to do with beautiful souls; I am a Hegelian to the end: if the Real is rational, the forms of consciousness that go with it are not. The philosopher always arrives too late, but his task is to drive a wedge between the Real and consciousness.[34]

Hence the importance of a new translation of Rumi: it forces the reader to reconsider the Real from a decentered Western gaze, relieved of its essentialist assumptions about itself and about Islam.

Accordingly, Jambet's translation of Rumi strikes the reader as much by its form as by its content, which is inflected by this continental philosophical idiom. On the inside title page, we find the words شمس الحق ["Sun of the Real"] printed between the title and subtitle. Throughout the course of the book, several poems, seemingly selected at random, are printed both in Persian and in French translation. The overall effect is that the reader is never too far away from the script of the original.

Equally striking is Jambet's long introduction, which is cast in an elegant idiom somewhere between Mallarmé and *Tel Quel;* the text neither pulls stylistic punches nor makes concessions to those seeking an easy read. Starting with the concepts of loss and grief as founding moments, Jambet's text plunges directly into an exploration of the link between the conceptual and the poetic: "Everything starts with loss. Rumi's poetry only exists through loss, it is nourished by the exultant melancholy and sad clamor provoked by disappearance."[35] Now, this is also the starting point of *Rumi: Poet of the Heart,* where we see a close shot of an actor playing Rumi turning around a pole in his grief, and Robert Bly rejoicing at the fact that Rumi explores "all those emotions that we prefer to avoid." But the image and sound bite do little to account for the nature and quality of the lyrical explosion that is Rumi. Here now is Jambet on the genesis of the lyric between Rumi and Shams.

Poetry encircles the divine Real and, having failed to express it, keeps trying to do so obsessively. This is poetry as negative theology, attempting to go beyond all the names it puts forward in order to exhibit a certain minute unsayable remainder. . . . Shamsoddin is the embodiment of the unsayable: he is not just one creature among many, he is that amazing living being who has the power of making manifest the very thing that the poetic act talks around without ever being able to say [*ce que l'acte poétique cerne sans pouvoir le dire*].[36]

While it is probably safe to assume that this introduction will only be read and appreciated by readers with some training in philosophy, its very existence along with multiple pages of Persian script speaks to the institutional difference between the French- and the English-language versions of Rumi: the former has no qualms about making serious demands, intellectual and metaphysical, on the reader. The opposition between the mind and the heart, while certainly operative in Rumi's poetry, does not preclude exercising the mind with a solid introduction to an elegant set of translations.

The next two translators of Rumi are both from Iran but live in France. Leili Anvar-Chenderoff teaches Persian at INALCO (Institut des langues et civilisations orientales, the last avatar of Colbert's École des jeunes de langues [1669] and the center of gravity of French studies of the Middle East, North Africa, and Asia), having completed a thesis on Rumi's lyric oeuvre. Her *Rûmî* was published in 2004 by Entrelac's new series, "Sagesses éternelles," under the editorship of Sophia Tazi-Sadeq, as part of a triple inauguration next to books on Meister Eckhardt and Maimonides. The innovative cover design is used to drive home three key points: Islam, the Mawlawi order, and love. On the front cover we read, "Mohammad Djalâl al dîn Rûmî (1207–1273), poète mystique de langue persane, inspirateur de l'ordre des derviches tourneurs" (Mohammad Djalâl al dîn Rûmî (1207–1273), mystical Persian-language poet, inspiration of the order of the whirling dervishes).[37] With this one sentence the author emphasizes Rumi's identity as a Muslim—it is highly unlikely that anyone other than a Muslim would be named Mohammad—and his status as the founder of the whirling dervishes, whose ritual is probably better known than the text of Rumi's poetry. Farther down, we read, "il fut initié à la religion de l'amour par un mystique derviche, Shams de Tabriz, qui bouleversa sa vie et fit de lui un poète et un chantre de l'amour mystique" (He was initiated into the religion of love by a dervish, Shams of Tabriz, who changed his life and turned him into a poet and a cantor of mystical love). The words *la religion de l'amour* are in a larger font and different color. Again, the emphasis is on the foundation in theology upon which the mystical edifice of the religion of love is built. Even before opening the book, therefore, the equation "Islam—Religion of love" is firmly embedded in the reader's mind.

Anvar-Chenderoff's skill as a translator, whereby a great deal of Rumi is rendered into French rhyming couplets, gives the reader a feel for the rhythms of the original. Her translations start with a short extract from the *Valad Nāmeh* that operates as an apologia for Rumi. As she explains, "The fact that Soltan Valad felt the need to justify his father's behavior indicates that it was not always acceptable for a religious teacher [*maître spirituel*] to write poetry."[38] The reader is thereby reminded of the tension between Rumi the *faqīh* and Rumi the Sufi, another aspect of his life that disappears in the Barks-Bly-Reiss approach, where the explosion of love and poetry are all that matter after the disappearance of Shams. (The reader is also reminded of the fact that Rumi was a family man rather than a mere love-crazed otherworldly individual.) The extract from the *Valad Nāmeh* further emphasizes the grounding of Rumi's poetry in a vast hermeneutic enterprise built around the language of God as expressed in the Qur'ān.[39]

The most remarkable of the recent French translations of Rumi, Manijeh Nouri-Ortega's *Le Sens de l'amour chez Rûmî*, published in 2004 by Dervy, brings multifarious innovations to the task at hand. Using an art book format sold with a CD of recitations of Rumi keyed to the selected translations, the book has an outside cover with dividers separating French from Farsi sections. Nouri-Ortega presents a thematic translation of sorts, focused on the presence of the word *'eshq* (love) in both the *Divān* and the *Mathnawī*. Based on an article of quotations that eventually became the foundation for a course on Rumi at the Université de Paris III by Abdul-Ghafūr Rawan Farhadi (later ambassador of Afghanistan to the UN), and combining bilingual text with sound, Nouri-Ortega's aim is to bring to the reader the lived Persian experience of Rumi: less as a translation than as a multimedia recreation of that experience with a focus on the theme of love.[40] The pedagogical dimension is further deepened by a section on the music and rhythm of Persian verse, aimed at nonspeakers.[41] Finally, this is one of the few translations of Rumi to include a section on the methodology of translation, explicitly stating the translator's decision-making strategy.[42] A student of the Swiss specialist of Sufism Fritz Meier, Nouri-Ortega is also a practicing Jungian analyst familiar with the work of Robert Bly and professor at the Institut Catholique de Toulouse. Despite her affinity with this circle, however, her version of Rumi is diametrically opposed to that of Barks: tight and exacting, proud of its academic origins, and unrelenting in binding the head and heart, Nouri-Ortega patiently applies the same strict standards to which she was held in Tehran, Basel, and Paris to the texts that she translates.

The irony of all this is that it is in the United States, where freedom of speech is theoretically sacrosanct, and church and state at their most separated, that the compromised, user-friendly, not-quite-Muslim Rumi made the greatest impact on the general public; while the openly Muslim Rumi has found a warm welcome in France, where the centennial of *la laïcité* was celebrated in 2005, *le foulard islamique* can still provoke apoplexy, and, as of this writing, the niqab was banned despite the small number of those who wear it on French soil. Why the vast personal and civil liberties in the United States generate this deep-running conformity, one can only guess, though the answer probably has something to do with the increasingly Darwinian social and economic apparatus in the years since Barks discovered Rumi.

The differences between the French and English translations of Rumi speak to the historical construction of an imagined community. In the American context we see a Rumi shorn of his identity in order to feed a population "hungry for spiritual nourishment." In France, on the other hand, we are constantly reminded of Rumi's identity as a Muslim, his activity as a theologian, the roots of his writing in the Qur'an and tradition in order to show France itself that its Muslims cannot be reduced to the extremist rabble that they are often made out to be. The excessive simplicity of the English-language Rumi leads to an image of Islam that is barely recognizable—after either reading Barks or watching *Rumi: Poet of the Heart,* one is still at a loss to understand the difference between *sharī'a* and *ṭarīqa,* and might be forgiven for not realizing that Rumi was a Muslim. In France, the stakes are different: what matters on social and cultural levels is forging a communal ethics that includes France's Muslims without dissolving their identity.[43] This gives rise to a much more politically-engaged strategy of reading and translation, one aimed at actively opposing oversimplification and caricature. Whether or not this pattern, born of intellectual commitments and the development of a wide reading public, survives the current rightward shift in French domestic policy remains to be seen.

NOTES

I have learned a great deal from conversations and informal interviews with Manijeh Nouri-Ortega, Leili Anvar-Chenderoff, and Abdul-Ghafūr Rawan Farhadi. Their generosity with their time, counsel, and material is hereby gratefully acknowledged. I would also like to thank the editors for their very careful reading and valuable feedback.

1. Franklin Lewis's authoritative study of Rumi devotes ample space to the history of his discovery and adoption in the West. *Rumi—Past and Present, East and West: The Life, Teachings and Poetry of Jalâlal-Din Rumi* (Oxford: Oneworld, 2000), 499–643. See also Amira El-Zein, "Spiritual Consumption in the United States: The Rumi Phenomenon," *Islam and Christian-Muslim Relations* 11, no. 1 (2000): 71–85.

2. Alexandra Marks, "Persian Poet Top Seller in America," *The Christian Science Monitor*, November 25, 1997, 1; Heather Grennan, "Introducing Rumi to America," *Publisher's Weekly*, September 23, 2002, 319.

3. Lewis, *Rumi*, 533.

4. The list is far from exhaustive, and the quality of the results far from even. See Lewis, *Rumi*, 581–610, 643–44.

5. Reynold Alleyne Nicholson *Rumi, Poet and Mystic* (1207–1273). London: George Allen & Unwin, 1950, 5.

6. David Barber, "Rumi Nation." In *Parnassus: Poetry in Review* 25, no. 1–2 (2001): 176–210.

7. George Steiner, *After Babel: Aspects of Language and Translation.* Third Edition. Oxford: Oxford University Press, 1998.

8. Barber cynically describes Barks's Rumi as one "who sounds as if he's been busy misreading Rilke." Merwin gives a more sober assessment of this style in "Echoes of Rumi," *New York Review of Books* 49, no. 10, June 13, 2002, 39–41.

9. Coleman Barks, *The Essential Rumi: Translations by Coleman Barks*. San Francisco, CA: Harper San Francisco, 2004.

10. Nevertheless, the heterodoxy of Barks's approach is immediately apparent in the autobiographical note and recipes that close *The Essential Rumi*. Few of Barks's reviewers seem to have responded to this section, though one took the trouble to call attention to its exoticist overtones: Lawrence Butler, review of *The Essential Rumi: Translations by Coleman Barks, 1995. Lambda Book Report*, May 1997: 29–30.

11. Jerome W. Clinton, "Rumi in America," Review article. *Edebiyât* 10 (1999): 149–54.

12. Haydn Reiss, *Rumi: Poet of the Heart* (Magnolia Films, 1998).

13. Lewis, *Rumi*, 10.

14. Jamal Eddine Bencheikh, "Khamriyyah," in *Encyclopaedia of Islam,* vol. 4, Second Edition. Edited by P. Bearman, Th. Bianquis, C. E. Bosworth, E. van Donzel, and W. P. Heinrichs. Brill, 2010. 1038–39; Maḥmūd ʿAzab, *Al-Ḥubb wa-l-Khamr,* Love and Wine, from Worldly to Sufi Poetry: A Critical and Analytical Study (Cairo: Hala, 2005) 77–99.

15. Barks, *Essential Rumi*, 100.

16. Barks, *Essential Rumi*, 100–101.

17. Original R. A. Nicholson, *The Mathnawí of Jalálu'ddín Rúmí*, Vol. 4: 4:5 London: Cambridge University Press for Luzac & Co., 1925–1940, 128–30, translation, 4:6:121–22, commentary 4:8:267.

18. Barks, *Essential Rumi*, 100.

19. Barks, *Essential Rumi*, 101.

20. Nicholson, *Mathnawí*, 4:6:122.

21. Nicholson, *Mathnawí*, 4:6:122.

22. Nicholson, *Mathnawí*, 4:8:267.

23. In an unpublished paper on the life of Rumi, Ibrahim Gamard and Abdul-Ghafūr Rawan Farhadi go further:

> Very rarely does one read in English the words, "Rumi was a Muslim." In most of the English popularized translations and versions of Mawlânâ's poetry, Mawlânâ's strong adherence to Islamic piety is minimized or ignored. Verses are changed or skipped in order to avoid references to the Qur'ân, the Traditions of the Prophet Muhammad. Even references to prayer and the mention of God are often avoided. Such minimizations of Mawlânâ's commitment to

Islam have also helped interpretive poetic versions of his poetry to become so amazingly popular. "The Life of Mawlânâ Jalâluddîn Balkhî-Rûmî," 2006. I am grateful to Professor Rawan Farhadi for bringing this text to my attention.

24. On the increase in and the vagaries of the representation of Islam and Muslims in French media, see Franck Frégosi, "La perception de l'islam en France," in *HI*, 962–64.

25. See the online discussion on notions of academic freedom in France and the United States on H-France during April–May 2006.

26. Although a proper account of the reception history of *Orientalism* in France is beyond the scope of the present essay, a good idea of the tone of the initial response might be gleaned from Maxime Rodinson's *La Fascination de l'Islam*, 1980. Paris: La Découverte/Poche, 2003, especially pages 13–15. Good reviews of the current state of the question are found in Daniel Reig, "L'Orientalisme savant," in *HI*, 601–20, and "De l'orientalisme à l'islamologie," in *HI*, 998–1019, as well as Sarga Moussa, "L'Islam au miroir de la literature," and Henry Laurens, "L'Orientalisme français; un parcours historique," in *Orientales III: Parcours et situations*, 53–67. Paris: CNRS, 2004. On October 3, 2008, a roundtable discussion was held at the Institut du monde arabe (IMA) in Paris marking the thirty-year anniversary of the publication of *Orientalism*. The opinions voiced by the participants—François Zabbal of the IMA, Lucette Valensi, professor of history at the École des hautes études en sciences sociales (EHESS) and founding codirector of the Institut d'études de l'Islam et des sociétés du Monde Musulman (IISMM), François Pouillon, professor of anthropology at the EHESS and member of the Centre d'histoire sociale de l'Islam méditerranéen (CHSIM), and Guy Barthèlemy, a professor of theology affiliated with the CHSIM—all bear witness to the extent to which the arguments of Edward Said's *Orientalism* are actively contested within the French cultural sphere. "*L'Orientalisme, trente ans après.*"

27. One notable exception being Alain Gresh, editor in chief of *Le Monde diplomatique*, who makes this point in his *L'Islam, la République, et le monde* (Paris: Fayard, 2004), 361–79.

28. Although French law prohibits questions about religion and ethnicity during official census-taking, most recent estimates place the number of Muslims in France at somewhere between four and five million, of whom approximately three million are of Maghrebi origin. In its report "L'Islam dans la République" (2000) the Haut Conseil de l'Intégration presented data suggesting that the total number of Muslims in France was just over four million (26). On the difficulties of establishing a reliable figure and the extent to which the numbers often fluctuate, see Michèle Tribalat, "An Estimation of the Foreign-Born Populations of France," *Population* 59 (1, 2004): 49–80; Alain Boyer, "La Diversité et la place de l'islam en France après 1945," in *HI*, 762–83; and Xavier Ternisien, *La France des mosquées* (Paris: 10/18, 2002).

29. Éric Geoffroy, "L'Attraction du soufisme," in *HI*, 827–36.

30. Ternisien, *France*, 199–206.

31. Rumi, *Mathnawî: La quête de l'absolu*, 10.

32. Mitchell Abidor, "La Gauche Prolétarienne" In *Marxist Internet Archive. History-France*, 2004. http://www.marxists.org/history/france/post-1968/gaunche_proletarienne/introduction.htm; Christophe Bourseiller, *Les maoïstes* (Paris: Sevil, 2008) 159–86 and on Jambet in particular, 167–71; Jean Birnbaum, "Christian Jambet, l'Islam dans le désert," *Le Monde*, 26/01/2003, Culture.

33. An allusion to French journalist and writer Alexandre Adler, whose book *J'ai*

vu finir le monde ancien (Paris: Grasset, 2002; the world in question being the one that existed before September 11, 2001) was published to great acclaim and awarded the 2003 Prix du livre politique.

34. Birnbaum, "Christian Jambet, l'Islam dans le désert," translation mine.

35. Jalâloddîn Rûmî, *Soleil du Réel: Poèmes d'amour mystique.* Edited and translated by Christian Jambet (Paris: Imprimerie Nationale, 1999), 7.

36. Rûmî, *Soleil,* 37.

37. Leili Anvar-Chenderoff, *Rûmî. Sagesses éternelles.* Sophia Tazi-Sadeq, gen. ed. (Paris: Entrelacs, 2004).

38. Anvar-Chenderoff, *Rûmî,* 206.

39. Anvar-Chenderoff, *Rûmî,* 206–7.

40. Manijeh Nouri-Ortega, *Le Sens de l'amour chez Rûmî* (Paris: Dervy, 2004), 10.

41. Nouri-Ortega, *Sens,* 25–28.

42. Nouri-Ortega, *Sens,* 29–31.

43. To a certain extent the development of this ethics over the last twenty years bears witness to the success of the policy of "vivre ensemble" ("living together" or "getting along"), first promoted as an alternative to the policy aim of "integration" by Georgina Dufoix during her term as minister of social affairs in 1984. A recent report by the Haut conseil à l'intégration explicitly equates the two terms, arguing that "intégration" is a certain form of "vivre ensemble." "Charte de la laïcité," 396–97; Catherine Wihtol de Wenden, "L'Intégration des populations musulmanes en France trente aus dévolution," in *HI,* 800–21:807.

FIFTEEN

"Axising" Iran
The Politics of Domestication and Cultural Translation

R. Shareah Taleghani

Of a Persian Letter and Preemptive Strikes

On May 8, 2006, Mahmoud Ahmadinejad sent George W. Bush a letter—the first, formal, direct contact with a U.S. president by an Iranian leader since 1980. The official U.S. response to the eighteen-page letter, replete with religious references and condemnations of U.S. foreign policy, was dismissal; it offered no solution to the issue of Iran's nuclear ambitions.[1]

While antiwar commentators debated the exact meaning of Ahmedinejad's rhetoric, the Bush administration had already demonstrated its awareness of the potential disruptive power of translation.[2] In September 2003, in an intellectual preemptive strike, and by activating long-dormant regulations, the Department of the Treasury's Office of Foreign Asset Control (OFAC) announced a publication ban on any text written by an Iranian living in Iran.[3] At first, articles by Iranian scientists were targeted, but the new policies also affected literary works, and violations of the regulations could result in imprisonment and fines up to one million dollars. Under such regulations, as pointed out by Nahid Mozaffari, the editing and translating of literary texts by Iranian authors would also "constitute aiding and abetting the enemy."[4] The OFAC gave new Orwellian meaning to the concept of *traduttore, traditore*. After several lawsuits were filed by publishers as well as translators and writers, in December 2004 the department eventually altered its position to allow for the publication of texts from countries on the "enemies list." Meanwhile, however, the policies had delayed the publication of several works—among them the memoir of Nobel Prize winner Shirin Ebadi.

The attempt to stifle the translation of works by Iranian authors marked another volatile moment in the ongoing political standoff between the United States and Iran. The OFAC's embargo on Iranian writing merely added official impediment to the already limited distribution of translations of foreign-language works in the United States. With the exception of Rumi's poetry, most translations of Persian literature have limited circulation in the United States.[5] Though a number of translations of contemporary literature from Iran have been published in recent years by academic and specialty publishers, these works have "modest" printings and sales.[6] Statistics on UNESCO's Index Translationum indicate that between 1979 and 2005, only 253 English translations of Persian texts were published in the United States.[7]

Although in the United States there is a lack of Persian literature in translation, Iran, nonetheless, has surfaced in many cultural forms. Significantly, in terms of commercial and mainstream critical success, in the past decade, an explosion of English-language Iranian memoirs, authored primarily by women, has hit the book market. The ur-text of this deluge is *Reading Lolita in Tehran* (2003) by Azar Nafisi. Numerous other autobiographical accounts have appeared including Marjane Satrapi's graphic memoir turned Academy Award–nominated film, *Persepolis* (2003).

The political and commercial marginalization of Persian literature rendered into English, and the celebratory reception of certain English-language Iranian memoirs appear in the context of a series of translational lacunae. Translation, within poststructuralist theory, is an interpretation, a transference, a movement from one position to another, a transformation as well as the act of turning a written or oral text from one language into another. Representations of Iran that surface in the United States and across the globe are enmeshed within and generate encounters of cultural translation in ways that incorporate all of the definitions above. In tracing these encounters, it becomes clear that Iran, as an imagined object-to-be-interpreted, is confined to a stationary axis—defined by the coordinates of the dominant trends of political *domestication* upon which U.S. cultural translation rests.

Historically, as Lawrence Venuti has shown, domesticating translation theories stressing fluent rather than foreignizing interpretation have been emphasized in the Anglo-American tradition of literary translation.[8] Domestication creates the "illusion of transparency"; a fluent translation produces an interpretation partial to English-language values that reduces and excludes the differences inevitable in any translative act. The following

Fig. 15.1. "Silence" and "Lying is forbidden," Valisar Street, Tehran, June 2009, courtesy of Amir Moosavi.

examination of two English-language Iranian memoirs and the fate of translated Persian literature analyzes the notion of translation in broad political and cultural terms. Here, translation will be considered in three intertwined ways: first, the conception of translation as an ethnographic process through which Iran comes to be textually, politically, and culturally transmuted to be read, received, and reinstated as fluently coherent and monolithic; second, the idea of particular writers as "authentically" entitled and authoritative cultural translators; and finally, the notion of the reception of Iranian memoirs and Persian literature in the United States as a series of translational acts that result in distinctive patterns of omission.[9]

Axes of Domestication: Lolita and Lipstick

Since 2000, more than a dozen memoirs by Iranian women have appeared on the U.S. book market. Iranian memoirs written in English appear to be so "hot, hot, hot" that they merit reviews covering multiple texts.[10] Authors frequently stress the idea of countering Western stereotypes of Islam, especially negative images of Muslim women.[11] In addition, some writers, such as Marjane Satrapi, hope to tell their story of Iran "from the inside" in order to avoid abstract reductionism; they seek to present a narrative of Iran that counters the dominant portrayal of the country in U.S. or European media outlets.[12] However, discrepancies exist between their publicly stated intentions, their depictions of Iran, and the reception of the texts in the United States.

Why have some Iranian women's memoirs enjoyed publication success, and just how do they generate encounters of cultural translation? The prevalence of these texts has coincided with a trend in the general ascendancy of the memoir genre in the United States at the turn of the millennium.[13] In addition, in the aftermath of 9/11 rhetoric directed against Iran in the so-called War on Terror, there has been a marked increase in interest in books on the Middle East in general, and Iran, Iraq, and Afghanistan in particular. Reviewers, and readers, often see memoirs and autobiographies as being written by "authentic insiders" who provide factual and seemingly demystifying accounts of life in foreign nations.[14] Authors use realist techniques that work to confirm the apparent "authenticity" and/or validity of their narratives. Despite obvious differences in the content and structure of the two bodies of texts, the interest in Iranian women's memoirs mirrors in many ways the popularity of Latin American testimonials in the 1980s. As with *testimonios,* reviewers often fail to see Iranian women's memoirs as constructed, mediated representations of Iran.[15] Also, readings of Iranian memoirs in the United States tend to assume an illusionary metonymic relationship between the author and her national community or country of origin.[16] This assumed metonymic relationship results in authorizing particular writers to be cultural translators of Iran based on a premise of "authenticity." However, the texts and their reception are always subject to the manipulative processes of reductions, exclusions, and constraints involved in the act of cultural translation, undermining any claim that a single memoir can authoritatively represent Iran.[17]

Generally, the autobiographical memoirs of life in Iran that currently circulate on the U.S. book market have been written by women who have immigrated to the United States or Europe, grew up outside Iran, or currently live in exile. Many have been educated outside Iran in English or other Western European languages. They are viewed as occupying positions as "cosmopolitan" authors or as "interpreters and authentic voices of the Third World"; yet, this belies the fact that though they are identified with certain locales, they address their work to readers in the West and identify with their tastes.[18] Authors of English-language Iranian memoirs have become "the privileged mediators and translators" of Iranian culture, politics, and history in the United States. Although copies of the recently published memoirs circulate in Iran, very few of them have been translated into Persian.

Most of the writers of such memoirs grew up in middle- to upper-class families, and with a few exceptions, these texts present Iran through a secular lens; the practice of Islam in Iran by the majority of Iranians is obscured or even reviled in some of the texts.[19] The authors' class, location, and religious engagement inform the text. Despite the publication of numerous memoirs, there is a lack of representative diversity in terms of the positionality of writers and the chosen genre. The circulation of such narratives in the United States cannot simply be taken as "evidence of decentering hegemonic histories and subjectivities."[20] Thus, in the case of the most popular memoirs, the productive aspects of liminality are circumscribed by how the writers translate Iran and by how the texts are received. The selective celebration of contradictions and hybridity does not erase differences and boundaries between and within nations and communities.[21]

Reading Lolita in Tehran: A Memoir in Books (2003) has been the most commercially successful of all English-language Iranian memoirs. In it, Azar Nafisi depicts her experiences as a professor of English literature from 1979 to 1997. A large portion of the narrative describes a private English literature class she held at her home with a group of female students. The initial success of Nafisi's text repeats a long-entrenched pattern of cultural and political conflation in the United States of Iran with Iraq, or Iran with the Arab world, through writings that are viewed as offering depictions of Islam's negative treatment of women. Published by Random House in March 2003, the book reached the *New York Times* best sellers list for nonfiction almost immediately. The first edition (March 23, 2003) of *Reading Lolita* coincided directly with the beginning of Operation Iraqi Freedom (March 20, 2003). The timing of the publication of Nafisi's text parallels the belated commercial appeal of the book and film *Not Without My Daughter* during Operation Desert Storm in 1991.[22]

The reception surrounding *Reading Lolita* is an instructive example of the complexities of memoir as cultural translation. Nafisi's narrative has now become a key point of reference for comparison in reviews and readings not only of subsequently published memoirs but also of Persian literature in English translation.[23] While it is deemed "extraordinary and thought-provoking" by most reviews in the mainstream press, the book has produced extensive academic criticism published primarily in academic venues.[24]

These discussions of the problematic content and reception of *Reading Lolita* have been written primarily by scholars of the Iranian diaspora situated in North American universities. Drawing on postcolonial theory and provoked by both the extreme popularity of the text as well the extremely limited and derogatory vision of Iranian intellectual and cultural life offered in it, critics, such as Roksana Bahramitash, Hamid Dabashi, Negar Mottahedeh, and Mitra Rastegar, offer a series of relevant critiques of *Reading Lolita,* and their reviews suggest why the memoir is a preeminent example of the domestication inherent in U.S. cultural translation.

Accordingly, the appeal of *Reading Lolita* rests in the fact that it consciously deploys the Orientalist tradition; it reiterates a binary opposition between East and West in which the West maintains its positional superiority by Nafisi's reinforcement of the notion that the ideals of democracy are only accessible through Western cultural sources (English novels) and that Iranian women are passive victims of the all-encompassing control of the Islamic regime.[25] Bahramitash, for example, asserts that Nafisi's "contempt for Islam as a religion" and her "lack of empathy" for the majority of the Iranian population pervades the text.[26] Some of the critics also argue that the author is not representative of the average Iranian woman because of her Western education, her secular orientation, and her class position.[27] Both Rastegar and Bahramitash note that Nafisi erroneously avoids depicting Iranian women as active agents of change during the time period depicted.[28] In addition, all four critics raise the issue of Nafisi's failure to historicize; unlike Marjane Satrapi or Shirin Ebadi, Nafisi offers no account of the historical conditions that led to the revolution.

A central point of these critical evaluations is that *Reading Lolita* and its author are complicit with and supportive of the "neo-conservative" agenda that has called for U.S. military intervention in Iran.[29] Nafisi has dismissed these criticisms either by deeming them unworthy of response or by charging her critics with censorship.[30] Yet, in parallel to the Bush administration's easy dismissal of Ahmadinejad's letter, her absolute denial of these critiques reveals a disingenuous failure to engage in the democratic debate she claims to support. *Reading Lolita*'s commercial success is not remarkable given that Nafisi, as a cultural translator, presents a rendition of Iran that coincides with the traditional Anglo-American representation. She deploys a familiar lexicon laden with the dualistic rhetoric of Bush's "Axis of Evil" so prominent in the mainstream U.S. media. She provides a cohesive interpretation of Iran through her "translatese" that erases cultural and historical complexities and integrates, as its base vocabulary, the binary opposition between East and West, the notion that Islam (and with it all Iranian men) victimize passive

Iranian women, a reverence for English as opposed to Persian literature, and an erasure of class, religious, and ideological differences.

Those who uncritically applaud Nafisi's book without recognizing her "politics of location" also enact a form of translation through the process of interpreting the text.[31] This translation-as-interpretation is informed by the "horizons of expectations" of the reader that include his or her past and present experience of the way Iran is overwhelmingly represented in the United States.[32] Particularly with its highlighting of the so-designated *redemptive* power of English literature, Nafisi's memoir neither forces such readers to engage in a "dialogicity of literary communication" in which one must be willing to acknowledge and accept otherness, nor does it provide an encounter of cultural translation in which one's expectations are expanded or revised by the experience of the other.[33] Rather than staging a "strategic cultural intervention," *Reading Lolita* betrays the potential democratic ideal of alternative modes of translation.[34]

However, the trouble with the memoir is not solely that it reproduces Orientalist discourse (which it does) or that it can be used to buttress calls for war against Iran (which it can).[35] The problem is not simply that Nafisi does not represent the average Iranian woman—this presupposes the possibility of a single, definitive, representative text that would be more "authentic." If *Reading Lolita* is "dangerous" because Nafisi's depiction of Iran provides an uncritical reconstitution of the familiar for a U.S. audience, it is also problematic because in its reception, it has gained a privileged status of representing Iran in a myopic field of cultural translation that appears, though is not, empty of alternatives.[36] The text has become an authoritative translation of Iran in part because the mechanisms of the U.S. book market and mainstream reception do not allow for a translation of Iran that could resist dominant cultural values.[37]

While *Reading Lolita in Tehran* presents a portrait of life in Iran prior to the greater visibility of the reform movement, *Lipstick Jihad* offers an "illuminating" narrative of Azadeh Moaveni's experiences as an Iranian American journalist in Iran primarily between 1999 and 2001.[38] Having grown up as part of a large, affluent Iranian American community in Northern California, Moaveni returns to Iran after the student demonstrations in 1999. The memoir presents her self-reflective explorations of the dilemmas of her various hybrid and syncretic identities, and calls attention to the presence of an Iranian minority in the United States. Most of the text describes Iran during the years 2000 and 2001 from the perspective of a "returnee."

Originally, Moaveni had intended to write a book about Iran in the multiple voices of Iranian youth, but she has commented that due to

Americans' "cultural isolation" and market forces, it made more sense to have a "narrator with an American voice."³⁹ The notion that a single, specifically "American(ized) voice," as opposed to a number of Iranian voices, carries greater weight for commercial success in the United States suggests a privileging of the perspective of the "individual," the "I," that narrates a memoir or provides an intimate narrative that metonymically stands for a collective. Reviews of the text confirm the expectation that an "American voice," via its fluency in U.S. popular cultural references, frequently evoked and at times ironically altered in the text, will offer a more appealing, more accessible, more *domesticated* rendering of Iran.⁴⁰ Reviewers cast Moaveni in the role of "native informant" and assume that as such, she provides the unequivocal truth about the entire religious and cultural system of Iran.⁴¹

Drawing on statements made throughout the text that indicate that Moaveni speaks of and for an Iranian collective as a cultural translator, many reviewers reiterate as totalizing truisms her observations on Iranian society. Many mainstream critics embrace *Lipstick Jihad*'s perspective on Iran, especially the negative portrayal of Islam.⁴² Reviewers often do not recognize or acknowledge that Moaveni's experience of Iran is primarily located in a specifically middle-upper-class, urban, secular milieu, and instead, they take her text as a translation of the true "semantic equivalence" of Iran more broadly. Unaware that their own reading of Iran is shaped by the predominant way in which it has been depicted in the United States as a premodern, isolated, repressive, ascetic site, the vast majority of reviews express surprise at the "surreal" world Moaveni depicts.⁴³ Most reviewers focus on Moaveni's depictions of the "shocking" presence in Iran of fashion shows, plastic surgery, ski trips, yoga, women's gyms, heroin addiction, "techno-Ashura parties," satellite television, women wearing makeup, and men wearing Armani.⁴⁴ Many reviewers also stress the presence of specifically identified-as-American products, cultural and otherwise, such as Ally McBeal, Carson Daly, and miniskirts, and in doing so suggest that (young) Iranians, especially women, are attracted to such products because they allow them to engage in "multiple daily acts of personal freedom that expressed their defiance of the myriad restrictions imposed on them by the Iranian government."⁴⁵ These translations of Iran rescript it as recognizable, Americanized (instead of demonized) terrain, and they cast various American cultural signs, much like the English literature in *Reading Lolita*, as providing the only means of personal liberation. A large number of reviewers also foreground the "ominous" atmosphere and general repression in which Iranians are seen as living. This juxtaposition creates a picture of Iran in which there is an overly simplified "clash" between "fundamentalist mullahs and younger Iranians" who want, as indicated in the memoir, a more "Westernized, modern" Iran.[46] They focus on the "hypocrisy of mullahs," described as lecherous because of a scene in the narrative in which one cleric asks for Moaveni's phone number. Some reviewers also highlight the discussion of sexuality in Iran and see Iran as a society obsessed by or "fascinated with sex."[47]

In their attempt to provide *their* readers with a transparent interpretation of the book, reviewers construct a particularly domesticated image of Iran. They also tend to ignore certain elements of the text. Although some view *Lipstick Jihad* as an identity narrative and note Moaveni's depictions of hostility toward Iranians and Muslims in the United States after both the hostage crisis and 9/11, many gloss over her portrayal of her life in California or her views on U.S. foreign policy. Very few reviewers take notice of the various other details of Iranian cultural life—food, customs, literature—that Moaveni integrates into her text. Instead, a process of translational neutralization occurs.[48] In the reviews, U.S. cultural supremacy is reinstated (Ally McBeal equals liberation) and difference is either transparently reconsolidated via Orientalist tropes (the hypersexuality of Shi'i clerics) or excised completely (Madonna not Simin Behbahani). Iran's translation, for the most part, is rendered fluent rather than disruptively foreignizing.[49]

Lost in Translation?

While English-language memoirs such as *Reading Lolita* and *Lipstick Jihad* have caught the attention of a large U.S. readership, a 2005 State Department report called for a renewal of American cultural diplomacy, and therefore translation, as a form of "soft power."[50] Translation, the report recognizes, is at the heart of any cultural diplomacy initiative; American policymakers may lack insight, but their views of other countries can be "mediated, by contact, *in translation,* with thinkers from abroad."[51] Recognizing that only 3 percent of books published in the United States are English translations of foreign-language texts, the final recommendations reiterate a request for a supplemental fund that would help finance the publication of translations of international literature. However, the report elaborates more fully on the idea of creating an "American Knowledge Library" in which the "best" American books would be made available in other languages for the "dissemination of information and ideas." The State Department's vision of cultural diplomacy appears to present translation as another strategy of containment—one that emphasizes the exportation of American literature in other languages over the translation of foreign-language texts into English.[52]

At the same time, commercial engagement with and reading interest in contemporary Persian literature in translation remains minimal. This disparity in popularity is indicative of what Harish Trivedi refers to as a new "dystopic world of cultural translation" that marginalizes literary translation in general. Yet, several English translations of Persian literature have been published in the past decade and are available on the market. Such texts range from the PEN anthology of modern Persian literature, *Strange Times, My Dear* (2006), Shahrnush Parsipur's novel *Women Without Men* (2004), and Iraj Pezeshkzad's novel *My Uncle Napoleon* (2004).[53] However, reviews of these works remain nominal and most frequently appear in academic journals.[54]

There are many reasons certain English-language memoirs are preferred. Many of the modern literary works by Iranian authors that have been recently translated into English also represent a broad range of experimental literary styles that differ significantly from the traditional first-person, reportage form of the memoir. Most of the translations of Persian literature available on the U.S. book market are published by small, independent publishers or by university presses without the large-scale marketing mechanisms of mainstream commercial publishers. Persian literature in translation appears to be marginalized commercially because avant-garde literary works are generally viewed as commanding a narrower literary market, and from the point of view of the publishing industry, it is more costly and less profitable to publish translations rather than texts already available in English.[55] The preference for English-language memoirs written by Iranian women might also be based in an interest in literature that addresses the status of women in Iran. However, a number of translated novels and anthologies of literature by Iranian women writers have been published. In fact, in recent years, English translations of Persian literature written by Iranian women outnumber the translations of works by male writers, and many of these translations evade the perspective of "Orientalist feminism" so pervasive in the production and reception of works like *Reading Lolita*.[56]

Persian literature in translation still faces some of the forms of the metaphorical embargo that Edward Said once described in reference to Arabic literature in translation in the United States—an embargo momentarily turned political reality with the aforementioned OFAC ban on texts by Iranian authors in 2003.[57] The chair of PEN America's Translation Committee, Esther Allen, reached her own conclusions about the attempted enforcement of such laws that would have strictly curtailed the publication of English translations of Persian literature and other works by Iranian writers and scholars. For her, the OFAC embargo was due to the desire of the Bush administration to maintain the image of Iran as "a backward and demonized denizen of the 'axis of evil' populated by ignorant religious fanatics," rather than a nation whose scientists were internationally competitive. The ban stands as an example of domestication at its most extreme; the attempt to suppress texts by writers from specifically targeted countries shows the extent to which translation can be manipulated as a strategy of containment. It has also placed emphasis on censorship in the marketing of some of the affected books; for example, the Words Without Borders anthology *Literature from the "Axis of Evil"* (2006) was initially marketed as the book "the Bush administration does not want you to read."[58]

A number of parallels can be drawn between the status and reception of contemporary Persian literature and Said's discussion of Arabic literature in the United States.[59] For Said, one reason for the lack of interest in Arab writers is the long entrenched prejudice against Arabs in Western culture, as well as the critical reductionism that maintains a traditional Orientalist perspective of Western cultural superiority and the dehumanization of the Other.[60] Despite the publication of works that offer alternative perceptions, Persian literature in translation suffers from a lack of readership and critical reception in the United States.

However, an increased recognition of works of Persian literature in translation and some of the less commercially successful memoirs could produce far more nuanced encounters of cultural translation of Iran in the United States.[61] In particular, many of these texts critically confront the conception of Iranian or Muslim women as voiceless, passive victims of ahistorically represented religious and cultural tradition. The anthology of stories by Iranian women, *A Feast in the Mirror* (2000), features works reflecting not only a wide variety of literary styles, but also a broad range of social and class issues in modern Iran.[62] These stories include Zoya Pirzad's "Sour Cherry Pits," which tells the story of a friendship between a young Armenian boy and a young Muslim girl; Fereshteh Sari's "The Absent Soldier," which details a moment in the life of Homa, a young mother coping with the fact her husband is missing in action in the Iran-Iraq war while trying to maintain her daughter's happiness; and Nuhshin Ahmadi Khorasani's "That Day," which describes the efforts of Shadi and a group of Iranian women to come together on International Women's Day despite official prohibitions against such gatherings. Shahrnush Parsipur's novel, *Women Without Men,* offers a surreal series of interconnected portraits of Iranian women that, like many of the English memoirs, can be interpreted as being extremely critical of the status of women in Iran, but it does so in a surreal, heavily allegorical fashion. The use of allegory, polyphonic narration, and surrealism in such a work calls on the reader to question his or her own assumptions about the inherent meaning of the text. At the same time, these literary works debunk the idea that a single text can stand as a privileged example of the cultural translation of Iran or that a monolithic interpretation of Iran can exist.

In addition, one can also seek alternative modes of cultural translation by turning to different Iranian women's memoirs not in order to seek confirmation of American or Western cultural superiority, but to examine the authors' perspectives as forms of cultural intervention. In her memoir, *Iran Awakening* (2006), Shirin Ebadi provides detailed criticism of the history of U.S. interference in Iran—including the 1953 CIA-supported coup that removed Muhammad Mossadegh from power. At the same time, she details her own struggles with the government as a human rights activist working within and resisting the Iranian system of laws. In *Jasmine and Stars: Reading More than Lolita in Tehran* (2007), Fatemah Keshavarz combines a critique of Azar Nafisi's memoir with analyses of both classical and contemporary works of Persian literature and descriptions of her memories of Iran and experiences as an Iranian American. Juxtaposing Nafisi's memoir and the works of Forough Farroukhzad and Shahrnush Parsipur, among others, Keshavarz not only interrogates what she calls the "new Orientalist narrative" but also introduces her reader to works of Persian literature as a counternarrative to the privileging of Western literature in *Reading Lolita*. It is clear from these brief examples that the possibility remains for a greater presence in the United States of the heterogeneity of images, literary styles, and voices that Persian literature in translation and different memoirs grant. Such works offer more complex encounters of cultural translation and thus provide resistance through cultural translation against ethnocentrism, racism, and "cultural narcissism" in the interest of more democratic geopolitical relations.[63]

NOTES

I would like to thank Ella Shohat and Evelyn Alsultany and the anonymous reviewers at University of Michigan Press for their comments on earlier versions of this essay. I am also grateful to Faedah Totah, Nader Uthman, and Shane Minkin for their insights during the rewriting process, Shiva Balaghi for her help with references, and Mitra Rastegar for providing me with an advance copy of her article.

1. Karl Vick and Colwn Lynch, "No Proposals In Iranian's Letter to Bush, U.S. Says," *The Washington Post*, May 9, 2006, http://www.washingtonpost.com/wpdynl-contentlarticle/2006/05/08/AR2006050800l4l.html.

2. See Jonathon Steele, "Lost in Translation," *The Guardian*, June 14, 2006, http://www.guardian.co.uk/commentisfree/2006/jun/14/postl55, for a discussion of the debate over Ahmedinejad's speech on October 6, 2005.

3. Esther Allen, "Doors, Windows, and the Office of Foreign Assets Control," *Words Without Borders: The Online Magazine/or International Literature,* 2005 http://wordswithoutborders.org/article/doors-windows-and-the-office-of-foreign-assetscontrol.

4. Adam Liptak, "The Crime of Editing: U.S. Tells Publishers Not to Touch a Comma in Manuscripts from Iran," *The New York Times*, February 28, 2004, A8; Nahid Mozaffari is co-editor of *Strange Times, My Dear: The Pen Anthology of Contemporary Iranian Literature*, a work that was also affected by the new OFAC regulations. Works from Iraq, Syria, Sudan, North Korea, and Cuba were also banned.

5. While I am aware of the numerous debates about the use of Farsi versus Persian in English to refer to the language of Iran, I am choosing to follow general scholarly consensus about the correct use of the terms in English. I am using the term *Persian literature* to indicate contemporary and classical texts written in the Persian language. In this essay, I use it to refer to works by Iranian authors or authors of Iranian origin, but the term also includes texts written in the same language by other authors of other nationalities as part of the same literary heritage. Because I am specifically referring to translation statistics from the Persian language into English, I am deliberately avoiding the use of the term *Iranian literature*, as in my definition of the term, it designates texts in any language, including English, written by Iranian authors or authors of Iranian origin. For a discussion of Rumi's popularity in the United States, see Ptolemy Tompkin, "Rumi Rules," *Time Magazine*, October 29, 2002, http://www.time.com/time/magazine/article/0,9171,356133,00.html and Ali Alizadeh, "Confused about Sufi Poetry?," *Saloni M*, 2005, http://www.innersense.com.au/salonim/articles/sufi.html.

6. Richard Seaver, president and editor-in-chief of Arcade Publishing, personal email communication, June 14, 2006. See also Stephen Kinzer, "American Yawns at Foreign Fiction," *The New York Times*, July 26, 2003, http://www.nytimes.com/2003/07/26/books/america-yawns-at-foreignfiction.html?pagewanted=all&src=pm.

7. Based on a search conducted through the Index Translationum Database.

8. Lawrence Venuti, *The Translator's Invisibility: A History of Translation* (London: Routledge, 1995).

9. Talal Asad, *Geneaologies of Religion: Discipline and Reasons of Power in Christianity and Islam* (Baltimore: The John Hopkins University Press, 1993), 189.

10. Michael Leaverton and Hiya Swanhuyser, "This Weeks Day to Day Picks," *SF Weekly*, September 7, 2005, http://www.sfweekly.com/2005-09-07/calendar/this-week-s-day-by-day-picks; for reviews of multiple memoirs, see for example: Tara Bahrampour, "Orphans of the Revolution," *The Washington Post*, March 20, 2005, http://www.washingtonpost.com/wp-dyn/articles/A45476-2005Mar17.html; Carey Harrison, "Islamic Enlightenment: 4 Memoirs That Add to Our Understanding of the Muslim World," *Chicago Tribune*, June 19, 2005, http://articles.chicagotribune.com/2005-06-19/entertainment/0506180 191_1_islam-dalai-lama-muslim-world; Sam Hurwitt, "Reading Memoirs About Tehran: A Steady Stream of New Chronicles by Iranian Women Offer Glimpses of the Islamic Republic," *East Bay Express*, February 23, 2005, http://www.eastbayexpress.com/ebx/reading-memoirs-about-tehran/Content?oid=1076848; Carol Memmott, "Women Write About the Iran They Know," *USA Today*, March 29, 2005, http://www.usatoday.com/life/books/news/2005-03-28-iran-books_x.htrn; and Melani Tournani, "Another Country," *The Nation*, May 2, 2005, http://www.thenation.com/article/another-country. It should also be noted that autobiography, as a specifically defined literary genre, has not been a major component of the classical and modern Persian literary tradition although autobiographical modes of writing can be traced in various other literary genres and within the past decade several works of *"khaterat"* have appeared in Iran. See Afsaneh Najmabadi, "Veiled Voices: Women's Autobiographies in Iran," in *Women's Autobiographies in Contemporary Iran*,

ed. Afsaneh Najmabadi et al. (Cambridge: Harvard University Press, 1990), 1–17. See also Farideh Goldin, "Iranian Women and Contemporary Memoirs." *Iran Chamber Society,* 2004, http://www.iranchamber.com/culture/articles/iranian_women_contemporary_memoirs.php.

11. Shirin Ebadi, "Bound but Gagged," *The New York Times,* November 16, 2004, http://www.nytimes.com/2004/11/16/Opinion/16ebadi.html.

12. Edward Guthmann, "Weed, Sex, Paranoia—Iranian Graphic Novelist Marjane Satrapi Lets It All Out in 'Perspolis' Sequel," *San Francisco Chronicle,* October 2, 2004, http://www.sfgate.com/cgi-bin/article.cgi?f=/c/a/2004/10/02/DDG2J9150Ul.DTL&ao=all.

13. Leigh Gilmore, *The Limits of Autobiography: Trauma and Testimony* (Ithaca: Cornell University Press, 2001).

14. Uma Narayan, *Dislocating Cultures: Identities, Traditions, and Third-World Feminism* (New York: Routledge, 1997), 142.

15. Amal Amireh and Lisa Suhair Majaj, Introduction to *Going Global: the Transnational Reception of Third World Women Writers,* ed. Amal Amireh and Lisa Suhair Majaj (New York: Garland Publishing, 2000), 10.

16. Robert Carr, "Crossing the First World/Third World Divides: Testimonial, Transnational Feminisms, and the Postmodern Condition," in *Scattered Hegemonies: Postmodernity and Transnational Feminist Practices,* ed. Inderpal Grewal and Caren Kaplan (Minneapolis: University of Minnesota Press, 2006), 153–172.

17. Susan Bassnett, "The Translation Turn in Cultural Studies," in *Constructing Cultures: Essays on Literary Translation,* ed. Susan Bassnett and André Lefevere (Clevedon: Multilingual Matters Limited, 1998),123–143. Venuti, *The Translator's Invisibility,* 310.

18. Timothy Brennan as cited in Anuradha Dingwaney, "Introduction: Translating 'Third World' Cultures," in *Between Languages and Cultures: Translation and Cross Cultural Texts,* ed. Anuradha Dingwaney and Carol Maier (Pittsburgh: University of Pittsburgh Press, 1995), 5–6.

19. Shirin Ebadi who describes herself as a "practicing Muslim" is an exception. A few of the authors, such as Roya Hakakian, describe their experiences as Jewish women growing up in Iran.

20. Chandra Mohanty as cited in Amireh and Majaj, Introduction, 2.

21. Ella Shohat, "Notes on the Post-colonial." *Social Text* 31/32 (1992): 99–113; Caren Kaplan, "The Politics of Location as Transnational Feminist Practice," in *Scattered Hegemonies: Postmodernity and Transnational Feminist Practices,* ed. Inderpal Grewal and Caren Kaplan (Minneapolis: University of Minnesota Press, 2006), 149.

22. Azar Nafisi, *Reading Lolita in Tehran: A Memoir in Books* (New York: Random House, 2003). See also, for example, Amal Amireh, "Framing Nawal al-Saadawi: Arab Feminism in a Transnational World," in *Intersections: Gender, Nation, and Community in Arab Women's Novels,* ed. Lisa Suhair Majaj et al. (Syracuse: Syracuse University Press, 2002), 33–67. Amireh discusses the increase in popularity of Nawal al-Saadawi's work in the aftermath of the Iranian Revolution. It should also be noted that Iranian women authors, in turn, have been asked to comment, as "experts," on the situation of women in Iraq and Afghanistan. See the CNN interview with Azadeh Moaveni entitled "Defining Iraqi Feminism; Lipstick Jihad" in which Moaveni's book is introduced as describing Iraq, not Iran.

23. See, for example, *"Even After All This Time: A Story of Love, Revolution and*

Leaving Iran," *Kirkus Reviews,* January 15, 2005, https://www.kirkusreviews.com/bookreviews/afschineh-latifi/even-after-all-this-time; see also Kelly Hartog, "Mullahs, Mini Skirts, and Carson Daly: A Look Inside Iran with Azadeh Moaveni, the Author of Lipstick Jihad," *California Literary Review,* June 19, 2005, http://www.calitreview.com/Interviews/moaveni_8015.htm and Carol Memmott, "Women Write."

24. Lynnell Burkett, "Finding a World Through Books." *San Antonio Express News,* August 22, 2004, http://www.sananto.com/sanews.html&pagenum=81&what=expresnews.

25. See Mitra Rastegar, "Reading Nafisi in the West: Authenticity, Orientalism and 'Liberating Iranian Women,'" *Women' Studies Quarterly* 34.1–2 (2006):108–128; Hamid Dabashi, "Native Informers and the Making of American Empire," *Al-Ahram Weekly,* June 1–7, 2006, http://weekly.ahram.org.eg/2006/797/special.htm; Roksana Bahramitash, "The War on Terror, Feminist Orientalism, and Orientalist Feminism: Case Studies of Two North American Bestsellers," *Critique: Critical Middle Eastern Studies* 14.2 (2005): 221–235; Negar Mottahedeh, "Off the Grid: Reading Iranian Memoirs in Our Time of Total War," *MERIP Interventions,* September 2004, http://www.merip.org/mero/interventions/mottahedeh_interv.html. For a brief critique of Nafisi's problematic position as a "native informant" representing the figure of the Muslim woman, see Minoo Moallem, *Between Warrior Brother and Veiled Sister: Islamic Fundamentalism and the Politics of Patriarchy in Iran* (Berkeley: University of California Press, 2005). For the construction of gendered identities in Iran pre-and post-Revolution, see also Minoo Moallem, "Muslim Women and the Politics of Representation," *Journal of Feminist Studies in Religion* 24.1 (2008): 106–110.

26. Bahramitash, "The War on Terror," 234.

27. Rastegar, "Reading Nafisi"; Dabashi, "Native Informers"; Bahramitash, "The War on Terror."

28. See Dabashi, "Native Informers," for a deconstruction of the cover picture of the book.

29. Dabashi is especially vitriolic in his condemnation of Nafisi, and his review has generated debate about whether or not Nafisi is simply a "pawn of the neocons."

30. Richard Byrne, "A Collision of Prose and Politics: A Prominent Professor's Attack on a Best-Selling Memoir Sparks Debate Among Iranian Scholars in the U.S," *The Chronicle of Higher Education,* October 16, 2006, http://chronicle.com/free/v53/i08/08a01201.htm. Nafisi and other authors raise a series of human rights issues that *do* exist in the Islamic Republic. My intention here is not to argue that they do not exist in Iran but to highlight how these images are unproductively translated in the United States.

31. Chandra Talpade Mohanty, *Feminism Without Borders: Decolonizing Theory, Practicing Solidarity* (Durham: Duke University Press, 2003), 106.

32. Hans Robert Jauss, "The Identity of the Poetic Text in the Changing Horizon of Understanding," in *Reception Study: From Literary Theory to Cultural Studies,* ed. James L. Machor and Philip Goldstein (New York: Routledge, 2001), 8.

33. Ibid, 9.

34. Venuti, *The Translator's Invisibility,* 20; Gayatri Chakravorty Spivak, *Outside in the Teaching Machine* (Routledge: New York, 1993), 182.

35. See, for example, the use of quotations from Nafisi's book in George Will, "The Iran Dilemma," *The Washington Post,* September 23, 2004, http://www.washingtonpost.com/wp-dyn/articles/A43384-2004Sep22.html.

36. Byrne, "A Collision."
37. Venuti, *The Translator's Invisibility,* 24.
38. "*Lipstick Jihad: A Memoir of Growing up in America and American in Iran.*" 2005. *Kirkus Reviews,* January 15, 2005, https://www.kirkusreviews.com/book-reviews/azadeh-moaveni/lipstick-jihad/; based on Lexis-Nexus, Wilson-Omni, and Proquest Databases searches, I located at least 21 reviews of *Lipstick Jihad* in U.S. journals and newspapers.
39. Hartog, "Mullahs, Mini Skirts."
40. For example, see Harrison, "Islamic Enlightenment."
41. Moallem, *Between Warrior Brother,* 109.
42. Moaveni's critical assessments, and, at times, denigration, of Islam and the ruling clerical establishment are a running theme throughout the text. These include referring to clerics as lecherous and lazy, describing the rules of fasting as "human rights abuse," and derogatorily referring to "chadori women" in the text; Azadeh Moaveni, *Lipstick Jihad: A Memoir of Growing Up Iranian in America and American in Iran* (New York: Public Affairs, 2005), 100, 103.
43. The issue of Moaveni's class and location is addressed in Maria Bagshaw, "Lipstick Jihad: A Memoir of Growing up in America and American in Iran," *Library Journal Reviews* 103 (2005):140; Kevin Walker, "Book Review: *Lipstick Jihad,*" *Tampa Tribune,* March 13, 2005: 10; Michiko Kakutani, "As if the Mullahs Were All Young at Heart," *The New York Times,* February 25, 2005, http://www.nytimes.com/2005/02/25/books/25book.html?_r=1; Toumani, "Another Country."
44. See Kakutani, "As if the Mullahs"; Anne-Marie O'Connor, "The Other Battle in the Middle East; Curiosity Spurs a Market for Books on Youth and Women Struggling with Cultural Restrictions," *Los Angeles Times,* April 30, 2005, http://articles.latimes.com/2005/apr/30/entertainment/et-middleeast30; "*Lipstick Jihad: A Memoir of Growing up in America and American in Iran,*" Publishers Weekly Reviews, January 17, 2005 http://www.publishersweekly.com/978-1-58648-193-3; "Book Takes Us Inside Iran Before *9/11,*" *Deseret Morning News,* September 8, 2005, http://deseret-news-salt-lake-city.vlex.com/vid/book-takes-us-inside-iran-before-81091870; Ann Marlowe, "The Politics of Home," *LA Weekly,* March 18, 2005, http://www.laweekly.com/content/printVersion/39784/; Debra Ginsberg, "An IranianAmerican Journalist Confronts Life in Iran in 'Lipstick Jihad,'" *The San Diego Union Tribune,* March 20, 2005, http://www.signonsandiego.com/uniontrib/20050320/news _lz1v20jihad.html; Erica Noonan, "A Cultural Bridge Between Iran, US," *The Boston Globe,* April 12, 2005, http://articies.boston.com/2005–04–12/ae/29216575_1_tehran-ayatollah-lipstick-jihad.
45. O'Connor, "The Other Battle."
46. Bagshaw, "Lipstick Jihad."
47. See Kirkus, "Lipstick Jihad"; Marlowe, "The Politics"; O'Connor, "The Other Battle"; Gelarah Asayesh, "The Two Faces of Iran," *St. Petersburg Times,* March 27, 2005: 4P; and Elaine Margolin, "Iran Exile's Search for Roots Takes Her Within," *The Atlanta Journal-Constitution,* March 20, 2005: L6.
48. Spivak, *Outside in the Teaching Machine,* 181.
49. Similar patterns can be seen in reviews; see Marjane Satrapi, *The Complete Persepolis* (New York: Pantheon Books, 2007) and Shirin Ebadi with Azadeh Moaveni, *Iran Awakening: A Memoir of Revolution and Hope* (New York: Random House, 2006). In particular, Satrapi's negative experiences in Vienna and her family's experiences with

SAVAK prior to the Revolution are glossed over. With Ebadi, reviewers frequently ignore her critique of U.S. foreign policy—including CIA involvement in the overthrow of Mossadegh in 1953.

50. U.S. Government: Dept. of State, Report of the Advisory Committee on Cultural Diplomacy. *Cultural Diplomacy: The Linchpin of Public Diplomacy,* September 2005, http://www.state.gov/documents/organization/54374.pdf.

51. Ibid, 12.

52. Susan Bassnett, "The Translation Turn"; Harish Trivedi, "Translating Culture vs. Cultural Translation." *91st Meridian,* May 2005 . http://www.uiowa.edu/~iwp/91st/may2005/trivedi/trivedi2.html.

53. Nahid Mozaffari and Ahmad Karimi Hakkak, ed., *Strange Times, My Dear: the Pen Anthology of Contemporary Iranian Literature* (New York: Arcade Publishing, 2005); Shahrnush Parsipur, *Women Without Men: A Novel of Modern Iran,* trans., Kamran Talatoff and Jocelyn Sharlet (New York: The Feminist Press at the City University of New York, 2004); Iraj Pezeshkzad, *My Uncle Napoleon,* trans., Dick Davis (Washington, D.C.: Mage Publishers, 2004).

54. For example, using Lexis-Nexis, Proquest, and Wilson Web, I located only five reviews for *Strange Times, My Dear.* Arcade Publishing lists eight reviews for *Strange Times.*

55. Amireh and Majaj, Introduction, 4; Kinzer, "America Yawns."

56. Bahramitash, "The War on Terror."

57. Edward Said, "Embargoed Literature," *The Nation,* September 17, 1990, 278–280.

58. Alane Mason et al., ed., *Literature from the Axis of Evil: Writing from Iran, Iraq, North Korea, and Other Enemy Nations* (New York: New Press, 2006). See also the back cover of *Strange Times, My Dear* that details the OFAC 2003 regulations and the lawsuits brought against the Treasury Department in order to publish the book.

59. See also Jenine Abboushi Dallal, "The Perils of Occidentalism: How Arab Novelists Are Driven to Write for Western Readers," *Times Literary Supplement,* April 24, 1998, 8–9.

60. Said, "Embargoed Literature."

61. Trivedi, "Translating Culture."

62. Mohammad Mehdi Khorrami and Shouleh Vatanbadi, trans. and eds., *A Feast in the Mirror: Stories by Contemporary Iranian Women* (Boulder: Lynne Rienner Publishers, 2000).

63. Lawrence Venuti, *The Translation Studies Reader* (New York: Routledge, 2004).

SIXTEEN

"The Uneven Bridge of Translation"
Turkey in between East and West

Shouleh Vatanabadi

On the home page of the official website for the Office of Turkish Culture and Tourism there is a music video clip showing a digital billboard advertising Turkey juxtaposed over the neon-lit Nasdaq building in Times Square. The song that plays, "Here I Am" from Turkish pop singer Sertap Erener's recent English-language album *No Boundaries,* goes:

> Here I am
> Ready for you, here I am
> I'll never run away
> I have made my connection,
> Seen my reflection in you.
> So here I am.
> Living under a lonely shadow
> I have seen from the other side.

The music video captures an image of the new Turkey of the neoliberal era for the global tourist; an image indicating the passing-through of boundaries, the crossing of a civilizational divide, from the quintessential "East" to the quintessential "West." The advertised image of Turkey, one of triumphant transnational crossing and coming out of the "lonely shadow" of its isolation into the global community, might speak of full-scale Turkish integration with global capitalism as a result of the post-1980 military coup and the subsequent open market policy. And yet, in the realm of cultural politics and geographies of identity informed by the complexities involving local, global, and regional power relations, the bridge has instead become a demarcation for the divides between "the East" and "the West."

As Salman Rushdie once said, "[The bridge in Turkey], depending on how you see these things, separates or unites, or, perhaps, separates and unites, the worlds of Europe and Asia."[1] In other words, the "bridge" is constructed as the contact zone, that space "where cultures meet, clash, and grapple with each other, often in contexts of highly asymmetrical relations of power."[2]

The enduring, ambivalent metaphor of Turkey as a bridge is caught in a double bind of geopolitical asymmetries that characterizes the era of globalization. While the discourses of transnationality, diversity, and transparency of boundaries on the one hand could translate the bridge as a detached zone of in-between-ness, the discourses of clashing civilizations of "East" and "West," "Orient" and "Occident," "U.S.-Europe" and "Middle East-Islam" continue to translate the bridge as a momentous site delineating these very divides. Discourses of "crossing" and "in-between-ness" as indications of a transgression beyond the Occidental and Oriental constructs, detached from the intricacies of global, regional, and local power configurations, remain; they reproduce the confining discourses of essentialized and territorialized differences.

The "bridge" has a certain potential for collapsing the dichotomous vision of the mutual exclusivity of East and West. However, it runs the risk of being so remote and abstract as to appear to be unaware of the uneven terrain below. Metaphors of bridges, like hybridity and syncretism, have ignored power relations. As Ella Shohat reminds us,

> A celebration of syncretism and hybridity per se, if not articulated in conjunction with questions of hegemony and neo-colonial power relations, runs the risk of appearing to sanctify the *fait accompli* of colonial violence.[3]

In this essay I intend to trace the functions and politics of translation as captured within the enduring and ambivalent image of the bridge, as it reflects the asymmetries of cultural exchange and cultural production across the geographies of the Middle East and the United States and Europe, with the "West" as an enduring site of knowledge production. Examined through the perspective of translation, the metaphor of a bridge exposes the complexities, contradictions, and, above all, the asymmetries involving politics of culture and representation across the axes of "East" and "West," along with the persistent and shifting constructs of "Orient" and "Occident" in new geographical configurations. Turkey offers a possible way of looking at how the competing paradoxical discourses play out to mark the disparities involving identities and nations, cultures and languages. As Tejaswini Niranjana writes, "The problematic of translation becomes significant for raising questions of representation, power, and history. The context is one of contesting and contested stories attempting to account for, to recount, the asymmetry and inequality of relations between peoples, races, languages."⁴

Reading Pamuk across the Bridge

Orhan Pamuk's receipt of the Nobel Prize for Literature in 2006 brought the issues of transnational in-betweenness and clashing civilizations again to center stage with the image of the bridge between East and West as its backdrop. The Nobel Committee's citation describes Pamuk as a writer who has "discovered new symbols for the clash of interlacing cultures," a highly oblique formulation, in Sibel Erol's words.

> The deliberate choice of "clash" is a coded, evocative way of simultaneously bringing up the now well-worn phrase "the clash of civilizations" and disavowing it by replacing "civilizations" with "cultures." This is also carefully balanced with the more positive word "interlacings." However, the impression remains that concerns of political correctness on the Academy's part have affected their language formulation more than their actual thinking. After all, does not the reformulation of this cliché convey cum grano salis the same message as the original that was alluded to, indicating that Pamuk's main problematic is the clash of civilizations?⁵

On the other hand, Pamuk's work is received as an example of a postmodern hybridity that finds voice beyond the boundaries of East and West, given his desire to "be a bridge in the sense that a bridge doesn't belong to any continent, doesn't belong to any civilization, and a bridge has the unique opportunity to see both civilizations and be outside of it. That's a good, wonderful privilege."⁶ A wonderful privilege that remains an abstract ideal.

When it comes to writers from the Middle East, the political and the territorial remain the languages into which the authors themselves as well as their work are translated. When another Middle Eastern writer, Naguib Mahfouz, was awarded the Nobel Prize, Edward Said noted that Mahfouz was taken to be "a hybrid of cultural oddity and political symbol, with not much mentioned about his formal achievements . . . or his place in modern literature as a whole."⁷ Pamuk's reception in the print media and scholarly discussion over the past decade as the author positioned between the East and the West compels him to contradict himself. "I am neither a bridge nor a wall," says Orhan Pamuk, "I am myself."⁸

Pamuk, with his masterful narrative, brings into his work a performance of innovative interpreting and reinterpreting of tales between the geocultural spaces marked as "East" and "West." The wide reception of his work in English translation seems to interpret his work in either the discourses of clash or the discourses that remove the author and his work from the nuances of the very geography from which he articulates.[9]

In many ways the hierarchies established between the languages and cultures of the Middle East and the West have their roots in modernization via Westernization, which itself was a process of translation. This process structured the region's modernity, historically and discursively, around European technologies, cultural practices, and epistemologies within a field of power where anything less than equivalence was a sign of ontological backwardness.[10] This was a field of power that continued to inform the discourses of national identity and construction of boundaries in the Middle East even while nationalist movements resisted the intervention of European colonial powers in the region and in the local traditions, religions, and absolutist regimes. Translation was part of the violence, then, through which the colonial subject was constructed.[11] Within this field of power, nationalist discourses regarding culture and identity, brought to the surface through the mechanisms of translation, consequently ushered in anxieties over purification of "national" languages from their past "backwardness," attributed to their interconnectedness with the language of the other in the region. The project of modernity in the different regions of the Middle East defined as *Tajadod* in the Persian world, *Tanzimat* in the Turkish world, and *Nahda* in the Arab world, was for the most part a process of translating the West. This translation in many ways became a mirror for the Middle Eastern subjects to see their own reflections. A looking glass of Oriental and Occidental fantasies, with what lay in the Other of the East locked in the spatiotemporality of the past associated with the "backward," "static," tradition and religion of Islam, and with the West primarily as a site of progress for the dynamism of the future. This is a persistent paradigm that has continuously informed the process of translation in the Middle East and its efforts to "cross" in between the "East" and the "West" from the nineteenth century to the present. For Turkey, as a bridge between the East and the West, similarly, perhaps even more so, the bridge of translation of modern history has consistently produced a reflection of the ambivalent spatiotemporalities of the Orient and the Occident in a contested field of power.

Modernity as Translating the West

The remarkable history of the process of translating Western, mostly European texts, into Turkish dates back to the late eighteenth to early nineteenth centuries, when Ottoman power began its decline and thus compelled the Turks to seek salvation by turning their gaze westward. As manifestations of enlightenment, classical literary texts from the European tradition were translated into Turkish with the aim of transforming Ottoman culture and society and enabling it to catch up with the advancement of European power. This process introduced European literary genres such as the novel, the stage play, and the newspaper to Turkish society, and replaced the "outdated forms" that had been based on Persian and Arabic classics known as *Divan* literature. As one of the Ottoman intellectuals of the day stated:

> European classics! Europe, which has reached the highest stage of progress by experimenting with everything for three or four centuries, is a model for us at all levels of material beauty. Literary classics are also the works of great success that Europe is extremely proud of, and that need to be loved and taken as model by us.[12]

Employed as significant means of social reform, these literary works begat the new genres during this period of Ottoman history as *Edebiyyât-ı Cedid,* or "New Literature." This "New Literature" represented the anxieties, debates, and aspirations of a society in transition from a traditional, Muslim, and Eastern "backwardness" into a modern Westernized society. Namik Kemal (1840–88), Shinasi (1826–71), and Ahmet Mithat Efendi (1844–1912) are among the representative writers of this period. The process of translation of Western literary texts as projects for modernity sparked many debates and discussions in the different Middle Eastern societies. These debates reflected a variety of outlooks on the process of modernity, in response to the changing societies, and point out that the course of translation was not solely the import of texts from the West by a "passive" receptor in the Middle East.[13]

Translating the West took a more forceful shape with the establishment of the Turkish Republic under the leadership of Mustafa Kemal Ataturk at the end of World War I. Within the first decades after the establishment of the Republic, a vigorous, systematic program of translation was embarked upon to further introduce the literary canons of Western classics as models of universal notions of the humanities to Turkish society. These Western classics were translated to educate the general populace and to create a foundation for the modern Turkish identity that would draw on the Turkish pre-Islamic heritage and traditional folklore as a source of "culture" and on the "West" as source of superior civilization. A significant tool for the realization of the occidental fantasy of the Kemalist official state ideology, an institutionalized policy of translation was deemed necessary to create the ideal conditions for the advancement of the new nation. Toward this goal, a Translation Bureau was established within the Ministry of Education in

1940, with an extensive plan to translate the Western literary canons. This undertaking was considered essential to the drive to bring about a Turkish cultural "Renaissance" based on a corpus of Western humanities. "The roots of civilization of which we want to be a part of are in ancient Greek," proclaimed Hassan Ali Yuncel, the minister of education at the time, adding, "The Republic of Turkey which wants to become a distinguished member of Western culture and thought [should translate] the old and new works of the modern world into its own language and strengthen its identity with their sensitivity and thought."[14] Thus from 1940 to 1967, during its period of activity, the Translation Bureau produced some thousand translations of canonic literary works, beginning with Greek and Latin texts and followed by the major works of the European tradition, embracing everything from Shakespeare's plays to the poetry of Baudelaire, to be incorporated into the national Turkish educational curriculum.[15]

And yet among the most drastic translational measures was the modernizing project of the Kemalists in language reform and the adaptation of a Latin alphabet to replace the Arabo-Persian writing system. Geared toward the breaking of ties to the Ottoman past, with its linguistic connections to Persian and Arabic, both associated with the Muslim world, a project of purification of the Turkish language was set in motion. Purification, it seemed, meant purification from association with the rest of the Middle East, as many French terms were introduced at this time. This project successfully left the past and its cultural connections in oblivion, inaccessible to the new generations born after the Republican Era. For in the process of constructing a "modern" and "Western" Turkish identity, the bridge between "East" and "West" served as a crossing into the "West" and created a disconnect with the rest of the "East." This disconnect continues to inform the dominant paradigm of historicity in a non-Western context with the "non-Western other rendered invisible in the hegemonic conceptions of Western modernity."[16] It also explains the inconsistencies and gaps reflected in the process of translation, reception, and contextualization of contemporary literary texts across the "East" and "West."

Translations of Turkish Literature in the West

In the decades following the Republican Era, many Turkish writers of both poetry and fiction emerged, representing a variety of literary trends and the diverse contexts of Turkish life. This rich body of modern Turkish literature, like the literature of other areas in the Middle East, has not had a smooth path crossing the uneven bridge to the West through translation. Indeed, "the vast literary output of Ottoman and modern Turkish cultures is represented only in a limited number of translations in English."[17] The limited, sporadic number of translations of Turkish modern literature available in English and in other Western languages points to a larger problem of translation: the asymmetries of cultural exchange across the "East"/"West" axis, with the West maintained as a perpetual site of discursive hermeneutic power for the production and circulation of knowledge. The discursive field of power of translated Middle Eastern texts governed under this imperative is dependent on selection, translation, and circulation. Translating Turkish texts relies on a logic that for the most part is inconsistent with the complexities of the source culture and dependent on the cultural politics within the context of its reception. It is shaped by discursively constituted notions of othering and territorialized differences, and consistent with Orientalist epistemological frames. Venuti's theory of domesticating and foreignizing regarding the asymmetries of cross-cultural translation[18] as well as the observations of many translation studies scholars in recent years on the ethics of translation, such as the collection of essays in Sandra Bermann and Michael Wood's collection *Nation, Language and the Ethics of Translation,* find a special meaning in this context. Translations of modern Turkish literature into English often reflect the same consistent pattern that generally governs politics of translation of Middle Eastern literature. Yet, more specifically, it is the ambivalently assigned notion of Turkey as the "bridge" across the East and the West that becomes territorialized and essentialized through the Orientalist gaze. Most of the literary texts of the Middle East, from Iran to the Arab world, are culturally translated as representations of a predefined space in the East, locked in "the Orient." In contrast, Turkish modern literature in translation finds representation as an Other that fluctuates and is suspended in the "in-between-ness" stretching across the "West" and the "East," captured and characterized by the bridge itself.

The sporadic, limited translations of Turkish literature into the master languages of the West, primarily English, operating within the same power-laden cultural production, point to an inclination of Western readership toward the exotic East. Such desultory representation sets each individual text in a disconnect from the complexities of its context; intertexts are read as singular and independent spectacles of a Turkey that is not quite the "West" and not altogether the "East" but an uneven bridge across constructed variables, at times showing a divide and at other times a suspended "in-between-ness." Either as best sellers for the general public or as texts with their utility for the American circuits of academic knowledge production, some examples of literary texts carried into the Anglophone world point to this ambivalent representation in translation. Such works represent an intriguing trend in the pattern of translation of Turkish literature, as representing the divide between the East and West, with more narrative styles as "realisms": sociopolitical documentaries of the unknown mixed with the abstract narratives of postmodern fragmentations as they relate to contemporary Turkish life.

Only a few literary names have found relative recognition among Western readers. Among these is Halide Edip Adivar (1884–1964), whose work represents the modernizing nationalist discourse as it related to women in Turkey. In addition to her writing, her fame is also due to her wide exposure through travel and career experience in Europe, the United States, parts of the Arab world, and India, along with her activism as a woman living at a significant moment in time. Her position as a controversial feminist from the Middle East, an oddity for the Western perceptions of Middle Eastern and Muslim women, adds to her fame. Her translated novels include *Ateşden Gomlek* (1922; translated into English as *The Daughter of Smyrna,* or *The Shirt of Flame*), an account of the Turkish War of Independence. She later wrote and published another novel in English, *The Clown and His Daughter* (1935; translated into Turkish in 1936 as *Sinekli Bakkal*). For the most part, Adivar's work depicts the contradictions revolving around the decisive and turbulent years of the Ottoman decline at the end of World War I, the occupation of Turkey by the Allies, the War of Independence, and the early years after the establishment of the Turkish Republic[19]—a period informed by the dominance of European colonialism, nationalist and anticolonial sentiments, and demarcations of the boundaries of nation-states.[20]

Resat Nuri Guntekin is another writer of this generation. His novels *Çalikusu* (*The Autobiography of a Turkish Girl,* 1922) and *Akşam Guneşi* (*Afternoon Sun,* 1926) were translated into English in 1949 and 1951 respectively. The reason for translating *Calikusu*, as Saliha Paker tells us, was given by the translator, William Deeds: it "revolutionized the novel in Turkey because it was the first Turkish novel about ordinary and real people, written in straightforward spoken Turkish, without any claim to literary effect."[21] This is a disturbing reminder of the ways in which literature from this part of the world is persistently valued more highly if it can be read as an informative document over and above any claim it may have to literary effect. The same translator later translated the novel *Bizim Köy* (1950; translated as *A Village in Anatolia*) by Mahmut Makal (1930), a writer whose work became an inspiration for the genre of "village novels" that dominated the literary scene in Turkey until the 1980s. The novel, in the context of Turkey, had much to do with the turning point in giving the rural population a voice and the political shift that ended the era of single rule of the "People's Republican Party" (CHP), established with the founding of the Republic. The choice of title for the translation of this work in contrast to its original Turkish title is very telling. Where the Turkish title, *Bizim Köy,* literally means "Our Village," indicating the localness, the personal, the particular place with its special meaning in the Turkish context of its time, the translated title, *A Village in Anatolia,* speaks of the depiction of life in a distant land, which, in the context of the reception of this translation abroad, maintains the same appetite for looking into the life of the Other in the Unknown.

Among the most celebrated Turkish writers of the "Village Novel" genre who found fame through translation is Yashar Kemal (b. 1922), a Turkish novelist of Kurdish descent, whose works translated into English lasted through the decades of the 1960s well into the 1980s. Kemal, a powerful and lucid storyteller, depicts the lives of the downtrodden in the Eastern Anatolian region of Turkey. Mixed with legends and folkloric tales, his work addresses the disparities, injustices, and economic hardships experienced by people located on the peripheries of Turkish urban centers. An activist with a leftist ideological position who spoke out against the ethnic discriminatory measures suffered by the Kurdish population of Turkey, Yashar Kemal exemplifies the socially committed writer at odds with the ruling power. The translation of his work into English started with his novel *İnce Memed* (1955), translated as *Memed, My Hawk* in 1961, followed by *The Wind from the Plain,* translated in 1962; *Anatolian Tales,* translated in 1968; *Iron Earth, Copper Sky,* translated in 1974; and *The Legend of Ararat* and *The Crush of the Serpent,* translated in 1991. Most of the translations were done by his wife, Thilda Kemal. Also among the Turkish writers of this generation, famous and perhaps translated for their political perspective as well as literary value, is Aziz Nesin (1915–95), known for his satirical works exposing bureaucratic corruption. The best-known translation of his work appears in the English version of his memoir, *Istanbul Boy* (1977). Meanwhile, the anthologies of Turkish literary works translated into English are *Contemporary Turkish Literature: Fiction and Poetry,* edited by Fahir Iz and the well-known translator and scholar, Talat Sait Halman; and *An Anthology of Turkish Short Stories* (1990) and *Short Stories by Turkish Women Writers* (1994), both edited by Nilüfer Mizanoğlu Reddy.

With the post-1980s transformation of the Turkish political and economic structure, which brought Turkey closer to the neoliberal global market, the urban centers of Turkey became center stage for political and economic tensions and conflicts.[22] Indeed, the military coup itself and its toll on the lives of the people became a dominant theme for many literary works translated into English at that time, such as Adalet Agaoglu's *Uç Beş Kişi* (1984; *Curfew,* 1997) and Bilge Karasu's novel *Gece* (1985; *Night,* 1994). With the dominance of a neoliberal economic structure enveloped in the competing discourses of secularism and Islamism, and the migration of a large number of the rural population into the urban centers, the years after 1980 have indeed made the metropolitan sites of Turkey complicated scenes, contradictory and unsettling. Latife Tekin's depiction of this complexity through a literary language suited to this magical-realist moment appears in her novel *Berci Kristin: Çöp Masalları* (*Berji Kristin: Tales from the Garbage Hills,* 1993), a surreal depiction of life in the shanty towns, the Gece Kondus, of Istanbul. Another of her novels is *Sevgili Arsız Olüm* written in 1983, translated as *Dear Shameless Death* (2001).[23]

The English translations of most of the Turkish literary texts, appearing in a scattered pattern, involve far more works than I have mentioned above. These translations represent a Turkey with its complexities of modern and postmodern reality informed by the complications of political, economic, and cultural factors at the crossroads of the East/West: a bridge across divides. A more recent trend in the Turkish representations through translation emphasizes an identity for this geography that attempts to move beyond the constructs of East and West. Orhan Pamuk's example is very much a case in point here. Whereas many other readings of literary texts from Turkey find interpretation far removed from the complexities of their context and intertext, Pamuk's finds reviews that remain within the frame of analysis dominated by the Western lens; either in a reformulation of a clash of civilizations or as a work suspended on a bridge, disconnected from the unevenness of its end points in the East and West. Indeed, many scholars point to a missing link in understanding Pamuk, a link connecting him to an intertexuality with other Turkish writers who are less known or unknown in the West.[24] Pamuk's genealogy can be traced to such writers as Ahmed Hamdi Tanpinar, a major earlier literary figure who has articulated Turkish identity through much of the contested discourses of the East as well as of the West.[25] Such oversights, pointing to the inconsistencies of literary translation, often continue the persistent deficiencies in reading literatures from the Middle East that, like other literatures, are products of intertextualities and dialogues and of historical and geographical overlaps and intertexts, albeit informed by power contestations and masked by orientalized and neo-orientalized discourses of knowledge, producing exclusions and silences, disconnects.

Many initiatives in Turkey, such as the project established in 2005 through the Turkish Ministry of Culture and Tourism, to encourage a wider profile of Turkish writers in translation, are attempts to rectify this problem. To cite one example from the Turkish literary site Zaman online:

> Publishers in the West saw Turkish literature from an Orientalist point of view. Turkey was unable to promote both its classic literary

works and its contemporary pieces to the rest of the world. The days, months and years passed, and Turkey barely translated 100 books into different languages. But interest in Turkish literature has recently increased in the world. The fate of Turkey's literature changed after Orhan Pamuk won the Nobel Prize in Literature in 2006 and Turkey received an invitation to join the Frankfurt Book Fair as a guest country. Turkey's bid to join the European Union has made the West more curious about Turkey. The selection of Istanbul as a European Capital of Culture for 2010 has helped to facilitate the promotion of Turkey and the project called the Introduction of Turkish Culture, Art and Literature (TEDA) has served as a turning point. As part of the project which is led by the Ministry of Culture and Tourism, close to 600 publications have been translated into different languages since 2005, giving foreign readers the opportunity to get to know 150 Turkish authors.[26]

Although a commendable project, the primary targets for the translation of Turkish literature initiated by TEDA are Western countries. "TEDA is a translation subvention project running in developed countries such as England, Germany and the US. Foreign publishers that want to translate Turkish works into their own language apply to TEDA."[27] Although the TEDA project is an initiative supporting translations of Turkish works all over the world, the majority of translation activities for this task are located in Europe and the United States, with fewer in the Middle Eastern countries for all their proximity to Turkey.[28] The Orientalist frame of knowledge production remains in place even from the site of the in-between bridge itself. The notions of transnationality and in-between-ness will be far removed from their liberating and transformative potential if one fails to see that the bridge is informed by relationships involving wider overlapping geographies. It would seem that the matter has come full circle. Originally the Ministry of Education began the process of translating the West for the benefit and improvement of Turks, and now the Ministry of Culture and Tourism has picked up the thread and is working to translate Turkish works for the primary benefit of the "West."

Intraregional Translational Disconnects

On the bridge of translation, though busy with the traffic of translating Western modernity for the East and translating Middle Eastern culture for the gaze of the West, the crossing indicates an unequal path, with the "West" as the site of the greatest number of both arrivals and departures. Although attempts to cross over this bridge create connections, though hardly symmetrical, with the West, they have at the same time created disconnections with Turkey and what lay further to the East, that is, the other areas in the Middle East. In fact, the process of modernization and Westernization has had the same impact for every area in the Middle East as it relates to interregional cultural exchanges. Due to the lack of direct dialogue among the Middle Eastern regions, knowledge within each area of other areas is primarily produced through the linguistic and hermeneutic power of the West. Therefore, the identities of the Others in the Middle East remain within the Orient, each seeing the other through the Orientalized gaze. The voids created by the loss of cultural linguistic ties going back centuries are now filled by Western cultural linguistic references.

At a fairly recent conference in Istanbul entitled "Woman of the East Ishtars at Our Doors," the invited participants were all either from Iran or other Arabic-speaking countries in the region. The working language for the event was English with simultaneous translation, since it is neither common nor practical for people in the Middle East to learn other languages spoken in the region. The language of communication among people then, is predominantly English, and most of the cultural texts circulate across the area through the mediation of English. Beyond linguistic limitations, however, the problem involves the hegemonic dominance of the U.S./European metropolitan site of the production, construction, and cultural translation of the Orientalized Other. This translation in turn extends beyond the U.S./European metropolises to inform and "affect what various 'Third World' readers themselves come to see as apt representations of their own and other non-Western cultures."[29] Hence, in the absence of a multilingual dialogue, the event in Istanbul was rather a display of the women of "the East," culturally translated and informed by "Orientalist" paradigms. Addressing the issue made evident by this event, which in many ways was an attempt to reconnect the Middle Eastern disconnections, Elif Shafak, a bicultural contemporary writer from Turkey, accurately identifies the heart of the problem.

> In general, in Turkey there is a prevalent indifference . . . towards cultural products and artists coming from the Middle East. This, of course, is not a unique problem here. Most of the Iranian readership is quite unaware of many Arab and Turkish writers. . . . How is it possible that with so much in common in history and geography, in their minds the people of this geography can be so separated from each other? The important question is to see if in the face of this unawareness some channels of dialogue and some bridges can be established. . . . I found the "Women of the East" conference to be

a shattered illusion . . . for publicity; the conference used a "sugar-coated" title, a title that if used for a book or an event, would attract attention. "Women and Islam" or "Women in the Middle East" as well as "Women of the East," are examples of such sugar-coated titles; generalizations that lead to further ignorance instead of understanding.[30]

The problem to which Shafak refers is largely perpetuated by the linguistic inequalities and asymmetries of translation involving the linear flow of translation as opposed to a multidirectional and interregional one. This is a problem that points to the lack of information and of direct, unmediated knowledge of the people of one region in the Middle East on the part of another. It is perpetuated by a situation of untranslatability across the different regions in this geography due to the hierarchies integral to the flow of translated texts in a field of power governed by the discursive sites of the global cultural market in the United States and Europe.

Although economic partnerships and political maneuvering among Middle Eastern countries are aspects of our market-driven society today, economies of cultural production are persistently defined within the frameworks of the Orientalist gaze and the discourses of cultural and civilizational divide. Crossings over the bridge and getting closer to the centers of the neoliberal global capital market in many ways force the disparities of class, social status, ethnic identities, and Middle Eastern interregional relations to be defined through the discourses of civilizational clash and new articulations of the Orientalist and colonial paradigms. A vivid example of divisions by class, social status, lifestyle, and ethnic and religious identities defined through a racialized and culturalized language can be seen in the expressions "white Turks" and "black Turks." Sedef Arat-Koç refers to the "white Turk" ideology in the context of the last few developments in Turkey. She relates

> the emergence of the new "white Turk" discourse to the economic, social, political and geopolitical developments of the post-1980 period. In defining the specificity of a "white Turk" discourse, it is important to remember that the "old" element of Orientalism gains new meanings and dimensions as it articulates with neoliberalism and the geopolitics of the post–Cold War period. . . . As an identity, "white Turkishness" involves two complementary and inseparable dimensions of identification and differentiation. First, it involves material connections to Europe and the United States as well as an identification with a certain conception of "the West"—as both the center and the standard of "civilization," and also as the center of

global Capitalism. Second, it involves differentiation and distancing of self from the "others," those who seem to be standing in the way of connecting with "the West."[31]

The demarcation of lines of inclusion and exclusion that take on literal meaning in the urban space by reproducing the Orientalist and colonial binaries are exemplified by the change of the name of a street in a gentrified old Istanbul neighborhood, from Algeria Street (*Cezayir Sokağı*) to French Street (*Fransız Sokağı*).[32] Such cultural demarcations of geographies of identity informed by the paradigms of civilizational divides also play out in the Middle Eastern regional relations.

> What is interesting about the recent discourses arguing for a new role for Turkey in the world and in the Middle East, especially those discourses developed since 9/11, is that they reflect, on the one hand, a continuing and a renewed disdain on the part of the Turkish elite for Arabs, Muslims, and those assumed to be the "backward" and "reactionary" masses of the Middle East. On the other hand, as it has become quite clear in the debates around Turkey's inclusion in the European Union, Turkey is aggressively marketing a new geopolitical identity as a "bridge" between the allies in the West and its "rogue" Middle Eastern neighbors. Central to this "bridge" role is the image of Turkey as a "good Muslim" or "model Muslim" country which attributes to itself what are otherwise thought to be the incompatible combinations of democracy, secularism, and Islam.[33]

With vacuous transnational connections, unmediated cultural exchange, and little translational and linguistic dialogue, knowledge of different areas within the Middle East is maintained only through a monolinguality of global power that translates difference along the demarcated lines of essentialized and clashing geographies of identity. Texts representing the Middle East, therefore, that find a special place in the U.S. and European circuits of cultural markets by their discursive performance along the civilizational clash as cultural translations of the Orientalized space, cross back over the bridge to represent the Other of the Middle East for another Other in the Middle East. These translated texts produce the necessary meanings for the constructions of new identities through bridging connections with the West.

A case in point here is the translation of the U.S. best seller *Reading Lolita in Tehran* by Azar Nafisi, in Turkey. Owing its status as a best seller to the special political atmosphere of post-9/11, *Reading Lolita* became a vivid example of a civilizational clash by framing its story around the cultural translation of ethnonarratives of the "East" and the liberating literary canons of the "West"; the mutually exclusive world of the "Orient," that is, Iran and Islam, and the world of the "Occident", that is, the United States, outside the complexities of their contexts; with both worlds, that of Iran and that of the United States, conceived as abstractions. The translation of *Reading Lolita*, a narrative of clashing civilizational abstractions, finds a special meaning in the context of Turkey, which, as Meltem Ahiska puts it, is a bridge caught in the "timeless fantasy" of "the West" in contrast to "the East" with an everlasting attempt to crossing the bridge.[34] *Reading Lolita* is marketed in Turkey with the same Orientalist depictions concentrating on such taxonomies as Women in Islam and the Veil. To quote a Turkish review on the book, "The young girls . . . wearing veils move around like insignificant shadows."[35]

A very small number of initiatives have been undertaken to open the path of intraregional translational cultural exchange. One notable recent example is a project entitled *Komşu Aç Kapiyi* (Open the Door Neighbor) initiated in 2004 by the translator Hashim Khosroshahi and renowned Turkic-Iranian writer Reza Baraheni. The project has brought together a number of Iranian and Turkish writers at gatherings in Ankara and Istanbul in recent years, aspiring to have more Arab writers join the effort for future activities of the initiative. On account of so few initiatives, only a small number of translations of modern literary texts from the Middle East are available in other Middle Eastern regions. Special issues of the Turkish literary magazine *Hece Öykü*, devoted to translations of Iranian, Egyptian, Syrian, and Palestinian literatures, as well as a very small number of publications of anthologies and other translated literary works of the region in Turkey[36] (and in the other Middle Eastern countries), remain on the peripheries of the circuits of publications and readership. Given the overall disconnects in intraregional cultural dialogue, the only Middle Eastern literary texts that find their way into the publishing market of the region are those finding fame in the global cultural markets of the U.S./Euro center first, to then get translated back in the different regions of the Middle East as translations of the translated within context of reception of the "West."

To demonstrate further the double bind of the ambivalent metaphor of the bridge as a label on Turkey with the competing discourses of civilizational divide and seemingly unrestrained notions of deterritorialized "in-between-ness," I turn to a reading of a novel, *The Saint of Incipient Insanities* by Elif Shafak. In many ways, through its sites of publication, processes of translation, and the story it narrates, Sharfak's text locates itself at that site of the in-between bridge.

Narrating the "In-between-ness": The Saint of Incipient Insanities

The Saint of Incipient Insanities was originally written in English and later translated into Turkish. In fact, in many of her works Shafak alternates between languages as she incorporates the lexicon of Ottoman Turkish with that of Modern Turkish and writes her novels either in English or in Turkish. The characters in most of her novels straddle borders of identity and geography. Shafak wrote the *The Saint of Incipient Insanities* in English in order to create a broader space for her writing. Her audience is not primarily located in America: she attempts to write the Middle East in America for her Turkish readers; that is to say, she writes in English with an eye to her Turkish readers. *The Saint of Incipient Insanities* was a best seller in Turkey. An imaginative narrative positioned in between the borders of "the Middle East" and "America," Shafak's novel *The Saint of Incipient Insanities* is a "carnivalesque" multicultural space with an array of characters representing a diversity of cultural, ethnic, racial, religious, and sexual identities. The setting of the novel is the transitory, nonstable space of an international graduate student house in Boston. Shafak's protagonist, the central female character in this text, is a bisexual, feminist American woman who feels more out of place in her native Boston than do those born outside it. As this central character shifts identities and names, from the unusual name "Zarpandit" to "Gail," she is linked with the Middle East through her love affair and later marriage to Omer, a graduate student from Turkey. Omer himself is not a character fixed in a particular place; he is not tied to any notion of stability. What brings the two together is a sense of a constant "nomadism"; they are both strangers and "tourists" who do not belong anywhere. Shafak, in this sense, attempts to situate these two characters in the "in-between-dom" of the Middle East and the United States, deterritorialized and fluid. In fact, the Turkish translation of the original English novel defines this place pointedly with its translated title of *Araf,* Turkish for "Purgatory."

Shafak, however, does not assign all her characters to this deterritorialized zone with fluid identities. In many ways, other differences are constructed through the "East"/"West" dichotomies, with identities in singular, fixed spatiotemporalities. The names of the protagonist's two cats are indications of this perspective. The female cat, "West," and the male cat, "[the] Rest," represent the divisions in the world. The text in many ways functions according to the logic presented through these designations. If, due to difficulty in pronouncing foreign, "unfamiliar" names, Omer from Turkey becomes Omar, Abed the Arab becomes Abdul. If Omer, with a fluid, flexible, deterritorialized identity, floats between the Middle East and America, the East and the West, Abed is constructed as being locked in the "East." It is through his mother that these dichotomies are further constructed.[37] On her visit to America, Abed's mother, who we later learn was cursed by a female *jinn* earlier in life, loses her mind and begins to acts strangely. To cast off this curse, she must sacrifice a ram, a ritual she has forgotten to carry out before her visit to America. Thus her entire voyage in the States turns into an ordeal of fulfilling this obligation: a practice she has brought with her from "the Orient," the world of mysterious, inexplicable superstitions. This Middle Eastern woman visits America with "Orient" attached to her.

The Turkish student Omar returns to the Middle East after living in the United States and takes his American wife Gail along with him on his visit back home. To avoid a narrow outlook on the Middle East during her visit, Gail attempts to "learn new things . . . while at the same time trying to unlearn some old things—Midnight Express, human rights violations, the Kurdish question, bits and pieces of tarnished information she had a sound feeling the Turks wouldn't like to be reminded of."[38] Gail has prepared herself for "anti-American sentiments" and to confront with the Middle Easterners a "series of political, international, religious and historical questions about American foreign policy in the Middle East, the clash of civilizations, ethnic conflicts, . . . colossal issue of Islam and woman, the war on Iraq, instabilities in the world oil market . . . ." But instead she finds that there were "neither religious matters nor sociopolitical debates"; that the people she visits are more concerned with knowing themselves through the gaze of their American visitor. The Turks, Gail discovers, are more interested in the basic question, "How do I look from outside?"[39] Through her gaze from "outside," Gail sees

> some sort of a duality that divided Turkish people into two camps. On the one hand, there were the more educated, the more affluent, and far more sophisticated who were irrefutably Western and modern; and then there was a second group of people, greater in numbers, less in power, less western in appearance. This discrepancy in between could transfer the members of the former bunch into "tourists" in the eyes of the latter group.[40]

It is through "East" and "West" dichotomies that people in Turkey and "the Middle East" are designated. Although her main characters, Omer and Gail, are "nomads" and "tourists," they are part of "the West"; Abed's mother, the visitor from the Other of the "West," is fixed in space, orientalized and essentialized.

On her way to the airport to go back to America, caught in the traffic jam on the Bosphoros Bridge, in between "Asia" and "Europe," "East" and "West," "North" "South," "the Middle East" and "America," the territorially detached Gail jumps off the bridge into the sea of "perennial borders," as Omer/Omar, detached from the world outside, tunes into the postpunk music of Iggy Pop, while the "Other," the Arab woman, remains, fixed, in her essentialized, territorialized geography. Shafak's text accurately represents the ambivalences of the "bridge" as an assigned metaphor for Turkey, for it demonstrates the entangled and interconnected discourses of divides and "in-between-ness." It demonstrates the attempts to move beyond the dichotomous discourses to deconstruct and deterritorialize the "Orient," yet in doing so it "orientalizes" the "Other" in "the Rest" of "the East."

Crossing over the bridge into the global economic markets might have been successful, as the advertisement for Turkish Tourism suggests, in getting closer to the center of global capital, Nasdaq. Turkey has been successful in its crossing; in political, interregional, and global relations it is trying to assume the role of a bridge between the East and the West. With the ways in which cultural politics play out across the in-between-ness of the bridge, the dichotomies of East and West, Orient and Occident, Middle East and United States / Europe continue to remain the framework into which culture and geographies of identity are translated. The popular song advertising the new image of Turkey for Tourism and its full integration into the West speaks of connections that are made across the bridge and reflections seen through translation in the West. Nevertheless, the bridge still lingers in its unevenness with the Other side, reflecting only a translation of the Orientalized shadow of the "East."

NOTES

I am indebted to Ella Shohat for her invaluable comments on this essay.

1. Salman Rushdie, "How Can a Country that Victimizes Its Greatest Living Writer Also Join the EU?" *Times Online,* October 14, 2005, http://www.timesonline.co.uk/article/0,,1072-1824869,00.htm.

2. Pratt, Mary Louise, "Arts of the Contact Zone." *Shaping Discourses: Reading for University Writers.* Ed. April Lidinsky, et al. Boston: Pearson Custom Publishing, 2002, 389–403.

3. Shohat, Ella, "Notes on the Postcolonial," *Social Text,* No. 31/32, *Third World and Post-Colonial Issues.* (Spring 1992), pp. 99–113.

4. Niranjana, Tejaswini, *Siting Translation: History, Post-Structuralism, and the Colonial Context.* CA: University of California Press. 1992.

5. Erol, Sibel, "Reading Orhan Pamuk's *Snow* as Parody: Difference as Sameness" *Comparative Critical Studies* 4, 3, 2007, pp. 403–432.

6. Orhan Pamuk, Interview with Elizabeth Farenzworth in "Bridging Two Worlds," PBS Online News Hour, Nov. 2002, http://www.pbs.org/newshour/conversation/july-dec02/pamuk_11-20.html.

7. Said, Edward, *Orientalism,* New York: Vintage Books, 1978.
8. Quoted in Hrant Dink article, "Orhan Pamuk's Epic Journey" Open Democracy, October 16, 2006, http://www.opendemocracy.net/arts-turkey/pamuk_journey_3998.jsp.
9. For a very insightful discussion of Orhan Pamuk's work see Azadeh Seyhan's "Tales of Crossed Destinies: The Modern Turkish Novel in a Comparative Context," in *Crossing* (New York: Modern Language Association of America, 2008).
10. Selim, "Nation and Transnation in the Middle East: Histories, Canons, Hegemonies," *The Translator,* vol. 15, no. 1, 2009:3.
11. Simon, Sherry, Paul St-Pierre, eds. *Changing the Terms in the Postcolonial Era.* Edited Ottawa: University of Ottawa Press, 2000.
12. Demircioglu, Cernal, *From Discourse to Practice: Rethinking "Translation" (Terceme) and Related Practices of Text Production in the Late Ottoman Literary Tradition,* PhD Dissertation, Translation Studies, Bogazici University, Istanbul, 2005.
13. The classics debate, *classicler tartişmasi,* in Ottoman society is an example of this dynamic. Saliha Paker in her article "Ottoman Conception of Translation and its Practice: The 1897 'Classics Debate' as a Focus for Examining Change," in *Translating Other* V.2, 325–48, provides an insightful discussion on the subject. Also see Kamran Rastegar, "Literary Modernity between Arabic and Persian Prose," in *Comparative Critical Studies* 4 (2007); as well as the special issue of *The Translator,* "Nation and Translation in the Middle East: Histories, Canons, Hegemonies," Semah Selim ed. St. Jerome: 2009.
14. Berk, Ozlem, "Translating the "West": The Position of Translated Western Literature within the Turkish Literary Polysystem" in RiLUnE, 4, 2006. 1–18.
15. For a detailed discussion of the activities of Translation Bureau, see Berk's article cited above and *The Politics and Poetics of Translation in Turkey* by Şehnaz Tahir Gurcaglar (Rodopi, 2008).
16. Ahiska, Meltern, "Occidentalism: The Historical Fantasy of the Modern" in *The South Atlantic Quarterly,* 102, 2/3, Spring/Summer 2003, pp. 351–379.
17. Paker, Saliha, "Reading Turkish Novelist and Poets in English Translation" in *Translation Review,* 68, 2004, PP. 6–14.
18. Venuti, Lawrence. *Scandals of Translation: Towards an Ethics of Difference.* London: Routledge, 1998.
19. Salihe Paker and Malike Yilmaz provide a very extensive bibliography of Modern Turkish texts translated into English in "A Chronological Bibliography of Turkish Literature in English Translation, 1949–2004," in *Translation Review* 68 (2004).
20. It is also interesting to note that Adivar's memoir was translated in India during the Independence movement with its special reading as an anticolonial text.
21. Paker, Saliha, "Reading Turkish Novelist and Poets in English Translation" in *Translation Review,* 68, 2004, PP. 6–14.
22. Special Issue of *The South Atlantic Quarterly* 102, no. 2–3 (Spring–Summer 2003) has many essays addressing the cultural politics of Modern Turkey; Izrik and Guzdere, "Introduction," 284.
23. An extensive body of translations of modern Turkish writers into English is also available on Bogazici University website; *Süat Karantay,* the collection of literary texts edited by Süat Karantay, is a very comprehensive resource for Turkish literature in English translation.
24. Seyhan, Azade. *Tales of Crossed Destinies: The Modern Turkish Novel in a Comparative Context.* Modern Language Association of America. 2008.

25. Tanpinar's novels are only recently being translated, such as *A Mind at Peace*, translated in 2008.

26. Konseli, Bonyamin, "World' s eyes on Turkish literature", in *Sunday's Zaman*, online, http://www.sundayszaman.com/sunday/detaylar.do?load=detay&link=177347, June, 7, 2009.

27. Ibid.

28. In a recent symposium entitled *Translation of Turkish Literature*, sponsored by TEDA, only one translator from Iran and two others from Arabic-speaking countries had attended.

29. Dingwaney, Anurandha. "Translating 'ThirdWorld' Cultures." Introduction. Dingwaney and Maier, eds. *Between Languages and Cultures: Translation and Cross-Cultural Texts*. Pittsburgh: Univ. Pittsburgh, 1995.

30. Elif Safak, "Doğunun kadınları konferansı ve sükut-u hayal" in Zaman online, http://www.zaman.com.tr/yazar.do?yazino=184403. June, 19,2005.

31. Arat-Koc, Sedef, "(Some) Turkish Transnationalism(s) in an Age of Capitalist Globalization and Empire: 'White Turk' Discourses, the New Geopolitica and Implications for Feminist Transnationalism," in *Journal of Middle East Women's Studies*.

32. Ibid., 45.

33. Ibid., 46.

34. Meltem Ahiska, "Occidentalism: The Historical Fantasy of the Modern" in *The South Atlantic Quarterly*, 102, 2/3, Spring/Summer 2003, pp. 351–79.

35. Sezer, Sennur. "Tahran'da Lolita Okumak" Evrensel Gazetesi. January 8, 2004, available on line http://www.evrensel.net/04/01/08/kultur.html#2.

36. The event (Neighbor Open the Door) resulted also in the translation of some Turkish writers who are not known in Iran, through translations to be published in a Persian Literary Journal, *Baya*, in 2004 (in general the only Turkish writers known are Yashar Kemal, Aziz Nesin, Nazim Hikmet, and Orhan Pamuk who have become known due to their translations in English).

37. I owe this point to my conversation with Sibel Erol on Elif Shafak's text.

38. Shafak, *The Saint of Incipient Insanities*, 330.

39. Ibid., 331.

40. Ibid., 330.

Contributors

Theresa Alfaro-Velcamp is Professor of History at Sonoma State University in California. She is the author of *So Far from Allah, So Close to Mexico: Middle Eastern Immigrants in Modern Mexico* (University of Texas Press, 2007). Her work has appeared in *Law and History Review*, *Hispanic American Historical Review*, the *Americas* and *Comparative Studies of South Asia and the Middle East*. She has also co-authored articles in *Cancer Epidemiology, Biomarkers & Prevention* regarding cancer incidence among Latinos/Hispanics.

Evelyn Azeeza Alsultany is an Associate Professor in the Department of American Culture at the University of Michigan. She is coeditor (with Nadine Naber and Rabab Abdulhadi) of *Arab and Arab American Feminisms* (Syracuse University Press, 2010) and author of *Arabs and Muslims in the Media: Race and Representation after 9/11* (NYU Press, 2012). She is the guest curator of an online exhibit, Reclaiming Identity: Dismantling Arab Stereotypes (www.arabstereotypes.org) with the Arab American National Museum.

Jacob Rama Berman is an Associate Professor of English Literature and Comparative Literature at Louisiana State University. He is the author of *American Arabesque: Arab, Islam, and the 19th-Century Imaginary* (NYU Press, 2012).

Christina Civantos is an Associate Professor of Spanish and Arabic at the University of Miami (Florida). She holds a PhD in Comparative Literature from the University of California at Berkeley and researches and teaches in the fields of nineteenth- and twentieth-century Spanish American and Arabic literary and cultural studies. Her work centers on Arab diaspora communities in the Americas, Orientalism in Latin America, nationalism, the politics of language, and cross-cultural representation in the Global South. Her publications include *Between Argentines and Arabs: Argentine Orientalism, Arab Immigrants, and the Writing of Identity* (SUNY Press, 2006).

Heba El Attar is an Associate Professor of Spanish and Arabic at Cleveland State University. Her research focuses on the Arab Diaspora in Latin America and the ensuing dialogue between Latin America and the Arab world. Her publications center on the cultural performance of Palestinian-Chileans.

Ziad Elmarsafy teaches in the Department of English and Related Literature at the University of York (UK). He recently published the award-winning *The Enlightenment Qur'an: The Politics of Translation and the Construction of Islam* (Oneworld, 2009). His next book, *Sufism in the Contemporary Arabic Novel,* is due out in 2012 from Edinburgh University Press.

Amira Jarmakani is an Associate Professor of Women's Studies at Georgia State University. She is the author of *Imagining Arab Womanhood: The Cultural Mythology of Veils, Harems, and Belly Dancers in the U.S.* (New York: Palgrave Macmillan, 2008), which won the NWSA Gloria Anzaldúa 2008 book prize. Additional publications have appeared in *Signs: Journal of Women in Culture and Society, American Quarterly,* and the edited collection *Arab & Arab American Feminisms: Gender, Violence, and Belonging.* She works in the fields of women's and gender studies, Arab American studies, and cultural studies, and she is currently at work on a book about the popularity of the "sheikh" hero in mass market romance novels, tentatively titled *Romancing the War on Terror: Mapping U.S. Imperial Desires through Desert Romances.*

John Tofik Karam is trained in cultural anthropology, and a core faculty member in the Latin American and Latino studies program at DePaul University. His book, *Another Arabesque: Syrian-Lebanese Ethnicity in Neoliberal Brazil* (Temple University Press, 2007), has won awards from the Arab American National Museum (AANM) and the Brazilian Studies Association (BRASA). Karam's current research excavates the history of Arab mercantile and political figures in the triborder between Brazil, Paraguay, and Argentina.

Sunaina Maira is a Professor of Asian American Studies at the University of California, Davis. She is the author of *Desis in the House: Indian American Youth Culture in New York City* and coeditor of *Youthscapes: The Popular, the National, the Global* and *Contours of the Heart: South Asians Map North America,* which won the American Book Award in 1997. Her latest book, *Missing: Youth, Citizenship, and Empire after 9/11* (Duke University Press), is on South Asian Muslim immigrant youth in the United States and issues of citizenship and empire after 9/11.

Junaid Rana is an Associate Professor of Asian American Studies at the University of Illinois at Urbana-Champaign. His book *Terrifying Muslims: Race and Labor in the South Asian Diaspora* (Duke, 2011) addresses the relationship of Islamophobia, the global racial system, and transnational labor migration.

Helle Rytkønen is a Lecturer in the Program in Writing and Rhetoric at Stanford University and teaches classes in humor, race, class, and gender. She is a native Dane who has lived in San Francisco since 1993. She holds a PhD from Stanford's Program in Modern Thought and Literature, and an MS and a BS in political science from University of Copenhagen. Rytkønen's work on contemporary European identity construction in relation to Muslim immigrants is situated in the intersection between feminist studies, postcolonial studies, cultural studies, and rhetoric. An earlier version of the analysis of the Mohammed cartoons controversy was published in the Danish Institute of International Affairs' Yearbook 2007. Rytkønen is also the author of "Whose Knowledge? How Race, Class, Religion and Gender Intersect and Interfere with 'Our' Intellectual Community," published in *Social Change in Diverse Teaching Contexts: Touchy Subjects and Routine Practices* by Barron, Grimm, and Gruber (2006).

Ella Habiba Shohat is a Professor of Cultural Studies at New York University. She has lectured and written extensively on issues having to do with Eurocentrism, Orientalism, postcolonialism, and transnationalism, and more specifically, she has developed critical approaches to the study of Arab-Jews in relation to the question of Palestine. Her books include: *Taboo Memories, Diasporic Voices; Israeli Cinema: East/West and the Politics of Representation; Talking Visions: Multicultural Feminism in a Transnational Age; Dangerous Liaisons: Gender, Nation and Postcolonial Perspectives; Le sionisme du point de vue de ses victimes juives: les juifs orientaux en Israel;* and with Robert Stam, *Unthinking Eurocentrism; Multiculturalism, Postcoloniality and Transnational Media; Flagging Patriotism: Crises of Narcissism and Anti-Americanism;* and *Race in Translation: Culture Wars Around the Postcolonial Atlantic.* Her work has been translated into diverse languages, including Arabic, Hebrew, Turkish, French, Spanish, Portuguese, German, Dutch, Polish, and Italian. Shohat has also served on the editorial boards of several journals, including *Social Text,* co-editing a number of Special Issues, including "Edward Said: A Memorial Issue"; "Palestine in a Transnational Context"; and "911–A Public Emergency?" Recently she was awarded a Fulbright research/lectureship at the University of São Paulo, working on the cultural intersections between the Middle East and Latin America.

R. Shareah Taleghani received her PhD in Middle Eastern and Islamic Studies from New York University. She recently completed her dissertation on contemporary Syrian prison literature, human rights discourse, and Arabic literary experimentalism. She has also worked as a literary translator and coedited *Salt On My Voice,* a collection of poetry by Faraj Bayraqdar. She currently teaches at the City College of New York.

Karim Tartoussieh is a doctoral candidate at the Department of Middle Eastern and Islamic Studies at New York University. His work focuses on the politics of culture and representation in the Middle East with an emphasis on new media, religion, and citizenship in Egypt since the mid-1990s. He has taught courses on cultural politics at the American University of Paris, The New School, and New York University. He has published articles on cinema and Islamic Revival, and Islam, media, and cultural policy.

Shouleh Vatanabadi teaches Global Cultures in the Liberal Studies Program at New York University. She has been a member of the NYU faculty since 1991. Her work focuses on the intersections of cultural studies and the politics of translation of Middle Eastern cultural texts and the global North and South to South cultural flow. She is the coeditor and translator of the award-winning book *A Feast in the Mirror: Stories by Contemporary Iranian Women* (Boulder: Lynn Rienner, 2000) and *Another Sea, Another Shore: Persian Stories of Migration* (Northampton, MA: Interlink, 2004). Among her recent articles are "Stories Beyond Histories, Translations Beyond Nations," in *Critique: Critical Middle Eastern Studies* 18, no. 2 (2009), and "Translating the Transnational," in *Cultural Studies* (special issue: Transnationalism and Cultural Studies) 23, no. 5–6 (2009).

Index

7th Heaven, 155
24 (television series), 30, 153–54, 155, 158–59, 160–61, 166–67
The 1001 Arabian Nights. See Menem, Carlos, and *1001 Arabian Nights*
1967 Arab-Israeli War, 200, 202

The A-Team, 161
Abdel-Malek, Anouar, 43
Abdel Wahab, Mohammed, 13
Abdul, Paula, 17
Abdulhadi, Rabab, 16
Abeer (MC), 197
Abi-Ackel, Ibrahim, 19
Abraham, Nabeel, 17
Abu Chakra, Hanine, 13
Abu Ghraib, 243
Abujamra, Antônio, 19
Adams, John, 48
Adivar, Halide Edip, 306
African Americans, 5
 representations of, 171; and U.S. foreign policy, 191–92n17
Agaoglu, Adalet, 307
Ahiska, Meltem, 313
Ahmadinejad, Mahmoud, 282
Aidi, Hishaam, 17
Ainouz, Karim, 19
Aksser, 197
Al Qaeda, 177, 186
Alabina, 13
Aladdin, 161
Alameddine, Rabih, 16
Alger Jr., Horatio, 69–71
Algeria, 6
Ali, Ayaan Hirsi, 6–7

Alienation, 31, 188, 196, 215, 219, 228
 belly dance and, 141–43
Allen, Esther, 291–92
American-Arab Anti-Discrimination Committee, 16, 202
American Association of University Professors, 245
American Enterprise Institute, 6
Amireh, Amal, 17, 57
Amusement parks, 133–34
Andalusia, Al-Andalus, 260
Anglo-Saxonism, 47, 60n11
Animalization, 227–28
Another arabesque, 92
Anthologies, 78n8
Antiracism, 7
Anti-Semitism, 26, 52
 in Argentina, 109, 111
Antonio the Turk, 53
Anvar-Chenderoff, Leili, 276–77
Appadurai, Arjun, 216
Appropriation, 201, 204. *See also* belly dance; co-optation
Arab American hip-hop, 30
 challenges to the War on Terror and, 203–5; commodification of, 209; critiques of Orientalism in, 198, 204–5; gender and, 204–5; Palestine and, 199–200, 202–3, 206–7, 210–11n8; as response to racism, 198, 205–6, 209; tensions in, 208; transnational, 195–98, 205–7
Arab American literature
 the canon and, 68–69; contemporary, 75–77
Arab American National Museum, 16

Arab American studies, 16–17, 27
  cultural studies and, 22
Arab American University Graduates, 202
Arab Americans, 30–31
  activism and, 202; Amr Khaled and, 221–22; multiculturalism and, 202; queer, 31, 219, 224–28; racial identity and, 200–201, 209
Arab Film Festivals, 16
Arab Latin Americans
  and counterrepresentation, 256–62. See also *Al-Damir*; Massís, Mahfud
The Arab Summit, 198–200, 203, 205–6
Arab Women's Solidarity Association, 16
Árabe, 97, 99
Arab-face, 183
Arabic Assassin, 197
Arabness
  as corruption, 84–87, 90–92, 93–94n18; discourses in Mexico, 97–98; and Mexican *turco* stereotype, 97. See also Lebaneseness
Arabs/Muslims
  as activists, 7; conflation, 156–57, 164, 173n5; as corrupt merchants, 19; fictionalizing countries of, 161; "good" and "bad," 170–71; organizations, 38n34; patriotic, 171. See also Muslims; stereotypes, Arabs/Muslims as terrorists
Arapeyat, 204
Arat-Koç, Sedef, 311–12
Arberry, Arthur John, 265–66
Area studies, 27
  diaspora and, 56–57
Argentina, 4, 11, 19, 28
  and immigration, 109–11, 113–14, 127–28n5; Orientalist representations of Arabs in, 108–9; relationship to Spain, 109–10. See also Gaucho; Menem, Carlos
ASH ONE, 197
Asian Americans, 56, 160, 184–85, 198. See also Pakistanis, as a U.S. demographic
Asmahan, 13
Assad, Talal, 44

Assemblage, 75
Aswad, Barbara, 17
Ataturk, Mustafa Kemal, 303
Atlas, Natacha, 13
Al Atrash, Farid, 13
Auto-Orientalism, 127, 252, 256–57
Axis of evil, 282, 287, 292

Baeza, Cecilia, 258
Bahramitash, Roksana, 287
Bakalian, Anny, 17
Ball, Alan, 226
Bangladesh, 5
Baraheni, Reza, 313
Barber, David, 266
Barghouti, Mourid, 208
Barks, Coleman, 264–67, 270–72, 278, 279n10
The Battle of Algiers, 6
Bayat, Asef, 216
Bayoumi, Moustafa, 17
Belgium, 5
Belly dance, 24, 29
  in Brazil, 3; commodification and, 133–34, 140–42, 149–50; as liberating for women, 134, 135–39, 140, 147–48; Orientalism and, 132–33, 136–38, 141–42; origin of terms, 151n16; popularity in United States, 130–31; and rhetoric of freedom, 144–50; United States history of, 131–35; and the War on Terror, 139–40, 148–49
Bellydance Superstars, 29, 140–47, 149
Bermann, Sandra, 305
Beyoncé, 12
Bittar, Doris, 16
Black Atlantic, 35n8
Black nationalism, 179–80
Bluitgen, Kåre, 233
Bly, Robert, 265–67, 269, 275, 277
Boikutt, 197
Bouyeri, Mohammed, 6
Bozorgmehr, Mehdi, 17
Brazil, 3–4, 19, 28
  Arab politicians in, 82–89, 90, 93–94n18, 94n19; Middle Eastern diaspora in, 56, 81–82, 93n6; and

modernity, 23–24, 54. *See also* racial democracy; São Paulo; Turco
Bremer, Paul, 148
Bridge (as metaphor). *See* Turkey, as "bridge" between "East" and "West"
Bucaram, Abdalah, 17
Buck, Joan Joliet, 165
Buck, Leila, 16
Bufalino, Jamie, 225–26, 228
Bunt, Gary R., 217
Burlesque, 132–33
Bush, George, 231–32, 236, 242, 245, 282
Bushrui, Suheil, 72

Cabaret, 132–33
Cahan, Abraham, 72
Cainkar, Louise, 17
Canada, 5
Canadian Arab Federation, 244
Carnivale/carnivalesque, 3, 130, 141–42, 314
Casting
  racial, 183–85
Caudillo, 108, 112, 114, 123–25
Centro Cultural Islámico de México, 103–4
Centro Libanés, 28, 98–99, 101–4
Cerruti, Gabriela, 114
Césaire, Aimé, 43
Challenging the Arab/Muslim conflation with diverse Muslim identities. *See* simplifed complex representations
Charara, Hayan, 16
Chile, 257–61. See also *Al-Damir*; Massís, Mahfud
Chittick, William, 265
Cho, Margaret, 130, 138–39, 149
Chodkiewicz, Michel, 274
Chopra, Deepak, 267–68
Christie, Robert, 242
Chronicle of a Death Foretold, 32, 253–56, 261–62
Civil rights, 7
  erosion of, 10
Clinton, Bill, 232, 242
Clotaire K, 197
Cognitive consonance, 254–56

Cognitive dissonance, 253–56
Collective memory, 172, 199, 243
Colombia, 18–19
  Arabs in, 254–55
Colonialism, 4, 44
  belly dance and, 132–34; French, 6, 272–73; settler, 178, 206; Turkey and, 306. *See also* neocolonialism; translation, colonialism, and
Columbus, Christopher, 50, 62n27
Commander in Chief, 161
Commemorative Day of Lebanese Independence, 87–90
Conquista, 26, 51–52
Contact zone, 20, 300
Containment, 189, 197, 227. *See also* cultural translation, as containment
Cooper, Ibrahim, 244
Cooper, Kurtis, 243
Co-optation, 148
Copeland, Miles, 143–48
Corbin, Henry, 274–75
The Cosby Show, 171
Council on American-Islamic Relations, 16, 29, 153, 173n2, 221, 244
Criollo, 109–10, 112, 114, 125, 127n4
Crusades, 6
Cuba, 12
Cultural diplomacy, 290
Cultural flow
  direction of, 215–16, 221–22, 228; and disjunctive flows, 216. *See also* cultural translation; translation; Turkey
Cultural production, 10, 15–16
Cultural studies, 25, 57–58
Cultural translation, 33, 282–84
  as containment, 290–92; English translations of Persian literature as, 290–93; memoir as, 284–90, 291. *See also* Rumi
Culture clash, 5, 300–301, 311–13. *See also* Huntington, Samuel
Culture talk, 157

Dabashi, Hamid, 287
DAM (MC), 197, 206–8
Al-Damir, 32, 257–62, 263n19, 263n22

Danish People's Party, 239
De Andrade, Carlos Drummond, 81
De Gomara, Francisco Lopez, 52
de Vitray-Meyerovitch, Eva, 267–68, 274
Deagon, Andrea, 134, 139
Dearborn, MI, 201–2, 244
Debord, Guy, 141–42
Decolonization,
　of knowledge, 59, 60n1
Deeds, William, 306
Def Poetry Jam, 14
Deleuze, Gilles, 75
Denmark, 5, 31–32, 231. *See also* Prophet Mohammed cartoons
Detention, 203–4
Diab, Amr, 12
Diasporic turn, 59–60
Diasporization, 27, 55
Digital citizenship, 224
Digital diaspora, 31, 214, 219, 222–24, 228
Digital spaces, 20, 31, 214, 217–19
El Din, Hamza, 13
Dissimulation, 182–85, 190
Domestication, 179, 283–85, 287–92, 305
Dorr, David, 11
Dox, Donnalee, 137–38
Duggan, Lisa, 225
Duncan, Robert, 265

Ebadi, Shirin, 282, 287, 293, 297–98n49
Ecuador, 17
Edebiyyât-ı Cedîd, 303
Éditions du Seuil, 274
Edward, Brian, 17
Efendi, Ahmet Mithat, 303
Eghbal-Mahdjoub, Zohra, 267, 270
Elia, Nada, 17
Emancipation (DJ), 204
Embargo, 127n1, 188, 283, 291
Erener, Setrap, 299
Erol, Sibel, 301
Esfiha, 80, 84–87
Ethnic studies, 16–17, 21–22, 27
　diaspora and, 56–57
Ethnographic cinema, 30, 179, 189–90
Euphrates (hip-hop group), 198

Eurocentrism, 5, 21, 27
　as encompassing Orientalism, 44; in pornography, 227; self-definition and, 48
Excentrik, 20, 30, 197–99, 201, 203–4, 206–9
Exceptionalism, 163, 206

Fabian, Johannes, 44
Facundo Quiroga, Juan, 112–14, 116, 122–23, 126
Fadda-Conrey, Carol, 17
Fakih, Rima, 10
Fanon, Frantz, 43–44, 227
Fantasy, 11, 69, 199, 273, 303, 313
　sexual, 215, 225–28
Farhadi, Abdul-Ghafūr Rawan, 277, 279–80n23
Farhat, Ilias, 19
Farroukhzad, Forough, 293
Fattal, Simone, 267–68
A Feast in the Mirror, 292
Fehr, Oded, 183
Feminism, 306
　belly dancing and, 134, 136–37, 139–40; Orientalist, 291
Feres Jr., João, 49–50
Fernandez Retamar, Roberto, 43
Fetish, 31, 69, 215, 227
Fez, 3–4
Fictionalizing the Middle Eastern or Muslim country. *See* simplified complex representations
Flaubert, Gustave, 132
Flipping the enemy, 166. *See* simplified complex representations
Flynn, Gillian, 164
Foreign citizens, 28, 99–101, 106n18
Foreign-making, 232, 242, 246
Foruzānfar, Badī' al-Zamān, 265
France, 5, 32, 251n87. *See also* Islam, in France; Rumi, in France
France culture, 272
Francophobia, 6
Fredwreck, 197
Freedom
　of speech, 31–32, 231, 238–40, 242–43, 246. *See also* belly dance

Freyre, Gilberto, 26, 53–54, 81
Fuentes, Carlos, 252, 262
Fung, Richard, 227

García Márquez, Gabriel. See *Chronicle of a Death Foretold*
Garib, Hanna, 84–87, 91
Gaucho, 29, 108–9, 111–14, 123–25
Gay pornography, 31, 215
  representations of gay Arabs in, 225–28
Gaza Strip (hip-hop artist), 197
Gaze, 179, 227, 275, 303–5, 309–11, 315
Germany, 5
Ghazouani, Abdelmalek Cherkaoui, 24
Gibran, Gibran Khalil, 19, 27, 66
  self-representation of, 71–73
Global racial system, 178–79, 189–90
Globalization, 131, 178, 185, 189, 197, 215, 300
Gomez, Michael, 53
Gray, Herman, 171
Great Britain, 5
Greater Syria, 111
Grewal, Inderpal, 215
The Grid, 154
Groupo Aisha Al-Hanan, 12
Gualtieri, Sarah, 17
Guattari, Félix, 75
Guntekin, Resat Nuri, 306

Hadad, Astrid, 17
Haddad, Yvonne, 17
Hadid, Zaha, 38n33
Hadith, 221
Hafez, Abdel Halim, 12
Hagopian, Elaine, 17
Hakmoun, Hassan, 13
Halaby, Leila, 16
Halal, 218–19
Hall, Albert P., 180–81
Hall, Stuart, 169–70
Hallar, Ibrahim, 113
Halman, Talat Sait, 307
Hammad, Suheir, 14–15, 195, 197, 201, 204–5
Hammer Brothers, 197
Handal, Nathalie, 16

Hansen, Jens, 235
Harem structure, 41n61
Harum Scarum, 161
Harvey, David, 148
Hasan Salaam, 197
Hassan, Adel, 236–37
Hassan, Jamelie, 16, 38n33
Hassan, Salah, 17
Hassoun, Rosina, 17
Hate crimes, 5–6, 9–10, 36n17, 155
Hatem, Mervat, 17
Hatoum, Milton, 19
Hatoum, Mona, 16, 38n33
Hattah, 260–61
Hayek, Salma, 17
Haza, Ofra, 13
Heteronormativity, 157, 225
Higgins, Justin, 243
Hip-hop, 30
  as countersurveillance, 203; origins of, 196; and racial identity, 201–2. See also Arab American hip-hop
Hispanismo, 109–10
Holland, 5
Holy Land, 11, 68, 218
Homonormativity, 157, 225
Homoterrorist, 224–28
Honduras
  Arabs in, 255–56
Howard, Douglas L., 172
Howell, Sally, 17
Høyer, Rasmus, 234–35
Humanizing terrorist characters. See simplified complex representations
Humor
  Muslim lack of, 233–34
Huntington, Samuel, 46–47, 49
Hussein, Lutfi, 17
Hvam, Frank, 233
Hybridity, 13
Hyder, Happy, 16

Imaginary, 73, 114, 252
  gay pornographic, 215, 224–28;
  Orientalist, 11, 20, 44, 51–55
Immigration, 5, 7–9
  and assimilation, 27, 68–70, 73;
  controlling, 189; early Arab, 66–67;

Immigration (*continued*)
  France and, 273; narratives of, 56;
    Palestinian, 200. *See also* Argentina,
    immigration and; foreign citizens;
    quota system; xenophobia
Imperialism, 4, 191n11
  benevolent, 178. *See also* Imperialism-
    through-freedom
Imperialism-through-freedom, 149
Index translationum, 283
India
  conflation with the Middle East,
    184
Indigeneity, 206
Indigenismo, 99–100, 105n13
Indonesia, 5
Inserting patriotic Arab or Muslim
  Americans. *See* simplified complex
  representations
Integration, 5
Internment of the psyche, 36n19
Intertextuality, 235, 305, 308
Introduction of Turkish cultures, art,
  and literature, 309
Invincible, 207
Iran, 33, 282–83
  contemporary literature from, 291–93;
    memoirs of women from, 284–90;
    the War on Terror and, 285
Iraq War, 6, 148, 205
Iron Sheik, 30, 196–97, 199–202, 204–6,
  208–9
Islam
  in Argentina, 126; clerics and the
    Internet, 219–22; and digital
    networking portals, 214–16, 228;
    European fear of, 5; in France, 272–
    78, 280n28; as incompatible with
    "Western values," 232–33; in Latin
    America, 18; matrimonial websites,
    217–19; multicultural, 180–81; in
    O Clone, 3–4; as oppressive toward
    women, 234–35; and patriotism,
    155, 174n12; racialization of, 156;
    stereotypes of, 122; Sufism and,
    268–70, 273–74. *See also* Muslims;
    post-Islamism; Rumi
Islam Hoy, 18

Islam Online, 222–24
Islamic Society of North America, 221
Islamophobia, 6, 15, 215, 224, 228
  in Denmark, 240–41; in early
    America, 52
Israel, 4. *See also* Israeli-Palestinian
  conflict
Israeli-Palestinian conflict, 183–84, 199–
  200
Iverson, Dan, 168–69
Iz, Fahir, 307

Jabor, Arnaldo, 86–87
Jacir, Annemarie, 16
Jacir, Emily, 16
Jamal, Amal, 258
Jamal, Amaney, 17
Jambet, Christian, 274–76
James, C. L. R., 44
Jarrar, Randa, 16
Jay-Z, 12
Jefferson, Thomas, 48
Jews
  Brazilian racial democracy and,
    95n37; conflation with Muslims, 53;
    Sephardic, 26, 51, 53, 105n11
Jobrani, Maz, 15
Joseph, Suad, 17
Jyllandsposten, 234–39, 245

Kaffiyeh, 209
Kahf, Mohja, 17
Kaldas, Pauline, 17
Kamel, Ali, 19
Kanazi, Remi, 197
Kaplan, Caren, 215
Karasu, Bilge, 307
Kashmir, 5
Kemal, Namik, 303
Kemal, Thilda, 307
Kemal, Yashar, 307
Keshavarz, Fatemah, 293
Khaled, Amr, 216. *See also* Islam, clerics,
  and the Internet
Khaled, Cheb, 13
Khater, Akram, 66, 73–74
Khorasani, Nuhshin Ahmadi, 292
Khorrami, Mohammad Mehdi, 57

Khosroshahi, Hashim, 313
Kyrgyzstan, 4

The L Word, 184
La Organización Islámica Para América Latina, 18
La raza cósmica, 20, 34
Labaki, Na'um, 19
Lagos, Ricardo, 260
Lahr, John, 226
Laroui, Abdallah, 43
Latinas/os, 3–5, 47–48, 156, 160, 181, 184
    hip-hop and, 198, 201, 207
Latino-American Dawah Organization, 18
Lebaneseness, 98–100
    economic agency and, 101–2
Lebanon, 19, 66, 197, 200, 239
    Mexico and, 81, 87–90, 99, 102–4
Leonard, John, 165
Lethal Skillz, 197, 206
Levy, Herbert, 82
Lewis, Franklin, 265, 270
Liberalism, 144–46
Lil Kim, 12
Limpieza de Sangre, 51
Lipset, Seymour Martin, 48
Lipstick Jihad, 33, 288–90, 297n42
Little Egypt, 141
Little Syria, 8
Loras, Sheikh Jalaluddin, 268
Lorimer, Linda, 244–45
Lowe, Lisa, 142
Lubin, Alex, 17
Lugones, Leopoldo, 109, 112–13

Macias, Enrico, 13
Al-Madfai, Ilham, 13
Maghreb, 273
Mahfouz, Naguib, 301
Mahjar, 27, 66–67, 257
    strategies of, 68; as transitional identity, 74
Mahuad, Jamil, 17
Maira, Sunaina, 183
Majaj, Lisa Suhair, 17, 57, 68, 76
Makal, Mahmut, 306–7
Malcolm X, 180

Malek, Alia, 16
al-Maluf, Fauzi, 19
Maluf, Paulo Salim, 82–84
Malufismo, 83
Mamdani, Mahmood, 157, 170
Mami, Cheb, 13, 143
Mansour, Shadia, 204
Marketing, 209, 265, 291–92, 312. *See also* belly dancing
Maronite, 101
Massignon, Louis, 274
Massís, Mahfud, 32, 257–58, 262
Mathnawī, See Rumi.
Mattawa, Khaled, 16
Matrimonial websites. *See* Islam, matrimonial websites
MBS, 197
McAlister, Melani, 17, 172–73
McCormack, Steve, 242–43
Meade, Michael, 267, 269
Meddeb, Abdelwahab, 272
Medved, Michael, 163
Meier, Fritz, 277
Mencia, Carlos, 12
Menem, Carlos, 18, 28, 108, 111–12
    and *The 1001 Arabian Nights*, 123–24, 126–27; charges against, 127n1, 128–29n13; and the gaucho, 113–14; Orientalism and, 114, 116–23, 127
Merwin, W. S., 265
Meshal, Iman, 77
Mestiçagem, 80–81
Mestizaje, 99
    and the gaucho, 112
Mestizo, 20, 99–100, 110
Mexicanidad, 98–100, 104
Mexico, 19, 28
    European discourses in, 100–101; Muslims in, 102–4, 107n25–26. *See also* Lebaneseness; Mestizaje; Mestizo; Mexicanidad
Michel, Albin, 274
Middle-East-in-Europe, 5
Middle-East-in-the-U.S., 4–5
Middle East studies, 16–17, 27
    critique of Said within, 57–58; expanding of, 58–60
Mignolo, Walter, 26, 49–50

Migrant labor, 185–90
Mikkelsen, Brian, 232–33
Moallem, Minoo, 17, 57, 217
Moaveni, Azadeh. See *Lipstick Jihad*
Modernismo, 109, 113
Modernity, 24–25
  compatibility of Islam with, 221–22; Mahjar literature and, 73–74; Turkey and, 302–4, 306
Møller, Per Stig, 242
Monjardim, Jayme, 22
Moors, 26, 51–53, 107n25, 109
Moral geography, 241
Morandini, Norma, 122
Morocco, 3–4
Mosque
  construction of, 5, 7, 126; King Fahd Islamic Center, 18; in Mexico, 103
Mossadegh, Muhammad, 293
Mottahedeh, Negar, 287
Mozaffari, Nahid, 282
Multiculturalism, 147, 160, 201–2
  commodification of, 170; as dangerous, 180–81, 189–90; in the United States, 5, 20
Music, 11–13
Music videos, 12
Muslim Americans. See Muslims, in the United States
Muslim Public Affairs Council, 244
Muslims
  anti-Americanism and, 30, 177, 181, 188, 315; in Denmark, 232–33, 245–46, 248n27, 250n69; in Europe, 6, 232; as pawns, 158; polls about, 9, 241; racialized, 30, 176–79, 184–90; as terrorists, 153–54, 156–57, 215; in the United States, 232, 243–44. See also Arabs/Muslims; Islam; Mexico, Muslims in; racism, Muslims and
Mutamissik, 204
MWR (MC), 197, 206

Naber, Nadine, 17, 67
Naff, Alixa, 70–71, 73
Naficy, Hamid, 17
Nafisi, Azar. See *Reading Lolita in Tehran*

Nakba, 200
NaR, 204
Narcel, Jamal Abdul. See Narcycist
Narcycist, 20, 198, 203–4, 209
Nash, Geoffrey, 72–73
Nashef, Rola, 16
Nassar, Raduan, 19
Nation of Islam, 180–81
National identity, 20, 26
  Argentine, 113; British, 273; Chilean, 257; French, 273; Mexican, 100
Nationalism, 26
  Arab, 202, 257–58; Argentine, 110–12, 125; Brazilian, 81; Chilean, 257; Islamic, 217; Mexican, 100, 105n13; United States, 157, 191–92n17
Native Americans, 5
Native informant, 289
Near Eastern studies, 43
Nelson, Cary, 245
Neocolonialism, 143
Neoconservatives, 6, 46–47, 287
Neoliberalism, 123, 144, 149, 188, 214
  Turkey and, 299, 307, 311
Neo-Orientalism, 58–59
Neshat, Sherene, 16, 38n33
Nesin, Aziz, 307
New Age. See belly dance
Nicholson, Reynold Allen, 265–66, 270–72
NOMADS, 197–98, 204
Nostalgia, 54, 110, 199
Nouri-Ortega, Manijeh, 277
Nye, Naomi Shihab, 16, 78n8

O Clone/El Clon, 3–4, 9, 22–24, 252
Obama, Barack, 228
Obeidallah, Dean, 15
Occidentalism, 26, 50–52, 55
Occupation, 183, 196, 199, 205–9, 240, 306
October Arab-Israeli War, 200, 202
Odalisque, 29, 108, 124–25, 255–56
Offendum, Omar, 20, 198, 203–4, 206
Office of Foreign Asset Control, 282–83, 291
Ojo de Tormenta, 257–58
Oklahoma City bombing, 168

Operation Desert Storm, 286
Operation Iraqi Freedom, 286. *See also* Iraq War
Orfalea, Gregory, 16, 202
Orientalism, 3–6, 10–11, 21, 26
  and belly dance, 132–33; in the early Americas, 50–55; in France, 273; homoeroticism and, 227–28; in Latin America, 252–53, 256–57, 261; in memoir, 287–88, 293; Turkey and, 304–5, 309–10, 312–13. *See also* Arab American hip-hop, critiques of Orientialism in; Argentina, Orientalist representations of Arabs in; Auto-Orientalism; Menem, Carlos, Orientalism and; Neo-Orientalism; Self-Orientalizing
Orientalism (book), 26
  academic disciplines and, 45; anticolonial precursors to, 42–45; as Arab American studies text, 46; area studies and, 46; ethnic studies and, 46; in France, 273, 280n26
Ottoman Empire, 8, 19, 33, 52
  Latin America and, 81, 91, 97–99, 102, 108–11, 252; Turkey and, 303, 304–6
Oviedo, Jorge Luis. See *La Turca*

Páez Oropeza, Carmen Mercedes, 101
Paker, Saliha, 306
Pakistan, 5
  conflation with the Middle East, 177, 184, 187–90
Pakistanis, 30
  as dangerous, 186–87; as a U.S. demographic, 176–77
Palestine
  and Latin America, 258–61, 262n4, 263n19; as symbol, 183–84, 189. *See also* Arab American hip-hop, Palestine and; *Al-Damir*; immigration, Palestinian; Israeli-Palestinian conflict
Palestine Rapperz, 197
Palestinian Street, 197
Palumbo-Liu, David, 79n22
Pamuk, Orhan, 33, 301–2, 308–9

Parsipur, Shahrnush, 291–93
Partition
  India and Pakistan, 184–85; Israel and Palestine, 185
Passing, 182–84, 190
Patriarch (hip-hop artist); 197
Patriarchy, 136–37, 147
  Arab/Muslim culture as, 25
PATRIOT Act, 10, 241
Peddlers, 73, 81, 111, 119, 255
Perez, Gloria, 22
Perl, Richard, 6
Persepolis, 283
Peru, 4
Pezeshkzad, Iraj, 291
The Philistines, 197–98
Pirzad, Zoya, 292
Pitta, Celso, 84–87, 94n27
Pluralism
  religious, 123, 125–26
Poetry, 13–15
Poli Heat, 197
Political correctness, 162–63
Politics of containment, 197
Pornography. *See* gay pornography
Portugal, 4
Postcolonial studies, 5, 25, 27, 34, 45, 50, 58
Post-Islamism, 214, 216
Post-race, 30, 154, 171–72
Postwar seismic shift, 42–44
Pound, Ezra, 266
The Practice (television series), 155
Press, Joy, 163–64
Profiling, 203–4
Projecting a multicultural U.S. society. *See* simplified complex representations
Proof of Life, 161
Prophet Mohammed cartoons controversy, 31, 231–36
  Danish responses to, 231–32, 238–39; Muslim responses to, 236–40, 244, 250n61; Orientalist responses to, 241; United States responses to, 232, 240–46
Puar, Jasbir, 157, 216, 225
Public Enemy, 197, 216

Public service announcement, 153–54, 173n4, 173n6
Public sphere, 17, 21, 90, 195, 202, 272
 virtual, 31, 214–15, 224

Qaradawi, Yusuf, 222
Quota system, 81
Qu'ran, 6, 221

Rabinowitz, Dorothy, 163
al-Rabita al-Adabiyya, 19
Al Rabita al-Qalamiyya, 19
Racial democracy, 28, 80–81, 92n2
 place of Jews in, 95n37; place of Arabs in, 90–92
Racial formation, 19, 30, 176–79, 184–85, 188–90
Racism
 anti-Arab, 30–31, 92, 111, 116, 198–202, 205, 252; in Brazil, 81; cultural, 188, 190; enlightened, 171; hip-hop as a response to, 196–98, 203–8; inferential, 170; institutionalized, 171; Muslims and, 178–79; phenotypic, 184, 188; in pornography, 227–28; in the press, 91; scientific, 51. *See also* Arab American hip-hop, as response to racism; global racial system; post-race
Raffo, Heather, 16
Ragtop, 30, 198, 203, 205–7
Al Rahbani, Ziad, 13
Rai, Amit, 216
Rainbow Atlantic, 47n8, 55, 62n39
Ramzy, Hossam, 12
Rasmussen, Anders Fogh, 236, 238–39, 249n41
Rastegar, Mitra, 287
Razack, Sherene, 17
Reading Lolita in Tehran, 7, 33, 283, 286–88, 291, 293, 312–13
Reconquista, 26, 51–52, 109
Reddy, Nilüfer Mizanoğlu, 307
Refn, Lars, 235–36
Reiss, Haydn, 267–70
Resistance, 31, 43, 73, 258, 293
 cultures of, 16, 203–10

Rice, Condoleeza, 242, 282
Richburg, Keith, 242
Ricupero, Ricardo, 93–94n18
The Right, 7
 anti-immigration and, 47; Christian, 10, 34, 48–49. *See also* simplified complex representations, responses to
Rihani, Ameen, 19, 27, 66
 and contemporary Arab American writing, 75–77; and contradiction, 66–68; and negotiation with Orientalism, 74; Pan-Arabism and, 65; self-representation and, 75
Riis, Jacob, 69
Rio de Janeiro, 3
Rodinson, Maxime, 43
Rose, Flemming, 233–34, 245
Rouba mas faz, 83
Roy, Fatimah, 179
Rumi, 32–33, 264
 de-Islamicizing, 264–72, 278; in France, 264–65, 272–78; in the United States, 264–72, 277–78
Rumi: Poet of the Heart, 275. *See also* Rumi, in the United States
Rumsfeld, Donald, 6
Rushdie, Salman, 300
Russia, 4

Said, Edward, 17, 26, 291–92, 301
 and cultural studies, 57; *Culture and Imperialism* and, 44. *See also* *Orientalism* (book)
The Saint of Incipient Insanities, 313–16
Salah, Tahani, 204–5
Salaita, Steven, 17
Saliba, Therese, 17
Salimpour, Jamila, 131, 144
Salimpour, Suhaila, 137, 144, 148–49
Salloum, Jackie, 16, 207
Salloum, Jayce, 16
Sanctions, 187–88
São Paulo, 28
 corruption scandal, 80, 83–87, 90–91, 94n22. *See also* Brazil; Commemorative Day of Lebanese Independence

Sari, Fereshteh, 292
Sarmiento, Domingo F., 109, 112–13
Satire, 15
Satrapi, Marjane, 283, 285, 287, 297–98n49. See also *Persepolis*
Saz (MC), 197
Schimmel, Annemarie, 265
Schmidt, Arthur, 100
Scopic pleasure, 132–33, 146–47
Seikaly, May, 17
"Self-orientalizing," 11, 59, 204
Sephardi-Moorish Atlantic, 26, 50–55, 34n1, 62n34
September 11, 6
    in poetry, 14; as rupture, 149
Sex and the City (television series), 137
Sex and the City 2, 11, 137
Sexuality
    belly dance and, 132, 134; in Iran, 290; repressed, 157. See also Arab Americans, queer; gay pornography
Shabib, Samih, 259
Shadeed (MC), 197
Shafak, Elif, 33, 310–11. See also *The Saint of Incipient Insanities*
Shaheen, Jack, 17
Shakir, Evelyn, 17
Shakira, 11–12, 17
Shamieh, Betty, 16
Shams, 269, 274–77
Shapiro, Samantha A., 219–20
Shinasi, 303
Shohat, Ella, 216, 227, 300
Shryock, Andrew, 17
Sikhs, 10
Silva, General Costa e, 82
Simão, José, 86
Simmons, Russell, 12
Simon, Pedro, 88–90
Simplified complex representations, 30, 154, 170–72
    critic responses to, 161–65; strategies of, 155–61; viewer responses to, 165–69
Sirio-Libaneses, 99
Sleeper cell, 160, 183
Sleeper Cell (television series), 30, 154, 155, 156–57, 160
critic responses to, 162–65; the racialized Muslim and, 179; viewer responses to, 165–69
Slim Helú, Carlos, 98, 100, 105n8
Smith, Huston, 267, 269
Soft power, 58, 290
Son Cubano, 13
Sosa, Omar, 13
Spain, 5, 252
Stam, Robert, 216, 227
Steiner, George, 266
Stereotypes, 29, 170
    of Arab "corruption," 92, 111, 124–25; Arab hip-hop and, 204; Arabs/Muslims as terrorists, 153–54, 162, 169, 172–74, 225–26; belly dance and, 135, 142; in gay pornography, 226–28; Orientalist, 44, 50, 252–53, 257; South Asians and, 184–85; in television, 153–55, 162, 170–72; of the *turco*, 97, 116, 120
Sting, 13, 143
Street Arab, 68–71
Submission, 6
Suleiman, Elia, 16
Suleiman, Michael, 17
Sutherland, Kiefer, 153–54, 173n4, 173n6
Sweden, 5
Switzerland, 5
Sympathizing with the plight of Arab Americans post-9/11. *See* simplified complex representations
Syncretism, 266–67
Syria, 19, 66, 70–71, 80–82, 102, 111, 198–200
Syriana, 30, 179, 185–89

Taliban, 177, 186
Tanpinar, Ahmed Hamdi, 308
Tashweesh, 197
Tattered Tom, 69–71
Tazi-Sadeq, Sophia, 276
Tekin, Latife, 308
Tel Quel, 274–75
Telemundo, 4
Telenovela, 3
Temporality, 141

Threat Matrix, 154, 155
Tibawi, Abdul-Latif, 43
Timz, 205
Topographical reductionism, 24
Translation, 33
   colonialism and, 302; of Persian literature, 282–83. *See also* cultural translation; Rumi; Turkey
Treaty of Tripoli, 48
A Tribe Called Quest, 197
Trivedi, Harish, 291
Trudeau, Garry, 242
La Turca, 253–56, 261–62
Turco, 8
   in Argentina, 110–11, 116, 120–21; Brazilian opinions of, 91; and commercial acumen, 97; in Mexico, 97; origins, 80–81; as stand-in for corruption, 80
Turcophilia, 32, 253, 256, 261–62
Turcophobia, 32, 252, 256, 261–62
Turk
   "White" and "Black," 311
Turkey, 4, 33
   as "bridge" between "East" and "West," 299–302, 304–5, 308–10, 312–16; and Middle East intraregional cultural exchange, 309–13; politics of translation and, 300; and translation of Turkish literature, 304–9; and translation of Western literature, 302–4
TV Globo, 4, 86
Twain, Mark, 11
The Two 1492s, 26, 50–54, 61n21, 61n26

Umrah, 229n14
Unión Nacional de Jóvenes Mexicanos de Ascendencia Libanesa, 101–2
United Auto Workers, 202
Unwin, Allen, 265
Unwin, George, 265

Al 'Usba al-Andalusiyya, 19

van Gogh, Theo, 6, 233
Vasconcelos, José, 99
Vatanabadi, Shouleh, 57
Venezuela, 4, 19
Venuti, Lawrence, 284, 305
Village novels, 306–7

The Wanted, 154, 167
War on Terror, 6, 29, 139, 177
   as civilizing project, 236; immigration and, 47; Muslim women and, 178; television dramas and, 153, 166–68, 171–72. *See also* belly dance, and the War on Terror; Iran, the War on Terror and
Washington, George, 48
The West Wing, 161
Westergaard, Kurt, 234, 236, 245, 251n84–85
Whinfield, Edward Henry, 265
Whirling dervish, 264, 276
Willis, Deborah, 172
Winger, Debra, 267–68
Winnubst, Shannon, 146
Women's/gender studies
   diaspora and, 57
Women's liberation movement. *See* feminism
Wood, Michael, 305
World's Fairs, 132–33

Xenophobia, 100, 110

Yale University, 244–45
Yaser, Juan, 113
Youmans, Will. *See* Iron Sheik
Youth culture, 31. *See also* hip-hop
Yuncel, Hassan Ali, 304

Zionism, 199